Vive Moi!

BY THE SAME AUTHOR

Novels

A Nest of Simple Folk
Bird Alone
Come Back to Erin
And Again?

Short Stories

Midsummer Night Madness
A Purse of Coppers
Teresa and Other Stories
The Stories of Sean O'Faolain
I Remember! I Remember!
The Heat of the Sun
The Talking Trees
Foreign Affairs

Biography

Constance Markievicz
King of the Beggars
de Valera
The Great O'Neill
Newman's Way

Travel

An Irish Journey
A Summer in Italy
An Autumn in Italy

Criticism

The Short Story
The Vanishing Hero

Play

She had to do Something

Translations

The Silver Branch

Miscellaneous

The Irish
The Story of Ireland

Vive Moi!

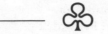

SEAN O'FAOLAIN

Edited and with an Afterword
by Julia O'Faolain

SINCLAIR-STEVENSON

This edition first published in 1993
by Sinclair-Stevenson
an imprint of Reed Consumer Books Ltd
Michelin House, 81 Fulham Road, London SW3 6RB
and Auckland, Melbourne, Singapore and Toronto

A CIP catalogue record for this book
is available from the British Library
ISBN 1 85619 376 4

Phototypeset by Intype, London
Printed and bound in Great Britain
by Mackays of Chatham plc, Chatham, Kent

Contents

☙

Acknowledgments

The author wishes to thank the following for
permission to use copyright material:

The Hogarth Press Ltd for permission to
reproduce 'When They Are Roused' and an
excerpt from 'The City', from *The Complete
Poems of Cavafy*, translated by Rae Davlen.

The Estate of W. B. Yeats and Macmillan &
Co. Ltd for permission to reproduce twenty-
seven lines from *The Collected Poems of
W. B. Yeats*.

Faber & Faber Ltd for permission to
reproduce twelve lines from 'Journey of the
Magi' by T. S. Eliot, from *Collected Poems
1909–1962*.

The Trustees of the Hardy Estate and
Macmillan & Co. Ltd for permission to
reproduce nine lines from 'Weathers' by
Thomas Hardy from *Collected Poems of
Thomas Hardy*.

F. W. Bateson Esq for permission to
reproduce four verses from his poem 'Spring in
Massachusetts'.

Afterword

by Julia O'Faolain

——————— ♣ ———————

So dear Sean,

Here ends the long dialogue between you, the rest of us, and your several selves! Your remains, even as I write, are being dissected in the Dublin Medical School to which you willed them. That choice saddened me since, in life, you hated to see things reduced to their elements.

Did you, I wonder, make it from love of paradox? Or to thumb your nose at the Church which, at the time, was still forbidding people to leave their bodies – 'temples of the Holy Ghost' – to science? If so, perhaps rending your temple's veil was a last *non serviam*?

Just as you did not fear to imagine the dissector's scalpel, so you never minded my probings. On the contrary. They helped test your camouflage. Hiders invite seekers – as *Vive Moi!* shows, for it is written flirtatiously. So let me, one last time, play the role to which I am conditioned, having been formed by you as trees are formed by a prevailing wind.

In my childhood you truly were an Aeolian force whose words drew music from the air. You, Sean, were a tropical boon in my life, as bountiful as the Gulf Stream which thaws our chilly island. But – how evade a curmudgeonly, Philip Larkin-ish 'but'? – you also gave a skewed notion of the way things were. Like a playful uncle, you were evasive and a touch untrustworthy – a worrying thing in a father. 'They fuck you up, your Mum and Dad,' wrote Larkin. Even the best of them do, and since, without their fucking, we wouldn't be here, how complain? I'm not. Only saying that I seek because you hid, and *you* – well, you

vii

explain that when you say here – in Chapter 9 – apropos of Joyce, Yeats and Frank O'Connor, 'Some defensive reaction is inevitable in every writer whom the gods drop into an anti-pathetic environment, a threat against which the artist must sooner or later concoct an anodyne to preserve his personality.'

Squid-like, then, the Irish writer squirts – or used to – his ink to blur the waters, and your own method shows up in your metaphors. Aeolian, you played with clouds. Your proem to this memoir muses on how you missed them in places such as Italy, where 'whenever a cloud occluded the ruthless sun I felt my senses at once leap in whatever part of me irrevocably belongs to this island of dark green brooding under a sky which is one vast pearl.' Over and again, clouds float through your writing. In life as in fiction you used them as a scrim to blur edges, magnify effects and keep what you called 'realism' at bay.

'You,' you sometimes said pityingly to me, 'are a realist!'

Well, growing up in your prismatic dazzle, what else would I be? Myth-makers breed demystifyers and romantic realists. A lot of Irish people had, by my time, begun groping for light rather than cover and were less awed by that 'vast pearl' which still peers down on them like the eye of a cataract-ridden but intrusive God.

In this, to be sure, they were partly following your lead for, 'half-dreamer' though you claimed to be, you had your Prome-thean moments. More accurately: there were successive Seans and the one you called the 'integrated citizen', the ex-IRA acti-vist who defended liberal values against your dodgy old com-rades when they came to power, was a stripper away of veils. You relinquished the role slowly between 1946, when you gave up the editorship of *The Bell*, and 1964, date of the first edition of *Vive Moi*.

That edition wound down the polemic with the Irish *res publica*, signalling the withdrawal to privacies about which you were so loath to write that your narrative, on reaching the late 1930s, mantled itself in mist and did a fade-out. Citing Mauri-ac's *Mémoires intérieurs* as support, you used to argue that an autobiography's proper subject was a life's inner trajectory rather than its external accidents.

Your real reason for censoring these was reluctance to hurt

Eileen. Having managed – you hoped – to keep your private life compartmentalized, you had now, like a kindly Bluebeard, to stop her discovering the memory-chamber which contained other women. So, you sealed it up – and it at once began to obsess you. Increasingly, you took to reliving your love affairs and, on my visits, there was always a hot, shy moment when you would reminisce, your mind steaming over sunbursts of memory. As writing grew difficult, they became the one topic which could rouse you – which is why I persuaded you to defy your own ban and write them down.

'Write a candid supplement to *Vive Moi*,' I urged. 'It need not be published yet.'

So you did and here it is, gleaming like a web in the mist, ambushing and throwing light on painful memories – then fracturing it to conceal the pain.

Candid? Yes and no. The omissions are striking: Eileen's stress-maladies for instance, brought on by your philandering with Honor Tracy – and Honor's attempts to win you for herself. Were you really able to blind yourself to these?

'She was,' you used to say of her, when remembering your lovers, 'the best of the lot!' And I wondered whether you felt this because you liked the man you were when you knew her: the 'integrated citizen' who needed no cloudiness to dress up his feelings? And because she had an eye like a laser beam for cutting through clouds.

'Could you have lived with that for long?' I asked you once and you stared into the distance, then took off at a tangent, confusing your tracks like a ringing fox.

I remember Honor. She *was* fat and had no ankles but, to make up for that, had a thrilling laugh and a candour which astounded me. My mother disliked her – is this an understatement? Probably. I: pained, priggish and adolescently blind to how people looked, was confused by my own crush on this exotic Englishwoman who, alone of the people I knew in the Ireland of the 1940s, called a spade a spade. With wit! And relish. In her seductively musical voice. Surely – I think now – this was a tactic? A way of digging you out? Wanting you for herself, she must have seen Irish clannishness and double-think as inimical. A moderate scandal – did she hope? – might shake you free. At all events, she provoked a few. One occasion of universal betrayal can surely not have escaped your memory. I remember it like this:

You and Eileen had arranged a family holiday in your old haunt of Gougane Barra in West Cork. It was a pilgrimage to commune with memories and with old friends who synchronised their visits. That year you had hired a horse-caravan and driven it from Cork city, pausing in places where you had been on the run during the Civil War playing cards in back kitchens, splashing through floods – it was a rainy summer – and sending bulletins back to a Dublin Sunday paper which published them with snapshots of us, of the caravan, and of the fat hired mare called, I remember suddenly, Scarlet!

Then Honor, the Scarlet Woman herself, turned up. Uninvited? Almost certainly, for no booking had been made and by then we were in Gougane, whose hotel was full. Every cabin with a spare bed was full – so she slept, to the scandal of native and tourist alike, in the caravan, which was parked in the hotel yard and could be suspected of being a trysting place for your adulterous visits.

We were ostracised. Pointedly and painfully. The old friends held loud, convivial parties to which we, alone among the hotel's guests, were not asked. Even my mother was excluded which, in retrospect, seems odd – unless, from pride, she deliberately joined the ranks of the pariahs? I don't know. I was thirteen and baffled and began to see what had been happening only years later when, as I sat with friends in the bar of a Dublin restaurant – I was now at the university – you and Honor came down the stairs and I saw that you had been dining together. She and Eileen had by now fallen out; she no longer visited us and I hadn't known you were seeing her.

When you broke with her, she rented a small, Gothic-Revival tower a stone's throw from our house, which was on the edge of a village where everyone knew everyone. An Impatient Griselda, she lived there defiantly for years while publishing satiric pieces about Ireland for which you got the blame. She couldn't, went local wisdom, have raked up all that muck by herself. I think of her with sorrow. She had spirit and rose above her physical drawbacks in a way which was surely harder to do then.

In my years as your agony aunt, I could never get you to say why you fell for increasingly plain women. Each, to be sure, had other qualities. Yet the pattern was odd – especially as you had chances with pretty ones, including two acknowledged beauties in whom you took very little interest. Timidity? Hardly.

Quite early on, I remember your being chased by a woman who – you told me years later – froze you in your tracks by saying, 'I want *everything*!' That was not your style and you backed off at speed. She was handsome too – unlike your chosen three. But then so was my mother, although she was not photogenic – or perhaps was never photographed by anyone who could handle a camera? When I was in my twenties and met Ernie Simmons who had known her when she was my age, he carried on like an old Greek remembering Helen of Troy. Maybe that was why she was able to put up with your misdemeanours? Whatever you were after implied no flaw in her. And, I suspect, you must secretly and passionately have conjured her to stay. For you were devoted to her at the end, and, when she died, went briefly out of your mind.

To return to the woman who wanted everything, I remember her dropping by one morning when a dustily aproned Eileen, the washerwoman, the skivvy, and the man who dug the garden were busy with chores. The visitor wore green eyeshadow – which none of us had seen before. Was this what brought the aproned chorus into the drawing room? Or had they been there anyway, doing something like spring cleaning? All I recall is our common stupefaction as we stood marvelling at this green-eyed bird of paradise, whose manic state seemed to have no explanation, while waiting for you, Sean, to emerge from your study and, somehow, ratify the occasion.

Throughout my childhood, 'la Bowen' – as my mother called Elizabeth Bowen – was an offstage source of contention in that she invited you, but not Eileen, to house parties. 'They're professional gatherings!' you would argue with lofty perfidy, as you packed your bag.

Was it quite perfidy though? Reading here that you were 'half in love' with her before you met her, I see that your affair was indeed an *affaire de tête*, a willed encounter between you and your Irish Turgenev and between the Irelands your fictions had portrayed. Her *The Last September* had seen the Troubles from the viewpoint of a Great House and your *Midsummer Night's Madness* from that of the men who burned such houses down. Sex, then, as synechdoche? A 'professional' conjunction after all? Interestingly, even in this candid memoir, you have less to say about her than about her work.

The one time I met her, when she came to our house in London in the early 1970s, she revealed with relish that her name for you was 'Johnny'. A tease? A dig? A bit of closet imperialism? I wonder if you ever called her 'Eilís'? Hostilities, to be sure, can give a liaison zest. As the actress, Arletty, is said to have said when accused of sleeping with a German during the war, 'Gentlemen, my heart is French, but my c— is international.' Even as a child, I guessed that 'la Bowen' had no great hold on your heart.

Hints and intimations: I am seven or so; my bedroom is on the ground floor and, very early one morning, the curtains part and you appear at the window. 'How fresh you look!' you exclaim. 'The ladies I know never look fresh so early in the morning!'

Ladies? What ladies? I can tell that you mean to puzzle me, but not why. The occasion is baffling and because it is, I remember it. Then one Christmas, I ask for a gift of *The Child's Encyclopedia*. You demur, then consent, adding a bottle of appleblossom fragrance as a counterpoise. I must not, you warn, become a blue-stocking. Literary ladies grow hair on their faces! 'Like,' you add ungallantly, 'Elizabeth Bowen!' Later you bring me a Spanish fan made of gilded paper with images of posturing peacockish bull-fighters. It is a gift from her whom I have never seen and adds to my sense of a contrived relationship. Over the years, further satiric quips confirm the impression.

By contrast, Kick Erlanger, your last lover, was shrewd and likeable, had a very short attention span, and seemed to flick through the end of her life as through a glossy bestiary. She was knowledgeable about horses, dogs and birds, having written about poodles and worked with the US Army on mine-detecting.

If poodles were not in the end used for this, it was, she swore, because they were too clever for the men. Her spell with the military was acrimonious and she was amusing about the addle-pated top brass who did things like classifying her reports as so secret that she herself could not get access to them.

Here, Sean, is my Last and Final diagnosis as your agony aunt.

Your three great loves – 'la Bowen', Tracy and Kick – had wounded personalities. Stendhalian and histrionic, their galled wit gave them that doubleness to which you were addicted since the days when your mother kept such lodgers as Long John Silver and the Ghost of Hamlet's father. The stammering Elizabeth Bowen, whose mad father and declining family fortunes drove her to snobbery and fiction, Honor tormented by her bulk, and Kick, your aging 'Miss Information' – already aware of her cancer? – all found relief in fantasies which delighted you. Yet they were capable too of taking a courageous look at life, and so incarnated your beloved Stendhalian mix: realistic psychology validating the absurd-but-thrilling claptrap of romance, such as the rope ladders from which Julian Sorel climbs through the heroine's bedroom window and the pistols with which he shoots her in church. (And Honor's damp and avid, phallus-shaped, stone tower?) This play of sense and non-sense, illusion and truth, pluralised experience for you – and gave you what you craved. It was when Honor tried to pin you to a single reality that you backed off. (A wonder she didn't shoot you!) Kick's misinformation was more to your taste, so you played along with it. She was in her mid-seventies at the end and so withered that, despite your indiscretions, none of us could believe you were having an affair.

In this connection, it is piquant to see you misreport my meeting with her old acquaintance at Villa San Michele. Nadia, so far from being as you describe her, was then outrageously wearing haute couture mini-skirts and having an affair with a sailor. And, not only did I not ask her Kick's age but, no sooner did I mention Kick than Nadia, fearing to be taken for her contemporary, exclaimed: 'Don't tell me *she's* still alive? She must have sold her soul to the devil! She's ancient, you know!'

When I told you this – remember: we didn't know of your affair – you, I suppose, mentioned Nadia to Kick who, fearing in turn to be 'dated' by association, thought up the story about how Nadia dressed old, dyed her hair white, and used quaint expressions like 'My child'. In short, she turned the thing on its head and you happily accepted it, just as you did when she told you that her own gilded hair was natural. Its true/false gleam brought back the thrill of the old Cork Opera House in a way that the natural blondeness of my beautiful friend S., who was eager to flirt with you, did not. Doubleness was all. Thrills and kinks go back to childhood, a time when – even without an Opera House spilling its coiled canvas sky into your street – simultaneities of belief and disbelief can occasion paroxysms of anxiety and glee.

And that brings me to that traumatic beating by your mother which must be the Larkin-ish source for a lot! Could it, I wonder, explain that old puzzle: the fact that you invested Eileen with every quality – beauty, idealism, etc. – then looked for your pleasures elsewhere? 'Eileen,' you used to say, when remembering the women in your life, 'is in a different category.'

The true wife-and-mother must be kept separate from the false one and the good woman from the adventuress! Such soothing dichotomies are common in folk tales where cruelty is often ascribed to stepmothers or other intruders who assume the true mothers' appearance! Your own mother had switched abruptly from kind to cruel and, like the old tale-tellers, you couldn't face the blend – but neither, unlike them, could you bring yourself to write about it until the very end of your life.

Instead, look what you did with her in the oral history of our family and in those stories of yours where she appears! You Bowdlerised her! Applying to her the very Edwardian gentility with which you reproached *her*, you turned an aggressive creature, whose wilful ways – pissing standing up and, if I read you aright, at or towards you – aim to reverse her gender, into a meek, caricature Irish mother! Passive and two-dimensional. Remembering her photograph, I feel I should have suspected this image! In the one I have, she is seated but looks likely to stand as tall as her husband and three sons – you, the smallest, were just under six feet and, between you, you could have fielded a basketball team. She had a strong jaw and sad eyes and, despite my distress for you, I have a feminist fellow-feeling for her.

Her misdirected violence must surely have been a kind of wild protest at her lot? One thinks of Medea. Without minimising the mischief wreaked on you, I cannot but wonder what lay behind it? Shame at her own half-perceived urges? Jealousy? Loneliness as she saw you step away from her and go to your peers? The words are husks, since I lack information to plump them with guesses. But there is a strikingly similar mother-and-son scene in one of Robertson Davies' novels. I wonder what you would have made of that if you'd read it? Might you have been soothed? The fact that you didn't yourself try for the catharsis of writing out the memory tells me how badly it had maimed you.

To come to her pissing. The small James Joyce became, as we know, so excited while watching a female servant doing just this that, later, he got his wife to do it over him. Was it really a female servant, one wonders. Might it not, more probably, since the impact on him was so lasting, have been his mother? Then might not he, using the same device as the old tellers of folk-tales, have tidied up her memory by ascribing the incident to a servant? This would explain the fact that his mother is such a faceless figure in his fiction, being indeed the ur-example of the effaced and pious fictional Irish mother – *fons et origo* of a long line of moaning Minnies.

Suppose instead – a wild (?) surmise – that the writers' real Mums were so unacceptably earthy that their sons felt obliged to suppress this side of them in literature? Thus leaving them doubly cloven and, indeed, halved? Might the real ones' true role-model have been Queen Maeve, Prime Mover in our pre-Christian saga, the *Táin*? That, you'll remember, starts in one version, with a pillow talk during which Maeve and her kingly husband lie in bed comparing possessions and she finds that, though she can match all his other riches, he has a fine black bull the like of which she does not have. Piqued, she sends her men out to seize one belonging to another king and declares that she won't piss until they bring it back. When, after many feats, the raid is over, she empties her bladder and makes the biggest lake in the British Isles: Lough Neagh. Eileen loved that story. She had an earthy imagination, despite living under your idealising bell jar. You see – you tidied her up too.

Oh, but I shouldn't spar with you now, Sean, since this time you can't answer me! So I'll admit that when I first read your account of my grandmother's goings on, I was sufficiently upset to contemplate doing my own bit of Bowdlerising! I thought of cutting it out. But how could I, having urged you towards candour?

Perhaps if we'd tamed it in talk, you might have got a story out of it and come to terms with the memory? If I'd spun my nonsense about Queen Maeve for you over a glass – or more – of Irish whiskey, might you have? Just as, years ago, you and I and Lauro, my husband, got tipsy together on one of your visits to LA and you told us about the little girl whom you and your mates used to pay when you were small to 'show' her private parts?

'Write a story about it,' we advised. But you said you were too embarrassed. 'When embarrassed, write!' cried we, made sage by drink. So you wrote that gentle, lyrical story, *The Talking Trees*.

But perhaps it was even harder to write about such things as fact? I am reminded of Yeats' poem about his poetry which ends,

> I must lie down where all the ladders start,
> In the foul rag and bone shop of the heart.

Your new *Vive Moi!* does that gallantly. Bravo, Sean, and long may your memory live! *Vive ton moi!*

Proem

Under this Irish tent of clouds the trees are inky-green, so deeply
pitted by dark caverns, so dark against the paleness of the clouds
that at twilight I sometimes find it hard to distinguish the ash
from the copper beech. When my eyes lift from this silhouette-
greenness in search of the veiled heart of light they remain wide
and wandering for a long time, and whenever I look down again
I imagine that the caverns have become even darker than before.
The trees, except on the wildest days, seem immobile and pon-
derous, too heavy with long-soaked-in moisture to stir. Whenever I look up again I often find it impossible to tell whether
the cloud floes are moving at all, for it is the whole mass that
floats, ever so slowly. I love the windy days when the clouds
roll and the sky is as if somebody had flung a scatter of watercolours into it to dissolve and spread. I love the autumn when
there are fields of yellow and brown, beige and chrome, saffron
and gold with ripening oats, barley and wheat, and the leaves
glow and burn. But I love far more those two colours of my
childhood, the raingod's green, dark as passion, and this pallid
immensity of the sky. All the other colours of Ireland are sub-
dued by these dominant two – the violet slates of old houses,
the brown thatch over the buttermilk cottages, the salmon-pink
of Georgian brickwork, the old sausage-meat walls of outhouses
made up of bits of brownstone, sandstone, limestone, greeny
shale and peeling cement, the leaden rivers, the grumbling lakes
with their tawny streaks of foam, the solemn, wine-stained sea,
the shadowed skins of the beech, the ash, the holly, the alder.
All these gleam only when the rain falls and the sun follows,

and then the rain soon returns to darken them again. I was starved as a child for colour and hardness. I used to long to eat those crisp violet roof slates, crackle them under my teeth like biscuits. When, as a grown man, I first laid eyes on northern Italy what overpowered me was the colour blazing in churches and palaces faced with marble and mosaic, the tesselated pavements, the houses painted in fading and peeling ochre and pink; and when I went on southward to Calabria's heap of brittleness hanging on over the edge of the emerald Ionian I was at once enslaved by its caked and cruel earth, by the tawny, dusty dryness in its crepe-skinned gypsy flesh. And yet, whenever the clouds occluded the ruthless sun I felt my senses at once leap in whatever part of me irrevocably belongs to this island of dark green brooding under a sky that is one vast pearl.

It is in this chaste and chastened mood of surrender and acceptance, all boasting done, that I call this book *Vive Moi!* I am where and what I was born. The two wry words of French came to me from a long brick wall in Paris on which somebody had chalked the words VIVE PÉTAIN, which another hand had crossed out in favour of VIVE BIDAULT, and another crossed out in favour of VIVE MENDÈS-FRANCE, and yet another rejected to write VIVE DE GAULLE, until one last wavering, wandering drunken hand drew a line through the whole bang lot and signed himself with a flourish VIVE MOI! I imagine this happy roisterer as passing that way the following morning with a throbbing head, rolling his eyes up under their lids as he sees his midnight flourish on the wall. He is not a burly fellow. He is a slight, even a small man. His wife has given him hell, his children have given him delightedly sardonic glances across the breakfast table. He hastens on, chastened but impenitent, self-accepting with a shrug, head into the wind, muttering the two words obstinately out of the corner of his moustache. So, in his footsteps, do I write now, borrowing his piece of chalk – What was he? A cooper, a tailor, a sign painter? – and his midnight and his morning mood.

2

Double Doors

I

Our house on the corner of Half Moon Street looked across the River Lee flowing or ebbing between deep limestone quays. Except for the seagulls and the fishermen nothing ever happened in this part of the river, which was always empty except for a couple of moored rowboats spotted by seagulls' droppings. The edge of the quay was guarded by a series of limestone posts joined each to each by iron bars. Over these bars brown fishing-nets were hung to dry when in the spring the salmon fishermen sat on the pavement and mended their nets with little wooden bobbins shaped like boats, and then boiled them in big iron pots or round sitbaths full of bubbling creosote. For months afterwards those sections of the quayside were spidered with cobwebs of brown and black. Now and then an old woman walked there, slowly, on fine days. A bit farther up the river there was a slip, or slope down to the river, absolutely forbidden to us three children – I had two older brothers – but we naturally visited it often; it was irresistible at high tide, when bobbing bits of flotsam, cork, wood, empty boxes or the like gathered there for the taking. Our house was over a pub. It was Number 16.

From these quayside windows we saw, on the farther side of the river, the pillared, limestone façade of the Church of Saint Mary, bearing on top of its triangular pediment a statue of the Virgin, on whose halo one nearly always saw a perched seagull. Beside this white church front was a graceful Italian campanile in reddish brick with white limestone quoins. Below it stood a wide Georgian house, also in brick with limestone quoins. Next came a store on whose slated roof one read (as soon as one could read) the big white words CHAS. DALY BUTTER STORES. Next to that was a big hoarding or billboard bright with large-scale advertisements. At the foot of this gaudy coloured hoarding six policemen gathered in a line every morning within minutes of nine o'clock before dispersing for their rounds of duty when Shandon struck the hour. Policemen's shifts were from nine to three, from three to six, and from six to eleven, after which special night duty began. My father was one of those half-dozen bobbies.

Above and behind this riverside façade an army of blue-slated houses went clambering up the hills, and topping their cliff, up against the clouded sky, rose the tower of Shandon. This, Cork's emblem, consists of four immense boxes, each smaller than the one below, rising from a base of solid red sandstone with white limestone quoins that outline each of its four edges and its tiny arched windows. The whole of this fantasy is crowned by a tiny green dome bearing, for its weathervane, a golden fish swimming into the wind. On each side of the tower there is a clock-face. In time with it Shandon's bells rang our lives away, quarter by quarter, all through the day and night. The clouds fell down into the river's stillness. The bells sank into the water and were drowned. Far to the left and right were other hills with dark-green trees against the pale sky. I must have gazed and listened for hours, especially when, sometimes, the verger would play carillons or whole tunes, such as *The Last Rose of Summer*, or *Come Back to Erin*, for the city spread far below. The tunes had to be simple since the chimes were limited to a single octave of eight naturals, so that whenever there should be a sharp the poor man had to use a natural, and if he ever wanted to go above his range he just banged his top note and hoped for the best.

Those were the background noises of my childhood: the chiming bells; the constant squawks of silver seagulls endlessly gyring, wheeling, volplaning on to the water; the distant murmur of the busier streets in from the river; the bells of the city's churches, ringing for the Angelus, for Mass, for the

4

evening devotions. Occasionally one would hear a hoot like a cockcrow from a ship farther down the quays about to cast off for Queenstown and the Atlantic. After dark we heard little except the comings and goings from the pub below us, though sometimes a group of boys and girls would circle the Opera House nearby, singing the music hall songs of the day in improvised harmony. The nights were deathly silent except for Shandon's hourglass dropping time into the darkness and past of this little city in whose valley-cradle I slept.

I am filled with awe when I think of those night hours. They make me think of the many other lost hours, lost years – lost because as completely vacant in my memory – that I spent beside those quiet quays in the waking sleep of childish content, a hibernatory cocoon of total happiness. The very thought of those contented years frightens the life out of me when I consider all that I was taking in, all that was being put into me, unknown to my will. I fear those dark nights, that gentle river, those silent quays, from which I must often have embarked out of my motionless body.

I am much clearer about Half Moon Street itself, the little street on which our side-windows looked out and on which our door gave egress. I remember it with accuracy. On our side of this street – moving from the river in towards the centre of the city – there was, first, an ancient cooperage, composed of sheds, and an old cobbled yard, smelling of wood shavings, old iron, beer barrels and wine vats; then came a series of stables, smelling of hay and horse dung; then came a forge, smelling of coal smoke and annealing iron, clanging all day long; then came a minute store or factory where somebody concocted a condiment still known as Kandy Sauce; and, lastly, an electrician's shop, at Number 5, effectively Number 1, over which we were to live in later years when our first house, Number 16, grew too small for our ambitions.

Along the other side of this street – we are moving back, now, towards the river – there ran, first, the rear of the municipal School of Art, a not ungraceful building, in the usual pink brick faced with limestone; and then – the real interest of Half Moon Street for me, the core of its wonder and the reasons why I remember it with such devoted satisfaction – the dressing

5

rooms, scene docks, and stage door of the Cork Opera House. This tall double door, arched and high-flung to give room for the scenery to enter and leave, was always open by day, venting stale air otherwise imprisoned for almost a hundred years, and that particular smell of all theatres, which seems to be made up of dust motes, ropes, canvas mouldering, the gluey size laid on scenery under its paint, cigarette smoke, beer, sweat, and, unless I am now imagining it, scent, powder and the fading stink of greasepaint. Frozen applause. The ghosts of words. Behind this arched door a wide stairway, iron-tipped, led up to the backstage area, generally closed off by a second double door guarded by old Downey, the stage-door keeper. In the summer it was often thrown open for ventilation, and then we small peepers on the pavement below could see hints of what was going on inside.

I would see men and women passing to and from the stage, hurriedly or slowly, a robed king with a crown, a pirate with a cutlass, ladies and gentlemen in rich clothes, beautiful girls in pink tights and tiny skirts, their arms, backs and bosoms paper-white, soldiers in red coats, armed cowboys, a Negro in chains, or a tattered beggar. It is not their strange costumes that I remember with passion but their Indian-coloured faces and red mouths, and their great eyes darkened and staring. It was, of course, explained to me that these were actors and actresses. Far from resolving my unappeasable and delighted bewilderment – an experience repeated week after week, through year after year – this explanation merely intensified my astonishment at seeing the here constantly become the elsewhere, the solid dissolve, the familiar become unfamiliar, things and people become most persuasively whatever they were only when they were least whatever they had been so persuasively before and would, just as persuasively, become again a few hours hence.

Every Sunday morning or Saturday night I would see at this arched door the departure, and every Sunday afternoon or Monday morning the arrival of forests, waterfalls, mountains, grey castles, panelled halls, mossy rocks, cannons, candelabras, bundled swords and muskets, gold chairs, thrones, white clouds billowing up from or subsiding down on great drays drawn by hairy-legged draft horses. But who carried the golden throne, the grey castle or the mossy rock out of the dusty gloom into the sunlight? It was Tommy Mulvaney or Jim Dooley who would then, darting across to the pub for a pint, pat me on the head and ask after my father. Who bore the blue skies, sagging like thirty-foot-long furled flags, up from the street to the stage's dimlit maw? It was Lazy Casey or Georgie Cantwell, who might, tomorrow morning, be whitewashing the ceiling for my mother, or holding up the street corner by the quay waiting for the pub to open. There were no borders in my mind between this actuality and that fantasy. It seemed entirely natural to me when one day the doors were flung open (in the middle of a matinee of *A Royal Divorce*) to allow the acrid smoke of the Battle of Waterloo to creep out into Half Moon Street, and pouring out through its pungent clouds came the entire Napoleonic Army, sometimes called the Cork Butter Exchange Band, clutching the instruments with which they had been playing the *Marseillaise*, dressed in Grand Army uniforms, hastening across to the Alaska Bar for foaming pints quaffed with rolling eyes and hearty moustache-sucking in the middle of the street. I was no more surprised the day I found Cinderella's white-and-gold coach standing in the cobbled yard of the cooperage. One afternoon an ambulance from the North Infirmary arrived in our streets to bear away two bleeding *sans-culottes* (from *The Scarlet Pimpernel*), one of them still wearing his tricoloured cap. They proved on closer inspection to be my old friends Lazy Casey and Tommy Mulvaney, who had become so transported by the heat of battle in a mob fight as to have momentarily become what they had been persuaded to pretend to be.

I hold a column of thick golden coins, napoleons, given to me by one of my scene-shifter pals. In my palms they are about eight inches high, beautiful, shining things. A clutch of urchins gathers about me at once, asking for one for me, and one for me, and I give them out royally until I have only one left. On the face of my one coin is the profile of the Emperor. On the back of the pasteboard I read, printed black on white: *A Royal Divorce*, NEXT WEEK, 8 P.M. NIGHTLY.

My mother decided presently to take in what she called *arteestes* as weekly lodgers which meant that soon I began to meet the most interesting people face to face in our kitchen. I do not myself remember the day, but one of my brothers vouches for it, when a bearded gentleman with a deep voice paused at the kitchen door to have a friendly word with my father, tipped my chin with a smile and passed softly on. 'A very nice gentleman,' my father said when he was gone. 'Very well spoken. He is the ghost of Hamlet's father.' Simon Legree helped me every evening for a week with my simple arithmetical problems; he was much more helpful than Long John Silver, who later did my Latin translations for me so badly that on each morning following I was given a sound wigging in school for his piratical mistakes. Has anyone heard of the great Kentucky play *Mrs Wiggs of the Cabbage Patch*?* She used to come down to our kitchen every morning plump in a pink kimono for a cup of hot tea with my mother and a dekko at the *Cork Examiner*. It was to her my father announced one morning, with sad solemnity, that there would be no performance of her play in the Opera House tonight.

'W'y not?' she asked in astonishment. 'Has the blessed theatre gone up in smoke or sump'n?'

'His Majesty King Edward the Seventh died last night.'

Mrs Wiggs sank to the floor in a beautiful faint.

I recall with tenderness a lovely young creature, whose name I never knew, the only woman whose empty Player's Navy Cut cigarette carton I have kissed with tears, and the only woman I have ever personally known to be sawn in two every night, by an illusionist known as The Great Lafayette. I have established that he was burned to death in 1911 in an Edinburgh theatre while gallantly trying to save his pet ponies, so I cannot have been much over ten when I adored her. Such is the frailty of love and memory that I cannot remember a single thing she said to me, although I do think that I know that she told me a lot of interesting things about the private life of the late King Edward. I suppose I don't remember them because I did not listen to her, so exquisite she was to look at.

They came to us in the kitchen, they passed me on the stairs, they sent me on errands, out of *The Light That Failed*, *Two Little Vagabonds*, *Bella Donna*, *The Sorrows of Satan*, *The Sign*

* By Alice Hegan Rice, 1901.

8

of the Cross, East Lynne, A Bachelor's Romance, When a Man's in Love, Brewster's Millions, A Bunch of Violets, The Bells, Alone in London, Sweet Lavender and ten hundred more, typical, I now know, of the English theatre at its lowest ebb since about 1699. There were, in justice to Cork, to the period and to my own infatuation, exceptions: Shakespeare above all, with Sir Frank Benson, Alexander Marsh and Charles Doran (Sir Ralph Richardson began his acting career with him), an occasional Sheridan, Goldsmith, Wilde, Pinero and the then daring Shaw, fair wallops of grand opera with Moody Manners and others, lots of Gilbert and Sullivan, and some quite inexplicable personal visitations – these must have been down on their luck – from Maud Allan the dancer, Esmé Percy and Mrs Pat Campbell. Plays and actors, good or bad, they introduced me to art and to England, they made London my capital, they inflamed my imagination and fanned my senses, they doped me and benzedrined me. I was their willing Trilby, a name that names them and their age, Edwardian in all its blissful somnambulism. Zena Dare, Phyllis Dare, Sir James Matthew Barrie, Jerome Klapka Jerome, José Collins, *The Arcadians*, Henry Arthur Jones, *The Silver King*, Sidney Grundy, Marie Corelli, *The Prisoner of Zenda*. By all the laws of chance I did not stand a chance of ever understanding the real nature of the world into which I was dropped. It was, as you may say, the age of other people too, Thomas Hardy, Cunningham Grahame, Max Beerbohm, Verhaeren, Claudel, D'Annunzio, Ibsen, Sudermann, Monet, France, Zola, Samuel Butler, Gissing, Forster, and if it comes to that of our own George Moore and Willy Yeats. But how in hell could I, could Cork, could any of us know about *them*? I am between twelve and fourteen at the time I am now describing. I was sixteen or seventeen before I heard of or read any of them.

When our lodgers leave our house at night for the theatre I wander wonderingly through their rooms, their fires banked cosily for their return at half-past eleven, a late supper laid out for them on white napkins spread over the soft Paisley table-covering of ink-stained chenille. I gaze in awe at their exotic belongings – the travelling clock in red leather, the whiskey bottle with the patent lock, photographs of themselves and their friends in silver frames, all signed, their specially ordered bits

9

of outlandish food on the sideboard, Gorgonzola, Smyrna figs, piccalilli, Palmyra grapes, Peak Frean's rusks, Whitbread's ale, Yorkshire relish, cold veal pie, their foreign papers and magazines, the *Stage*, the *Performer*, the *Red Magazine*, the *Strand*. I touch a lady's snow-white furry slipper. I lift and let fall a diaphanous nightgown. I examine, do not know the purpose of, yet have, it seems, not forgotten a travelling douche. I smell a man's pipes. For fifty years afterwards I wanted an Austrian meerschaum with an amber mouthpiece in a red leather case because the first one I met had such an exquisite smell. Once or twice in *London Life* I stared, transfixed by shame, fear, and delighted wonder, at my first pictures of lusciously naked women. It is my impression that in these Edwardian times women were expected to be bulky, have big shoulders, breasts, thighs, all the old solid, reliable Renaissance idea of lusciousness in large quantities. The 1914–1918 war changed all that. Men stuck for years in muddy, sodden trenches dreamed of tender, innocent, pig-tailed girls, 'birds', 'flappers', as the women thought of them as 'boys'. Foreign smells were all over the house. The air of our solitary bathroom was dyed in heliotrope and verbena. Our single lavatory stank beautifully of female shit. It all made me long for far-off places with alluring names – Swansea and Blackpool, Newcastle and Dundee, Aberdeen (that name was like a spell), Perth, Burton-on-Trent.

On Sunday mornings as each latest group left us, waving their cheery and elegant farewells to 'Ma', off to those desirable, distant places, my heart would become darkened and troubled with sad longings. If, presently, I heard a faint, far whistle coming softly on the wind from over the hills behind Shandon as their train emerged from Cork's mile-long railway tunnel, it was like hearing a long, sorrowfully exhausted sigh bleeding all beauty white. I would remain sad until the door knocker thumped late in the afternoon and some new envoys from far away would enter, with more smells, more exotic belongings, more checked coats and caps, more cheery English greetings, more incitations to my by now unshakable belief that all beautiful women are good, that all handsome men are brave, that courage and love triumph over everything, that every sorrow has its balm, that virtue will always find its due reward before life's brown safety curtain (fireproof) sinks heavily behind the foot-lights – bearing the proud motto of Cork City: *Statio Bene Fida Carinis*, A Safe Harbour for Ships, written in a scroll in gilt under our city's armorial bearings, two castles and a homing barque.

I could evoke the flavour of that never-never world in which I grew up much better if I had a little music box inserted in the back of this book to tinkle out the songs of the city's other theatre, its music hall, called the Palace, much frequented by the British military then garrisoned on us to the shame of our nationalists and the satisfaction of our shop-keepers. If you are under eighty you will have never heard them. *If Your Lips Could Only Speak*, *I Didn't Want to Love You but You Made Me Do It*, *I Wonder If You Miss Me Sometimes*, *Miss Me When the Twilight's Blue*, *By the Side of the Zuyder Zee*, *Fall In and Follow Me*, *By the Light of the Silvery Moon*; songs from *Floradora*, *The Country Girl*, *The Merry Widow*, *The Girl in the Taxi* ... If my music box could croon them out to you from those days of hobble skirts, harem skirts, Phul Nana scent, hats two feet wide, violets in furs, pipe clay belts, brass buttons and puttees, barouches, muddy streets, crossing sweepers, trailing skirts held up to show buttoned boots, you might then better see a small boy apparently lost, at least wandering, in wide-eyed wonder, through this Oriental bazaar called Cork.

Only one feature of this life irked me – touting for tenants, meaning that if by any Saturday my mother still had a disen-gaged room she would dispatch me on Sunday afternoon to the railway-station where, around 4 p.m., the morning train from Dublin would arrive bearing its actresses and its actors, the paraphernalia of the play due to open the following night, its scenery, its load of effects, its great creaking travelling baskets of costumes. Most of these travellers would of course have already reserved rooms in established boarding-houses, but it was my task to spot among all the passengers on the train any who, by their dress or/and accents, looked English and among these any who looked at a loss about where in this city they might lay their heads for the next seven nights. These I would approach, holding out a printed visiting card, bearing my mother's name and address, and some such encomium as

Reasonable Apartments, or *Highly Recommended Lodgings*, or *Three Minutes From Your Stage Door*, saying politely as I did so 'Quite settled apartments?' Now, if my name were Guy de Maupassant, or Saki, or Anton Chekhov, or James Joyce, or Honoré de Balzac, and if I knew that one day all this stuff was going to be grist to the mill of my worldwide fame as a brilliant evocator of Bohemia's mechanical backgrounds I would have revelled in these contacts with not just merely back-stage but off-stage life, in short with the raw material of fiction, drama, and conceivably romance. As things were I think I performed a striking conjuring trick by transforming the whole thing into an Oriental bazaar.

2

Often at night two trickles of pedestrians would pass one another under our windows, going in opposite directions, to the play and to the church. As soon as I was old enough I thus visited another theatre – Saint Peter's and Paul's, every Sunday morning for Mass and Communion, every Monday night for the weekly Confraternity of the Sacred Heart, and every afternoon in Lent, at my mother's command, with my two older brothers, to do the rounds of the Stations of the Cross. It was, to my eyes, an immense church, red sandstone and grey limestone, high, dim, silent, yet never without its few sighing worshippers. I was baptised there, I made my first confession and took my first Communion there, I was confirmed there by our bishop. My father and mother were to lie there in the cold mortuary.

It was full of legends. Its pulpit of carved pine, spired by a tapering fretted pinnacle, was, we believed, the tallest pulpit in the world. The church was lit by trident-like gas standards held by a row of carved angels along each aisle. We were told that a former parish priest, in showing these to a stranger, informed him that they were the work of a great German woodcarver.

'Not so,' said the man. 'They were carved by John Hogan.'

The priest smiled unbelievingly. 'I know whom you mean, the famous Irish sculptor. But Hogan never did anything as fine as these angels.'

For answer the stranger led the priest to one of the angels, drew out a carved quill from one of the wings and showed, carved thereon, the signature *John Hogan*, saying: 'I am John Hogan.'

My mother often led me to pray at the tall crucifixion in the dim southwestern corner, hard by the baptismal font where so many generations of poor children had been christened. As we knelt there under the pendent body of Christ, with the Magdalen, Saint John the Divine and the Virgin grouped sadly beneath, she never failed to whisper to me that the Virgin's foot had performed many miracles of healing. And sure enough (what further proof did I want?) I would, now and again, see a poor black-shawled woman pause there, rub the Virgin's foot with her spittle and then rub the spittle to her eyes, nose, lips, throat and heart, genuflect, sigh upward at the bleeding face of the Redeemer and shuffle away. The painted foot was worn to the marrow of its plaster by these pious rubbings.

Farther down the same aisle was a full-sized carved and coloured figuration of Purgatory, set in a niche large as a small chapel, lit from above by an orange light. There I saw, among the red and yellow plaster flames, the suffering souls, young and old, kneeling with their hands stretched up appealingly from the fire to the Christ Child leaning forward benevolently from His mother's arms. I liked to kneel there and pray for them, fascinated by the girl highest in the group, always almost redeemed, her long, fair hair always falling to her waist, her manacles always already parted, her uppermost hand always just out of reach of the Divine Child's foot. All about me would be the wide lofty church, the wind whispering in the roof slates, the mouse-noise of a candle guttering in the iron candelabra beside me, the far hum of the streets, a groan from some invisible visitant like myself.

The Stations of the Cross were a story. There was a story in every coloured window – Joseph and his brethren, the loaves and the fishes, the birth at Bethlehem. Story after story fell from the lofty pulpit – bearing, often, great phrases of faith – the humble water at Cana that saw its Lord and blushed, the mustard seed that grew up to be the tree of the kingdom of heaven among whose woven tresses the birds sang, the proud centurion at the Crucifixion who created the great and humble prayer *Domine, non sum dignus ut intres sub tectum meum, sed tantum dic verbo*, Lazarus, the seed that fell on stony ground, Not by bread alone, Behold the lilies of the field, Henceforth thou shalt be a fisher of men, Make friends with the mammon of unrighteousness, But the greatest of these is charity.

Many of the ceremonies of the Church are of their nature dramatic, but for me the most dramatic were the matins and lauds sung on Wednesday, Thursday and Friday of Passion Week and called Tenebrae because at the beginning of the office fifteen brown lighted candles on a black triangular candelabra were extinguished one by one, at intervals, until the last, a white candle, representing the Light of the World, was removed and hidden behind the altar, whereupon all the lights in the church went out, and the whole packed congregation clapped loudly to symbolise the confusion following the death of Christ. There were other dramas to excite my devotion and emotion: the stripping of the altars; the washing of the feet; especially the blessing of the Paschal candle, when the priest scattered the water of the font to the four corners of the world, breathed on it in the form of a cross, plunged the candle thrice into it, and poured a drop of oil and chrism into it to signify the union of an anointed King with His people.

How much of all this was a good prospectus for life? Very little, if by 'life' one means a recognisable course or mode of mortal existence.

A major part of the reason is in that coloured window of the birth at Bethlehem. The Virgin is beautifully dressed, every fold in place, her hands slim and delicate, her hair smoothly curled as if, instead of rising from the rending pains of childbirth, she has just come from Charles of the Ritz. Her newborn baby has curly hair and a full set of pearly teeth. Saint Joseph ... Not until years and years after my childhood was over did I realise what I had been doing to myself, what 'they' had been doing to me, during those sentimental years. Then I read Mauriac on his youthful religion; rather, on his youthful religiosity, distinguishing sadly and scornfully between religious intelligence and religious emotionalism. I, too, used the thurible as a scent bottle, luxuriated in the sacraments, enjoyed the ceremonies as I enjoyed the play, got cosy feelings out of the birth and death of Christ. I am speaking of myself as a child and a young boy. I could just as well be speaking of myself in my twenties, when I also found out that

> The Holy Spirit wreaks a terrible revenge when life suddenly confronts the man who has emerged late from a spineless adolescence. What help will he find in a religion which has never been more to him than ... a source of feeble delectation ...

When I first read those lines, late in life, I squirmed. Not that I blame myself as a child (how could I?) or disown my youthful religion, meaning by that last word 'religion' my first contacts with humanity's endless quest for the values of the ideal life. I might as well hope to repudiate my genes, womb, cradle. I do, indeed, repudiate vast stretches of the Roman Catholic church's systemisation of the original, noble adventure which came to be known as the Christian quest. Who, for example, could without a deep sigh discover that 'The Church' took three and a quarter hundred years after the execution of Jesus Christ to decide that he had not been a man but a god, which was finally decided at a secular gathering or assembly or parliament in a town in what used to be called Asia Minor simply by taking a final vote on it, i.e. counting hands up For and thumbs down Against. (This was known as the Nicene Creed.)

Another thing I shall always resent, because it caused me so much suffering as a boy, is the delicate-mindedness, or over-protectiveness, or mealy-mouthedness, whichever it was, of the Irish Church, and the sentimentalised picture of life, especially in relation to sex, that it presented to us through its teaching orders and from the pulpit, except when some tough Redemptorist took over to give us a bit of straight-forward, realistic hell. I think it was chiefly over-protectiveness; as if they believed that if nobody mentioned sex organs we would not notice that we had them, or as if they had decided that in all such matters as the flesh familiarity breeds desire, or as if they considered that God, in creating desire for woman in man, had been guilty of a lapse of taste about which the least said the better. Some of those allusive sermons that I hung on in my nubile years were so euphemistic – as when sexual desire was nicely referred to as 'company-keeping', or birth control approached either with jovial circumlocution via mocking warnings about 'twin-bed marriages' or stern but vague references to 'a woman's duty to her husband' – that I often sat listening to them in wonderment as to what the blazes the preacher was driving at. One simple result was that I remained ignorant about such a simple matter as childbirth for longer than I would now believe possible if I did not remember that I was two years at college – that is, I was twenty – when a medical-student friend pityingly pointed out to me one sunny afternoon in the quadrangle, on reading a poem I had written containing the phrase 'Mother Ireland's teeming navel,' that as far as his knowledge of the history of medicine went no mother had yet been known to eject a baby through her belly-button. A few skilled anatomical drawings on the back of my poem completed my education, and then, to dispel the last of my romanticism and my ignorance, he pleasantly quoted Origen's famous phrase *inter faeces et urinam nascimur*; after which, the group of Joyceian students who had gathered about us proceeded to proffer me some rude and facetious alternatives to my unfortunate word *navel*. (There is no doubt about it, the best classroom in every university is the quadrangle.) A worse result of this niceness and genteelism of my clerical teachers was that, as boys, whatever we learned, mostly incorrect, about our bodies was learned in dark corners and huddles of shame from brutal words and coarse jokes that associated all passion with filth. Whenever I think of the turbulence and agony of nubile youth, the terror of a boy at his first discovery of his manhood, of a young girl at her first bleeding experience of womanhood, I can only rage at our pious elders who so sweetly, so virtuously, so loftily and so benevolently sent us naked to the wolf of life.

I think back to the first teen of the century and to my startled bewilderment when nature informed me clammily that my familiar fifth limb possessed a wilful night-life of its own – this absurd protrusion which I had hitherto accepted as casually as one does a water-tap. How indifferently likewise I had observed that little girls possessed no such fifth limb but could, I now found, at times, for that very reason, emanate an agreeable appeal both when they were present and when they were merely conjured up by my memory, whereupon my water-tap, other-wise inert, would respond in a manner that was both embarrassing and pleasant. What to this day I do not fully understand is whence there at once crept into me a horrible sensation called guilt, rather than a glow of joy or a throb of pleasure such as calls the birds in the trees and the animals in the fields to leap laughingly on one another in the spring. This filthy sensation of guilt I suffered for years – quite unnecessarily I discovered far too late.

Why should I have felt like a sinner? What are sinners like? I recall the Monday night meetings of our Confraternity of the Sacred Heart of Jesus. As the years passed I came to recognise everyone in our local section or guild – Canty the tinsmith, Stuttering Looney the cork-cutter, Bagsy Flynn the basket-weaver, the one-eyed man who made boiled sweets, the bowler-hatted man who made Kandy Sauce, big, fat Nicky O'Connor the publican, the two neat little Mr O'Sullivans who were coopers, an anonymous coal-heaver whose eyes were always ringed with the mascara of the day's coal dust, Jacky MacCarthy the pawnbroker, with whom the poor women from the lanes about us pledged their husbands' suits every Monday and from whom they recovered them every Saturday, Buster Duggan the net-fisherman, whose wife was a dresser in the Opera House, Lombardi the statue-maker, all of them bawling away at the heartening hymns, *Jesus, Lord, I ask for mercy, Let me not implore in va-a-ain*, or *Hail, Que-e-en of Heaven, Thou ocean star, Guide of the wanderer he-e-ere below* . . . Sinners? I knew the chronic drunks; I knew the poor devil who once lured me into his office and to my embarrassed astonishment began to unbutton my fly; I knew the hunchback who (I can only believe, no other explanation fits) was 'persuaded' by the local priests to marry the local frail – she was not a whore, she was a beautiful girl who, as we used to say, 'went with officers from the barracks' – to give a name to her bastard; I knew the day labourer who regularly threw his wife out into Paul Street late on Saturday nights, he drunk as a lord, she in the rain-swept street appealing up to him at the window from which would come flying all her little ornaments – crash, tinkle, a rolling tinny noise, a big crash, each accompanied by his triumphant, defiant yells. I think how my pretty 'religious' toys broke in my hands again and again, as theirs, poor wanderers, must also. Naturally I picked up my broken toys again and again, and patched them together in tears, hoping they would work this time. Naturally many times in later years I threw them away in despair or anger, as some of my fellow wanderers may have done too, until in the end I learned that what were only toys to my adolescence – toy Christs, doll Virgins, tinsel heavens – could be to my manhood little matches of light, glow-worms in my palm. They could not tell anyone anything about 'life' but they might cheer one through its dark woods, tiny talismans, minute constellations, engravings on a ring, stars hidden above dark branches, obscure amulets. They would have their use if only to impress on me always that most of the so-called Facts of Life are irreducible and inexplicable atoms of mystery wandering about in the infinity of mortal existence.

They were my first symbols and metaphors. And what does one do with metaphors anyway? With the lilies of the field? The resurrection of Lazarus? Balthazar, Melchior and Kaspar? Gold, frankincense and myrrh? Believe in them? I am sure that I never really did believe in them as facts. I think I believed in them as I still believe in them, as phrases or images of the mystery of creation. I believe in them as Eliot's kings believed, in *Journey of the Magi*:

All this was a long time ago, I remember,
And I would do it again, but set down
This set down
This: were we led all that way for
Birth or Death? There was a Birth, certainly,
We had evidence and no doubt, I had seen birth and death,
But had thought they were different; this Birth was
Hard and bitter agony for us, like Death, our death,
We returned to our places, these Kingdoms,
But no longer at ease here in the old dispensation,
With an alien people clutching their gods.
I should be glad of another death.

That pretty, sugary, German-made window, signal-red, mustard-yellow, Reckitt's blue, showing the birth at Bethlehem is only a shadow of an answer. Mauriac was right – sensibility needs intelligence. Yet, sensibility is not useless even without that, nor is it totally unrelated to the common round of life. One must begin with sensibility. It can then, fertilised, become a mustard tree. I defend my seed of childhood not for what it was but because of what it became.

3

I should here make a confession, much as Henry James did when he wrote in his autobiography, a bit surprised, that he was writing 'the history of an imagination.' Perhaps my sense of 'reality' was never strong. Perhaps it is not so much that the Theatre, or the Church or the Empire bred my imaginative tendency as that they fostered what they found. It is partly to find out if this is so that I pursue myself.

Other people, I presume, went to the play and the church for other reasons than mine. Certainly as a boy I went only for reasons of the Imagination: many others, doubtless, for reasons of the Reason. I never abstracted intellectually what I experienced in the church or the theatre from its context of lights, words, colours, gestures, voices, sounds, or smells. It is true that as a child and boy the theatre did indeed fill all my days with undeniable and irresistible images of what I took to be nobility, beauty, courage, loyalty, happiness, love. But I did not translate them into brain-stuff about actual life. I related them to life only insofar as they formed a transparent film across my eyes so that I saw life through them. The theatre and the church were the first ingredients of my built-in filter. They were the two greatest influences of my lonely childhood and boyhood: without them my first fourteen or fifteen years would have been a virtual blank.

It was enough for me to watch the ceremony of the Benediction in the church, to smell the aroma of incense; enough to stand in the smelly canvas wings, just barely catching the very last of the footlights on the farther side of the stage, see a lower lip shine in the bright lights, see eyes and teeth glisten more brilliantly than they could ever glisten by daylight, see gestures form, hear words take shape with power and grace, watch a story round its parable act by act, in order thereby to enjoy the ecstasy of what I now take to be that transformation, or idealisation, of common life which is at the heart of the most admirable ceremony as well as of the most meretricious art.

For years the play was to me what Charles Lamb tells us his first play was to him – feeling absorbed in vision; an experience so hypnotic that he wanted to become a Mohammedan immediately he saw the fires before the idols of Persia. I was like him lost in what he called the 'enchantment and dream.' As time passed I was to lose this natural inflammability of my innocent years, their elemental gift for being consumed emotionally, imaginatively, sensually by what I saw, heard or read, of being charged by their fires like a burning match into some other substance by the rearrangement of its molecules. For a long time I have thought to blame my later teachers for this imaginative loss, who would have had me spend my days brainily analysing, discussing, criticising. I have long since come to realise that we are all victims of the widespread delusion that it is a child's *mind* that is led, or pushed, or lured from the 'low' state of chanting Longfellow to the 'high' state of pondering Wordsworth, from the simple state of being thrilled by *A Royal Divorce* to the complicated state of being both torn asunder and delighted by *The Three Sisters*. The truth is simpler. Literature teaches nothing. It merely confirms Life which leads, lures, pushes, drags us mindlessly into our own heartburning longings or frustrations. Seeking about us, then, for clearer images of our inbuilt longings and frustrations, we alight on Wordsworth or Chekhov and cry: 'That's marvellous! That's true! That's good! I recognise it! *It's me!*' – and there is the end to Longfellow and *A Royal Divorce* – as, likewise, we may one day pass on another inch or two beyond even Chekhov and Wordsworth. All art is thus a form of autobiography, as Claude Edmonde Magny so impressively says by the very title of her *Les Sandales d'Empedocle*, her image of the philosopher who, to prove himself a god, before flinging himself into his last adventure in the heart of Etna, removed his sandals and laid them on the crater's edge. So every man, certainly every artist, before passing into death, leaves behind him *his* testament, *his* witness, *his* book, *his* poem, *his* picture, *his* music, *his* play, *his* autobiography which we take up with more or less reverence, delight and understanding according as *our* life seems to resemble his. We cherish only what we recognise as a mirror of our own nuclear selves.

2

The Old Grenadier

I

My father, whose name was Denis Whelan, was a police constable in the Royal Irish Constabulary. He came from a small farm near the hamlet of Stradbally, about fifty miles southeast of Dublin in what was then known as the Queen's County, a region named after Queen Mary I, the wife of Philip of Spain, when it was first planted and shired by English settlers. It is known today by its old Gaelic name of Laois.

When I first became consciously aware of my father I chose to see him (being at the time very much under the influence of the Baroness Orczy) as a Napoleonic grenadier, tall, finely built, his back straight as a musket, his air distinguished, his eyes grey-blue and clear as if they forever reflected the snows of Moscow, his greying hair soft as dust, his neatly brushed moustache gone white before its time. I was not far wrong in romanticising him as a grenadier. He was a modest, pious, trusting man, upright, honest as daylight, and absolutely loyal to the Empire as only a born hero-worshipper can be. I have no doubt at all that certain rebellious people today would call him a square, and that, if he had ever met a couple of beats, he would have quietly advised them to go home to their mothers. He would not have raised a finger to them, least of all have tried to make or fake a charge against them – I do not believe he ever charged anybody in his life: he was too gentle. I am not idealising him. He always evoked my respect, and sometimes my admiration, but, although I am sure he loved me with a father's love, he rarely warmed me to love him. Not that I thought about it while he lived, but now I know why it was so. He was the humble but priceless foundation-stuff on which all great states and empires have raised themselves, deviously, to power and glory, and I was a natural, if mild, rebel.

I believe my father's humility was really a form of proud reverence growing out of his job. Because of this, I have occasionally told my English friends in my later years that he was a product of Sandhurst, which would be like a gendarme's son saying his papa had been through Saint-Cyr. Then I would entertain myself by explaining just what I meant. I meant that the Royal Irish Constabulary, or the Force as it was popularly called, was mainly officered by Sandhurst types – in religion mostly Anglicans, or what we called Protestants; in politics Anglo-Irish imperialists to a man – whose great ambition was to infuse and inspire the lowest ranks of the Force with the officers-and-gentlemen traditions of the crack regiments of the British Army. Only those who have known, or can imagine, the earthy simplicity of the Irish youths recruited into the Force, practically all of them poor, inexperienced young men of Catholic peasant stock, will realise the enormity of this ambition. If I may judge by my father, it succeeded absolutely; it is my impression that it also achieved a good deal of success among natives in Delhi, Colombo, Accra, Nassau, Hong Kong, Nairobi, and elsewhere.

In his dark bottle-green uniform, black leather belt with brass buckle, black helmet or peaked cap, black truncheon case and black boots, my father embodied the Law. What was far more important, he embodied all the accepted and respected values and conventions of what we would nowadays call the Establishment. In simple language, his language, he considered that the highest state in life that anyone could achieve was to be a Gentleman; and he wanted each one of his children to grow up as a Gentleman. The most easily observable effect of this on me was that, in dutiful imitation of him, I took over, holus-bolus, the accepted hierarchy of the imperial way of life.

At the top of this hierarchy was the bearded, jovial, rotund, elegant father figure of His Majesty King Edward VII. How amor-ally jovial he was never entered my father's devoted and loyal head. Had somebody told him the now common stories about Eddie's mistresses and concubines, about, say, Cora Pearl being brought in naked after dinner on a vast silver tray borne by six footmen, or about his gay goings-on in Balbec or Baden-Baden, or about the selfish caddishness he showed towards his friends, so painfully described by Christopher Sykes in *Three Studies in Loyalty*, my father would have thought the storyteller mad, obscene, blasphemous, a traitor and a blackguard; or else he would not have understood a word of it; or it would all have floated in and out of his ears as happened to me when The-Girl-Sawn-in-Half told me all those other wonderful and, alas, forgotten stories about 'dear Eddie'.

From His Majesty my father would trace what he called 'the line of precedence' from the First Lord of the Admiralty and the Chief of the Imperial General Staff to the First, Second, Third and Fourth Sea Lords and their corresponding Field Marshals and Admirals of the Fleet, generals, major generals, rear admirals, lieutenant generals, vice admirals, colonels and captains, down through the civilian galaxy of the Lord Chief Justice and all his judges of lower title, down to our own resident magistrates, our district inspectors and county inspectors, down and down to our local Lord Mayor, his sheriff, his aldermen and, I presume, his fur-hatted, red-cloaked mace-bearer. I am not sure how my father would have place our Lord Bishop, our canon at Saint Peter's and Paul's, or certain rich city merchants and rich county folk like, say, Brigadier Winterbottom, who used to drive into the city in a grey tilbury drawn by a trotting bay, his fawn bowler on the side of his head, his white moustaches bristling, his gloved hands held high on the reins. But I feel sure that after all those my father and I began to waver. We could not really admit *all* the city councillors – they were too near to us, much too like ourselves. It would have been hard, for instance, so to uplift Danny Gamble, a vociferously eloquent tinsmith, a member of the Cork Corporation for our ward, who lived around the corner from us, who rarely wore either collar or tie, and whom we occasionally saw at Mass robed in the brown garments of the Third Order of Saint Francis, his belly wound about with a cream cincture, collecting the offerings of the faithful. Was he a Gentleman?

'Mind yourselves, now,' my father would say to us three brothers as we set out on our regular afternoon walk, always the same walk, up Wellington Road, and down Saint Luke's. 'Mind you behave properly in the street. You never know who might be walking behind you. It might be Alderman Jimmy Simcox. Or the Lord Mayor. Or Brigadier Winterbottom. Or the canon. Or, the Lord between us and all harm, maybe the district inspector himself!'

Because of this hierarchy-worship, certain Sunday mornings provided me, like the theatre and the church, with some highly emotional images of the Admirable Life. On these special mornings my father would lead the three of us up our all too familiar Saint Luke's or Wellington Road, and on beyond it to Wellington Barracks, under the arch, into the barrack square, there to join other loyal citizens watching the church parade of whatever regiment was quartered on us at the time. I have forgotten now what form of drill took place. All I remember is that either the Union Jack or else the regimental flag was shown, and that at the end the regimental band solemnly played *God Save the King*. My brothers told me in later years that they felt a little embarrassed at this point – two loyalties, to the Empire and to Ireland, conflicting. There was no such conflict in the Old Grenadier or in me. He would thrust out his chest, stand to attention like a ramrod and glare straight in front of him. I, at his knee, would whip off my cap, throw out my chest, glare, and feel almost choked with emotion at the sonorous brass blare of:

> Send him victorious,
> Happy and glorious,
> Long to reign over us,
> God save the King.

When the drums rolled and the brass shook the air I could hear the sabre clash, the hoofbeats, the rifle fire of all the adventure books I had read – mainly Henty's: *The Dash for Khartoum*, *With Kitchener in the Soudan*, *One of the Twenty-eighth*, *Under Drake's Flag*, *Winning his Spurs*, *Saint George for England*, *With Wolfe to Canada*, or *Won by the Sword*. As we walked away my father would be completely silent, or he would touch a stone in a wall bearing the broad arrow and the carved letters WD (War Department) and nod at us sagely and proudly. We belonged.

This pride nourished in him a strong fire of ambition for his sons. He was to make his eldest son, Patrick, a priest, an ambition of high priority with all Irish parents, and he was madly proud of his second son, Augustine, who later entered the British Civil Service and became a Revenue Inspector.

'To think,' he would then muse, 'that a son of mine is examining the incomes of men as rich, aye and richer than, the judge and the district inspector!'

He nearly went out of his head with delight the day my brother, then stationed in Bournemouth, one of the wealthiest centres for rentier incomes in England, told him that he had a retired field marshal on his books.

'What next?' he moaned, throwing his hands up to heaven in delight. 'What next?'

Still later he put me through university. After I got a fellowship that took me to Harvard he used to write me letters, in his neat copperplate handwriting, so full of humble respect that they used to make me squirm at my own ingratitude and inadequacy. Remember that all this was achieved on a policeman's salary of about fifty-two pounds a year, eked out with the few pounds my mother made on her lodgers. This ambition for their young was a universal mark of the old RIC, and its source is as obvious as its history is long. Indeed, when I think now of that regimental parade I wonder whether, among our own most ancient ancestors, living on the boundaries of another empire, another such father may not on occasion have stood watching from a hilltop, in a similar blended mood of smoored pride and parental ambition, the imperial eagles passing far below along the Aurelian and the Julian Way into nether Gaul, and wondered, like my father, whether his son might one day carry them.

My pride in my father was at its greatest when the assizes opened and he would be among those allotted to guard the judge at the Courthouse. The British managed these things well. The judge, gowned and bewigged, was always borne in a horse-drawn carriage, open if the weather was clement, through the streets of the city, accompanied by detachments of mounted police and military trotting, tinkling, and clanking gallantly, fore and aft. These mounted police, now gone, were a smart body of men, dressed in tight black breeches with knee-high boots of shining leather, the belt worn diagonally across the chest over one shoulder, little black pillbox hats held gaily on the sides of their heads by patent-leather chin straps, their long truncheons dangling from the pommels. I remember that many of them had a way of affecting small waxed moustaches. As for the foreign soldiery, I recall with a special pleasure a detachment of cuirassiers with gleaming breastplates, helmets with long red plumes, and drawn swords. The foot police, my father among them, wore full-dress uniform, spiked helmets with silver chin straps, patent-leather belts and gloves. On his arrival at the Courthouse the judge would alight from his carriage and in stately grandeur climb the long flight of steps up to the entrance, where a row of officials stood waiting respectfully to receive him – all native-born Irishmen. It was an impressive sight. A political system had been established. We the people had accepted it. Our Church blessed it. Our politicians tolerated it. The law of the land was now about to apply it.

Meanwhile, downstairs in the waiting rooms, or in the cells, about to be herded into the dock, there would be another bunch of native-born Irishmen. Most of them would, under any system, have to be considered lawless men; but at that time others would have been there thanks only to inherent injustices in the law itself. One might be a peasant farmer who, in despair, had resisted eviction from his minute cottage and holding by the local agent of some landlord residing in London or on the Continent who rarely, if ever, laid eyes on his property. Another man in the dock might have got involved in some internecine feud with his neighbour because of some real or imagined injustice arising out of the same complicated land system. Another might be a youth whose hot blood had led him to knock down or wound a policeman for no better reason than that he disliked the law of the land without knowing why he disliked it. All such protesters, for whatever reason, against the established system were, I am sure, accepted by everybody present as criminal.

I, certainly, thought them criminals whenever, through my father's almighty influence, I was slipped into the court to witness the drama of their trial, judgment and sentence. When I saw, hanging around the dim halls and corridors, the mothers, fathers, sisters, wives, or other relatives of the men on trial – old brown-shawled women, frieze-coated countrymen, rude denizens of the hills and the fields – whispering in corners with bewigged counsel, apparently overawed by their strange surroundings, fearful for their kin, I never felt for them anything but a sense of vicarious fear blended with awestruck wonderment at their folly in getting themselves into such a mess.

2

There were, now and again, undercurrents. A sense of fear and wonder used to visit me every time I drew my father's pinewood baton from its leather case. As I slowly fingered the smooth, hard weapon I felt repulsion and something bordering on disgust. There was nobody to make the mental connection for me with Henty's rattling rifle fire, flashing sabres and galloping hooves, yet, in some dim way, I do think that I here first began to feel the unpleasant reality of power when combined with brute force. I felt something of the same sort when, a couple of times a year, my father would be on late duty in the Bridewell and I and one of my brothers would be sent down there with welcome bowls of soup for himself and his comrades. By way of reward, we would be shown over the cells with all their paraphernalia of restraint. Once, to amuse me, one of my father's colleagues locked my wrists in the cold handcuffs. Another time we were shown the straitjacket for violent prisoners, a contraption of stout canvas with heavy leather belts. The cell was cold, dirty-white, with a smelly water closet in the corner, and a yellow fan of light bubbling in an aperture over the iron door. On that evening my brother lay down in the straitjacket and they buckled him up to show how it was done. 'Get out o' that, now, Mr Houdini!' laughed one of the constables, standing over him in his grey shirt and braces. I trembled to see him lying there, trussed like a mummy, smiling boyishly up at my smiling father and his jolly friends.

I loved the weeks, not more than one a quarter, when my

father was detailed as night watch in the streets from midnight on. He looked very big, powerful, and handsome in his special night duty uniform: a long black-belted overcoat down to his shins, a domed helmet, if the weather were bad a black waterproof cape, and short black stubby leggings. Our small city was free of serious crime, so that he and his comrade had nothing to do all night but kill the long hours pacing the empty streets, or standing in doorways watching the rain make bubbles in the lamp-lit pools, slant in the wind, hiss and moan up the river – Cork is a notoriously wet and windy city – hearing nothing except some late reveller or late night worker beating his lonely way home, or, on the cold gusts form the north, Shandon's tireless bell. One reason why I loved those occasions was because my father and his companions ate a special late supper of chops, potatoes and strong tea just before going on duty, and I was allowed either to stay up late or come down in my nightshirt to partake of bits and scraps from his plate like a puppy dog. No piece of chop has ever since tasted as sweet as those bits of tail-end from his piled-up plate, I sitting on his knee, wearing his belt wound twice around me, my face and head half extinguished under his vast helmet. The fire in the range would be glowing. The steel of the fender shone bayonet-bright. The red tiles of the kitchen looked as warm as their colour. The wind in the already deserted streets shook the windows. The two policemen would presently buckle on their belts and truncheons, button up their collars, hook their capes, slip baby bottles of whiskey into their pockets against colds and pneumonia, and adventure out into the darkness, emptiness, and rain of the city streets, whereas I was about to clamber between my two brothers into a nicely warmed bed. I particularly liked the nights when his companion was one Constable Jim Hedderman, a pleasant, lean-faced, redheaded fellow who had established himself as the Brains of the Bridewell. He was always full of chat and odd stories. He had ambitions to get the two stripes, that is to become an acting sergeant, and was forever studying for the necessary examination – which he never passed. His two favourite subjects were orthography and astronomy. My father said he used to pass the night producing hard words to spell, or, if it were a clear sky, reading the stars:

'That is Cassy-o-paya. How would you spell that, now, Dinny? That is Orion's Belt. I bet you think that is spelled "O'Ryan." It is not, then. I will now relate to you the story of Orion . . .'

My mother would take the holy water bottle and bless the pair of them with a wild scatter of it. She and I would then peep down through the corner of the window as they started their slow pacing around the corner of the School of Art, encased, immense, transformed, no longer just Father or just Jim, padding out of sight, once again the embodied and respected Law.

One afternoon I ran into the kitchen, divesting myself of my school satchel, eager for my dinner, and was halted by my mother's pale face and pointing finger. There, on the old battered sofa in the kitchen, lay my father, his head bandaged round and round, his right hand wrapped in layers of cotton wool and more bandages, looking solemnly up at me. She told me that he had been sent out that morning to a place called Watergrasshill, a rural hamlet a few miles northeast of Cork, where he had joined a squad of police forcibly evicting a tenant farmer and his family from the small house and farm whose rent they, presumably, could or would no longer pay but which they refused to surrender. He may have been a shiftless and worthless farmer or a hardworking and over-burdened man; his landlord may have been indulgent and patient or he may have been a ruthless tyrant; all we knew was that the man had barricaded himself in his house, cottage, or hut, and that the police had come, as was usual on such occasions, to break in the door with rifle butts and a battering ram and throw him and his family out, with their belongings, on the roadside. In the mêlée my father had been hit with a heavy stone, and when somebody inside thrust an iron bar out through a hole in the window he had grasped it. The bar looked black, but it had come, one minute before, red-hot from the hearth. It had seared his hand to the bones. As I looked down at him, gazing silently up at me, I could not have felt more overcome if he had been a boxer in the ring and I had just seen him knocked on the flat of his back to the canvas. Beside me my mother was at one moment commiserating him and at the next upbraiding him for 'putting himself forward' in the fray.

'Sure, you were always a quiet man! Too quiet! Too soft

altogether for this world. Never in your life summonsed a living soul. What call had you to be making a hero out of yourself? How fair it was you were the foolah to catch the blow and snatch the bar! Always a good father, and a kind husband. Oh, the blackguards! To do such a thing to such a quiet man . . .!'

And, indeed, this was all true. How often had I not heard him at night in his little attic room, when we were all in bed, praying aloud for us all, in a soughing, undulating, pleading voice, on his knees by his bed, his hands joined, his eyes to the ceiling and, as always, his braces hanging behind him to the floor like bifurcated tail:

'Oh please, dear kind Jesus, look after my poor little children, Patrick, and Augustine, and John. Watch over my poor wife Bid. Guide them and guard them. Help me to work for them as long as I live . . .'

It was his silence that wounded me, and the bewilderment in his eyes. Could it have been that he was shocked by this passionate clash with his own kind of small-farmer folk in that early morning tussle on those windy uplands? If so, it was well for him that his retirement age came before the revolutionary spirit after 1916 spread all over the country. During the Troubles, as we were ironically to call those not so dangerous and very happy years, the Force was to stand to its guns against the rebels almost to a man; so, I am sure, would he have done, stubbornly, however bewildered by it all, not, to be sure, after any deep conscience-searchings about the conflicting demands involved in the idea of loyalty, but for a quite simple and unarguable reason: 'Oh please, dear kind Jesus, look after my poor little children . . . Help me to work for them as long as I live . . .'

Men like my father were dragged out, in those years, and shot down as traitors to their country. Shot for cruel necessity – so be it. Shot to inspire necessary terror – so be it. But they were not traitors. They had their loyalties, and stuck to them.

3

I feel downcast that I can only remember my father like this as a figure, almost as a type, rather than as a person. His own inner, private life is hidden from me completely. He is to me more of a myth than a man, a figure out of that time, out of that place, a symbol of childhood. Does it always happen when we live closely and long with a person or a place that we come to know them less and less, whether wife, husband, child or town? With him this happens when I seize even on the one or two privacies of his life, such as his little brown locked box, always on the shelf in the kitchen. To my mother this was Bluebeard's chamber about which she used to tease him, to his great annoyance, saying: 'I wonder what have you at all, at all, in that little brown box? Maybe a little roll of pound notes? Ha?'

I think it contained his razors, possibly a few family letters, possibly a couple of pound notes. I associate it with his one relaxation, a bet on a horse now and again. After all, he had been born in the Queen's County, which borders on County Kildare, both famous racing counties. Down there he had a friend who was supposed to be 'in the know', one Philly Behan, a starter or a starter's assistant on the Curragh. To Philly, now and again, he would send a present of a ham, and from Philly there would come, now and again, a letter which my father might, though rarely, leave on the shelf and which my mother would guiltily read. 'There is some talk about a promising three-year-old, Flyaway, trained by Hartigan, for the June meeting, and if Gus Hogan is up I would say he would be worth a bet both ways.' But when I would hear those words I would not think of his tremors or expectations so much as of the green wonder of the Curragh plain, about which he often talked to us, or of the Great Heath of Maryborough, near his boyhood home, and of all that far-off country from which he, and therefore I, had come. For me that little brown box held green fields, yellow heather, and galloping horses. In this way he really was a bit of the Irish myth and a bit also of the imperial myth, and through their blended ambitions and pieties he achieved wholeness.

He would not have understood one word of this, and if he had he might not have agreed, because he had one other precious dream. Every so often there would come in the post a copy of a local paper from Kildare or the Queen's with advertisements of forthcoming auctions of farms marked in red ink: 'Four miles from *Emo*. Thirty acres of useful grazing land. Farmhouse and outhouses ... *Kildangan*. Twenty-seven acres, three roods of fine arable land ... Near *Kiladoon* ...'

It was the pipedream of a man who had not enough money to farm a window-box, the uprooted peasant longing for his Mother Earth – incomplete, unwhole, mortally vulnerable away from it. There must have been thousands like him in the Force. He reminds me that we had a semipermanent lodger one year named Ross, a retired sergeant of the Force. He was a finely built man, now grey, though you could see by his eyelashes that he had once been redheaded, with flowing moustaches still russet, partly from his pipe but also from rude persistent health. He was a figure of fun to us children because he was always talking aloud to himself, so loudly that even through the ceiling we could sometimes hear him in his room mixing up his memories of barrack yard and farm haggard:

'Yessir! Nosir! At once! Attention! Dismiss! Halt! Whoa, back, whee! Gee up! That's the gurl! G'wan! Pike it up there, Jim. Fine hay! Dismiss! Yessir! Nosir! At once sir!'

He had never married. He lived and died on his two memories.

Last night I read with deep emotion this little entry in Cesare Pavese's *Il Mestiere di Vivere*, written at the height of his success as an author in Turin:

> Isn't it curious that at the moment when you first left your home in the country ... it never occurred to you that you were starting out on a long journey through cities, names, adventures, pleasures, unforseeable worlds which would make you realise in the course of time that that one moment had been one of the richest parts of your Future, wherein the everlasting mystery would prove to be that childish You whom at that time you made no effort to possess.

I wonder what my father dreamed on his happy nights? When we talk about squares how we simplify! In every square is there a buried myth? I think I am trying to persuade myself that there is. I want desperately to believe that my father was larger than I must otherwise think. He was, so evidently, so accusingly, a good man, a loyal servant, an upright citizen, a pious Christian, a good father, that I cannot believe in him as

33

a man at all unless he had, also, some purely personal dream outside those social virtues. I do not want to think of my father as a Father. By being my father he is lost to me, as, for all I know, I am lost to my children. Perhaps I must accept the truth, miserably: that he, happily, lost himself in his children. It makes me feel so ungiving, so helpless, now that it is too late to explain to him that if he had been less good I might now admire him less and might then have loved him more.

3

A Happy Schooling

My mother's maiden name was Bridget Murphy. She came from a twenty-five-acre farm called Loughill on the banks of the little River Deel, two or three miles from the town of Rathkeale, deep in the flat, flat lands of West Limerick. She was very tall, slim as a reed and quite beautiful, with liquid sapphire eyes shadowed by an inborn melancholy. She laughed a lot, and when she laughed she swayed over like a reed in the wind. I am always reminded of her when I see, or evoke, the little blue lochs of Limerick, its pale albino sky, its grey stone walls, its winding limestone roads, dust-deep or mud-greasy, its outcropping rocks, its soft meadows, its wind flowing over them as if they were water. She had that blend in her of the soft and the hard, the melancholy and the tender, the dreamy and the harsh, the pitiable and the pitiless. As a boy I loved her dearly, as a youth I ceased to love her, as a grown man I pitied her. She was deeply pious, but it was not a happy piety. Her religious melancholy withered everything it touched, like a sirocco.

My mother shared my father's ambition for her children. She expressed it in a phrase that she dinned into us day after day: 'Rise in the world!' To do this we must be educated, which meant that we must be educated to get good jobs. Since the word had no other significance for either of them, this, as time went on, naturally made things a bit difficult for me, who in the process of being educated for a purpose began to discover the infinitely superior joys of being educated for no purpose at all.

The first school I was sent to was as cracked as blazes. It was the Lancasterian National School, so called because it had been one of the first, if not the first, of the Irish Bell and Lancaster schools. I did not discover this until long afterwards, and at the time associated the name only with the House of Lancaster. I very much wonder if the good monks who taught us, and who were mentally and emotionally rather like children themselves, ever thought at all about the origin of the name. They and we all called it the Lancs. Even as a building it was crazy. I do not know what it was originally: it may have been a factory, or a barracks, or a poorhouse, or it might have been a madhouse, or it may even have been some eighteenth-century lunatic's idea of how a school should be built. After all, the Bell and Lancaster schools arose out of a pamphlet written by Mr Andrew Bell, in 1797, entitled *An Experiment in Education Made at the Male Asylum of Madras*.

The school was composed mainly of two enormous rooms. The bigger of these two rooms, to my childish eyes as big as a cathedral, was, like the nave of a church, lighted by clerestories high up on either side, that is, long lines of glass, that is, bits and patches of glass, and under these clerestories the various classes would 'toe the line' about horseshoes chalked on the floor. The centre of this main hall was occupied by lines of desks, like benches in a chapel. Every second boy did literally toe the line: he was barefooted, with the mud of the streets drying between his frozen toes, and zoomorphic tracery on his shins from sitting in the ashes of his laneway home. At play-time, when other classes were howling outside in the yard, I have often seen boys standing so, each with an open book balanced on his head like a circumflex accent, in order to protect his skull from the penalty of falling glass. That was because the great game in the yard outside would be what I have since heard called the Roof Game. It began by throwing a ball, a thing made of paper and twine, sideways up on the slates, and then there would be a mad rush and a mad tangle struggling under the gutters to catch the ball when it fell – or I should say if it fell, and did not go right through the clerestory and send glass showering over the room inside.

East and west of this nave were two aisles divided into a couple of smaller classrooms. Behind the apse the infants were tucked away in much the nicest room in the place; and somewhere back here, too, was a black hole where chronic criminals were sometimes flung to whimper among the coals and the rats. For playground a slim gravelled yard ran along each side of the building. The lavatories lined it behind, malodorously near a tumbledown caretaker's cottage piled up with thrown-out copybooks and dilapidated desks which were used for fuel. One room specially impressed itself on my memory, the science room. It acted also as visitors' room, office, and monks' lunchroom, and was much feared because it was the place where more severe and less modest forms of corporal punishment were inflicted on the real toughs.

I recall, with indelible distaste, an incident that took place in this room. One day the news trickled through our class, in the main hall, that our headmaster, a brother whom we called Sloppy Dan, had hauled into this room two boys named Feeney and Corrigan who had been, as we used to say, 'on the lang', that is, who had been roving the fields outside the city for several days instead of attending their classes. Now, the door opening from the entrance hall into this room had six small glass panes, painted an opaque white, but a small eyelet hole had long ago been scratched in one of the panes. A few of us got permission, one by one, to leave class on the usual pretense but really to steal a quick peep through the eyelet hole to see what was going on between Sloppy Dan and his two culprits. When my turn came I was struck with horror.

Those two boys were senior boys. Corrigan was a great burly fellow, so developed beyond his years that he looked about twenty, so strong that he could have knocked down Sloppy Dan with a blow. Feeney was slight, fair-haired, and back-bowed, but also more of a grown youth than a boy. Sloppy Dan himself was smallish but burly, with a round porcine face, always brick-red, big round glasses, a rounded, powerful back. His devouring pedagogic obsession was English grammar. He would wander from class to class to teach it, invariably carrying in his fist a punishment strap cut from a black leather harness trace, about one-foot-six long, two inches wide and a half-inch thick, and when, as he constantly did, he became excited over his parsings and analyses he had the odd habit of swishing his strap behind his back like a tail and roaring at the top of his voice like a bull. If we failed to give the right answer he would make us hold out our hands and give us one-two of the hardest he could draw. It was not the pain I minded so much as the sight of his round, empurpled face leaning over me with bulging eyes and bellowing mouth around which there would sometimes gather a pale-gray scum of frothy spittle.

This was how he looked now through the eyelet hole, holding Feeney by the left arm and lashing with his leather strap at his naked thighs and bottom. Even through the closed door I could hear Feeney screaming, probably not so much from the pain as from fright and shame. To make things worse, six or eight other boys sat on each side of the room at long desks engaged in the task we called 'making up the rolls', that is, adding up in the usual big blue attendance books the various totals required by His Majesty's Commissioners of Education. Their heads were bent low over their books in, I now guess, pity and embarrassment. The bigger fellow, Corrigan, stood by impassively watching the degradation of his friend. I must add, in justice to Sloppy Dan, that there were some very rough boys in that school. In those days – to illustrate what I mean by rough – we did not work our arithmetic on paper with pen or pencil: we used slates and slate pencils, after each calculation spitting on the slates and wiping them clean with the underside of our sleeves. Many of those slates were framed in wood, but by no means all, so that the edges were often bare, chipped and sharp. It was not unknown for a boy, driven too hard or of a bad temper by nature, to let fly one of those sharp-edged slates at a teacher's head. 'I'll split him!' was a common boyish threat. I am still surprised that the burly Corrigan did not 'split' Sloppy Dan that afternoon. I gave no more than one glance in at the, to me, bestial scene in the science room, turned and fled out to the evil-smelling jakes and hid there, shivering, until the school closed.

It is possible that certain manly readers of these lines will laugh at me and say that it probably was no more than Feeney deserved, or say that they themselves often got leathered and add (the usual phrase) that it didn't do them a bit of harm – as if they could possibly be sure of this. Or my reader may say that Sloppy Dan was exceptional. The whole tenor of my memories of that school informs me that Sloppy Dan was as exceptional as a plane crash. There was, so far as my experience went, only one other dangerous driver in that school. This other brother was a man of great height, breadth, weight and strength. I have forgotten his name, but I know that when we discovered his obsession, which was boxing, we called him Battling Billy. In his class, as in every class, there were children so poor that they did not bring anything to eat at the lunch hour, when everybody else above their level of poverty would take from his satchel bread and butter sandwiches with or without a corked bottle of milk. For these poor boys he would kindly save from his own doubtless meagre lunch a few pieces of bread and butter. Other boys told me that his practice – I only saw it happen once – was to produce these pieces of bread and butter at the end of the day and offer them to any two of those poorer boys who would fight one another bare-knuckled for the food. On the day I witnessed this procedure I saw two boys exchange a few aimless blows without interest or enmity, and then, food or no food, sullenly refuse to continue.

These instances of cruelty apart – and I recall only those two objectionable teachers in some six or seven years – my school has often since reminded me of Lowood School in *Jane Eyre*, because in spite of the cold, the dirt, the smells, the poverty and the vermin, we managed to create inside this crumbling old building a lovely, happy, faery world. And when I say 'we' I mean the brothers and ourselves, because those brothers were brothers to us, and I think we sincerely loved them. After all, they were not much more than boys themselves, country lads with buttermilk complexions, hats so much too big for their heads that if Providence had not supplied them with ears to keep them up they would have extinguished their faces; hands as big as and still rough from the spade, feet still heavy from walking the clay. They were entirely unselfconscious, which did not prevent them from blushing like girls in the presence of adults. They had nothing at all of the keep-the-boy-in-his-place attitude that I became familiar with later on in my secondary school.

In general it is their simplicity that I recall now: their jokes that were not made simple for our benefit but were born simple of simple parents; the hearty way they used to kick ball with us in the yard, just like kids themselves – the ball, of course, being a bit of stick or, again, a lump of paper tied around with twine; their innocent inquisitiveness about our home lives, we being city boys and they being country boys; and their natural piety that threw a benignity over all our days. I recall their general and particular innocence with a general and particular delight. I once wrote a childish essay on 'Fishing' for my Brother Magnus, in which I described cheekily how I went fishing up the Lee and fished up a girl. I can still see three or four of them crowding over this essay, full of joy, gloating in their superior knowledge of worldly wickedness. As I was only about eleven or twelve I naturally did not understand why they kept looking at me as if I were one of the Borgias. To reverse the roles, how wicked Brother Patrick made us feel when he began to warn us about the temptations of summertime, and how he actually had heard that some little boys went swimming without any bathing togs at all. But in general it was innocence versus innocence, as when Brother Josephus asked each one of us to bring a book to start a library and I brought Kingsley's *Water Babies*, with a picture of baby mermaids on the cover. When he refused to accept it, and indeed was rather cross about it, three or four of us gathered about the book, scratching our heads to know what on earth was wrong with it.

'Sure, what is it anyway but an ould book about babies?'

As to their more particular sort of innocence, or ignorance, I remember it, I hope, not with the slightest feeling of superiority, but because even we knew, and liked to know, that their weight of knowledge did not divide them far from us. They commonly mispronounced common words, saying 'New*found*land', and 'coinci*dence*', and they were as free as ourselves with their epenthetic vowels, as in 'cathedaral'. They spoke eighteenth-century dialect when they said 'tay' for tea, and 'contrayry' for 'contrary', and 'they do be' for 'they are'. At one of the science classes we were told that combustion was due to phlogiston.

When I once asked what the Feast of the Circumcision meant I was told that circumcision is a small circle cut from the foreheads of Jewish children. (My brother confirms that he was told the same, exactly.) At the classes in science they had to make do without Bunsen burners – gas was not laid on – and, instead, used painters' blowlamps, occasionally with startlingly pyrotechnical results. On the other hand I will always think admiringly of old Brother Philip, who offered sixpence to any boy who could extract salt from seawater, and when one or two did it, offered a silver watch to anybody who would extract sugar out of a turnip.

The charm of that school was that we were all working together as in a family, as when we conspired against inspectors from the Board of Education. One day an inspector of hygiene came to lecture us on cleanliness – a lecture badly needed in that school. It was, unfortunately, a lecture delivered from a remote distance, as if from another and far superior world, taking no account of the utter poverty in which most of the boys lived. That man made us as embarrassed as if he were giving a lecture on sex. When he was gone Brother Josephus, who had been standing behind him with a slow smile on his lips, swept us into his bosom forever and ever in one warm wave of indignation by saying, 'Boys! That man thinks we're filth!' It was the 'we' that won us.

I know I am doing them all an injustice, and doing those years an injustice too. They were happier, and these teachers (generally) more kind than I can ever suggest. The lovely thing about that time was that the days had no aim, no object: we did not go to school in order to get somewhere; we just went to school. Later, when we went up to the secondary school, all this changed. Ambition reared its nasty nose there. Up there we were pressed every day to eat the apple of knowledge which gives one power over good and evil, and makes the world fall into fractions, and makes everything not an end but a means to some end, always invisible, padding out of sight around the corner. End? We knew nothing about ends in the Lancs. We just learned because we liked to learn, as we came to school because we liked to come to school. What end is there anyway to child education except to learn a few necessary technical things and

41

after that to shock the intelligence, stir the sensibilities and warm the imagination into some sense of the mystery, horror, and beauty of life?

What of those pouring wet southern days when so few kids came to school that the few who did felt such a close sense of comradeship that we hated to return home? Were they not education? The rain lashed the windows and we huddled over the fire and talked of the tawny Lee rising in flood, and of all the things coming downstream on its foam, branches and trees, and dead sheep, and hencoops, 'and a whole grand pianah and a coffin with two ducks sittin' on top of it . . .' Days when we rounded our cheeks and rolled our eyes and hunched up our backs and said 'Oooh!' to the wind under the door. Up in the other school we never said 'Oooh!' to the wind under the door. We'd have been ashamed to. They just told us up there what wind was, out of a textbook.

Do not, however, begin to imagine that we learned nothing useful in our old tumbledown Lancs. They ground the three r's into us, unforgettably – reading, 'riting and 'rithmetic. They gave us a solid basis for whatever we might later wish to build. Before we finished, or as we used to say were 'out of books', we had learned fractions, proportion, compound interest, the nature of stocks and shares, of bills of exchange, of discount. We were introduced to the rudiments of physics and chemistry – very simply but none the less impressively (even if the painters' blowlamp did bust the retort); the nature of oxygen, why a teapot handle has an inset of nonconducting material, that metal expands when heated, the lever, the law of Archimedes, and so on. Above all, we got (even if it *was* done by Sloppy Dan with the black strap) a thorough knowledge of parsing, grammar and analysis. I suppose it depended on each boy how much interest in literature he got out of our English Readers – I know I loved to recite poetry aloud from them and became vain of my power to do it readily if not well. There was, of course, no language-teaching, so that when at the year's end we sang 'No more Latin, no more French, no more sitting on the hard old bench' we were copying the, later, secondary school. We learned our Religious Catechism so well that to this day I can rattle off all the answers, often to questions whose nature I did not yet understand. And, by what magic I know not, none of this seemed to be work for us, though I am sure it was for our teachers.

The simple truth about that old wreck of a school is that it was not a break in the routine of living. It was part of living. Even those casualties from falling glass, or from stones flung in the fierce yard fights, were welcome, because it meant you were led off to the Mercy Hospital by an older boy to be stitched or bandaged, a pleasantly terrifying experience during which you wondered if you were going to die and wished it had not been so long since your last confession. It was a delight to be sent out into the street just before roll call to hasten the laggards, and to tell the shivering wretches that Sloppy Dan would KILL them when he got them inside; magical to be sent in search of a missing pupil down among the leaning lanes of the city, in and out of Featherbed, or Cut-throat, or Three Hatchet where the shifts and shawls drying from window to window glowed in all the canopied colours of a papal procession, and every dark doorway under the thatch shot its blob of firelight to delay our already lingering steps.

In the last few days before breaking up for summer holidays we used to feel both glad and sad that the term was ending, days when we did little but clean the white inkwells, and roll up the maps and disclose on the walls behind them stored blasts of light, and shove dusters down one another's backs, and crush closer than ever about the skirts of the brothers to talk about our homes and our holidays, and their homes and their holidays, and our future – which for us meant next year – and theirs, that meant, alas, poor grown-ups, so much less, so much more. At the last moment we looked back at the crumbs on the floor, and the dust under the desks, all empty, and felt the crumbs of the year at the bottom of our satchels that suddenly having lost all their importance smelt only of vanished days, before we turned away as to a happy exile.

3

That wreck of a school is gone now: not a stone remains upon a stone; a modern red-brick boot factory stands where it once stood. It has been replaced, a little out of town, by a fine modern school, all tiles and hardwood floors, and it is beside fields, and below it there are trees through which one sees the flowing river with cows chewing the cud in other fields beyond. In our old place there were just a few ragged trees growing out of gravel, and not one blade of grass.

I have often asked myself this question: If that old school were still there, and I lived near it, would I send my own children to it? I know that many who read these pages will be surprised, even shocked, when I say that I have hesitated before saying no. I have wavered partly because I was so happy in that crazy school, in spite of the hardship, the cold, the dirt, the all-pervading smell of poverty, in spite even of those occasional outbursts of cruelty. I have wavered, too, because cruelty, except for the very few – if you consider the whole range of life – is an inevitable experience. I have, at last, said no only because who-ever else may suffer cruelty, children must not. We elders can, in some sense, absorb it, or, as we say, take it. Besides, while we are all, in a sense, co-partners in the guilt of mankind for the perpetuation of cruelty, these innocent ones must be pro-tected from our guilt as long as they remain defenceless in their minds against it. One blow can destroy a delicate instrument forever. There was a time, one may believe, when Judas was a happy child, and a terrible moment after when he was not. In the childhood of Judas what man or woman, perhaps what teacher, betrayed Christ?

In my childhood and boyhood brutal manners were so common that nobody took any notice of them. By the calendar we were in the 1900s. In countless other ways we were still pre-Waterloo. I am not thinking of such well-known facts as that it was not until 1901 that the law indulgently raised the minimum age for child workers to twelve, or that the legal working day for all was generously limited to ten hours, with two hours for meals, to which can be added at least two more for journeys on foot back and forth to home, making in all about a fourteen-hour day for six days each week; or from about seven in the morning to nine at night. I am thinking of how the big foreign ships were unloaded on the quays of Cork by hefty coal-heavers or grain-baggers wearing ripped sacks as cowls, an endless stream of men each carrying his basket on his back, humping in and out along springboard lines of gangways, out full at a trot, in empty at a weary walk, a nonstop, day-long, livelong slave race. I am thinking of the barefooted women gleaning like beetles over the mounds of coal dust; of the old rag-pickers, their age, their unforgettable smell; of my mother's Dickensian slavey, paid half a crown a week, who rose at seven, went to bed at eleven, was let out only at night, got no free day, dressed in my mother's castoffs, yet was as gay as a cricket, buxom, strong, her hair puffed out with pads made of rolled-up newspaper, so that, on occasion, one might read a bit of headline between her lavish locks.

It was almost a popular sport to see women fighting in the street. They would first hurl their coloured shawls on the ground, let down their long wild hair – the word *maenads* always evokes those old-time Cork shawlies to me – clap their hands swiftly many times to their bawling mouths to produce a fierce drumming, self-exciting noise, pour out abuse at one another, dance a few mad steps around the street, and finally each would leap at the other's mane in order to drag her enemy to the ground and, if possible, jump on her. After that – blood, moans, wails, the encouraging shouts of the onlookers, and then the police whistle up the street to scatter everybody. When British soldiers (Synge's 'walking khaki cut-throats') fought civilians, they used to unfasten their belts, hold the end with the holes in it and swing the heavy brass buckle into the eyes of their opponents. All this naturally went with the lines of crowded pubs, maybe a dozen of them shoulder to shoulder in places near the docks. No wonder we never went into certain streets after dark.

My father and mother always referred to these very poor as 'blackguards', quite without any desire to insult them. 'Come home straight from school and don't talk to any little black-guards on the way.' Or: 'We need to get the kitchen white-washed: there's a blackguard outside there holding up the wall of the pub – he'll do it for a pint of porter.' It is not surprising that, as a matter of course, all policemen were trained in the use of firearms.

Cruelty, then, and rough ways one took for granted. But still, not in school! Above all not in an otherwise happy school where kindness normally lulled us into total trust. All children live in a sort of dumb search for the Pattern, for a polestar by which they can set their compasses for life. Would I send a trusting child along a street full of uncharted open manholes? A child to whom a wind is a simoon, a slip a landslide, a tremor in the solid ground an earthquake, threatening his confidence, his integrity, his wide-eyed belief in men?

Like my father and mother I had only one escape: humbly to accept the Will of God. It is the escape from bitterness that we Irish have taken for centuries, and it has not worked out too badly, insofar as we have come through all sorts of oppressions and misfortunes a cheerful, good-humoured, loyal, hardworking, tenacious people. The Will of God prevailed for a long time with me. I went through most of my boyhood unquestioning Heaven. What broke it apart, in the end, was pity and anger: the first for my mother, whom I loved so dearly that I could not bear the sight of her unhappiness; and the second, far later, for my people, in a bitter rage that they should be obliged to endure so much.

If this early pity grew in my home, that later anger, strangely enough, grew in me at school. His Majesty's Commissioners of Education had taken every precaution to keep from us the bitter, ancient memories of our race. From various unguarded sources the ancient memories nevertheless escaped through – in a phrase, or a word from a teacher, or no more than an inflection in his voice, or in an uncensored passage in a history book about the bravery of Irish soldiers in the Jacobite or European wars, until, drop by drop, the well-springs of my being became brimful, and finally, when I was sixteen, which was the year of 1916 and of the last Irish Rebellion, it burst in a fountaining image of the courage of man.

It was not, then, a good school, and it was not a completely bad school. It at least let in the virtues of tenderness, kindness, loyalty, affection and warmth of heart. Its fatal weakness was that virtue cannot exist in a vacuum, and can even become a destructive vice if not accompanied by moral courage and the honesty of a free and inquiring mind, two things which Irish (or is it Catholic?) education rarely thinks about.

In the end these were to come not from our schools but out

of our rebellion against everything, chiefly the domination of an alien and privileged class who encouraged, even demanded the tribute of resignation, and then sneered at us for the evasions and circumlocutions that have always been the last wretched, self-destroying weapons of the poor and resigned the world over. If I say a final no to that school, what I am really saying, then, is a no to that Ireland. I am saying no to my own boyhood, my own youth, even to my own parents, to everything that, had I not rebelled against it, would have mismade me for life.

4

Poverty No Bar to Happiness?

To any outsider observing us three brothers we must have
seemed to lead a wretchedly dull life, we were so severely disciplined. Our daily routine was adamant. We rose at eight, except
during Lent, when my mother would awaken us at half-past six
for seven o'clock Mass, often having to tear the bedclothes
aside before she could rouse us from our drug of sleep. At such
moments you must see the three of us strewn in one big featherbed like three white-robed puppets, a bed so big that it almost
filled our attic bedroom at the tip-top of the house.

I must pause at the mention of these attics. They were garrets
that had originally been intended as boxrooms. Their ceilings
sloped to the floor like tents, and they were lighted and venti-
lated only by skylights which were raised by means of notched
bars. When it rained heavily we could not open the sloping
windows more than an inch, and in the hottest weather they
could not be opened higher than the length of the brief bar. The
result was that in the summer the garrets were too hot and in
the winter too cold: there was, of course, no way of heating
them. Nevertheless, when we moved into this new house – 5
Half Moon Street – my mother seeing at once that if we used
the garrets as sleeping quarters she would have more bedrooms
for her lodgers occupied one garret, my father occupied another,
we three children slept in a third, and the servant girl, or slavey,
had the fourth. Since my mother used the large space outside
these four partitioned-off garrets as a drying room, we often

made our way to bed between damp curtains of shirts, sheets and tablecloths. That we slept in attics was therefore not so much a measure of our poverty as of our parsimony, and another token of the thrifty principle that dominated all our lives – my father's and mother's constant anxiety to make enough money to give their three children a good education. Here I am not trying to suggest that we were not really poor: a father of three children earning one pound sterling per week was a poor man even by pre–1914 values. I am saying that we, that is my father and mother, were of that class of ambitious poor folk who refuse to accept their poverty and all the natural and easy compensations of poverty. One may be happy though poor; to be poor, frugal, parsimonious and ambitious is quite another matter. It leads to a dull and disciplined life. This dragging us out of our warm cocoon of sleep at half-past six of a cold morning was part of it.

As we three sleep-heavy children stirred or turned in the unwelcome cold my mother would cry heartily to us: 'Up! Up! I come, said the Lord, like a thief in the night seeking whom I may DEVOUR! Rise from your slumbers! Woe to the weak and lukewarm of heart – I spit them out of my mouth. Up! Up! Come to me, all ye who labour and are burthened and I will refresh ye. Think of the poor souls suffering in Purgatory at this minute, waiting for your prayers. Think of poor Ned Keating who used to let ye in free to the Opera House and died only last month. Is this your return to him? There he is down there burning like hot coal! Up! Up with ye! Say but the word and my soul shall be healed. A fine bright cold hardy morning, with the crow putting out his tongue and ye still in bed!'

At that raw spring hour, mid-February or early March, the sky would be as beautifully cold as a mackerel, bluish-white at its base, everywhere else a dark bruise-blue except where gas lamps in the streets gleamed green-whitish-yellow, and to my memory it seems as if always there had just been a soft fall of rain. The slavey would still be snoring in her attic, the kitchen fire black, the streets empty and silent, damp and cold, the church suddenly glaringly bright, but also cold, and I fear my prayers were mostly damp and cold too. There was however always for me an exciting, strange beauty in those dark and

49

empty streets in contrast with the suddenly bright church. Afterwards they were less interesting. The sky had lightened, the lamps were extinguished, a few other people were abroad, a milkman, the first tram, early workers. I felt less special.

After breakfast we went off to school, the three of us together, walking there in all weathers since pennies for trams were as scarce as pennies for pocket money. Not that we ever had any such thing as pocket money, barring a halfpenny now and again to buy sweets, shared between us with meticulous justice, so that if an odd sweet were left over we drew lots for it. From school we returned at three o'clock, directly, strictly forbidden to loiter on the way, and, above all, forbidden to consort with 'barefooted little boys', 'corner-boys', or 'blackguards'. This meant that we never met with or played with our fellows out of school. Indeed, throughout my entire childhood, I did not have a single friend. After dinner, eaten in the kitchen, our sole living room since every other room was given up to the *artistes*, we were sent off, again in a bunch, for the usual walk up Wellington Road and down Saint Luke's, dropping in along the way to some church to say the Stations of the Cross. On our return from this daily walk we would sit at the long kitchen table to do our homework until suppertime, and after supper we would study again unless it was our night for the Confraternity or one of those divine nights when we had a free ticket for the play at the Opera House. And so to bed, up the long stairs, carrying a candle in a candlestick, first on the carpeted stretch, then on the lino stretch, and lastly on the bare boards with the nails shining like silver, into the attics.

2

It took me a great many years to see why it was that we three boys led such companionless lives, especially after school when our companions were playing and shouting and generally enjoying themselves in the streets or playing fields. Yet the reason was under my eyes. We were an Irish cop's family, which involves something quite different to being an ordinary civil policeman's family in say at random Britain or France or the USA or indeed any fully autonomous country in the world. The Royal Irish Constabulary had been established not merely to keep the civil peace but, if the need arose, to maintain British power in Ireland. The police were here an adjunct to the military units stationed in various military barracks throughout the island. As a small token of this fact they were given an elementary arms training, though they never wore side arms. They did not need to. The country as a whole had been so peaceful for so long that the mass of the population had become content with the colonial system in all its details, satisfied to leave it to their lawfully-elected representatives as British MPs in the British parliament to seek and sometimes win reforms therein. But the police chiefs in Ireland never forgot that they were an occupying force as well as a peace-keeping force. Accordingly very quietly and very effectively, they discouraged all fraternisation with the 'natives'. Hence those bits of fatherly advice (given, I must insist, in all innocence of their latent political import) about not talking to 'blackguards', i.e. the common population, on our way home from school. Hence, finally, those lonely, restricted walks repeated day after day up Wellington Road and down by Saint Luke's. In short, to be a cop's son in that Ireland meant to be either a rubber-stamp conformist, a secret rebel or a loner. My two brothers were natural conformists; the older conformed to the rule of Rome and ended as a Monsignor of his Church; my other brother, completely Anglicised, conformed to the rule of the Empire as an Inspector of Taxes in London; I became, step by step, a loner, a recusant, detached, an *étranger*, an observer, an alien, a spy, a writer. But this liberty was many miles ahead of me in these years that I am now recalling – years when my only escape from dullness was through the gate of the imagination. Did I even know at the time that my childhood and first boyhood really was dull? I cannot tell. Perhaps all mortal creation is, in Saint Augustine's tremendous image, no more than a vast sponge in the middle of a sea of infinity, in which case the only part of us which may not be the absorbent sponge is our surfaced brain peering consciously around like a greedy cormorant while all the rest and perhaps best of us is deep in the glaucous sea, incontinently forgotten. Dull? Dreamy? My whole childhood? In an effort to find out if it really was so I struggle to submerge. (After all did not Cesare Pavese say, 'The richest part of our memories are those we have lost.')

What do I come up with? Buttercups. My mother used to love us to gather them along the roadside for her pious altars in our attics, yellow, greasy flowers shining like wet lacquer. I dive again. Some boy at school once gave me a single scarlet-runner bean that I planted in a pot. I was amazed when it actually broke into flower on the windowsill of our bathroom overlooking roofs, river, homes, Shandon's tall bell-tower, the hills of Cork. Another memory? A boy casually gave me half a dozen strange things that he called *chessies*, that is chestnuts. I removed the prickly burr and there like some dark, precious stone on white velvet lay the fruit shining like mahogany. I rushed back to him to ask where did these things come from. From the earth? From trees? His laughter at me was that of a necromancer.

What about books? There were, of course, at first fairy tales, later *The Magnet*, *The Gem*, or the (was it weekly?) adventures of Sexton Blake, Tinker and their bloodhound Pedro. Later still the Free Library gave me all Henty, Dumas, Fennimore Cooper. Our first 'moving picture' was *Quo Vadis*. If only we had then had radio and television! As it was, without the Opera House I might have been living in the middle ages. Indeed, when the Great War came, it did not so much break out as sneak out in our town. We three sons of a Cork cop had, like ninety-nine per cent of the British Empire, never heard of Sarajevo, or Bismarck's *Eisen und blut*. It may well be that it is from some warm evening of that same June of the Archduke's murder that I recall the *Cork Evening Echo* startling its readers with the frightening announcement on its pink front sheet: RUNAWAY HORSE IN PATRICK STREET!

3

Rebellion! Indeed? Although I did actually once really and truly *mit eisen und blut* rebel – about a coat. This coat was sewn together for me by my mother out of the material of one of my father's castoff uniforms. Now, these tough uniforms were made of a material so closely woven, and then shrunk , or felted, that they could have kept out everything except a bullet, so that in spite of all my mother's art as a seamstress she failed to control the obdurate material, with the result that when she had reduced the paternal jacket to the size of a boy's body, the Coat curved out like a church bell all around my bottom, my two shoulders peaked up like two epaulettes, and my two arms were encased in two tubes. The next day, clad or confined in it, I went, most unwillingly, to school, where my companions laughed so mercilessly at me in the schoolroom, at playtime, in the yard, on my way home, that I refused to wear it again. My mother could not, or professed not to be able to, see what was wrong with it, holding it up, admiring it eloquently, fitting it on me again and again. To no purpose! I still looked like a sable-skirted fay, a minute South American mute. My mother begged. I insisted, obstinately and tearfully. In the end I had my way. The Coat lay around, or rather stood around, for months, until one day the Bottle Woman called.

This woman was a barefooted, beshawled shrimp of a creature who came to our door periodically to buy empty bottles and our castoffs. (*Our* castoffs!) The usual heap was thrown on the tiled floor of the hall and the usual bargaining began. A shilling for this. Sixpence for that. Suddenly she spied the Coat, snatched it up, held it up, turned it around and around, and then, with a wild peal of laughter, she cried: 'For God's sake, Missus Whalen, what in Heaven's name is *dat*?'

My mother snatched it from her and flung it on the heap.

'Sixpence,' she said.

The Bottle Woman shook her head sorrowfully, as if she were saying, 'Now, I'd like to be a philantropist, Missus Whalen. But!' She shook her head at fivepence, and at fourpence, and even at tuppence she would not have the coat. I, leaning over the balustrade, prayed that the Bottle Woman would at least give a penny for it. My mother would not stoop that low. Preserving her dignity as a true lady, she said grandly: 'You may have it as a handsel.' The Bottle Woman was too polite not to accept the gift, too honest to suppress a sigh as she took the piece of armour; and with as deep a sigh I leaned up from the balustrade and went upstairs to my attic window to inform all Cork of my blessed release from the shame of our masquerade.

For this was what our whole life was: a pretence that we were not what we were, a bobby, a bobby's wife, and a bobby's kids, living on the edge of false shames and stupid affectations, caught between ambition and fear, between struggling and striving, never either where we were or where we hoped to be, Janus-faced, throwing glances of desire and admiration upwards and ahead, glances of hatred or contempt downwards and behind. But I wonder, even as I talk about this life of the shabby-genteel that I saw on all sides of me as a boy and a youth, whether anybody today can form any idea of what genteelism meant in the British Isles before the 1920s began to make hay of it and the 1940s finally threw it out of the door. Certainly none of my American readers will understand the term or be able to form any feeling for what it once meant. Even their dictionaries – if the one before me is typical – do not know what the word means; for what this lexicographer says it means is: 'Belonging or suited to polite society, well-bred, refined, elegant, stylish.' The true meaning points to the effort to be all those things, and the transparent failure to be any of them. One has probably to go back to the novelists to get the tragicomic sense of the word. Thackeray gives it to us – *The Book of Snobs*; so does Dickens, Gissing, Wells, Bennett, Italo Svevo; it outcrops in Forster; it is all over the stories of V. S. Pritchett. Of American writers, only one drew inspiration from this half-grey life of the ambitious half-poor, and she, being a Bostonian, had not the courage to depict more than a quarter of what she knew so well and had so painfully experienced – Louisa Alcott in that much under-estimated novel *Little Women*.

In the end however I was saved, or anyway partly saved from the virus of genteelism not by rebellion against it but by escaping from its breeding-grounds in the city to that sole reliable basis of the traditional Irish mind, the country. I went behind the anglicised urban rot to the simple rustic life my father and mother cast aside, had to cast aside, when they entered the rat-race of Cork's metropolitan ambitions.

5

Love's Young Dreams

I

Every summer, when we used to leave Cork to spend at least a
month in the country we did so because fresh air and country
food were supposed to be good for us, especially the fresh air.

'Drink it in,' my mother used to say, as if it were some form
of nourishment, and she, my brothers and myself would stand
in a row in the fields of Limerick with our mouths like four O's
drinking in the pure air, much as her own country folk used to
go to Kilkee or Kilrush to walk into the wavelets up to their
calves and drink cupfuls of health-giving seawater. In Limerick
we stayed with my mother's sister, my Auntie Nan Cosgrave,
who had lived all her life since she was married in a long low
cottage, thatched and whitewashed, its mud walls bellying with
layers upon layers of lime, on the edge of the market town of
Rathkeale. It was a pretty cottage; it had Jacoby geraniums in
the windows; it was a step lower than the road; it flanked a long
neglected orchard surrounded by a very high wall. Otherwise we
stayed with my father's sister, my Aunt Kate, who lived in
various parts of the counties that border on Dublin.

We always left the city in July or August when the theatre
closed and it was the harvesting season in the country, so that
by April we were already planning every inch and moment of
the holiday. Our ritual walks up Wellington Road and down
Saint Luke's began to disintegrate more and more often into
anticipatory visits to the terminus of the Great Southern and
Western Railway, a wide, generally empty station, smelling of

smoke, steam, soot, oil, dust and crates of goods awaiting transport. Not that there was much to see there; but the least thing associated with travel was by now an excitement to our senses – the jarvey cars lined up in the yard outside; the coloured travel posters; the four-wheeled porters' trucks; the bookstall, which sold such unlikely papers as week-old *Echos de Paris* or that old monthly travel periodical for children called *Je Suis Partout*; the empty rails bright as four knives, narrowing away between the platforms into the arched maw of the tunnel through which every northbound train has to pass underneath Cork City into the open fields beyond. Again and again we would stand before the poster showing the timetables of our trip, learning the timing of those necessary changes at the junctions along the way which would be its main hazards, learning by rote the names of all the stations to be passed – Cork, Blarney, Rathduff, Mourneabbey, Mallow, Buttevant, Charleville, Kilmallock, Knocklong, Limerick Junction. Usually we diverged off the main line at Charleville for the town of Croom, where Uncle Tom Cosgrave used to meet us with his sidecar and drive us across country to save us further train fare. If he could not do this we would persist to the Saint Patrickswell junction, a tiny, silent place where one waited for maybe an hour or more for another train, with nothing to look at except one hand truck, a cow in a field, and a single bright rail vanishing in perspective under the eye of the next bridge. All this, and much more, we foresaw whenever we three stood in a half-circle before the printed poster in that windy terminus in Cork.

We foresaw hazards. We knew that for months to come my mother would waver, funds would waver, aunts and uncles would waver. Even when the dates were agreed on, even when my mother had begun buying elegant, second-hand clothes for the trip – for, of course, she had to arrive home in regal fashion, a success returning from the big city – we remained tremulous. There could be a crisis even on the very last night, when the trunk was being packed, a troubling ceremony on which my mother and father spent hours long after we three had been sent off to our bed, lying awake thinking and talking of tomorrow morning, or listening fearfully over the banisters while the packing ceremony went its usual way downstairs. Things would not fit into the trunk; things had to be taken out; things were put back, taken out, put back again. The presents for the relatives had to be displayed, considered, priced, approved; a highly delicate matter, since all the relatives would be at pains to find out what the others got – so very delicate that the presents were sure to be taken out again and again, reconsidered, repriced, thought adequate for some and not for others, reshuffled as to their recipients, still thought inadequate, argued over crossly, finally approved as being 'much too good for 'em' or simply packed in despair.

Sooner or later the whole of this ritual would evoke in my mother so many sad-happy memories of her girlhood that she would sit back on her hunkers and weep, at which stage she had to be comforted with a half-glass of brandy, became even more emotional on the strength of it, and in the end so aggravated my father waiting impatiently to rope the trunk (no peasant ever, anywhere, trusts in mere locks!) that the night and the packing invariably ended in pious and impious invocations to the Holy Family, individually named and personally appealed to for patience and comfort, with my mother's wails mounting up through the empty house to us three, by now halfway down the attic stairs in our nightshirts, terrified lest the whole adventure be abandoned at the last moment.

Of course, in the morning all was smooth as milk. We drove royally on our hired sidecar through the city, so early that hardly anybody was out in the streets; the train was there, its engine hissing madly, breasting the tape to be off; my father commended us to the guard, the conductor and to God. If we were lucky we had a carriage to ourselves, one in each corner, each loudly extolling his position above the others. Then, at the very last moment, my father pressed into each clutching fist a bright sixpence, our holiday pocket money, ordered us sternly to be good boys, kissed my mother, made us close the windows tightly, stood back with a little salute, and the train slowly chugged into the tunnel where the windows at once went grey and we heard an occasional drip of moisture on the roof.

Then there was the sudden blaze of the open country, cows and horses in fields, blue and pink donkey carts trundling by with bright churns to the morning creamery, countless other things that meant much rushing from one window to the other. There were the *Gem*, *Marvel* and *Magnet* to be read, the stations to be noted, the changes to be made, the waitings to be enjoyed, until at last we came to the last junction of all with the solitary porter calling out in his flat Limerick accent, 'Ballingraane, Ballingraane, chaange here for Askeaytin and Fynes' – and there were the lake and the spire of Rathkeale wheeling slowly about us while we excitedly grabbed our belongings to be ready to alight at the next station, mount Uncle Tom's car, drive through the straggling street of the town, turn into Roche's Road, and pull up at its last cottage, over whose half-door Auntie Nan would already be leaning out to greet us with peals of red-faced laughter, open arms, shouts of welcome and floods of happy tears at the sight of her favourite sister.

As for me, I was by then already away and gone. Immediately we had turned the corner of Roche's Road a tang of turfsmoke had fallen from the high roof of Normoyle's pub like the swish of a headman's sword decapitating time. When Auntie Nan – a slattern old woman, her hair streeling, her eyes filled with tears, her hands speckled with the dried flecks of the meal she had just been feeding to the hens – squashed me to her bosom I was with the ages. I was where nothing ever changes, where everything recurs – the dull sheen of morning sifting through the holland blind on the sacks of meal crouched in a corner of my bedroom, or the last of the sun glinting on a bit of brass in a horse collar hanging from its peg in the bellying wall, or the lighting of the lamp when the blue twilight fell and the town was wrapped in veils of silence for the night. Only the clouds would move, and they barely, and they were always the same clouds, the same weather, like the same scenes going around and around in the wheel of a magic lantern. Everything was as solid as the fields, common as a cow, yet timeless and tenuous as a faraway, fluting cock-a-doodle-doo or a distant, milk-heavy mooing. Habit and custom ruled here. It was a place breathing its own essence. Nothing was imposed, nothing made, everything grew as softly as the morning light through the blind. Here there was no up W. Road and down Saint L., no watch-your-step, no for-God's-sake-mind-who-is-behind-you, nothing except Nothing – the lake, a road, a path, a spring-well tasting

58

of iron, the swish of a scythe, a rock to lie on, a hillock to stand on with your mouth open like an O to the wind over the clover fields or the bogland heavy with mint and thyme, and over it all Limerick's westering sun as pale in the albino sky as if she had been frozen to a moon.

What did I do in Rathkeale? Nothing. I once described Rathkeale in a travel book as a dead, lousy, snoring, fleabitten pig of a town, adding that I can never think of it without going as soft as a woman. Nobody ever came to Rathkeale unless he came there from his mother's womb or for business: a banker, a dentist (in my day maybe twice a week, or once a week, from Limerick), cattle-drovers, cattle-buyers, the parish priest, a parson, the teacher, a midwife. We used to see some of them pass sedately along the road for a walk, the chemist's wife, bank clerks, the teacher, returning as sedately an hour or so later. I do not know what else these exiles had to do to pass their free hours. Perhaps they played cards, had a drink in one of the pubs, read a book occasionally. Maybe it was 'something to do' to go to Benediction. I used to see Auntie Nan lean over the half-door a dozen times a day to look up and down Roche's Road. Remembering this habit of hers, years later, on my last visit there, I leaned over the half-door, looked sideways down the road and took a photograph. It came out as the empty road, the long ten-foot-high wall of her orchard on the left, a tumble-down low wall of round stones on the right, one telephone wire following the long perspective of the limestone road, and on the single telephone wire a crow. If my picture had had a sound track, I would have heard nothing but a humming in the wire, although if I had held the sound track open for long enough it might also have picked up a basso hen clucking somewhere, or the soft *croc-croc* of a donkey and cart passing by the other end of the road on the Main Street. There was no cinema. Later they got some sort of library. Once a year a one-tent circus came, with, on one occasion, a small, sad elephant. I feel I want at once to take out Yves Montand singing *Saltimbanques*. What a life! *Di dolce far niente, di dolce absolutabloodywellutely far niente.*

But no! This is the wrong style. This is the cowardly, evading style that fears the heart. Ask me that question again so that I may answer it simply and honestly. 'What *did* I do there?'

I answer: 'Nothing!' Nothing that can mean anything to anyone unless he grew up there, or unless all this land around the little River Deel is holy ground to him because it is his mother's country. Limerick is to the traveller who travels only with his eyes one of the most uninteresting regions in the whole of Ireland. Flat, monotonous, colourless, shaggy, half asleep, a sighing land, wet underfoot and often wet above, a land of crinkling alders, little grey-lichened walls, tiny lakes, brown haystacks wind-ruffled, streams willow-edged or reed-clanking, poorish land sometimes breaking into good heart and high meadows, sometimes declining into scrawny, reedy fields, and all of it canopied by that unmistakably pallid sky. *Splendeur et magnificence des pays plats!*

I did nothing. I sat by a well and saw a spider race with delicate legs across the cold water from out of his cold cavern. I did the rounds of a Pattern (that is, a place dedicated to a Patron Saint) at the Holy Well of Nantenan near Ballingrane, with scores of old women come from long distances in their pink carts to pray as they circled, and to hang when they finished a medal or a bit of cloth on the sacred thorn tree by the well until it looked as ragged as a servant's head in curling-papers in the morning. I saw a line of cows pass along a road, their udders dripping into the dust. I went with Uncle Tom, each of us seated on a shaft of the donkey cart, jolting out to his bits of fields in the Commons near Lough Doohyle, taking with us for the day a bottle of cold tea and great slices of wheel cake cooked in a bastable, plastered with country butter and cheap jam. While, all day, he went slowly up and down the ridges on one padded knee thinning his turnips, I wandered. I saw a row of twenty poplars whispering to the wind. I picked and chewed the seeds of the pink mallow. I saw how the branch of a thorn tree in the armpit of an alder had worn itself and its lover smooth from squeakingly rubbing against it for forty years. I saw an old ruined castle and a Big House with the iron gates hanging crookedly from its carved pillars. And all the time away across the saucer of the lake there was the distant church spire of Rathkeale, like a finger of silence rising from an absolutely level horizon.

You see? Nothing! A fairy tale, a child's memory, a cradle song, crumbs in a pocket, dust, a seed. I lay on my back among lone fields and wondered whether the cloudy sky was moving or stopped. Childhood, boyhood, nostalgia, tears. Things no traveller would notice or want to notice but things from which a boy of this region would never get free, things wrapping cataracts of love about his eyes, knotting tendrils of love about his heart.

What a boy does not think he stores up. It was not until twenty-five years had passed that I suddenly remembered that Uncle Tom had a wen as big as a billiard ball on the back of his neck, and something near to a hump on his back. Suddenly all that had been timeless and tenuous became timefull and tense. Auntie Nan was not Auntie Nan, she was Nancy Murphy, a young woman being married in the church of Rathkeale to a man with a hump and a wen. My mother Bid, her sister, would have been there. There were – I have forgotten the precise number: six or eight or was it ten? – other sisters. They also would have been there watching the wedding. They had no brother, and the father was dead. They would have considered that Tom Cosgrave had two sidecars, a small contract with the post office for carrying bags of mail to some nearby station; that he had the cottage, the orchard, those few bits of fields on the Commons. It was a good match – that would have been the judgement of her mother; of her sister Bid, then behind the counter of McDonnell's Hardware and Grocery shop in the Main Street, 'serving her time'; of all her sisters, fated to emigrate to Australia and America, for what else could my old grandmother Mag Murphy (born a Power) do, a widow without even one son, with so large and helpless a family of girls on twenty-five acres of land in this wide, flat, soggy riverbasin of the Deel, rank with streams and dikes that feed into one small river, and from the small river, with many others, into the great River Shannon beyond? Nancy was lucky. As my mother had been to have caught the eye of young Constable Dinny Whelan, then stationed in Rathkeale. The ones who had to take the emigrants' ship? I have no record of any of them but one, an aunt whom I met many years later in Brooklyn. All the rest have vanished. That was the pattern of our line. Of our race.

Our visits to the farm, three miles west of Rathkeale, always took place on Sundays, and then only on fine days. Uncle Tom had a neat little tub-trap, drawn by a donkey, into which my aunt, my mother, one of my brothers and I would crush. The third brother would cycle. The brave little donkey would trot off down Roche's Road, down Well Lane into the New Line, and then having shown his paces to the town walk at his ease past Ballyallinan Castle, west past the Knockaderry crossroads, and so on until we entered the long, narrow, rutted *boreen*, or side road leading to the stone-strewn yard of Loughill. The farm-house had, visibly, once been a small thatched cottage, about twelve feet by thirty, no bigger than my present living room, where ten or twelve people had once lived – my grandmother and grandfather and their fatal line of girls. The eldest of them, when the last of the others had been shipped off or married off, had brought in her husband, a man named John Hough. These two, my Aunt Maggie and my Uncle John, and their family had, over the years, added a room or two, outhouses and a good metal barn. They were my first and unforgettable close-up of farmer stock, and I have to say that I did not wholly warm to them. Uncle John was a tall, bearded man, wearing on Sundays a swallow-tailed coat, with a gentle voice and smile, in whom I felt a tireless animal strength, a certain smiling contempt for Uncle Tom and Auntie Nan with their comical bits of scattered fields, and I knew he could be cruel, because we were often told about his wild son whom he had once stripped and whipped with a horsewhip so pitilessly that the youth had run away and never been heard of since. Aunt Maggie was equally tall and strong-shouldered, with a round, bellowing voice that you could hear two fields away, and teeth that could plough the earth; a dark, rough woman whom nobody would want to cross. I admired them and was in awe of them. Of their inner natures, of course, I knew nothing. I was conscious only of what I would now call the animus – never for a second at rest – bred in all peasants by the hostile gods of the earth and sky.

Over the summers things fell into place historically. That well where I saw a spider crawl over the cold surface of the water was (I gathered from my mother's memories) the well where her mother used to come late at night, under the stars, when her children were in bed, to drink cold water and worry over her debts. That castle I have mentioned was called Caislean Arandubh, or Blackbread Castle, which invoked the famine of 1847, of which Martin Ross once said that for generations after its snows melted its ice water still shivered in the veins of Ireland. At the Pattern of Nantenan the slowly circling, dark-shawled women would have had plenty to pray for and pray against. Those iron gates hung crookedly from the entrance pillars of the Big House where the landlords had lived. The thorn tree had rubbed the alder, and the poplars had fluttered in an Atlantic wind that could also lodge crops and bring brushes of rain down from the clouds to sweep the fields. I learned that the pretty pink mallow is the flower of marshlands and ruins. It is all over Limerick. When my own mother sighed, and then went to the press in her kitchen to look at her lean purse, and then went to the tap for a drink of cold water . . .

I loved those visits to the farm once I got over my first shyness and awe. We tumbled in the tall haybarn with the Hough children. We were put up on the mighty back of the working horse for rides. We chased the geese in the haggard. Once I stayed for a couple of nights on the farm, sleeping by the undying turf fire with my cousins John and Jer in the excitingly novel settle bed – by day a plain, long box of wood, at night its seat and side folding down flat on the floor – hearing the crickets whistling quietly behind the hearth, telling them about Cork City, and the theatre and my school, they telling me about the farm, and rabbit-catching and otter-hunting, waking in the dawn to see John in his dayshirt blowing the smoored ashes into flame under fresh turf. When they had milked the cows in the half dark I went rattling off in the cart with John to the creamery, there to join a line of other carts from the plain about. One night, for some reason, I went with Jer up to the hill of Knocka-derry. Below me a lighthouse winked on the Shannon. Twenty miles away a glow under the clouds meant Limerick town, their gateway to the world.

Our alternating holidays with my Aunt Kate were another world altogether. My father's sister had, like my mother, married a policeman, Uncle Owen Boyhan, and had by him three children, Tom, May, and Lil, or Lena. They always lived in County Dublin or County Kildare, a long train journey on the main line.

Uncle Owen, of whom I became very fond, was a warm-hearted man, big in belly and in moustaches and, it was whispered at home, big in thirst. He had retired at the rank of sergeant, and was now eking out his modest pension with various unexacting jobs. When I was very small he was the gatekeeper of a gentleman's country house in Celbridge, a crumbling village about twelve miles from Dublin, living rent-free in the gate lodge, whose pillared gates faced the end of the village street, so that whenever I passed between them to go to the sweetshop in the village I was never quite sure whether I was going in through them or coming out through them. On top of each pillar was a lion with a bare-breasted woman's head. A long, long, long avenue, linden-lined, led to a big, big house with hundreds of windows. I now know that this was a very famous and splendid building: Castletown House, built in 1715 by William Connolly, the Speaker of the Irish Parliament, so that two C's still link one another like hooked fingers on the gates. I have only one crumb of memory from that long-ago visit: the lively image of a red fox fleeing, all out, early one morning, across the long drive of the demesne, with the hounds and red-coated huntsmen in full cry after him. I just barely saw him. When all the others rushed from the lodge at the baying of the hounds I was left behind racing on my short legs, bawling at being deserted, until my cousin Lil Boyhan ran back to take me in her arms and race after the others. I remember that tender gesture as keenly as I remember the red fox fleeing, and I think that from that infantile moment I knew she was the softhearted one of the family.

Later, Uncle Owen was in charge of the public weigh-machine and market house in the military town of Newbridge, a few miles up the Liffey, living in an apartment overlooking another small demesne at the rear. Later still, they moved to a new house in the town, letting the top floor as an apartment to married officers. These, of course, were English, and I was much impressed by their elegance, their accents, their clothes, their dressing for dinner every evening, their silverware, their general proposal of distance, wealth and romance, especially when the war began in 1914. But this town, always a garrison town, was dyed pink and khaki. It had grown just after Waterloo, when the cavalry barracks was built, so that all along one side of the street we saw the high walls of the barracks, and all along the other the shops and houses which had once been the original sutlers' booths. I was often awakened in the mornings by bugle calls or by the jingling and rattling of horse-drawn gun wagons ambling down the street into the countryside on some military exercise, their drivers astride the leaders, chin straps fixed, wearing the steel shin guards that kept their legs from being crushed between the frightened horses in the roar of battle. There were always soldiers in the streets at night, parading before the lighted windows, up and down, up and down; poor bored, bloody English swaddies, as I now see them, fed up with this country town where there was nothing to do but get noisy in a pub or try to lure a girl under a hedge for a bit of mugging. There was no cinema, but every known denomination had its tin chapel.

For me the pleasures of Newbridge as of Limerick were all of the countryside: tramping the roads, visiting the Curragh plain, playing cricket in the fields, swimming in the Liffey, or going off with my third and oldest cousin, Tom Boyhan, a National Teacher, when he went shooting over the vast bogland behind the town. I at once fell in love with this infinity of purple heather and black peat, backed, so often, by sky-castles of snowy clouds, its silence broken only by a curlew's cry or a snipe rising with a whirr from the heather, its flat emptiness interrupted only by one hillock, as lonely as a stranded bottle on a beach, the Hill of Allen, or by an occasional canal village, sometimes with a derelict eighteenth-century flyboat hotel and immense warehouses for grain, or, when one got right into the bog, a distant thread of blue smoke from a lone turf-cutter's fire. But, above all, I loved the great open plain of the Curragh, two miles from the town. This immense rolling plain was empty except for its grass, a few grazing sheep and tufts of yellow gorse. In the distance one saw an occasional car slowly crawling across it like a beetle over a golf course. Ireland's most famous racecourse has written an oval in one corner of it. If I went there very early in the morning I would see the horses being worked out, their hooves followed by sprays of dew as they raced over the grass, or by flying tufts of peat moss from the specially prepared gallops. Afterwards they would be walked away, breathing whitely on cold mornings, wrapped in clouds of sweaty steam. Training stables all around the plain brought in here, too, a cosmopolitan touch, and far away, on the eastern edge of the Curragh, a faint red line as if drawn by a pencil marked yet another military settlement still known as the Camp, years, indeed three full centuries, after its canvas had turned to red brick buildings, tarred wooden huts and tin sheds. Here too one heard distant bugle calls wavering on the wind, the dull smack of rifles from the pits, the faint, smooth brass of a military band. On sunny days a heliograph winked across the bottoms.

More romance? That owl-lidded princess who has always smiled at me alluringly from the rim of life, and all too often caught me in her sea-puss claws? Though I wonder if I have the right to decry even by an adverb anything that has fashioned me as I am. This time she came gloved in the mud of Flanders trenches, breathing the cordite of its guns, smelling of the brown smells of India, the snows of the Himalayas, Egypt's sands (*With Kitchener in the Soudan*), all embodied in the tiny Union Jack on the tip of the far-off water tower high over the empty grass, the few cropping sheep, the rattle from the pits, the elegant and powerful horses, the casual words of stable boys about Newmarket, the Gold Cup, Epsom, or Longchamps; or evoked by endless, innocent prattlings from Lil and May Boyhan about which regiment was coming and which was going, the gay doings of the 'boys' in the camp (between 1914 and 1918 all soldiers were 'boys'), gossip about the private lives of owners, trainers and jockeys. All this, so very different from Limerick's wars with her hostile, earthy gods I was to pack years later, changed and heightened by the passion of memory, into a long short story called *Love's Young Dream*, which, I believe, is what it all was: our adolescent flesh becoming timidly excited by the first faint wavelet-whisperings of the world fretting in across our innocent bodies.

My cousin Tom was to be the first of us to answer the call. He was at that time my prince of men, older than any of us youngsters by several years, dark like all the Boyhans, handsome, debonair, dashing, reckless, full of animal spirits and, as I see now, always grasping madly at the grapes of life. Was he also evading gentility? When I first knew him he was earning only a simple National Teacher's salary but lived well beyond it. He liked me, possibly because he saw that I adored him. It was he who first showed me Dublin.

'I'll take you up to Dublin next Saturday,' he said to me with a grin one day, 'if Uncle comes through in time with a fiver.'

I believed him, but I did not know who Uncle was until I was awakened the next Saturday to find him beside my bed shaking my shoulder and gaily waving a cheque.

'Good old Uncle Ikey,' he was shouting, his brown eyes and his white teeth flashing with divilment. 'Off we go!'

In awe I found that he was, in my mother's phrase, in the hands of the moneylenders. Inside an hour I was among trams racing like thoroughbreds, packed streets, a ceaseless boiling and bubbling of noise, great ruby-red squares, towers, domes and spires. The first thing he did was to hand me half a crown. Then he took me to the top of the Nelson Pillar, in what was still being called Sackville Street, to survey the entire city. Then he had my 'sticky-back' taken, as we called the first of those semi-instantaneous (that is, wait-an-hour) photographs. He took me to sessions with his tailor and his gunsmith, to my first restaurant, redeemed his gold watch from his pawnbroker out of Uncle Ikey's money, showed me the swank shops in Grafton Street, admired the passing girls, allowed me to sit and watch him being trimmed, shampooed and manicured in a white-tiled hairdresser's shop, fed the ducks in Saint Stephen's Green with me, showed me the line of clubs ('I'll be in there one day!': he had not an ounce of envy in his body and he always identified himself upwards), and finally knocked me sideways by dropping into a chemist's shop, calling for a pill called Aspirin and throwing it back with a vigorous, 'That feels much better – always remember, John, to take one after a skite!' (Only on the stage had I hitherto seen anyone take drugs: in J. B. Fagan's *Bella Donna*, a steamy drama about dark passion on the Nile.) Within a year he was married to a local beauty, and had his officer's commission, and looked even more handsome and dashing than ever in uniform. Within a month of his arrival in France he was dead. I have just looked at his photograph. He has a moustache: it looks like a false moustache on the face of a smiling boy. Oh! All *very* different from Limerick! Perhaps that wild Hough son who had run away from home and not been heard of after was of the same mettle?

I am probably foreshortening the years. In my unthinking being everything about those alternating holidays in the plains of Limerick and in the plains of Dublin-Kildare has been for most of my life a mere scatter of blurs and blobs like dots on a radar screen. I am coalescing the blobs here only in the hope of discovering what they had in common, what they might have had to say to one another if they had ever met.

I pursue the Dublin-Kildare summers because a curious thing about them has suddenly arrested me. I recall that my father and mother, especially my mother, slightly disapproved of the Boyhans. It was not Uncle Owen who bothered them. He was a simple and unaffected man who never bothered anybody but himself; after all, as a member of the same police force as my father he was part of the same pattern of values and loyalties. It was my father's sister, my Aunt Kate, who made them feel uneasy, and whether they infected me with the feeling or not, she always made me feel a bit uneasy too. She was such a caricature of the genteel that she had not a natural turn in her. Though she was older than my mother, her hair was improbably and unpersuasively golden, and on all state occasions, such as going to Mass or visiting a neighbour, she squeezed herself so tightly into black satin that damp circles appeared under her armpits and perspiration came out in drops on her ruddy face. I associate her with large, too pink coral cameos and loops upon loops of gold chains. In public her manner was effusive and gushing. In private she was completely natural only when she fell victim to the 'megrims' and the 'vapours,' blinding head-aches to which she was prone, so that my abiding impression of her is either of an overdressed old peasant woman pretending

68

to be a grand lady, or of a sick old woman with cloths steeped in vinegar wound around her dyed head lying in a darkened room or wandering, moaning and inelegant, around the house like a tinker's wife after a battle-royal. She was an offence to all my romantic ideas in a way that warmhearted Auntie Nan in Rathkeale never was. I think she even offended my father's and mother's image of The Real Thing. Or did they uncomfortably see in her a mirror of their own citified pretensions? Or could it be that she was an obstacle to their real delight in these country holidays which was to escape from all that highfalutin' city stuff, back to the easy-going youth on their native heath, to open their mouths there and drink its pure primeval air?

I ought to be able to garner from each following summer as I grew a few more blobs and blurs of memory, but for weeks now I have been troubled to discover that when I peer into the radar screen of the three summers after Tom Boyhan was killed I can see clearly only one momentary, lovely image. This blankness frightens and excites me. Why have I forgotten all the rest? What was all that rest? I know that for one of those three summers we did not go to either of our aunts. We chose, instead, why I do not know, the dull seaside resort of Youghal, some thirty miles east of Cork City, where I was so miserable that I persuaded my mother to bring me home before the month was out. I have a photograph of myself from that summer. I am fourteen years old. I am wearing a flat straw hat with a wide band. My face is round as a berry and my mouth is soft and spread across it. I am fondly clasping my mother's arm. We are like a pair of lovers.

The next summer is a total blank. The summer after, I went to Kildare alone. By this time my Aunt Kate has died, and my Uncle Owen lives in the heart of the Curragh camp or barracks, with his daughters May and Lil. He has no job, and even over this item there is some cloud or shadow. The girls have some kind of secretarial jobs in the barracks and their address is something like Number 33, Row 6, Married Quarters, Block B.

I cannot understand why I went alone, for a holiday, to a military camp. All day long, while the girls were at work, I had nothing to do but wander about the plain looking for God knows what, or playing handball alone in the ball alley below the house. I discovered during those vacant days that this camp which had always stirred my imagination as a place full of every sort of excitement and gaiety was as silent and seemingly empty as a ghost camp. I never saw more than two or three soldiers at a time. All I saw was a sentry or two, a nursemaid or two wheeling perambulators, an occasional truck, two or three men lugging big dixies or big garbage cans across empty barrack squares. Even at night there was only the mildest stir around the cinema, its blue carbon lights sizzling in the open doorway of the projection box. Where do soldiers in big settlements like this go during the daytime? If they were on the plain, then the plain swallowed them. Do they go on long route marches by night and sleep by day? It might have been a monastery where the monks rose before dawn, were busy indoors or in distant fields all day long and never seen after that. Or was it that I, wandering around like a sheep on the plain, was lost in my own dreamy mind, enduring some strange and troubled shock, some tropism like a flower turning its blinded eyes to the invisible sun or absorbed by the gravitational pull of its earthbound body? The hearts and bodies of boys must often pass through this phase of suspended life, like an Indian fakir in a trance on his bed of nails, at that age when

> everything that is lovely
> Is a brief, dreamy kind delight.

I have wondered whether the girls, too, were not in some similar torpid mood, passive, on the brink of passion, hesitant like bathers stripped at the edge of the sea, hypnotised by the same siren-whispers that had called their brother, waiting only for one more stir of the will or of the flesh to call them to swim away to whoever or whatever waited for them out there in the darkness. Indeed, the next time I was to hear of them May had been married, to an officer – that of course – and Lil was living in London. When I heard this it came back to me that once or twice while they were out a young, smiling lieutenant, a replica of Tom, dropped into their living room, gay with blue curtains and blue cushions and simple posies, found me sitting there looking at him, silent and unresponsive, and left with bright, embarrassed cheerios after a few minutes.

My one brief, sunshot image of that summer is of one of the girls' friends, a woman whom we talked with for ten minutes one warm Sunday afternoon in the garden of a house on the other side of the Curragh, whether a wife or a daughter I have no idea. She seemed to me, suddenly swooning with silent joy, the most beautiful creature I had ever seen, large breasted, large-armed, her hair as fair as corn, her eyes sapphire or cornflower blue, her skin breathing like pale pink sweet peas, her white-toothed laughter a blast of sun. She was, in Stephen Daedalus's succulent phrase, softer than sound or odour. She was the first woman that I looked at as a man looks at a woman. There is no use in my saying to myself now that she must have weighed fourteen stone, or that she may have been the cook, or that she must now be an old blowsy, white-haired woman. When Lil and May and I left her to walk back across the shadowless short grass of the Sunday-silent Curragh into the empty camp, she walked with us, unknown to them. I have kept her image, her insoluble symbol for no reason known even to the heart, all my life.

You know Cavafy's poem 'When They Are Roused'?

> Try to guard them, poet,
> however few they are that can be kept.
> The visions of your loving.
> Set them, half hidden, in your phrases.
> Try to sustain them, poet,
> when they are roused in your brain
> at night, or in the glare of noon.

She is probably hidden somewhere, unknown even to me, in everything that I have written.

It was the last holiday I spent anywhere with those two girls, and the last time I saw them together. Boyhood and girlhood were done with, though once more I spent a summer on the plains of Limerick, my last. How few loves last! How often the apple falls from the tree into the soft grass so silently that we do not hear it. I did not know that I would not pass another summer in Rathkeale or in Kildare. How often it must have

71

happened that a man and his beloved have spent a long happy night together and on parting with passionate kisses until the morrow failed to hear the soft whisper of fate in the grass behind them!

6

Brimmings

Evidently, the world was not yet quite the world to me, nor I a being in it. As we say about halfwits, I was not all there. (I sometimes wonder if I have ever become 'all there'.) An existentialist would say I was not yet *un être dans le monde*, not aware enough of the world, indeed hardly aware of it at all. I had bypassed the canonical age of reason, which the RC Church and, I think, some states optimistically once put at the age of seven. Yet, as in the penumbral hour before sunrise, there were hints of light, much as the spring breathes invisibly on the ice of winter whose thaw has no fixed day. Understanding was on the way, in nuclear bits and pieces like a Salvador Dali madonna. She came as slowly as a well fills. All my moments of understanding have been like that – accumulations of minute experience, drop after drop, each unobserved at the time, brimming over at last as a little fountain of light.

Here is a small, absurd instance of this from much later, when I was twenty-five. I give it here as an illustration of what I mean by a brimming. For years I had enjoyed, as most Irish people enjoy, the hot and vivid pleasures of aimless disputation; for it is of the essence of the Irish love of argument that the destination of a discussion shall never be considered as interesting as the journey. Indeed it is considered rather bad form to arrive at any destination at all since this at once ends the pleasure of the dispute. Anyway, there is always somebody in every group of Irish talkers whose role it is to inject a joke whenever the discussion seems on the point of coming to the point, after which it can easily be resumed again at a safe tangent from this lamentable fate. On this brimming day, my twenty-sixth year, while I was walking somewhere beside a young professor, to whom I shall always be grateful for his unconscious gift of the good example, he stopped me dead in the middle of whatever logomanic argument I was unfolding in this happily aimless way, turned to me and, to my supreme astonishment, said: 'You know I think you have made a very useful point there in our discussion.'

Never before had any opponent granted me as much, or anybody granted the like in my presence to anybody else. At that moment something in my nature, hitherto only partially guessed at, fountained up so appealingly as not to be denied. I beheld, for the first time, stretching out before me, the calm and elegant satisfactions of constructive discussion as against the heady joys of purely contentious shindyism. If, at this, my good reader should find himself raising his shoulders in a prolonged shrug of astonishment, I assure him that I find myself doing the same. But not, possibly, for his reason. I shrug at the realisation that when this little fountain of light sank down, countless others elsewhere all over the world must have also been pulsing. I am happy to think that when I am dead those fountains of both the littlest and the largest knowledge will go on playing all over the world. I mean that I suspect most young people have those brimmings, though somewhat earlier than at twenty-five, and that it is in this way that we all learn whatever little or much we learn from life.

I recall from between the ages of thirteen and sixteen, or thereabouts, four specially important pools of understanding that began to lick the brims of my consciousness and finally overflooded it. The first of these brimmings has to do with the fact that up to about the age of thirteen I felt an intense love for that omnipresent figure my mother. For years we two had shared a warm pool of sympathy, understanding, mutual trust and reliance that may simply be called filial and maternal love, until the time came when – without, of course, realising it – I came to puberty, whereupon our tropical lagoon was visited by emotions that neither of us understood and that, now, an old man in his eighties, it pains me to as much as adumbrate. Even when fully grown and well able to understand these juvenile turbulences I found myself painfully disturbed by Proust's description of Marcel's (that is to say by his own) longing as a child for his mamma's goodnight kiss on one particular spot on his cheek; disturbed particularly by her obvious awareness of what that kiss involved, as shewn by her stern interdict against more than just that one single viaticum before the child unwillingly crept alone upstairs to bed; disturbed above all by Marcel's father's cool rationalisation of those Oedepal valedictions as 'just nerves'. So much sophistication, so much worldly wisdom made a mock of my mother's rustic simplicity, of the elemental, animal simplicity of her love.

What happened on the fateful evening I am recalling was that my 'Mamma' and I were on one of our solitary, delightful strolls together, arm in arm like lovers, when we came up with three or four of my young school companions. I left her side for one minute to exchange hellos with them. When I rejoined her side she violently rejected my hand from hers; she was, to my amazement, boiling with rage; she refused to speak to me; she turned at once for home. There she at once seized what was called the rattan: a length of tough Malayan cane commonly sold in any hardware shop for the express purposes both of beating carpets and children, always kept hanging by a string behind the kitchen door. Now we were used to getting a few cuts of this across the calves for such crimes as disobedience or impertinence; but this time was totally different. She followed my calves with lashes all the way up three flights of stairs, into my attic bedroom, there made me strip naked, and flogged me all over until she was exhausted and I was reduced to the abject and final subjection of unheeded sobs of shame. For it was the shame that mattered both to the victim and the aggressor. In my first year as a marriageable youth, *nubilis*, my masculine pride had been assaulted unforgiveably. I buried the memory but it lived on in its vault. The anger festered internally, though I naturally did not realise it at the time, nor indeed for many years after – my retaliation being quite unconscious.

From that moment on I began to strip her as she had stripped me. I did so by noting and silently recording imperfections,

75

lapses, crudities of her nature that I earlier had not registered at all; for when a couple are in the state of love neither beloved can do wrong. The truth forced itself on me that my once-beloved was not civilised. She was a boor. I began to disinter the ghosts of earlier incidents that – even still I am astonished at her insensitivity – continued to repeat themselves after the whipping incident. For example on similar affectionate strolls along one or other of the town's two pleasant, suburban, wide, tree-lined avenues – it could be the Marina along the river or the Mardyke, both untrafficked – she would still embarrass me by halting me, looking around to be sure no other pedestrians were close enough to observe her, bending low before me under the pretence of buttoning some part of my frontal clothing, spread her legs and pee standing up just as if she were a Pompadour or a du Barry or any of the lovelies of Versailles at an imperial ball taking advantage of a pause in a waltz to pee on the floor.

When I was in my fifteenth year I began to think, sadly, that my mother had not a great deal of brains. It took me only a very little longer to decide despairingly that she had no brains at all. I came to this sad conclusion because she, like her own mother, was always getting into debt, and always moaning about it. I loved her so much that I could not bear to see her miserable, so I resolved to help her by becoming her private accountant. I procured somewhere the remains of an old blue-covered ledger – so large that United Steel could have recorded their entire consolidated accounts in it – sat her beside me that very afternoon on the sagging horsehair sofa in the kitchen and said in a kindly but firm voice:

'Now, Mother, in future, I want you to keep your accounts properly. Your trouble is quite simple. If you are getting into debt you are spending more on your lodgers than you are receiving from them.'

'Ah, sure, child!' she assured me with a sigh and a laugh. 'I'm getting nothing at all out of them. I don't know why I have them at all, at all, only for the sake of the handling of the money.'

'But, Mother, there is no meaning to handling money unless

76

you can show a profit also. Now, let us begin. This lefthand side is the debit side.'

She looked at my vast ledger.

'Debit? Oh, faith, if that's where I put what I owe I can soon fill it for you.'

'No, no! Debit *in*. Credit *out*. This is not a personal account. This is a cash account.'

'Cash? Look at my purse. Four and sixpence, and it only Wednesday.'

'Let me explain, Mother. On the debit side you list what you take in.'

'Damn little, then!' she laughed.

'If that be so it means simply that you are not charging the *artistes* for everything you spend on them. But now that we are going to keep proper accounts this cannot happen ever again. You will see it all at one glance. Now! We begin here. We write down, *To balance*. That's what you have left over from last week.'

She stared at me.

'Are you joking? Sure I have nothing left over from last week!'

'But you must have something left over from last week! Otherwise you ran the business at a loss last week! Which is impossible! When the *artistes* go next Sunday you must sit down at once and write down your cash in hands.'

'I do be so tired, child,' she sighed. 'I do be very tired.'

'It stands to reason that by the time the *artistes* leave next Sunday you should still have something left from the batch of the week before...'

'Four and sixpence.'

'... or else all you are doing is spending exactly the same as you take in, week after week, and making no profit at all for yourself.'

At this she began to get annoyed with me.

'I spend far more than I take in! Every week of my life it's everything going out and nothing coming in. Sure, they have me ruined! Haven't I told you that over and over again?'

'Mother! I have explained to *you* that it is *impossible*. It could not happen. You would be bankrupt!'

'I am, and bankrupt forty times over.'

'Mother, when we keep these accounts you will see things very differently. You will be surprised. You will be delighted. Now, this left-hand side is the credit side. No! I mean this *right-hand* side. You are confusing me.'

'Ah! If I hadn't the credit where would I be? Only for Ma Sullivan trusting me, and Smith's in Patrick Street, and the butcher, and . . .'

'Mother! Debit *in!* Credit *out!* You're not listening to me. I'll give you a good slap. On the credit side you write down the total of all your bills paid out. No! Paid in. No! Paid *out!* You really mustn't interrupt me! Now that total must, simply *must* be much less than your debit side. So you must subtract what you paid out from what you take in and that is your balance to be carried down. That is called balancing your books.'

'Carried down!' she said, pointing.

'To balance your books,' I said, pointing left and right.

'To balance my books? That's an easy way, in faith, to balance my books!'

'Then you write that same amount of balance carried down as balance carried forward for the following week.'

Her voice rose here to a shocked squeak: 'But where did you get that seventy-five pounds you have written down there?'

'I just put that down for the sake of example. That's your profit to be carried forward for next week.'

'I told you five and forty times I make no profit!'

'But your credit *out* has to be less than your debit *in*. The bills you pay out to the grocer, and the butcher, and the bread man, and the coal man and all the rest of them *have* to be less than what you take in. It stands to reason!'

She laid her palm on the page of my ledger.

'My poor child, you are talking about what you don't understand. I am like my poor mother long ago in Loughill. Many and many's the time I saw her when she'd sell a cow or a pig at the fair of Rathkeale, and had the money in the heel of her fist, putting on her bonnet and tackling the pony and cart to drive up to Knockaderry. She'd pay a bit here and stop a gap there. So much against this. So much against that. When she had it she gave it. It's all I do from week to week. Rob Peter. Pay Paul. Carry on, as she used to say. Carry on until ye carry me out.

Carried down? Carried forward? Close your big book, alannah! You are very kind and very clever. But it's no use. You can't get blood out of a turnip.'

And she rose and went to the sink for a glass of cold water as I had often seen her do before, and as she, by her own telling, had often seen her mother do back in Limerick, creeping out under the stars, to sit with her beads by the well in the haggard when her family of girl children were in bed, and the weight of the worries came down on her like the fog over the River Deel.

2

From that day of my enthusiastic efforts to educate her in the art of book-keeping, the hopeless pathos of her life as I now saw it, oppressed me, first as an emotional burden and then as a moral problem – 'Why must life be like this?' – until I felt that I must share them both with somebody better able to handle them than myself. But this stage of the process was slow. Perhaps the earlier brimming had subsided? Perhaps by some sort of psychical underconscious the Divine Plumber had fed it away into another nearby pool, there to bring about the final and complete flood. This did not take place until at least another decade had passed over me, dropping more troubling thoughts into my 'Why must life be like this?' compartment. Those other thoughts and questions are the usual, largely sexual, mysteries that have troubled boyhood and early youth since time began, such as my wonder at God's knowledge, which ran somewhat like this:

'If God knows everything – and my Catechism had said that "God knows all things, even our most secret thoughts and actions" – does He follow the career of every blade of grass in every field throughout the vast spaces of the globe? In that case, is not everything I do of theological importance, even to the blowing of my nose? Otherwise why should men have noses at all?'

(The sexual symbolism is evident, as it also is in another of my questions about the importance of all our organs in the ontological argument for the being of God; namely: 'If existence is a property discoverable in the concept of a Creator, are not

79

all the sexual attributes of men's existence involved in our image of a Creator?')

As these and many other such irreverent wonderings increased and became unbearably insistent, I found that they all led back to my mother's sighs over her purse. They and she included and summed up everything: the sighing wind over the Limerick plain, her mother sighing by the well at midnight, Uncle Tom Cosgrave with his stooped back and the wen on his neck, Aunt Nan with her wide vacant laugh and her simple, childless life, all her emigrant sisters, that tiny farm of Loughill out of which so many lives, so many generations had been squeezed in tears and blood, the sudden killing of Tom Boyhan. My mother thus became for me Ivan Karamazov's one innocent child whom God allowed to be assaulted, a prime instance of the seeming monstrous and cruel world He created.

The day on which I came to the end of my tether I was eighteen and at the university, and the usual annual retreat for students was opening in the Honan Chapel, a pretty modern Romanesque building whose Harry Clarke windows disperse Beardsleyan purples and scarlets over the grey limestone walls and the cool mosaics on the floor. The retreat was conducted by a visiting preacher, an ascetic-looking man, rather like John Henry Newman in his Oratory days, and the cool mind he displayed in his opening sermon greatly pleased me. He appeared to me to be such a reasonable and kindly man that when, after two days, I knew that I was not going to complete the retreat, because my faith had now ebbed so low that unless I did something about it I would soon be left marooned on a sandbank in a sea of faithlessness, I decided to talk to him about my mother.

Now, this small decision of mine involves something that may not be apparent immediately to non-Catholics and possibly not even to Irish Catholics of a younger generation than mine; namely, that Catholic youths in my time did not normally talk to their priests about their problems – their priests talked to them. This relationship was based on the postulate that while the Catholic religion is intellectually impregnable, the gift of faith is too tender a plant to be submitted to the cold winds of private speculation. So, while our priests always treated sin with infinite kindness and pity, doubt was much more than likely to be considered either as a manifestation of intellectual vanity, or traced to the reading of 'bad books' or the keeping of 'bad company'. Religion in Ireland has always tended thereby to flower as a mystical experience and to wilt as an intellectual possession. Buttressed by emotional appeal and social habit rather than by thought or reason, it has even tended to disappear completely when transferred to other climates, unless, as happened with the close-knit Irish communities of nineteenth-century America, it meets elsewhere a familiar soil wherein to transplant, or replant, itself as cosily as before. Even today it is notorious that Irish emigrants are barely landed in England when they cease, in droves, to practise their religion; and yet when those same emigrants return to Ireland they at once resume the ways they had so lightly discarded.

It may be understood, then, that I was doing something rather unusual for my earlier period and place when I went one day, after the morning sermon, into the confessional and fully exposed my heart to the priest who was conducting the retreat. I told him that since I could not confess at all until I had cleared up my problem I would like to meet him for a frank talk outside the confessional. It was so arranged. I went to his rooms that afternoon and over the teacups I let all my misery pour out of me. He listened silently to my outpourings and my questions. Why should people be so poor and hard pressed? Why must their spirits be broken? My mother was a good woman, she worked hard, she was most devout, yet here she was without joy, without happiness, harassed day and night. I revealed the darkest of her secrets – that she was gradually being driven to take refuge in the brandy bottle. In plain language my over-worked mother was turning to the booze. Why, I asked again and again, must such things be? How could God allow them to happen?

His answer was to laugh.

'If I knew the old lady,' he said, 'perhaps I might be able to form some idea of her problem. But . . .'

'But it is not a question of *her* problem. The problem is mine. My question is why it has to happen at all?'

And I once more poured out all my Karamazovian doubts and despairs. We exchanged a few questions and answers.

Then: 'You come here,' he said at last, in, as I now see, an understandably exasperated voice, 'and calmly ask me to solve the insoluble problem of the existence of human evil! I ask *you*, "Why do you think it must be so?" I ask *you*, "What do you propose to do about it?"'

I have here to confess that I quailed. I suddenly felt the utterness of my folly in the justice of his question. I felt – perhaps he wished me to feel – a young ass. I began to retreat. I expressed my regrets. Seeing me become apparently contrite, he softened, spoke of the mystery of evil, promised to pray for me, and that was the end of our interview.

As I walked away from his rooms across the empty quadrangle I could hear the sucking noise of the ebbing tide. As I wandered through the unseen streets I knew that I was not only a fool but a damned fool. I had, like Stephen Daedalus and Karamazov, brought myself face to face with The Unanswerable Question. I must either accept the world humbly with all its insufferable malignities or, like Daedalus and Karamazov, declare a *Non Serviam* against it, an absolute revolt. I was not ready yet for that defiance. Instead I drove myself the next day to try another, local priest, choosing a church as far away as possible from my own parish. I entered at random the first confessional I saw. I was a little more circumspect this time, speaking generally, tentatively, and humbly. The shadowed face behind the grille spoke of trials, and crosses that we all must bear. I did not stress the burden and the weary weight of the intolerable mystery. I came away absolved, unappeased.

It took another fifteen years before that pool finally overflowed. I was then applying for a teaching post in the university. An acquaintance came to me and said: 'You won't get it, you know. Father X is against you.'

'Father X? But I know no Father X. I never met him.'

'Oh, yes, you did. You met him years ago at a retreat in the university.'

My belly turned over with the pain of betrayal. And yet, he had not broken the sacred seal of the confessional. For although

I had first met him in the confessional it was in his rooms that, as man to man, I had opened my heart to him.

3

My unhappiness at my mother's harsh life gradually abated as I saw that for her purposes she had had more intelligence than I had for mine. She had refused to keep out of debt not because she could not but because she did not want to. She wanted, for her children's sake, to press herself beyond her powers. She wanted to beat Time, get her job done before it caught up with her, keep the breath of life in us, like the pelican, with her breast's blood until we were ready to leave the nest, and then let the sky fall. In her love for us she despised the mean idea of measurement. Does a soldier contemplate death when he faces it? If she had so few personal wishes, apart from her immense and obsessive master wish for her children, it was because she, too, was of fighting stock, like all peasants placed by fate against nature.

She expected no return. She did not even seem to expect as much love as she gave, and, perhaps, for not thinking about it she did not consciously love us at all, being content to serve us. For herself she desired nothing. She had a slightly pathetic, because unattainable, longing for elegance, a good deal of natural vanity, as much house pride as she could afford, but apart from that never-fulfilled desire for pretty dresses she had no real capacity or desire for pleasure. The greatest joy of her life, she often said when she was old, was the joy she got out of us, her three children, when we were young. After we grew up emptiness fell on her like the slow closing of a tomb.

She was in the classical sense a tragic figure, aiming too high, guilty of *hubris*, doomed to be broken. She was also something of a heroic figure, because though broken she was not defeated. She did make a priest of one son, and give to the other the incomparable security of 'a job under the Crown'. My career gave her no satisfaction, much worry and some pain. I went completely outside any pattern she could recognise or understand. I often wonder what she must have suffered when my first book of stories was banned in Ireland as 'indecent and obscene'. I am sure that one of my deepest reasons for hating the Irish Censorship Board was what it did to her.

It would be agreeable to sum her up in this way – a tragic and heroic woman, admired and loved. Alas, as happens with all men and women whose lives are ruled by a master wish, the terrifyingly obsessive one-sidedness of her life cut her off from everybody's life. I was forcibly reminded of her when I came on Colette's observation on, of all people, professional courtesans: that any woman who devotes her life to love sacrifices all friendship. She had no time to be human, no time to be happy. She could not afford to let down her guard for so long. Her distrust of others was all-pervasive – though that may be another peasant weakness, their eyes always wandering fearfully up to the sky, their minds always reading the back of the other person's mind. She was more uncharitable than any other person I have ever met, though this also may have come from her desire to protect us from others. If she had been a bird she would have been uttering warning cries all day long. Like all women who become slaves to their children, she not only exhausted her own emotions but ultimately killed the emotions of everybody around her. Ever since, I have to struggle not to see all old women in her guise, self-worn as a seashell, drained at last of her life's devouring devotion, so indescribably disheartened and despondent at the end as to give me the impression that her spirit had already departed while her body was still waiting to die.

4

Another youthful revelation came when I was fifteen, and was to affect my whole career as a writer. It was the Theatre that started it one wet night in January, 1915, and probably on Monday because that was the night on which I got free entry to the Opera House. I went there with no expectations above the ordinary. The name of the play was *Patriots*, which might easily have suggested my favourite theme of the proud patriotism of Empire, celebrated by the stories of G. A. Henty, rather than the more common English country-house comedy opening with its classical exposition between butler and maid about master and mistress.

'Perkins! Do you realise that within five minutes, if the train to Maidstone is on time, the master will come driving up that avenue on his return from his honeymoon in Nice with his new wife, whom he met in Bombay, and that this very same evening his son by his first wife is expected from London accompanied by his fiancée, who is the daughter of the master's new wife by her first husband, whom she met in Cawnpore? Isn't that a ree-markable coincidence, Perkins? Most ree-markable!'

I did not even notice the name of the author of the play that I was about to see. If I had it would not have impressed me. It was as common as Jones or Smith. In fact it was Robinson. The theatre was half empty when the lights dimmed and the curtain rose – the old painted curtain showing the bay of Naples, with Vesuvius in scarlet spate, and the balustraded terrace in the foreground teeming with bougainvillea. On the lighted stage I beheld, with an astonishment never before or since equalled for me by any theatrical spectacle, the parlour of a house in an Irish country town, and my uncle Owen Boyhan. It will be gathered that I was seeing my first Abbey Theatre play, by Lennox Robinson.

I saw other familiars talking on the stage as naturally as if they were in my aunt's cottage in Rathkeale, or in old Bovanizer's parlour over his little provision shop in the Main Street, or in any other such house there or in Newbridge that I had visited during my various summer holidays. This parlour on the stage – But why do I say stage? It was reality itself – was over a shop, all its antimacassarish details, tenderly, delightfully, recognisably familiar: a geranium pot in the window, a chenille cloth covering the table, pictures of Robert Emmet and Pius X on the walls, old lace curtains, old padded furniture. As the talk went on I gathered that, as in my imaginary English country-house comedy, the husband was due to return home at any moment, though not from Nice – from several years in some English jail; and not with a new wife but back to his own wife, who had been slaving herself to the bone to keep the business turning over while he was away. There was a lame girl in the house, his daughter, prematurely born on the terrible night of her father's arrest by policemen like my father. The returning husband was a Fenian rebel. Had not a certain Uncle Paudh of mine, from County Limerick – it came back to me from some gossipings of my mother and Aunt Nan over the cottage fire – run off to Australia to escape arrest at the time of the Fenian uprising in 1867? I had also read about the Fenians, and I had heard my father utter harsh words about them. Presently I saw this actual Fenian, real and living, talking about Ireland's woes to young men not much more than six or seven years older than myself. It was all as exciting as when the lights of a passing motor car show up at night a familiar face, in a picture on the wall, never noticed before. The magnifying glass of the drama showed up my Uncle Paudh's face, though, confusingly, he – that is, the Fenian in the play – also looked like my Uncle John Hough back in Loughill: the beard, the aquiline nose, the cutaway coat, the height; though instead of horselike strength this man had an inner blazing power, unbroken by his back-breaking years in prison. It gradually transpired that he was still ready to lead the young men of Rathkeale in a fight for Ireland, and it also transpired that none of the young men wanted to fight for anything – they wanted only to go to that latest novelty, the moving pictures. Again, I had read of people fighting and dying for Ireland, but those had been people in cocked hats with gilt tassels and plumed feathers, waving swords like Lord Edward Fitzgerald or Robert Emmet, which in my view – or rather, in the view I had hitherto held – was the only proper and decent way for anybody to die for anything. The fantastic thought burst on me that in Rathkeale, even in Cork that night, there might be other real, living, exhaling-inhaling, dusty, scruffy, angry old men with these same noble, gallant, hopeless ideas. I will not say that I was changed, when I left the theatre and walked out into the wet streets of Cork. But I know that I was dazed.

If I were now to rationalise what happened there and then to that boy of fifteen, this is what I would say: Hitherto he had been led by the susceptibilities of his imaginative nature to form in his untutored mind idealised notions of everything. As far as the idealising goes, this was natural, and I hold it to be good. Youth should idealise. And, dammit, so should old age. Certainly there are plenty of precedents for this, and in art the greatest from Phidias to Courbet, Millet, Monet, the Fauves,

Gauguin, Degas, Cézanne. Is there indeed any art even among the 'realists', like Rembrandt, without some idealisation? But I have said 'idealised notions', and this is a very different matter. For a 'notion' is a more or less general, vague, imperfect, deluding concept that could no more survive one touch of earth's experience than a snowflake in June. I was the sort of boy who if given a chocolate-box picture of a girl would have said, 'Aren't girls lovely!' – unaware that I was looking not at an image of a real girl but at a bit of fancy shorthand, a hieroglyph, a pictograph or pipe-dream prettiness. At the same time, if I had been shown a painting of a real girl by Bronzino, Degas, or Holbein I might not have understood or liked it at all. These were men who had seen the inward beauty of real girlhood behind or through the outward appearance. They had seen actual life with heightened emotions. I had not. I had seen it only with the closed eyes of dream. They had dreamed with their eyes wide open. They had dreamed on the stone pillow of hard fact. In one word, they had lived. This boy that I was had yet to 'live'.

Still, he *was* warmhearted and sensitive, with honourable longings and desires, as well, no doubt, as dishonourable longings and desires, and life, though in its blind cruelty it often does, by the million, crush such creatures, never wholly betrays them, other than in those cataclysms that make us either throw our fists up to heaven, or whisper our last prayers to that X, that Somebody, that Spirit, that God, who, we still hope, on this side of near-despair, may know what He is doing. Life feeds such children as one feeds motherless birds with minute bits of scraps to begin with, and richer and perhaps tougher gobbets as their digestions grow in power. This boy had already seen touches of cruelty at school, hard poverty about him, wild street scenes, his father's shame in a moment of defeat, his mother's deep unhappiness, the tough lives of his forebears, heard their ancestral memories back to and behind the Famine of the 1840s. These and many other such hints were stored in his pool of memory, though he could not yet see them as a man sees them. Before he could truly see anything of what we call the nature of life these hints of 'real' life needed to be enlarged, enhanced, heightened. They needed to strike his imagination before they could pierce his intelligence, or his heart.

On that rainy night of Lennox Robinson's play, that was what happened to me. My double doors opened on these same scraps of real life enlarged now by the powerful glass of dramatic emotion, heightened by the hovering presence of truth, shaped by and for the intelligence. My doorways became, for the first time, doorways to that emotionalised reality which is the father of the truly creative imagination – life-based, life-transforming, what Berenson so often loved to call life-enhancing.

Still, they were only doorways. My fountain brimmed, common water out of the skies and the earth. It astonished, excited and delighted me, and I would dearly love to be able to say that it washed my eyes. Not yet! I may have always wanted to write, or may have wanted to write then about the common life around me, I cannot tell which, because when I began actually to write about that life it seemed to me that this was something I had always wanted to do. When I did begin to write – which was very soon – I was still stuck with a wardrobe full of theatrical posturings, swords and cocked hats, plumed grenadiers, gesturing sans-culottes, swearing pirates, lisping ladies, mere pictographs or notions about men and women, and only that one crumpled cutaway country-town Fenian's coat hanging like a ghost of real life among all the finery. That Fenian was still only a ghost to me although real to Robinson. I needed my own scenes, subjects and characters. But, at fifteen! Until life threw me, to sink or swim, into Life, I could only imitate other writers, as younger writers always imitate older writers, and as lesser, greater, and sometimes as even the greater the lesser whom they think the greater.

A year cannot have passed before I saw myself in print for the first time. It was a short story, in a weekly paper called the *Cork Outlook*, and it must have been one of the most remarkable stories to appear in either that or any other periodical before or since. I borrowed the opening from G. A. Henty, wrote the middle, very brief, myself, and swiped the conclusion from R. M. Ballantyne. This remarkable piece of collaboration was about a gallant British young cavalry officer sent with an urgent dispatch on the field of battle across enemy fire. As he galloped he waved his sword, and his plume danced in the wind, and it goes without saying that he was shot through the heart and died as nobly as only George Alfred Henty, Robert Michael Ballantyne and John Francis Whelan could do it between them. If Prometheus ever bothers with such small-fry activities I fear he must have sighed many times as he read that week's edition of the *Cork Outlook* and decided that it was really going to take an awful lot of experience to awaken this minute mortal to the facts of life.

The old Fenian's cutaway coat hung in my wardrobe for years and years. The finery gradually fed the fatted moth. Yet when I published my first novel, twenty years later, called *A Nest of Simple Folk*, there was the old Fenian, and my father, and my mother, and all my uncles and aunts among the fields, skies and streams of the plain of Limerick.

What a slow process! Or you may put it otherwise: what a slow development! You would be right. Somewhere, earlier on, when speaking of my father, and the Law which he embodied, I described myself as a mild rebel. But where is my revolt? Far from being an insubordinate child and boy, I was, it is more than evident, most dutiful. If I questioned at all, it was a mild and groping sort of business ending always in a lapse into the old submissiveness. I have tried to make this clear by calling this chapter by the name of *brimmings*, and that slow, tentative, always instinctive, never intellectual process of growth continued until my schooling ended and I was at last released from my boyhood by a double love.

7

Two Teachers and a Girl

From my crazy-happy Lancasterian National School I duly followed the trail of my two elder brothers into the secondary or higher school run by the same order, known to the public as the Presentation Brothers' College and to its pupils as the Pres, with the final *s* pronounced as a *z*. Fees here were a large worry to my parents, even though the headmaster kindly granted my father special rates. I could list other acts of kindness by him, such as the loan of expensive books like good dictionaries, efforts to throw a few pounds in my way for the private tutoring of backward pupils, and – I now suspect – much patient forbearance with a boy whom he must have considered egregious, or odd, or worse. Years afterwards when a friend mentioned me to another old brother who had passed me through his hands the good man said, 'Ah, yes! A nice boy, but . . .'. And he solemnly tapped his cranium. Shrewd man?

I can say and do the same precisely about him. Indeed, it is the burden of what I have to think and say about the Pres, since any school must be quite dotty that thinks it possible to reconcile a religious vocation with the teaching profession while controlled by a government of a totally different persuasion. Certainly, over the generations, certain compromises had already been fought for and won in 'Irish' education, or shall I say fought for and lost, since in such matters all compromises are tantamount to defeat. Religious instruction at fixed times was permitted; Catholic views were tolerated on such thorny subjects as the Reformation;

a limited number of alternatives were granted in the choice of texts, and so on. But the innocuous text is nobody's text. Tennyson's 'The Lotos-Eaters' was, in my time, considered a 'neutral' text. It might almost be a parable of the results of these endless compromises between Catholicism and Imperialism.

> Let us swear an oath, and keep it with an equal mind,
> In the hollow Lotos-land to live and lie reclined
> On the hills like Gods together, careless of mankind.

One year the commissioners selected *Pride and Prejudice* as a text. When protests at once arose from some teaching sisters dismayed at the loose behaviour of Lydia Bennett, the commissioners hastily replaced it by that Christian parable, *Treasure Island*.

The Pres, in my time, which is now a long time ago, was a fake in every respect except two. It provided some sort of pseudo-religious education, and it was a useful cramming factory for the sons of less well-heeled parents – clerks, civil servants, lay teachers and the like. In this latter it sometimes succeeded to remarkable effect when it got hold of specially bright students. It was also the useful gateway through which a small number of youths entered the local college of the National University, there, if they were industrious, to become doctors, engineers, secondary teachers, and the like. The majority went to modest posts in banks, insurance, the railways. If any reader feels that in doing so much the Pres did all it could do, I have to say that there were other schools, managed by priests, at that same time, and subject to similar governmental controls, which adapted themselves with subtlety and sophistication to the task of providing a Christian education with a humanist bias. One such was James Joyce's Jesuit School at Clongowes Wood, and whatever that school may now think of Joyce, he always paid high tribute to his Jesuit teachers. In fairness, however, we must remember that Clongowes Wood not only drew boys from much better-class homes than ours, but was a boarding school where the Jesuits had the boys all day long, for games, debating societies, and cultural doings of every kind. They did no less well at examinations than cramming schools like ours.

The worst about the Pres I must admit at once and be done with it – the place was snobby: it was the very essence of genteelism. It was an imitation of something else somewhere else. But, to be sure, the whole of urban Ireland at that time was an imitation of something else somewhere else; and it was the dilemma of the Pres, and all of urban Ireland, that it had to be so. To be of any use it had to accept the fact of life of the same imperial pattern and hierarchy that my father had accepted, to fit us all into it, to help us all to succeed within it. How few escaped, could escape, or wished to escape that trap! If James Joyce had had half an ounce of social conscience, of Stendhal's or Balzac's awareness of the molding power of the cash-nexus, he would have made this clear in his *Portrait of the Artist as a Young Man*. He made it most near to clear when he contrasted Daedalus the poor rebel – but not against *both* the Empire and the Church – with Buck Mulligan, who set out to conform. My school produced some rebels but not many; it produced conformists by the ton.

2

I have no wish to dally over my four years in the Pres. I have an idea that I have spent a good part of my life labouring under the same wish. My unhappiness there was chronic and suppressed. Even to this late day my two most frequent nightmares bring me back either there or to the period of the Troubles, each always leaving me with an identical, detestable impression of having been helplessly coerced. Those nightmares were often associated in my earlier manhood with the image of myself as a pea or a little glass marble under the towering overhang of a vast globe, large as the world, about to roll over me. If there is anything at all rebellious, obstinate or even mulish in my nature, and I think there is, it either began to take form at this time of subjection or, if it was latent in me from the moment of my birth, it flourished then like the banyan.

The prison gates closed on me the first day I started to cram French, Latin and algebra at breakback speed, an experience for whose drudgery it is not possible to find adequate language. Again, in fairness, I must say that although punishment was the sole spur within the school, by far the more painful spur came from outside the school: my father's and mother's repeated reminders that all this wonderful education was costing them great hardship and that, for their sake as well as my own, I must profit by it. Since there was no escape from this loving blackmail there were many occasions when I almost hated my parents for enduring so much for love of me.

I recall a typical occasion with a particular shame and bitterness. On this day the whole of my class, on being refused early release from school to go to the Cork Park Races, a great annual event which had always hitherto meant that classes were cut short, rebelled in a body and did not return after the lunch break – all, that is, except three boys, two others and myself. We pleaded, quite honestly, that we did not mind being punished, if punishment ensued, but that we could not bear that our parents should be, as we knew they would be, hurt and shocked. (The parents of the two other fellows were teachers in city schools.) The next day the massed rebels were duly caned, one by one, while we three sat, heads hanging, ashamed and unmanned. Remembering that day, I was to write one of my best stories, 'Up the Bare Stairs', about a man who went through that school and passed out of it to an eminent career inspired wholly by desire to escape from his parents' enslaving love.

I based it also, in part, on a remark of my brother's when in later life I said, to tease him: 'I have been told that there was only one examination in your whole career that you could not pass – a test in the Irish language. It was part of some scholarship examination that would have won you three years free at the university. Is this true?'

'Couldn't pass it?' he laughed. 'I failed it deliberately. I would have had to remain at home for years if I had gone to the university. My sole ambition was to get out from under at all costs.'

I wished he had not kept that secret to himself: we might have conspired to make home life more easy for both of us.

Only two subjects were presented to me at the Pres with enough feeling to fire my interest: Irish and Latin – the first because I could relate it to life, and the second because the headmaster, who was prior of the order, took a few of us brighter boys for Latin in our senior years.

93

He was the Reverend E. J. Connolly, known to us all as the Man, already old when I sat under him, so old that it was said that he had taught the grandfathers of some of my fellow pupils. He was a slight, smallish man, with a gentle, benevolent, commanding appearance, his white hair curling out from under his biretta, his voice always soft, his persistent attitude to us boys one of solemn amusement. He seemed to us a saintly man, yet at the same time we recognised in him, with admiration, a force of personality and a shrewd worldliness that none of the other brothers had. His large family of past students were by my time already scattered all over the world, and he had hung the portraits of about a score of the more distinguished among them in the main corridor for us to admire and emulate: officers in the British Army, colonial judges, men in the Indian Civil, and suchlike. Now and again one of these old boys would drop in to visit him, and he would always bring the visitor to see his old classroom. Once I remember an Australian officer, so tall that, as he looked at the old desks in the old room, and chatted with the Man, he leaned one hand on top of the door. Once a mayor from, I think, Johannesburg came. The Man thus gave us our first glimpse of the world's possibilities. We felt that he held the keys to all sorts of interesting careers in his hands.

He had the name of being a fine Latinist, and when he took us over he conveyed to us, if only by his mere tone of voice and his reverent approach as he recited the verses of Horace, Ovid or Virgil, at least some awareness of the sacred ground we were beginning to explore. I can still hear his caressing voice fondling the familiar phrases:

> O fons Bandusiae, splendidior vitro,
> Dulci digne mero non sine floribus . . .
> (O fountain of Bandusia, shining like crystal,
> Worthy of flowers and a libation of sweet wine . . .)

Or:

> Eheu fugaces, Postume, Postume,
> Labuntur anni, nec pietam moram
> Rugis et instanti senectae
> Afferet indomitiaeque morti . . .

94

(Alas, Postumus, Postumus, the flying years glide away, and our piety will not hold back the wrinkles, looming age, or indominatable death . . .)

The impression was indelible. Many years after, when following the steps of John Henry Newman in Italy, I visited Castrogiovanni, or Enna, perched high in the centre of Sicily. There I found, at its base, the Lake of Pergusa, where Pluto abducted that air flower Proserpina while she was gathering flowers far less fair. As I stood by the lake I suddenly heard his old, soft voice murmuring in my ear: *Terra tribus scopulis vastum procurrit in aequor Trinacris* (Sicily pours down to the vast sea its three promontories). And:

> *Tot fuerant illic, quot habet natura, colores:*
> *Pictaque dissimili flore nitebat humus.*
> (There were as many colours there as Nature holds:
> The whole earth painted with motley, gleaming flowers.)

I am sure that under a better system the Man could really have made young Latinists of some of us. He had no time. Too many examinations lay ahead like fences in a four-year race. There was no time to allow us to recite aloud, to talk to us about the authors of those poems or about classical mythology, even to show us a map of the voyages of Aeneas, to show us photographs of Cumae, or Lake Avernus, or the forum Romanum, or Sirmione, to do anything that would relate what we read to life and history. Yet he did give us a sense of form in poetry, he schematised eternal emotions, instilled a sense of immemorial piety, revealed to us that happy marriage of feeling and the intelligence which is the very heart of the classical way of life.

It goes without saying that he had time to do this only in a little way, could open only a postern gate – not even that, a cat's door; that we read no Catullus, or Juvenal, had to wait for our college days to open Pliny or Seneca; that when we read Cicero we had no time to think of Roman politics – in Cicero's day the most exciting politics in the whole history of Rome; that we pursued Caesar and Livy at such a pace that they became dull tasks in mechanical translation that bored us stiff. I suppose even the Commissioners of Education had their excuse for all

95

this savagery. Behind them, no doubt, there lay some other tyranny, including possibly the grim morality of Arnold of Rugby, whom many Latinists blame for cleaning up the classics, as certain other men cleaned up Shakespeare. (Had Sam Johnson gone to Rugby under Arnold, he would not have read his Catullus and Juvenal as avidly as he did at Lichfield.) Apart from what we got from the Man we had time only to cram for examinations to get jobs. That was the sum of it.

An absurd instance of this: one day our English teacher, Doggy Sheehan, said, as was his way: 'Learn off the first sixteen lines of Tennyson's 'Ulysses'.'

The next day the first boy in the class recited rapidly down to *And drunk delight of battle with my peers*, and stopped.

'Go on!' said Doggy.

'That's the sixteen lines, sir.'

'But where did he drink delight of battle?' Doggy implored.

'It's not in the sixteen lines, sir.'

'Not another line?' Doggy sighed. 'Even for the sake of *Far on the ringing plains of windy Troy*?'

But it was not merely Doggy's own mechanical way of saying 'The next sixteen lines for tomorrow' – as if all poetry were in quatrains – that had produced the result he deplored: both he and the boy were identical victims of a universal chain reaction started years ago and elsewhere.

In literary terms Doggy was an aged version of all Chekhov's schoolteachers, that weary, frustrated type we meet as younger men in *The Cherry Orchard* and *The Seagull*, become at last contented, no longer troubled even by remnant dreams. He was tall, thin, shambling, spectacled, bowler-hatted. His little briefcase bore his derisive nickname *Doggy* scratched by some boy on a patch of leather that had obviously been sewn there to hide the word *Doggy* scratched beneath it by some earlier tormentor. He had a flat Cork accent, saying 'flaat' for 'flat', or 'waey' for 'way', and all his th's, as in 'this' or 'that', had been, after the common Cork manner, dentalised into d's – 'dis' and 'dat'. He taught, that is he crammed, English poetry, drama and prose, English history, European history, Irish history, and world geography. His methods of cramming so much so quickly may be summed up by observing that the effective text for English

history was somebody's *Outline* handled by such injunctions from Doggy as: 'For tomorrow look up the reign of Queen Anne and pick out the dates.' Inevitably, he was a butt – nobody could hold the interest of a class of lively boys under such circumstances. He would be asked double-meaning questions, whose tenor he either ignored or reproved by a sniggering, 'Stop dat now!' His piles of books were slyly toppled from his table. He suffered constant inattention and occasional rowdiness. If it were not that in this senior classroom there usually were at least two other classes, and teachers, and, frequently, the Man himself in a corner coaching two or three boys preparing for special examinations, he would have been quite badgered by us. Yet, as his nickname may suggest, we all liked Doggy. He was harmless, he was necessary, and even we could see that he was put upon.

I more than liked him because he conferred a supreme gift on me. I had his open invitation to drop down, any night I liked, to his old dusty, murky house in the Lower Road, above the Railway Terminus, and there rummage among his books – mottled, dusty, foxed, unread, piled on shelves, chairs, the floor, up the stairs, in the hall, in boxes, on tables, under tables. (He must have spotted a potential book-lover in me: for which I revere him.) He lived in this old house alone with his mother, who was said to have been a midwife, a fat, heavy-breasted, warm old soul who gave to this drape of clothes on two sticks who was our Doggy and her beloved son the surprising personal reality of a name. She spoke of him as Jack. I would pick out a book, attracted by its binding, or its gilt lettering, or the decoration on the spine, and find I held Congreve's *Plays*. He would say, 'Dey're Congreve's plays. Some of 'em are dirty. Read 'em.'

I would find a sixpenny paper novel in my dusty hand.

'What's dat you have? Marie Corelli? Very romantic. Don't let your mudder see you readin' it.'

I have wondered whether the books he pressed on me were of his own taste or the midwife's: Hall Caine's *The Manxman*, George Moore's early novels ('Dat fellow was an awful blackguard!'), *Captain Kettle*, Hewlett's *The Forest Lovers*, William de Morgan's *Alice-for-Short*, Countess von Arnim's *Elizabeth* books, Rider Haggard's *She*, Barrie's *The Little Minis-*

ter, E. F. Benson's *Dodo*, mixed up with practically all of Shaw, Norman Angell's *The Great Illusion*, somebody's *Our German Cousins*, many books about Napoleon. (He had once visited France, and walked all over the site of the Battle of Waterloo.) He ignored the classics. ('I have dem all. But I'm all for the moderns now.') The reader will have noted that most of the books I mention were of the 1890s.

Did his preferences reflect early aspirations – sentimental, military, political? If so, he reached the apex of his ambition when he founded and became first, and last, president of the Cork Consumers' League, a body composed almost entirely of landladies, interested chiefly in the prices of domestic supplies.

Chekhov, clearly, exaggerated the sadness of the teacher type. Doggy was a drudge, but not a sad drudge. It is one definition of insanity to have an itch, and of sanity to have a niche. He had made his own modest image of himself. He had found a niche in the city's body politic to enshrine it. So much of life is a pure act of the imagination!

I have dallied with him because he makes an important point for me: that schools, colleges, clubs, all early, populous institutions are where we find our first references in life to and from that endless series of hypotheses that we call art. We may read Chekhov and remember our own Doggy. The Chekhovian hypothesis is thereby stamped on our minds. After that, whenever we meet a Doggy we will remember Chekhov. If we have not had our Doggy we cannot have our Chekhov – we cannot, that is, recognise the proposed type. But if we have original or obstinate minds we will not say, 'Doggy!' when we read Chekhov; we will say, 'No, not *our* Doggy!' and we will hold on to our own Doggy and make our own hypothesis about him, think or write our own play or story, not an imitation or pastiche of Chekhov. The challenge to think for oneself comes very early or not at all. Doggy had his complement in old Roche, a great hulking red-faced and red-nosed fellow, his clothes hanging baggily about his bloated body as if he had been even more bloated six months before when he bought the suit. The school fable about him was that he was the drunken remains of a great mathematical genius. Occasionally Doggy had to take what we called the Bankers, chaps hoping to get into a bank as a bank clerk, and give them lessons in mathematics. Doggy, in his corner of the room, would call out his tests for the evening on the lines of: 'If fifteen hundred pounds will produce one hundred and five pounds at a certain percentage in one year, by what percentage must the stock rise or fall for eighty-four hundred pounds to produce two thousand five hundred and twenty in five years?'

Roche, from his corner, would, to Doggy's supreme annoyance, say, at once: 'By one per cent.'

Doggy would then have to invent another test.

There were other talents whose waste impressed me, but I was most deeply marked by our one rebel, apart from the Man the only teacher there whom I fully admired. He was our Irish language teacher, who let fall, in odd words and phrases, hints about a far-off free country called the West where people talked only in Irish, wove and spun in it, fished and ploughed, drank and laughed in it, where – to me, at any rate, he gave this feeling – there was a wonderland where the star of Eden never died. I was also impressed by another teacher, Christy Flynn, to whom I had no opportunity to come closer than respect. He would pause in a French lesson at, say, the word *bois* to recall with a few fond words Le Bois de Boulogne, or at the word *invalides* to wave a hand across Ireland towards the Seine and Les Invalides. That was true education. In another not wholly dissimilar way the Man would leave a mark when, at five minutes to twelve, he would take out his silver watch, rub its glass between his thumb and his palm, halt lessons with a word he was always uttering, *'Gentlemen!'*, and talk for four minutes about somebody like Marshal Foch ('A daily communicant, gentlemen'), or of his regiment of cuirassiers drawn up before a priest for general absolution before entering battle. (This, of course, was right up my alley, plumes, swords, helmets and all that splendid fudge.) Then, while we were still seeing his picture, he would take off his biretta and lead us into the Angelus at the stroke of noon that, by then, sounded like a bugle calling us to charge!

I needed more of this satisfying kind of stuff-education by sheer incitation, persuasion, mesmerism, for my curiosity alone, unfanned, though highly inflammable, was *never* satisfied in the Pres. This may have made me a bothersome pupil. An incident to which I appear to attach a great deal of importance – for it keeps on returning and returning to my memory – illustrates this. One day an inspector walked into our chemistry class, ranged us about him in a half-moon, took a bit of paper, lit it and asked, 'What is happening?'

When various answers, such as 'The paper is burning, sir,' failed to satisfy him, I, clever little boy, raised my hand and said, 'Combustion is taking place, sir.'

This answer seemed to delight him. It gave me no pleasure because I dearly wanted to ask, but feared to, 'What is this combustion, sir?'

I still do not know what it was. If I look at a dictionary it refers me to oxidation, which refers me to oxide, which is supposed to be a compound containing only two elements, of which one is oxygen. But am I, and was he, sure that his bit of paper was all that simple? Would he not have needed, for a full answer, to analyse the constituents of this bit of paper?

I feel that this incident reveals in me that highly inconvenient kind of mind which is unable to accept any fact unless it knows all the constituents of it – which is far too inflexible and sceptical an attitude for everyday living since it can only be maintained by a scholar or scientist with or in contact with first-class brains. Soon after that day of the burning bit of paper I asked the Man to remove me from the chemistry class because I wanted to concentrate on languages, especially Latin. I regret to say that he was deceived by my flattery and did remove me from the chemistry class, much to my ultimate loss.

I must say more about our Irish teacher, Padraig O'Domhnaill: young, handsome, eager and quite uncowed. He, too, had his own self-image, as we all discovered the day the news ran through the school that he had been seen in the streets dressed in the full dark-green uniform of the Irish Volunteers (forerunners of the IRA) leading a band of what, I fear, the Man would have called *canaille*, on some military exercise. Had he been any other man I would have scoffed at him. I was on the Man's side, the saintly-worldly side, with Foch and his cuirassiers, with the Indian Civil, Sandhurst, gallant little Belgium, brave little Montenegro, and so on, beside all of which these Irish Volunteers were nothing but vulgar 'cornerboy' non-

sense. But I so admired O'Domhnaill as a man that this wind
of rumour about him ran over me with the shiver of a question
and a doubt. Besides, I gathered that he had worn a handsome
uniform with a hat pinned up on one side. 'Was there a plume
on it?' I asked eagerly, and felt disappointed when they said,
'No, no plume.' I have talked earlier of pools brimming and
fountaining. The brimmings one can more or less easily recall
and record; not so easily the last glorious moments of pouring-
over, of fountaining revelation, chiefly because they so often
come not with a sense of triumph but of surrender. So it was
with me and the revelation of the Rising of 1916 for which
young O'Domhnaill was preparing.

My heart did not burst with excitement and joy when I heard
that a rising had broken out in Dublin that Easter Monday
morning of 1916. I had not more than a week previous seen
somebody, who might have been Padraig O'Domhnaill, drilling
a shamble of forty or fifty men in the open place beneath our
windows in Half Moon Street – rudely accoutreed fellows, with
no uniform other than a belt around their ordinary working
clothes, only a very few bearing rifles. As I watched them
fumble and stumble my blood had curled against them, they
were so shabby, so absurd, so awkward, so unheroic-looking.
They were, as my father said, as the Man would have said,
disgracing our country: and this while real, glorious war was
flashing and booming in Flanders and France. When we heard
of the Rising my father and I raged at its betrayal. The British
Army would clean 'those fellows' up in twenty-four hours. Then
they would all get what they damn well deserved – the low
ruffians, the common corner-boys! Only bit by bit did my loyalties veer as the days passed, one by one, and I found that they
were still holding out. Dublin was shelled and burning, that
noble city I had traversed with poor Tom Boyhan, now dead in
France, but still they were holding out. There was a charge by
British cavalry down O'Connell Street, in the best G. A. Henty,
Light Brigade tradition of gallant lunacy, and I, who should have
been all for that splendid gesture, felt the world turning around
in my stomach when I heard, with satisfaction, that the ruffians

and cornerboys had mowed them down.* I continued to resist until the final surrender, and that broke me. Irishmen were surrendering to Englishmen, with dignity. That day I stole away up to my attic, and knelt on the scrubbed floor and looked out over the roofs of Cork under its tent of clouds, and I wept for them. When, in the following weeks, the British took out the leaders and shot them in ones, and twos, and threes, everybody and everything I had believed in began to tumble about me. Henty, my father, my home. The Man held out longest, because although he disapproved of the whole thing he was mild in his reproof. 'Foolishness!' he said. 'Foolishness on all sides!' For another long time, two years and more, I held out with him.

Besides, my body also held out. I was in that swoon of puberty that I have described when recalling my last visit to my Kildare cousins in the military camp on the Curragh, a boy doubly lost, to the objective world of action, in the subjective world of sexual desire, free of neither city, longing for the freedom of both. If only the outer world could be filled again, as it had been before, I might have struck a balance. I was aware only of my own emptiness and my body's frets. Was this the time in me that made that good brother say of me, 'A nice lad, but . . .' and tap his head? How can I tell, since these were years to which, as I have described, my memory is a near blank? Yet, not a total blank; I was not all that dotty. I remember the day I, without realising it, began to see light through a tiny circle.

I noticed once day that O'Domhnaill, who was still with us after 1916, was wearing a plain gold ring in his lapel and asked him what it meant. He explained that what he was wearing was *An Fáinne*, the Irish words for 'The Ring', a token which meant that whoever wore it could converse in our native tongue with anybody he met who also wore it. I at once told him I wanted to belong to this circle, and he encouraged me to prepare for the oral test. He began to talk to me in Irish whenever he had the chance. He told me I should start reading poetry and prose aloud, and loaned me a couple of books of Irish verse for the purpose.

One of these books contained the simple Gaelic verses of

* My imagination? Or a popular legend? In fact no such Charge of the Light Brigade occurred.

one Tomás O'Suileabháin, a Kerry postman of the nineteenth century. I kept the book for years. I cherished it solely for its frontispiece – a smudgy photograph showing a rocky promontory on the Atlantic, a ruined chapel, an old graveyard, a few small fields. Time out of mind I used to open the book at this photograph and gaze and gaze at it. Sea, chapel, graveyard, lonely rock, poor fields – they became my new symbols, transfigured by my longing for that liberty from my passionate flesh in a romantic, nobly patterned world which I now equated with remoteness, hardness, age and a traditional life whose pieties they rounded. It was not the place in the photograph that I revered or wished to possess but the absoluteness or essence of the entire life that I imagined made it, so that what I was really shaping in my mind whenever I looked at that photograph was a myth of life for which, so far, the only bodily vessel I knew was the wet, worn plain of West Limerick, with its lichened limestone walls, its distant sea, its battered Norman ruins, its dead, my dead. Gazing at that picture, I was creating a new legend, a new myth. I was unconsciously writing it, peopling it. I was engaged in every writer's first task – hypothesising life, imagining himself in it, as it, another Adam, self-created, fecund.

My new symbols were, of course – I say 'of course' because such is the course of nature – exhaustible symbols. Most symbols are. That apple, also, would fall with a whisper from its tree. Yet, before it fell life was to seem one long summer, many years of it, during which I was to know the reality behind those appealing images and during which the tree that bore them had to die for everybody else as well as me. All art, Pater said, is life seen through a temperament. One modifies one's views but one's temperament is a given thing, an indestructible and unalterable necessity.

Thanks to O'Domhnaill, I was wearing my Fáinne in the summer of 1917. That summer I went for the last time to County Limerick with my mother. I remember very little of that holiday. I remember my Uncle John, on the farm, laughing and saying, 'Haha, John, I see they're making a fine, tall, straight young man out of you!' I remember cycling about the country on my own in search of old abbeys and castles, such as the ruined castle of the last of the Desmond earls at Askeaton, or the friary of the Kildare earls at Adare. In a dim, general way I recall wandering around the Commons when my uncle would be at work on his humble plots of ground, or sitting daydreaming for hours by the lake, or walking the small white limestone roads – once with a purpose: to see Curragh Chase, where the poet Aubrey de Vere lived – or merely lying in the high-walled cottage orchard on Roche's Road reading, reading, reading, or idly watching the swifts dart like bullets into the ivy hanging a foot thick on the walls, or the Atlantic clouds passing ever so slowly from wall to wall, and not a sound but the inevitable crowing cock far away, or the dim clop of a straying horse's hooves.

The school year after that summer was my last, and it was climactic.

I was now eighteen, and by this time we were all for the Rebels, but still only as an idea, unembodied. The Pres, and the Man, so far changed as to allow a group of us to start a hurling team – hitherto the only game played in the school had been 'English' rugby. The Man gazed at me in amused surprise the first day he saw me going off with my hurley stick of new white ash and my togs. 'You?' he said. 'Games?' For my part, it was merely an effort to give body to my vague rebelly ideas, and it took some doing, because although Uncle John might say I was fine and straight I was also skinny, had never played any games, and was deeply conscious of how silly I looked with my long spindly legs in white shorts, running helplessly and uselessly around the field after the flying ball, so inept that my fellows had to beg me to desist because I was a danger to them (and to myself) with my wild swinging ash. That summer I won, with difficulty, an entrance scholarship to the university, and that summer the Man so far yielded to the new winds blowing over Ireland as to permit the college to be used as a summer school open to the public at large, men and women, young and old, for the teaching of Irish. Again encouraged by O'Domhnaill, I attended it. Here, having done his work, he drops out of my story. No other man has influenced my life so much and so quietly as he.

The immeasurable difference between that summer school

and any other place of study I have ever been in was that it was voluntary. We wanted – and how eagerly! – to be able to speak Irish well and fluently, not just as a useful accomplishment but because Irish was a symbol of the larger freedom to which we were all groping. The result was that, for the first time, study became wholly delightful. Through language we explored life. And not only this surrounding life of our own day but also that past, so often latent and unsuspected, which has the power to evoke from the most familiar and common words new, refreshing and revealing comments on the nature and habits of man. The study of any language can do this, but no language can do it so much as one's own when its images are embodied under our eyes – when, that is, one's own language really is the language of a vigorous life mode, is, in a word, a living language, as Irish once was but, alas, no longer is.

Think of any common word, say, *grocer*. Its subtler evocations must be quite lost on anybody unfamiliar with the English grocer's shop. Translate it into *épicier* and it creates another and quite different set of pictures. Translate it into American and we are at once presented with, or deprived of, still other associations, such as those attached to the word *saloon*, for which the words *corner grocery* are or once were sometimes used as a humorous euphemism in the United States; which word *saloon*, translated back into English, will in its turn make no clear proposals to minds which associate saloons only with ships, barbers, billiards and that kind of motor car which some Americans call by the archaic title of *sedan*.

Words are always local in their memories, images, emotions, ideas. *Girl* is a word with countless possibilities, but these do not include the images inherent for an Italian in *fanciulla* or for an Irishman in *cailín*. A *loch* is not a *lake*, any more than a *country lane* is a *stradella* or a *boithrín*, which we anglicise as *boreen*. Indeed, *lane* has no true emotive equivalent outside England. So, when we spoke Irish we simply evoked another country, another life, another people. *Mountains* were mountains, *roads* were roads, and *glens* glens (always Scottish); but when, for those things, we uttered the Irish words *sléibhthe*, *bóithre*, and *gleannta* we spoke passwords to another way of life. Irish became our runic language. It made us comrades in a secret society. We sought and made friendships, some of them to last forever, like conspirators in a state of high exaltation, merely by using Irish words.

On the very first day of the summer school I found myself sitting in class directly behind a girl with a black ponytail that had a provocative way of straying across the inkwell on my desk. At last I dipped the tip of her ponytail in the inkwell and politely handed it forward to her. She turned and laughed gaily at me. She had deep brown eyes, red, glowing cheeks, and white teeth one of which was gold-capped, an attractive little mole to the left of her upper lip, and a cloud of hair that I chose to think of as the colour of thunder. When we met after that first class I found that she was still at school and that her name was Eileen Gould, which meant that her people were originally (that is, some nine hundred years ago) either Norse or Norman, if Gould really is to be related, as she held, to the Irish word *gall* (pronounced gowl), meaning a Scandinavian.

She was full of animal spirits, of rude health, vital, wilful, romantic in the nineteenth-century Romantic way, her chap-books Byron, Shelley and the randy Irish poets of the eighteenth century. She was all for the recent Russian Revolution, hated snobbery, despised convention in dress – being so pretty she could afford to – and loved the country much more than the town. She knew its birds, trees and wildflowers, all its wild ways and wayward seasons, and took pleasure in sharing them with me in an affectionate if slightly scornful pity for anyone who knew only the city's pavements. She lived on the western edge of the city, in the district called Sunday's Well, so that all her walks took her, and me, directly out among the fields under the furzy slopes and wooded hills above the Lee. To come on her there, with her dog Rory, an old felt hat set jauntily on the side of her black hair, her cheeks damp from the rain, or warm from the sun, or reddened by the wind, was, to me, like coming on a heroic figure out of the West itself, the wonderful country, the far-off country, the Free Country as we came to call it, whose tiny blue mountains we could barely see when we climbed one of the higher hills above the quiet, pastoral river below us. Those hills became in time our regular haunt, where we would walk, and talk, and lie in one another's arms, whispering, listening to the flutterings or scurryings of the wild things about us, exchanging confidences about our lives, our longings, our symbols, all our inchoate dreams.

During that month she became my close friend, the first girlfriend I ever had other than my Boyhan cousins. From that we became intimate friends, from that intimate comrades, and on that chastely warm ground we pitched our separate tents for years. This may no longer be a normal relationship between young women and young men in Ireland; it was a common pattern during those idealistic years, and the more so as they grew more and more troubled. Certainly in the really hot revolutionary years all animal passion was sublimated in the overriding passion for Ireland and liberty. I should speak only for myself, since I do not know how it may have been for others, though I imagine that in those hot years far older men than I, engaged in the most dangerous adventures, strained constantly to the highest tension, must also have found a way of dissociating themselves completely from their own bodies, driving them before them like animals in a fierce anger, death-devoted to Saint Gun. We are not a people to record such things, but others have done so, as in those two terrible, confessional pages at the opening of Lawrence's *Seven Pillars of Wisdom*, proving that, on the other hand, idealists, though exalted from the body, are often amoral in their contempt for it.

Eileen did more than understand my new sacred symbols of the hard rock, the lonely sea, the forgotten ruins and the small fields. Every summer, while I had been going to Limerick or Kildare, it was her way to live among the Irish-speaking farmers or fishermen of the West Cork mountains, or the islands of the Southwest. This summer she was about to set off for the mountains again. Naturally I decided to go too. I borrowed a bicycle and set off westward, to where symbols and words became flesh and blood for my salvation.

8

The Free Country, the Unfree City

I

I had had no idea how near the mountains of West Cork are to Cork City. The Pass of Keimaneigh, which marks their southern spur, high above Bantry Bay, is only forty-one miles away. A bare thirty miles out you already feel them closing in when you top the little hillock this side of the village of Inchageelah and its long, lean lake, so indented and twisted that it seems to the traveller beside it not one lake but many. You feel their near presence a bare fifteen or twenty miles out if you take the unfrequented back roads through Kilmurry and Teerelton, as I was to do during the later years of the Troubles when making my cautious way to and from the city. In time they were hundreds of years away.

On the August morning of my first entry into the Free Country I was not more than five miles beyond the last suburb, climbing easily under Ardrum Woods above the valley of the Lee, before I began to feel the ascendancy of their Past. It seemed to flow out of the old furzy fields, an ancient stone bridge, worn rocks, a farmhouse that was as much part of the fields as the trees about it, a crumbling Norman castle at Carrigadrohid rising from its rock in the river, the very road under my wheels that had for centuries led travellers in from the Atlantic along the valley of the Lee to the port of Cork. Simultaneously everything to do with my own life became intensely precious to me because of this sudden sense of its brevity. Out there my love was waiting for me. I pedalled on faster, as if I were afraid that she might vanish before I arrived.

Less than two hours later I got off my bicycle on the hillock outside Inchageelah, always afterwards to be my mark of arrival in the true West. Beyond the first foothills, across the loose stone walls of the road, the outcropping rock, the sparse, wind-torn trees, the first few tiny fields excavated painfully by generations of cottiers out of a hard, infertile, sweat-making land softened only by the reed-edged lake, I saw the smoke-blue mountains now quite near. On their peaks white clouds, larger far than themselves, rose into the blue sky. I heard over my head a lark trilling invisibly. When I saw and felt all this, and knew that all about me people spoke an ancient tongue, that I could as yet only partly interpret, I experienced the final obliteration of time that turns a moment into eternity. In that moment the crude photograph at whose runic symbols I had gazed so often in the poems of Tomás Rua – the old ruined chapel near the ancient rocks, edging the sea – became clear as a mirror. Remounting my bicycle with a pounding heart, I passed through my mirror into reality. I pedalled on past the village, on beside its lake, now appearing, now disappearing, past small white cottages, through the village of Beal-atha-' n-Ghaorthaidh, after which I came on the Lee again, now a mere rocky stream, until I came to the farm and farmhouse, called Tuirín Dubh, where I was to stay.

It was not a picturesque house – little in these parts except the scenery is picturesque. It was a plain, cement-fronted, slate house of two stories. I saw an uncombed garden in front, red with fuchsias and old cottage roses. I saw a long stone loft and byres of uncemented stone to its left; a new corrugated-iron barn and more byres directly opposite across the road. Foothills rose rockily, front and rear. At the end of the path down from the house, beside the road, there was a well, separated from the road by a light fuchsia hedge. As I alighted from my bicycle I heard a girl's laugh from behind the fuchsias, and looking through it I saw Eileen's brown eyes laughing at me between its scarlet bells. She came forward, still laughing with pleasure, dressed in a brown frock, her skin almost as brown, her black hair astray, her cheeks fuchsia-red, and, standing on one muscular leg, she looked at me, as I did at her, quizzically and affectionately – our barrier and our bond. Then she brought me in and presented me to Bean Ui Tuama. The old lady welcomed me in Irish, as warmly as my Aunt Nan in Rathkeale would have done. At once, I felt at home.

We proved to be a company of about twenty or thirty men and women, youths and girls, all as lighthearted as children. Their gaiety was something I have never experienced before or since. The women and girls shared rooms in the house. The men slept in the dry stone loft, which had been turned for the summer into a simple dormitory. We ate in separate sittings, about ten at a time, at the long table in the dining room, and we always ate well. We spoke only Irish, often asking for a word, or a phrase, or a correct pronunciation from the more practiced. We had come from all parts of Ireland. They were clerks, students, craftsmen, carpenters, masons, an electrical engineer. Two, who were more serious than the rest of us, had been in the Rising in Dublin and had been released from jail in the general amnesty of the year before; but all of us were reborn of the Rising and all that led to it, so that the language acted both as a matrix to the tissues of our political faith and as its sign and password. Our zeal to speak Irish bound us into a community, a new, glowing, persecuted, or about-to-be-persecuted, political sect. One small sign of this was that we all adopted and, like myself, most retained for the rest of our lives the ancient, original Gaelic forms of our anglicised names, so, from being Whelan, I became and remain, as my children do, O'Faoláin. It is pronounced Oh-Fay-láwn.

In groups we spent the livelong days together. We spent half the day down in the village studying the language in the corrugated tin shed grandiosely called the College. The rest of the day we spent swimming in the rock pools, or climbing the mountains, or cycling to the farther glens, or dancing informally by the roadside at night, or more formally in the College, or boating on the lake if the moon was up, or simply sitting in the kitchen listening to some local boy or girl singing a traditional Irish song or playing old tunes on the fiddle, or we merely sat and conversed. Late hours were the common rule. I was always so pleasantly tired, so full of oxygen, that I could have slept soundly under a hedge or on a stone floor. On hot nights I often slept, in the clothes in which I stood, high up in the hay of the outdoor hay barn, waking only when I heard a horse's hooves on the road or somebody working in the stone byres below.

Nowadays, the learning of Irish has lost this magical power to bind hearts together. It has lost its symbolism, is no longer a mystique. This is entirely because the political fight of which it was then a part is over. Today we are not in the least concerned with translating the aspirations of those days into reality; we are concerned with translating the aspirations of these days into reality. For there has been, meanwhile, a shift of ambition. Then we foresaw the new Ireland as a rich flowering of the old Ireland, with all its old simple ways, pieties, values, traditions. Only the old men went on thinking like this; men like President Eamon de Valera. The younger men, proud to be called hard-headed men, indifferent to or even despising those traditional ways, now want a modernised country, prosperity, industrialisation, economic success. These ambitions have, for years, been demolishing the bridge with the past, stone by stone, until, inevitably, the Irish language, which is the keystone of that arch, will fall into the river of time. With it the life procession from the past into the present will cease. The language that once spoke to teeming life, and which is already speaking to fewer and fewer, will then speak only to ghosts, the language of the dead. Already, by 1958, a Swiss philologist could write in a publication of the Dublin Institute of Advanced Studies, 'We are dealing with the ruins of a language,' and report that Irish was the vernacular only in pockets of coastal Mayo, of Connemara, of Dingle, and of Donegal. English was infiltrating even into the Aran Islands. The Great Blasket Island was depopulated. Seven years earlier the institute reported that there were then (1951) not more than three thousand people in Ireland who could not speak English, and not more than thirty-five thousand in all who used Irish as their ordinary medium of speech. So the old life dies, the old symbols wither away, and I and my like who warmed our hands at the fires of the past are torn in two as we stand on the side of the bridge and look back in anguish at the doomed Ireland beyond it.

Of all our expeditions the most favoured by Eileen and by me was to the source of the Lee, beyond the small leaden lake of Gougane Barra, which is backed by a long, dark, dead-end valley or *coom*, known in Irish as Coom Ruadh, or the Red Coom, in English as Valley Desmond. All our symbols were concentrated in this glen. Near the edge of the lake, surrounded by steeply rising slopes or mountain faces, there is a tiny hermit island, now joined by a causeway to the mainland; on this drop of land there is a ruined chapel, beside a discreet little modern chapel in Romanesque style, almost hidden by the mountain ash and the rhododendrons that hang down over the dark water and are darkly reflected in it. There is also a small square cloister of 'cells' where, we believed, hermit monks once slept. Here, a thousand years ago, the patron saint of Cork, Finnbarr, lived and prayed. This is how I have described the quiet calm of this small lake, in one of the most satisfying stories I have written about this part of Ireland, 'The Silence of the Valley':

> Only in one or two farmhouses about the lake, or in the fishing hotel at its edge – preoccupations of work and pleasure – does one ever forget the silence of the valley. Even in winter, when the great cataracts slide down the mountain face, the echoes of falling water are fitful: the winds fetch and carry them. In the summer a fisherman will hear the tinkle of the ghost of one of those falls only if he steals among the mirrored reeds under the pent of the cliffs, and withholds the splash of his oars. Tiny muted sounds will then awe and delight him by the vacancy out of which they creep, intermittently.

We loved this valley, lake, ruined chapel and rude cloister because of their enclosure, their memories, and their silence. Many times then and in after years we entered the silent dead-end coom to climb the mountain beyond. Once we got lost there in a summer fog, aiming for the minute loch up there called the Lake of the Speckled Trout, dark as ink and cold as ice water, visited otherwise only by mountain sheep. When we reached the top of the coom after some tough climbing, the fog lifted and we came on another valley, and a vast view westward across other mountaintips far over the sunset sea. On those fortresses what could touch us? We enjoyed among them what I may well call a juvenile fantasy of grown desire, planning tiny cottages on either side of this lost valley or that, facing one another, so that by day we would descend to the lake and be together there and by night see, each, the other's beckoning light across the darkness of the glen.

Let me drag myself free of that dreamworld, that drunkworld, that heavenworld to try to look at it lucidly, now that it has left me and left all of us, sinking deep into the sea like a drowned bell, tolling more and more faintly as it sways downwards, to be heard in our day only by specially tuned ears like those sonic finders that yachtsmen use to take deep-sea soundings. Its gift was lovely, equivocal, dangerous and ultimately exhaustible. It was the gift of Proteus: to sport with whales and minnows and coloured fishes in the depths of an otherworld, or ascend, under any disguise one chose, to these mortal rocks, these shores. While I was Proteus I had no wish to lie for long on mortal shores. While I was in our Free Country I had no wish to think of any other. In that vast, shapeless, indivisible sea of timeless youth and age my being became an absorbent spirit rather than a perceiving intelligence.

Later, by painful experience, hard discipline, and perforce – because whether one likes it or not one has to cope with the mortal rocks – I added what I could of intelligence to intuition, a keel to keep me from toppling, a diver's case to keep me from being drowned, a compass to steer by whenever the gift of Proteus failed, as fail it must when time and the heart's winds veer. For while it was splendid then to need neither keel nor case nor compass, not to see but feel, swim not like a man but a fish, not to understand but know, fly not like a plane but a bird, not to reason as long as I could better imagine, we have to have other weapons when, with the years, the wagging world descends on us.

It is all a matter of how much one can save from boyhood as a man. Long after, twenty years after, when I had disciplined myself for this wagging world, and begun to travel Europe, I read what others – most of them my contemporaries and some by then my friends – had been seeing, thinking and doing in France, Austria, Italy, Greece, Asia Minor, the far Orient, such men and women as Robert Byron, the Sitwells, Morgan Forster, Elizabeth Bowen, Harold Acton, Christopher Sykes, Raymond

Mortimer, V. S. Pritchett, Cyril Connolly – in those fabled 1920s when you could travel often and widely for a few pounds. As I read I was often tempted to bewail my twenties, which I had spent arguing politics with young men, talking Gaelic to old men, in sun and rain, cowering under dripping hedges, sitting by cottage fires among the mountains. Was I mad to have spent my youth like that?

I could say that these, my friends, might well have envied me, and all of us who were driven by the winds of 1916 to touch off the first anti-imperialist revolt of the century. I could think that, by comparison with a revolution, travels in Greece or Asia Minor were mild adventures. I could think: 'Supposing I, aged twenty, heard of the Irish fight while in Athens or Vienna, what a fever of the blood I would have felt! What a sickening sense of being out of it!' And, yet, is the intellectual adventure really such a mild one? What about Joyce? That one Irish name which will always challenge us stay-at-homes? What heroism, and what martyrdom, that name evokes! He reminds us that there is no end to the dangers of the intellectual adventure, that a man could gamble a whole life on its hazards as surely as a soldier crossing a minefield, that it demands as much moral courage to think as I do, that every man must be lost in admiration of the scholar's persistence and heroic loneliness. After tormenting myself for years over my envies and regrets, I think the answer has to be threefold. Each man ploughs his fated field. If a man makes any mistake in the handling of his life it concerns less what he does than how he does it. And if my friends or I made any life mistakes at all it came not then but later, when each of us faced the challenge of art to recreate the experience of life.

That summer, and for many a summer after, I was either lost or found, so happy that I realised my happiness only when, each autumn, it was, for that year, over. Sadly we would say goodbye to freedom until the next year and return sadly to the city. To cycle back into the streets, so white after all the greenery that they looked sick, so busy in their own eyes, so empty to ours, was like facing a prison gate. Whenever Eileen and I parted then at the city's edge we would look at one another as if each wondered who the other was, our only comfort the thought that we were sharing the same fate and could soon meet to bewail it together. When we did meet, we used always to walk out along the uplands beside the Lee, and silently look westward towards our gods.

2

From then on my home meant nothing to me; but Cork City began to mean much more than it ever had before. This was because Eileen and her father, Jo Gould, were true Corkonians whose line had been for generations born within the sound of Shandon's bells. I had only explored Cork. They had the city in their bones.

He was a handsome man, and, or so I used to think whenever I met him out for a stroll with his dog, a bit of a toff, always with a flower in his buttonhole, carrying a silver-topped walking stick, bearded, wearing a slightly old-fashioned, well-brushed bowler. A certain amount of vanity and an Edwardian touch of affectation in his manner added to his distinction. But what really set him off from anybody else I had yet come to know in Cork was that he plainly had a romantic image of himself and his city, tenderly nourished by his memories of the larger, easier, more expansive world which Cork had represented in his youth and with which it was soon to lose contact forever.

The Cork of his boyhood, allowing for the usual Irish time lag, had been of the age of Dickens and was, his stories led me to believe, Dickensian. The most striking thing about it was that it did not sound a bit Irish, in the common stereotype idea of what Irish means, and yet was patently very much of its own region. His parents on his mother's side were Kidneys and Condons; his first employer was one Bob Helen, his second one Ebenezer Bogan; his later friends had such names as Meade, Bland, Curtis, or Bradley on the Catholic side, and Bond, Bolster, Scott, Newsom or Guy on the Protestant side. Not an O' or a Mac among the lot of them. The second most striking thing about his city was that he not only passed freely in it between Catholics and Protestants but had been a strong nationalist in his younger days, sometimes even calling himself a Fenian – that is, a member, associate or friend of the extremist semisecret society so called – and yet at the same time he had a great admiration for certain sides of English life, especially for its aristocracy; and, yet again, he was able to nourish, simultaneously with those two sympathies, a considerable distrust and even contempt for the native Irish countryman. One of his recollections, which I always enjoyed whenever he told it, acting it out vividly as he spoke, shows some of these sympathies working against one another, comically. This was his experience in a Cardiff music hall, when some stage-Irish comedians were to his mind, and one may accept it that he was right, mocking his country, to the delight of the audience. Unable to stand it any longer, Jo leaped to his feet, pointed here and there about the house and roared: 'There ye are! Murphys, O'Connells, Sullivans, Caseys, Driscolls, I know ye all, I can see it in your faces, laughing at your own country! Are ye men or are ye mice? Shame on ye! Shame!' He was jumped on, grabbed and thrown out on his neck. Music Hall? Yes! He loved that purely English institution, knew all its songs, loved to sing them and imitate the comics who sang them. But Ireland also claimed his loyalty.

His first job as a boy had been with a moneylender and pawnbroker on the South Terrace, old Bob Helen, whose wife dearly loved their young apprentice, and being childless hoped to build him into their lives and their business. He used to go around Cork collecting debts for the Helens, mounted on a white horse. He broke their hearts when he left them for his second patron, Ebenezer Bogan of the Cork Harbour Board, who planned to make a seaman of him by introducing him to the dredgers on Cork River. Thanks to that experience he soon knew every inch of the docks, every turn of the river, down to the great harbour of Queenstown, and out to the Sovereign Isles. The wide sea called him, he abandoned Bogan, and for several years he sailed around the world. Then he married, and he married an O', an O'Connell, his first and as far as I know last intimate contact with country folk from the green countryside beyond the walls of Cork. His wife died young, leaving him with five children, two sons, three daughters, and that ended his life as a seaman. When I knew him he had for some years been settled into a pleasant little job as overseer of the heating plant in a mental hospital set on a hill on the Lee Road half a mile from his tiny cottage and garden in Sunday's Well.

This, anyway, is how he might have phrased his biography. His associates in the mental hospital, warders and nurses, all countrymen and countrywomen – or as he would have scornfully said, 'In from the heath, thick in the head, strong in the back' – would have phrased it otherwise, deliberately cutting him down to size as Corkonians – a talented but acidulous and envious subrace – always love to do with everybody. They would have said that he was just an old sailor who had been a donkeyman on tramp steamers, after working with the Harbour Commissioners on their dredgers, and was now the boilerman in the madhouse. I think it was partly in resistance to and in scorn of these scornful thick-in-the-heads and strong-in-the-backs that he moved among them with the air of a retired Lord Rosebery, deliberately talked to them only of places like Pall Mall and Piccadilly, and refused to eat their bucolic meals, bringing instead to table pet concoctions of his own, such as curried brains, sweetbreads, stuffed crabs, crayfish, lobscouse, little jars of pickles that he had composed for himself, or, if he particularly wished to annoy or disgust them, snails that he had tenderly fed at home on herbs of his own growing.

In all this he was eagerly aided and abetted by old Walker, the mental hospital cook, also an old sailor, equally bored by the rough food he had to serve to the in-from-the-heaths. Sometimes these two far-travelled men would retire altogether from the dining room for private and exotic meals of their own in the boiler house, a cosy, dusty, enchanting place which Jo Gould had filled with plants, flowers and bird cages, and where he had absolutely nothing to do, since he was served there like a rajah by two 'good' lunatics who did all the work. He sat there all day, in an old basket armchair like a throne, reading back numbers of the *Illustrated London News* or the memoirs or biographies of the great men he had known about in the past – Parnell (his god), Augustine Birrell, Lord Balfour, the Marquis of Salisbury, John Redmond (his subgod), old plays, chiefly Shakespeare, local histories or local verse like the verses of John Fitzgerald, 'The Bard of the Lee', or paper chapbooks about the revolutionary Fenian Brotherhood with whom he had had that ambiguous relationship in his hot youth.

Irish readers will readily recognise the type and the period: a

Parnellite and a gentleman, not averse to a spot of physical force but only for so long as it was controlled by the constitutionalist Irish Party in Westminster. By now, however, his interest in politics was wholly historical. The fall of Parnell had broken his belief in Irish loyalty; he saw in the rejection of his subgod John Redmond by the new generation of Sinn Feiners yet another demonstration of anti-Parnellism; and foreseeing, quite correctly, that they, too, in time would come under the thumb of the Church, he had retired, literally, to cultivate his garden, a plot about the size of a pocket handkerchief, whose minute glasshouse he packed with boxes of seedlings and precious blooms raised lovingly from slips or bulbs given to him by his richer neighbours who shared his love of flowers, admired his sturdy, upstanding character, and enjoyed his free-wheeling conversation. Whenever I saw him sitting there in his garden on a kitchen chair, smoking, reading his books, surrounded by his blooms, cocking a careful eye over his glasses at me lest I as much as brush against a leaf, I always thought him the perfect image of philosophic content and burgher pride.

His talk about old Cork, and Eileen's echoes of it, as we used to sit side by side in his tiny garden on summer days, helped me to see the little city – spread far and wide beneath us, out beyond the cathedral's trident to the rolling hills of Lehenagh – with richly deepened feelings. Indeed, he made me see it clearly for the first time. He helped me above all to see its commonest habits as part of a longstanding tradition: the bands of Cork playing for band promenades in the Mardyke (we could hear the brass sailing up across the smooth-flowing river below Sunday's Well); the coloured rowboats dotting the Lee; the distant cheers from the athletic sports in the cricket field; the jaunting cars wheeling out the New Line for a Sunday's outing, with one man always perched on the rear seat to perform the double duty of playing the melodeon with his hands and ('just in case') concealing the car number from the police with his dangling legs; the old Cork custom of Maying, that is of visiting the countryside in every known sort of vehicle on May Sunday, when every horse in town and even our old ramshackle electric tramcars carried sprays of green leaves; the way you could tell the hours by the faint call of a bugle from the distant military barracks;

or the way you could tell the direction of the wind by the sound the ships' sirens made away down in the heart of the city as they entered the more trafficked part of the river. There, even still, a sign on the wall says DEAD SLOW as if to indicate to foreign sailors the sort of city they are approaching.

His memories of the Opera House and the Palace Music Hall were mellowed and glorified by time. He talked admiringly, without a trace of nationalist resentment or provincial inferiority, of the military tattoos; of every house in the city that possessed any interesting associations – where the painters Barry and Maclise had been born; where King Edward had stayed when he came to Cork as Prince of Wales; where the brothers Sheares, who had been rebels in 1798, had lived; where Baron Palles stayed; the Big House where the shipbuilder Pike had lived; or the burned ruins of another Big House where some Corkonian grandee had lived until, on one and the same night, his Cork house went on fire, his yacht in La Condamine burned to the water, and he lost his last sovereign at the gaming tables of Monte Carlo. He knew retired sea captains all over the city. He had acquaintances among his rich neighbours – Sunday's Well was at that time a select suburb – who were members of the City Club and the County Club, men who regularly went off to the Continent at least twice a year, and whom he would then advise about what to see in ports and places which he had once known like the palm of his hand. My father, had he had access to such succulent particulars of the social life of Cork, would have mentioned these burghers and merchants in respectful awe. Jo Gould had not a drop of that kind of human respect in his veins. He possessed the city; his line was as old as, or older than, any man's; his father had been a maltster, his grandfather a sea captain, his great-grandfather a glass-maker, and when pressed hard he would produce a seventeenth-century mayor of Cork, one Pierce Gould, hanged as one of the few real rebels of so-called Rebel Cork. It was this burgher pride in him that I most admired, it was so utterly at a pole from my father's pride. My father was proud to belong, looking upward along the rungs of the hierarchical ladder. Jo Gould's pride was a purely personal pride; he just did not give a damn about anybody while respecting, and admiring, everybody, rich or poor, who had his own spirit of independence. Because of this he was the most unprovincial man I ever knew.

You can see how easily I could fall in love with the Cork which Jo Gould typified and which he was the first man to reveal to me. I loved it and admired it for years in spite of many mental reservations about such things as its poverty and its bad housing, and the fact that it had not enough of anything for complete comfort – only one or two rattle-box cinemas, only one library, no elegant restaurants, no Little Theatre, no popular cafés or coffee shops but thousands of grim pubs. I admired its sedate air, its quiet sense of self-possession, its something that one can only speak of as an air or a tradition, indigenous and time-established, as old as Shandon's bells.

3

There was, for all that and all that, another side of Cork's small-town life that I must in honesty remember, hearing my own heel taps on many a night, wet and muggy, or windy and sharp, or just drizzle-wet-cold, along its suburban roads, narrowly held between walls, villas and gardens, matching the backs of houses that on the other side fall plumb to the pavement, fortress-blank except when broken by a door entry with a brass knocker or the gated arch of an old coachhouse; long slim suburban enclaves dimly lit by spaced-out streetlamps lightly touching the wet waving lilacs or the valerian on the tops of old sandstone walls, lean long suffocating *clausuras* of seclusion, smugness and security, images of the mental suffocation and total resistance to all new ideas of my city's damp, dark, miasmic valley.

I pass, under the green incandescence of a streetlamp here, and another farther on, and a third farther still, groups of two or three youths or middle-aged men killing the last hours before bed with an intermittent gossiping, no louder than night ducks, that falls silent as I pass them by. Like me they have nothing else to do. They are better off than I, who have nobody to talk to and am merely wandering the night down. They at least have these pools of light under which they can softly cluck. I am not like Jo Gould, an old man content to retire to bed and read about Lord Rosebery. I am a youth, supposed to be living, doing things, my blood hot, my imagination pulsing with vigour and ambition. This night has no vigour, my wandering will lead me only from one dark emptiness to another as I walk on and on, around and downhill out of this cloistered suburbia to old close-faced quays where the riverside's eighteenth century is crumbling into its final state of a modern slum; past a once noble house the left-hand side of whose broad limestone hand-cut steps are rotted clean away; past another once decent Georgian home one of whose many tenants has painted his square of property in whitewash, just the square bit around his own two windows, so that the house looks as if somebody had stuck a piece of sticking plaster over its wounds; past Saint Peter's graveyard bordered by a pitch-black slum laneway smelling of runnels, refuse, rags, and bugs; in through the markets, whose scattered debris strews the roadway and sweetly scents the night air with cabbage stumps and fish heads; on under the market buildings that house meat stalls, vegetable stalls, old scrap-iron booths, through whose ironwork gates I can see old clothes hanging gibbeted in the darkness and on whose limestone pediments I see the stonecrop fluttering in the nightwind. Lanes dive right and left. There are furniture and junk shops and eating houses suggesting the day's collation of bacon and cabbage. Everything is pulsing faintly with the breathing of sleep. I am only a few streets away from Half Moon Street and my sleep. All I hear is my own heel-tapping, or Shandon above us all on the hills grinding out a few more grains of time as it has done for so many generations of enduring poverty, quiet resignation, selfish ambition, and smug content. Oh all those damp and cloying nights! Oh breeding time of wild dreams, and smothering anger and terror of defeat! Oh my youth! Oh my city! I have loved, admired, feared and hated no city so much as you.

Do I then condemn my birthplace and spit it out of my mouth? The city was my shadow, and no man jumps off his own shadow. It was for twenty-six years my life; more than that it was Life – and one does not spit Life out of one's mouth. It is dyed into me, part of my way of seeing and feeling forever. Somebody else who lived there, unknown to me at that same time, might well see it differently, especially, perhaps, if he were wealthy, or more cosy, or more cushioned. But the lasting life-impress the city made on me was made through characters like poor old undefeated Doggy Sheehan, or my French teacher Christy Flynn thinking of Les Invalides as he looked out of the schoolroom window, or my father the policeman longing for the Queen's, or the Man ushering his boys out of it to triumph, perhaps death for the Empire in the farthest corners of the world. One feels for one's characters as one feels for (and against) 'the paradise, the grave, the city and the wilderness' that was their city, their wilderness, their grave. One quarrels over the fates of men and places – not with them. Otherwise, as we are warned and chided by old Cavafy in his poem 'The City', we will be always saying, 'I will go to another land, I will go to another sea, another city will be found, a better one than this . . .'.

> You will find no new lands, you will find no other seas.
> The city will follow you. You will roam the same
> streets. And you will age in the same neighbourhoods;
> and you will grow grey in these same houses.
> Always you will arrive in this city. Do not hope for any other –
> There is no ship for you, there is no road.
> As you have destroyed your life here
> in this little corner, you have ruined it in the entire world.

'What a man sees in the human race,' Mark Twain observed, 'is merely himself in the deep and honest privacy of his own heart.'

All the same, let me not be too bloody metaphysical! A man can, one hopes, outgrow his boyhood? Lugging it with him, yes; loving it, yes; but searching, also, for his manhood and his old age, which will be its completion. Cavafy, himself a migrant, was not writing objectively about Alexandria in 'The City'. He called it a poem full of *désespérance*. There are sixteen lines in the poem. He worked it over for fifteen years. He was writing about his life search – as I am. He found the answer in his poetry.

9

College Days

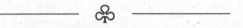

The University College in Cork stands on a slight hill overlooking what was in my youth the highly select suburb called the Western Road. One morning, in the September of 1918, I walked up its curving, climbing avenue in considerable pride and some awe to register as a student in the Faculty of Arts. I had been in the college grounds before now, but only as a visitor, almost as a trespasser, admiring and desiring them. Now I was here of my own right, conscious of my manhood. I was, like the century, eighteen years of age.

They were, and are, pretty grounds. To my left, after I crossed a bridge over a slight branch of the many-branched Lee, wooded slopes broke down to the tiny river. Down there, through the turning leaves of the beeches, I saw young men and women in elegant whites plonking at tennis in the grass courts. I at once wanted to be one of them. On the farther bank of the river pink and white houses backed daintily and discreetly down to gravel strands. Right and left of me, as I walked on upward, shrubs and trees bore leaden labels inscribed in Latin. I at once wanted to study botany and be able to talk of plants and trees by their Latin names. At the top of the avenue I passed beneath the high mullioned windows of a modern Tudor-Gothic hall in cut limestone, rounded it to pass under a tower with a modern Tudor arch and halted before a quadrangle of golf-green lawn surrounded by wide gravelled paths and enclosed on three sides by more Tudor-Gothic buildings with diamonded windows.

I approved.

Three students walked across the quad, gowned, bareheaded,

chatting and laughing loudly. Old hands. One wore a gown so ragged and acid-eaten that there was nothing much left of it except the shoulder pieces. I at once decided to have a gown just as stained and ragged. Nearer to me two youths with warm countrified complexions, very obviously in-from-the-heath, wearing very new-looking hats, were gazing respectfully at the three old hands. I pushed my hat on the back of my poll, leaned against the arch, and lit a cigarette. One of these days some former school chum would ask me *the* question. With a surprised start I would say, almost as if I had forgotten the answer: 'Oh no! I'm up at the university now.' Followed by, 'Where are you working?'

'Up at the university?' Or was I enjoying one of those classical mirages that at one and the same moment delude us with an earthly image and its aerial reflection?

What insistent and cruel bores knowledgeable old men are, exposing and betraying by every word the innocence of youth! Years later I read that Sir Bertram Windle, the president of the college in my time, described it, when he left it in dudgeon, as a *université pour rire*. I was cross with him for having been so devastatingly aware. Young men and old men have each their own unrealism; the one of illusion, the other of ambition. Each sins against modesty. It is true that my University College was far from its immodest notion of itself; yet if it was a joke it was not, as Windle saw it, merely a joke. It has often reminded me of the folk tale which tells how a bridegroom was bedded in the dark, enjoyed throughout that first night of passion complete happiness and total satisfaction, and woke in the morning to find himself lying beside a beautiful stranger. He lived on with her, happy ever after, though occasionally, I conceived, wondering in certain secret, smiling moments what that other lost girl might have been like. I was happy for some five years in that cheating bridal bed. What riches of the sense if not of the mind, of the emotions if not of thought, its library alone gave me! I spent countless hours lounging in the club or outside on its grassy banks, arguing, dreaming, hoping, mocking, conspiring, flirting and, so, learning from my fellow students. And how constricted my whole subsequent life might have been in some dead-end, menial job if I had not for those years enclaved myself in this slightly absurd Lilliput!

What would that other lost college have been like? Harvard? London? Oxford? Mr Bloom used to wonder, 'Happier now, happier then?' Happier here? Happier there? I cannot imagine that I could have been happier anywhere else, and one would need another life to try. It sufficed for me that I was not pushed, pulled, stuffed, crammed, directed, advised, admonished or controlled in any formal way. Nobody kept a roll call. If I did not want to attend lectures nobody seemed to care. If I did not want to study there was nobody to check me. Themes were rarely exacted. I enjoyed the total freedom of the free student in his free-roving studies. The set texts were mere starting points, and any bright student could have mugged them up in a couple of months: books like Newman's *Idea of a University*, Burke's *Reflections*, Palgrave's *Golden Treasury*, five or six plays by Shakespeare, a few essays of Matthew Arnold, Stephen Gwynn's *Masters of English Literature*. All one had to do with them was to learn impressive bits to quote. Certainly if one worked hard, that is, gave back dutifully everything the professor said, one would get an honours in the examination. But why bother? All that counted was the final degree, and between the end of the first year and the end of the final year there was no examination at all. I got a pass in my first year. I met my old headmaster soon after, and he smiled at me. 'A pass? You young rascal! You had a nice soft year!' From no other quarter did there come even a word of reproof. Nor from my conscience. I had been devouring that library.

We were not really all that free. I soon peeled off a few scraps of the illusion, which nevertheless persisted – I was no Joyce who saw through his college in Dublin within a matter of months. I peeled off one scrap the time I proposed that the Students' Club ought to have a small browsing library of modern Irish novels and other books of topical Irish interest. A local businessman, later a senator, James Dowdall, generously put up the money, I was appointed honorary librarian, and the books were duly installed. Within days the professor of education, a maiden lady of such highly genteel ways that we called her Feathery Ellen, observed among the novels Joyce's *Portrait of the Artist as a Young Man*. She at once had it removed. On another occasion I dropped into the suggestion box of the main library the proposal that it ought to have some of the novels of Emile Zola. I got the astonished reply: 'But who on earth wants to read Zola at this date?' It was vain for me to answer that I was curious about Zola and wished to understand the course of the modern novel. Zola was not added to the library. Intellectually speaking we led the Simple Life in UCC.

Had our little city down in its hollow, below the college on its outcropping rock, been a large and lively city, we students might have found there a balance to our own and the college's simplicities. How pleasant it would have been if we could have descended there to museums, art galleries, regional periodicals, a publishing house or two, a sister university, a symphony orchestra, all those things that commonly go with the long-continued presence of a cultivated tradition emanating from wealthy drawing rooms, old houses, old families. Cork, as I have tried to suggest, is a charming place in several ways, but it is not that kind of city. Whatever Jo Gould might think, his beloved city had decided limitations. Those of size and variety might be indicated simply by our common use of the definite, defining and confining singular article: the fountain, the Lough, the library, the college, the baths, the cricket field, the lower road, the top field, the regatta, the paper, the park, the statue. Only one of my professors seemed to realise the crippling effect of the mere size of the place on young people mainly drawn from a rural hinterland. He was old W. F. P. Stockley, my professor of English. About twice a year he would invite a group of us to his home, a charming old house with wrought-iron balconies, overlooking the wide Lochs of the Lee at Tivoli – now utterly destroyed by crude commercial ambition – its pink-washed stucco front covered in summer by grey-blue wisteria. There in his delightful drawing room upstairs he and his lively German wife would show us his pictures – he had some excellent Walter Osbornes – or arrange a play-reading, or she might play Chopin, or persuade her friend Frau Fleischmann, a highly talented pianist and most kindly woman, to play for us. The tea would be handed around ceremoniously, in old china on old silver, and they would struggle to draw us out of our shyness and awkwardness and lure us to talk as if we were not hobbledehoys but the grown men and women we pretended to be. If only for these gestures of kindness, as well as for his natural courtesy and dignity, if only indeed for his picturesque appearance, bearded, always capped and gowned, I am deeply grateful to his memory and the memory of his wife Germaine.

Alas, as a teacher he was a comical figure. This was unfortunate for me, because he was not only the sole English professor in the college but my main professor – I was taking honours in English. His mind was like a lady's sewing basket after a kitten had been through it. His lectures were a host of bright scraps of quotations and casual references all jumbled colourfully together without order, sequence or evident purpose. It used to be said of him that he was the only man who ever spoke and wrote without using verbs. We were lucky if we took away from an entire fifty minutes of him a single reference to a book, thrown at us with a commanding air that impressed us with its relevance or usefulness without conveying why it possessed either. We might carry away from his sonorous jumbles no more than one gnomic phrase like the words of a town-crier heard over the babel of a fair, and afterwards, in the quadrangle, cluster together to ask one another unhappily what this phrase implied. We might take away one name repeated so often that, like people hearing a ship's bell in a fog, we would guess at a presence that we would never see. He struck again and again on certain such favoured names, Burke, Newman and Arnold, and these we would relate to anonymous phrases like 'In religion it is the whole man that moves', or 'Opportunism in the *best* sense', or 'The world is governed by go-betweens', until we formed a firm idea that these must be men and matters worthy of our attention, though why they were worthy of attention he never could, anyway certainly never did, explain.

He was, I now think, an honorable soul without an iota of intellectual persistence who, over the years, possibly from lack of challenge, had ended up as something midway between a sentimentalist of literature and a playboy of a professor. He never brought written lectures with him, only a pile of texts. In the margins of their pages he had written brief notes, on top and bottom, to the right and left, so that his books and his head kept rotating as he reread them. He had also for many years stuck into his texts small scraps of paper bearing further notes, so that his books had swollen to twice their natural size, broken their backs, and been rebound with large strips of sticking plaster. He had an endearing way of pausing over one of those scraps, folding back his gown, unbuttoning his overcoat beneath it, unbuttoning his woollen pullover under that, searching wildly in his waistcoat pocket – all the time staring at a fixed point in his scrap of paper – and then producing an inch of pencil with which he would stab in a dot or a comma. It did not make for clarity that he would then proceed with the rest of his sentence, whose beginning we had by then forgotten if indeed we had ever heard it. He was really the complement of my old friend at the Pres, my English teacher Doggy Sheehan; for whereas that arch-crammer had distended our memories to bursting point with unrelated data, Stockley inflated us with cloudy mystifications unrelated to any data whatsoever. Scourged by his vatic cries we ran from book to book, wildly gulping here, madly scrabbling there, creating new hungers daily. When I left that college I did not know what a bibliography was, how to compile a clear course of reading, how to attack any subject, ignorant of the difference between a conflation and a collation, a prime source and a secondary source, objective analysis and subjective feelings, how to compose a résumé, how properly to organise a theme.

And yet, somehow, he did contribute something to us. He was like a man who had travelled to the Land of Literature as another man might have travelled to China or Greece and come back glowing, stuttering, incoherent, but so obviously fired that his listeners, who could not understand one word he said, felt that he really had been there and that it might be worth their while to go there too. He was the worst of messengers, but he brought back at least his excited stutter. His colleagues brought back nothing but grammars and texts. The thought of him and others far less endowed must have driven Windle mad. And rightly so. I must have been one of thousands who left the place with a fogged mind. This was not an irrecoverable loss to me. I had the rare good fortune to go on to a real university, to Harvard, where I learned to my surprise and pain the simple lesson that even in literature facts are facts, and that if you say something about literature, however flashing, you must be able to substantiate it from the text. Besides, I was fated to be a writer, and if I did leave the place more than somewhat befuddled I also left it widely read – thanks to my hours in the library – undisciplined yet undiscouraged, untrained yet unspoiled, and still full of curiosity. As an American friend once said to me when I talked to him about University College, Cork: 'Well, Sean, it may have been a bum joint but it evidently suited you down to the ground.'

Cuius regio eius collegio. In the Cork of my youth any other kind of college would have been as unthinkable as a Cork *Ulysses*, even more unthinkable since the individual may flee from his environment to exploit it. Colleges do not fly. They stay, and are exploited. Does this come down in the end to provincialism versus precocity? The precocial bird moves freely as soon as he is hatched, like Stendhal quitting Grenoble, Maupassant and Mauriac leaving Normandy and Bordeaux, Ibsen eviscerating Norway from Rome and Ischia. If one lingers one may become mentally delayed by the confining region. One may with less danger go and return – as so many artists have done who at first glance might seem to have exploited their narrow cages entirely from within – men like Hawthorne, Hardy or Faulkner.

I, for good reasons or bad, lingered a long time in Lilliput. Thinking back on it, I am not astonished at my slow development. For contrast, I think, again and again, of Joyce. Unprovincial, Jesuit-trained. There is no getting away from the power of environment, though there are those who would minimise its power. They are not always the best illustrations of what they assert; as when Edmund Burke once said, 'The road to eminence and power from obscure condition ought not to be made too easy, nor a thing too much of course; if rare merit be the rarest of all things it ought to pass through some sort of probation' – and then promptly shook the dust of Dublin from his shoes, lived, worked, died and was buried, in the greatest elegance, as far away as he could conveniently get from the country of his probation. Cork is in many ways a place of great appeal. Grant an extroverted man a fair number of piastres and a love of yachting, shooting, fishing or hunting and he could be very happy there. No intellectual or artist, however, could thrive there unless he got out of it frequently for refreshment.

In the whole history of the city *post urbem conditam* I can recall only one real writer who never left it, a most kindly, hospitable and sympathetic man, Daniel Corkery, who warmly encouraged Frank O'Connor and myself in our first efforts at writing. He was a teacher in an elementary school, a bachelor who, when I knew him, lived with a nearly blind old mother and a devoted, unmarried sister in a tiny suburban house on one of the north-eastern hills of the city. By unremitting self-discipline, for his profession was an exhausting one, he found time to start a Little Theatre, called *An Dún* (The Fort), wrote several romantic plays for it and published one novel of quality, *The Threshold of Quiet*, a far better novel than most Irish novels of the time, as well as some short stories of merit. Thereafter his environment exhausted him. His novel – a moving description of life in Cork City – bore the ominous epigraph from Thoreau: 'The mass of men lead lives of quiet desperation.' Its theme, less forcefully, even more disquietingly, points rather to a quiet resignation. Either might serve as a comment on the dehydrating nature of provincial life the world over.

In the boredom of Cork, I do not know what I would have done without his friendly door. How often, at night, sick of the college, even of its library, used I not come out of my front door in Half Moon Street, look up at the misty sky – it is a wet, damp city; its winters would give anybody *le cafard* – look right, look left, and not being a mixer nor a drinker have no place to go. Anyway, I had no money for drink. Dare I walk up the hills and knock again at Corkery's door? The poor man, having recovered from his day's slavery, was probably trying to get a few pages done. I would set off on an aimless walk, intending not to impose on him. I would impose on him. He never turned me away. After I got to know Frank O'Connor, he became an alternative victim. But he was three years my junior, fifteen to my eighteen, and I could not have counted on a fire in his house, or even a room to sit in, any more than he could have in my house, still full of lodgers and with, as with him, no other living room than the communal kitchen. If I did call on him we would walk around in the rain, sheltering in doors, talking literature.

Frank O'Connor as I knew him then, and later, was for years my only fellow-writer pal in that provincial city. The name 'Frank O'Connor' is the Yeatsian mask of a young fellow whose real name was Michael O'Donovan for whom, I once told him – we were rivals as well as friends from the start – the most interesting experience of his life was to meet me in a Gaelic League (Irish Language Revival) room one sleety night, over a hayloft in a side-street off one of the river-quays of Cork, called Queen Street after some queen or other from some such place as Saxe-Coburg. This room where we met was called *An Grianán*, which is the Gaelic for a queenly solarium. Horses champed in the stables on the ground floor. There was a gentle smell of old hay and fresh manure.

I was eighteen then, Michael was fifteen, slightly hooped, all specs, eyes and brow, the eyes myopic, the teeth ingratiating, the brow magnificent and prophetic of the genius he would display fifteen years later. He wore knicker-bockers, long, woollen, hand-knitted stockings and, to my fastidious distaste, black boots. With regard to those boots I realised that I must make allowances. I was, after all, a cut above him. His da, it seemed, was merely an ex-private of the Munster Fusiliers (RIP) while my father was a full constable of the Royal Irish Constabulary, the sort of man who put his sort of fellow into jug every night of the week for being drunk and disorderly, which, I soon gathered, Michael's da quite often was. This fine social distinction between us can be expressed in economic terms: when he had no money he was penniless; when, by some inexplicable oversight on the part of my dear parents, I had no money I was tuppenceless.

In spite of the black boots we took to one another at once and remained buzzums (*anglice* boozums, if not bessemas) for well over thirty years, fighting with or for one another against church (RC, tyrannical) and state; (Irish, free and even more tyrannical.) In other words we two youngsters lived in the blissful state of amicable antagonism natural to two rising young geniuses filled with sympathy for such failures as Balzac and Maupassant who had had no forewarning of the wonder-children coming after them. And if all the foregoing sounds a bit like a parody of the opening of one of 'Frank O'Connor's' more jocular and therefore embarrassing stories I must at once deny it. It is pure imitation, and no better than the original.

Michael's pseudonym symbolises several constants in his life and work such as his frequent and brilliant success in depicting characters whose genius it was to fail brilliantly and frequently in their zany efforts to strike some sort of a balance between their softer illusions and life's harder realities. Michael's contribution to these disasters was to make the illusions seem so reasonable and the realities so absurd that his readers, while enthusiastically applauding the elegance and the skill of his balancing act, could never be quite sure that it was not all being done by mirrors, rather like people at a conjuring show revelling in the joy of being conned. The pseudonym was also an act of prudent realism in so far as he adopted it only when he, very much later on of course, became a Dublin city librarian with a sword (i.e., a book about the Troubles) upstairs, shrewdly aware that if his employers were ever approached by one of the white-necked Black Mafia of that crazy period of unbridled censorship in Ireland which between 1930 and, say, 1950 must have banned as 'indecent and obscene' upwards of 10,000 books ranging from Amis to Shaw, Jomo Kenyatta to Brendan Behan, Defoe to Noël Coward, myself to both Kate and Edna O'Brien, those kindly employers could truthfully swear that they had no such man as Francis O'Connor on their books. 'What, Father! A man who would use such disgusting words as you have, alas, been obliged to mention – armpit, navel, tit, bottom! Unthinkable!'

His employers would protect him because they would subconsciously identify with him: most employers and employees of that later time had like Michael seen poverty close up.

It was only after he died and I could think of him not as a quondam friend but solely as a writer that I understood the origin of his technique. It was I feel sure his defence against the provincial environment of Cork just as Joyce's was his way of protecting his soul from (as he felt it) the spiritual paralysis of nineteenth-century Dublin: for the one, fantasy, warm laughter, drama; for the other, a Dantesque scorn, poker-faced satire and the stasis of his city-sized photograph album. Some defensive reaction is inevitable in every writer whom the gods drop into an antipathetic environment, a threat against which the artist must sooner or later concoct an anodyne to preserve his personality. Daniel Corkery observed that because of the British colonisation and conquest of Ireland we never enjoyed a Renaissance modernisation. He decided that the remnants of the old, preconquest Ireland, the apparently lost but actually merely hidden traditional Ireland was a medieval world, to be sought and still to be felt in our fields, farmhouses, lone islands, small towns and villages, with all their traditional rustic ways, especially when expressed in the already vanishing Irish language. He wrote one interesting if rather polemical book under the inspiration of these ideas, entitled *The Hidden Ireland*. In his old age he devoted himself wholly to the enthusiastic support of the Irish language-revival movement and to a stern disapproval, expressed in forcible English, of the unpatriotic practice of writing in English. He also ceased to be creative.

One sighs. There is none of us who does not make some lunatic misjudgment about the nature of his circumstances. The hard fact remains that it is all up with the artist who does not exploit his mistakes or obsessions, as Stendhal did with one amorous infatuation after another; as Yeats did all his life long, with the Celtic twilight, the Irish Republican Brotherhood, Maud Gonne, Madame Blavatsky, Rosicrucianism, spiritualism, spirit writing, even Fascism for one brief, idiotic moment towards the end of his career; as George Moore did with Bohemianism, Zola, the Irish language revival, the Irish literary renaissance; as Joyce did with religious mania – at one stage of his young life he used to recite the rosary piously while walking along the public street – with his calf-love for Mary Sheehy, with his drunken Bohemianism in Dublin, with his crazy plan for establishing a cinema circuit in Ireland. Otherwise it would seem that there are certain situations to which the only answer is a clean pair of heels from the soft smother of the provincial featherbed.

Smother? A smother, I think, of complacency chiefly, which is an offshot of vanity, which as we all learn to our cost can lead anywhere, from smugness to *hubris*. If Corkonians have any outstanding characteristic, apart from their immense drive and ambition, it is that of never thinking small beer of themselves. They will try anything, sometimes with embarrassing results. The other day, I came on a complete set of a tiny periodical called *The Day*, or in Irish *An Lá*, issued in my time by a small group of Cork intellectuals who had founded a club called the Twenty Club – twenty members – in the gallant hope of keeping the smother at bay. The very touch of it acted on me like the morsel of madeleine on Proust; for I used to attend the meetings of this club, in an upstairs room, in a back lane behind Saint Augustine's Church, paved in wood blocks to dull the sounds of passing horses and carts, almost directly opposite a secluded little stationer's shop, run by the Wallace sisters, where rather more realistic men, all unknown to us, had established the city HQ of the IRA. (I, equally ignorant of what those backroom boys were up to, used also to frequent Nora Wallace's shop to buy nationalist weeklies; and, again unknown to myself, was thereby suspected for a while of being a spy because I was a policeman's son.) I recall that I even read a paper to the Twenty Club, being then about nineteen, whose nature will indicate that all the club really achieved was another smother: it was a paper on Tolstoy written out of the abysses of total ignorance of my subject. I am grateful for having been allowed to do it. It was good practice. But even I could see that not more than three people present had read more Tolstoy than the little I had, and that most had never read anything by him at all.

We were not even provincial; we were parochial; and as I turn the roughly printed, hand-set pages of this long-defunct *The Day*, this is its pervading mark and signature. Little local jokes on the lines of: 'What a disgrace! No member of the Twenty Club has yet been nominated for parliament!' Or cries of patriotic despair on the lines of: 'Last Saint Patrick's Day we heard a woman buying a brush in a shop in Old George's Street say, "But it must be English, please!" '

Now and again, very rarely, a page lights up with a prose sketch by somebody like Con O'Leary, one of the ablest journalists his generation ever presented to Fleet Street, posted, alas, from London; or a piece in which I recognise the talented hand of Dan Corkery. I turn the pages in infinite sadness not unmixed with terror at the thought of the power of place to constrict, even to kill. Harder-minded men may say, 'Well, they should have got *out!*' But, as we know, people do not realise their danger when they are being played on passively. In those years I had no least sense of being in danger. All I felt was the pleasant feeling of the featherbed. I had no wish to leave Cork. I derided anybody who did. I was in love. And, soon, there was revolutionary politics.

I had not been up more than a term or two when a student approached me one morning in the quad and asked me if I would join the college company of Irish Volunteers. (We had not yet begun to speak of the IRA, which sprang from the Volunteers.) Straightway my whole life changed. The university became a conspiracy. I was now both a student and a revolutionary. Never will I forget the first day I stood in a field, in a deep glen, somewhere to the southwest of the city, with a score of other raw recruits, being given my first drill by some older student, while along the two hills overlooking the glen other Volunteers stood on the lookout for police or military. Before we were dismissed our captain, Ray Kennedy, a lecturer in the Chemistry Department, spoke to us about what we were, and were there for, about the coming fight, about secrecy and loyalty. It was an autumn day of sun and shower, and just as he began to speak to us a faint, gentle sprinkling rain began to fall on us, and then the sun floated out again and sparkled on every leaf and blade of grass as if some invisible presence had passed over us with a lighted taper, binding us together not only in loyalty and in friendship but in something dearer still that I am not ashamed to call love. In that moment life became one with the emotion of Ireland. In that moment I am sure every one of us ceased to be single or individual and became part of one another, in union, almost like coupling lovers. It was a supreme experience to know that you may not only admire your fellow men, or respect them, or even like them, but that you can love them so much that they have no faults, no weaknesses, so that you will never distrust them even for a second, and will forgive them every slightest minor fault or flaw as they will yours. This extraordinarily heart-lifting revelation, this gaiety, this liberation of the spirit, was to stay with us all through the exciting years to come. If any of the youths and young men of those days should chance to read these lines today I am sure that he will make no wonder of them. He will acknowledge that I am describing something very simple that happened to us all when we were not bald or grey, paunching, tired or sceptical, when in our generous youth we lived and were ready to die for one of the most wild, beautiful and inexhaustible faiths possible to man – faith in one's fellows.

'Yes, yes, no doubt!' the testy spirit of Sir Bertram Windle might say, still our president in University College on this eve of the Troubles. 'But you might have found and felt this faith anywhere! If you had been young enough you might have known this love of man on the fields of Flanders or the beaches of the Dardanelles. You might have even had your IRA if you had never gone to University College. All this has nothing whatever to do with that dreadful place!'

It is true. I might have. As a matter of autobiographical history this gift of faith came to me within those battlements of unlearning. It was not printed in the University Calendar. It never is. Students the world over write it in.

10

The Troubles and My Trauma

I

A student's war memoirs? One thinks of Fabrizio del Dongo's hussar's-eye view of the Battle of Waterloo. His experience of it lasted three minutes, and afterwards he said, 'Was that a battle, and if so was it Waterloo?' Fabrizio could, however, have said, years after, 'I once took part in a big battle', whereas many a man trained for guerrilla fighting has had to wait a year and more before taking part in even a small action, and most such men never fire a shot. I have met several men who were commandos in the last war and asked each of them how many men he had killed. One said one; the others said none. In my six years as a rank-and-filer of the IRA I shot nobody and I was briefly under fire once. I have no war memories to record except to say: 'Were those the Troubles? And if so was it a revolution?'

I was never cut out to be either a soldier or a killer. I did not feel like one, and I never looked like one. In my college days I opted finally not for rugby and a pipe, or tennis and flannels, but for a black poet's hat, long poetic hair, and Irish tweeds. I had grown so fast that I was as lanky as a stork. I think I looked like someone halfway between James Joyce and Willy Yeats when they were in their twenties. To have cast me for the role of gunman would have been like casting me as a bullfighter.

The great majority of us rank-and-filers were given such undemanding if essential jobs as the gathering of more or less useful information, watching over the billets of the fighters, scouting, carrying dispatches, doing police work, helping to trench roads or fell trees across them in order to hold up reinforcements when an ambush was due, marching in the public streets to defy some military order against it, perhaps standing guard at the public lying-in-state of some patriot, as it was my honour to do over the body of our Lord Mayor Terence MacSwiney, who died after seventy-four days of hunger strike in Brixton Prison in London. Otherwise we hung around, drilled, waited, felt nervy, groused, and were supremely proud and happy whenever even the most modest task made us feel we were really doing something positive in the struggle for independence.

There was only one thing that every one of us knew he could do well, and must do well if called on to do it, the least active rank-and-filer, the humblest citizen. If arrested and condemned for any or no reason, each man knew that he could die – 'For Ireland!' This is not romanticism; the time for being romantic about those years has long since gone; and any young man of those years, and they were enough, who died facing a firing squad may well have been white and terrified at the end. But it must surely have helped him to know that he was dying for something he believed in as fervently as we believed in Ireland then. I wish to God I could believe in anything as fervently now. I think there was only one thing we really feared in our bones – torture. The Black and Tans in their dark jackets and khaki trousers, and the Auxiliaries, generally a much finer body of men physically, in their Glengarry caps, tight waists, riding breeches and puttees, their guns strapped to their thighs, could be bastards at this. Nobody wanted to contemplate being stripped, having his testicles rhythmically beaten with a swinging revolver butt, his eyeballs persistently rapped with the ends of fountain pens, bayonets stuck in him, his feet stamped to pulp, his toenails pulled out, and more; all the things that English gentlemen just do not do, nor French, nor Jews, nor Irish, nor Americans, nor anybody, but are done by them all, are being done, one need have no least doubt, somewhere at this moment, and will always go on being done in time of war.

The Irish Troubles have been overdramatised, partly because they were the first successful fight against colonialism. In fact we got off lightly by comparison with later anti-imperialists like the Cypriots, Algerians and Africans. What would our lot have been supposing we had been a Mediterranean island fighting France after Europe had become thoroughly inured to the savage techniques of total war? It is true that fighters often had to live under conditions of almost unbearable strain; but for most of the people the Troubled Times, as they were modestly called, bore no comparison to the experiences endured so long and so tenaciously by later revolutionaries elsewhere. Think alone of the mere length of the Algerian struggle against France. In point of time our people did not have to suffer the full voltage of British military oppression for much more than the one year and a half that lay between the spring of 1920 and the truce of 1921. I remember the happy holiday Eileen and I spent in Cape Clear Island even as late as the summer of 1920. We were, indeed, aware, along the way, of the occasional presence of those new strange-looking units, half soldiers, half policemen, in khaki trousers and black police jackets, but we had as yet no suspicion of the brutalities of which this scum of England's earth was capable.

To give a fair measure of the strain during the full-voltage period I take two typical incidents. I remember the anger with which we read of the first in the newspapers – a shocked report that British troops had burned a village to the ground in County Tipperary. It transpired that a bunch of the local Black and Tans had burned down the market house of this small country town. No doubt the townsfolk were frightened and in danger. But after all, we *were* at war. Not, God knows, that I want to minimise what the country people endured: even one murder is infinite, one riddled and mangled body a total horror. When things really hotted up, any ambush was at once followed by a descent of Tans, Auxies and military on the whole area, and while they were berserk every village cowered, every lonely cottage was sleepless, every horizon glowed with houses burned and looted in reprisal. The other incident, one of the most outrageous lootings and burnings of the whole period, came to be known, and is still known, as the burning of Cork. That night military, Auxiliaries and Tans, infuriated by an earlier IRA attack, decided to inflict their own private reprisal. One lot descended howling and shooting like a posse of brigands on the main shopping street of the city after midnight, set a length of one side of it on fire and looted the shops wholesale; another lot, less interested in looting, burned the city hall. It all made a blaze as comparatively wicked, destructive and terrifying as a bad blitz attack on central London. Yet, it is not accurate to say that 'Cork' was burned, and there was only one fatal casualty.

It is difficult neither to exaggerate nor to minimise when remembering such things. The Troubles were like a fever chart, away up today, smooth enough tomorrow, blazing here, happily quiet there, every day unpredictable, and one tends to telescope them all in the memory. They have, too, been painted in over-dark colours by later writers. Nobody reading, say, O'Flaherty's fine novel *The Informer*, or coming away from O'Casey's famous play *The Plough and the Stars*, would guess that really for so many young men 'bliss was it in that dawn to be alive.' As my friend Dr S. C. Andrews, later top man in Irish Railways, then known as Tod Andrews, as active a fighter as Dublin ever produced, shrewdly pointed out, the albums so assiduously compiled in the internment camps during those years show that these men loved Ireland and loved life with equal fervour, loved poetry and song, were gay, not gloomy all through those troubled years.

The truth of it is that they were both wonderful times and nightmare times. Even still, after forty years have blunted my worst memories of them, I still frequently awake sweating from a nightmare that has whirled me back among them again. The worst of it was the war of nerves, for, in the long view, the aim of the British was not only to break the nerve of the fighters but to break a whole people; and before the end came they had, by countless devices, come dangerously close to doing just this. They closed life in on us tighter and tighter every month through a varied, incessant and inventive terrorism, constant and often pointless raids and arrests, humiliating and brutal beatings-up in city streets, casual murders on country roads, reprisals both unofficial and official – which usually meant the burning down in public of a sympathiser's home and business – early curfews that locked us up in our houses and reduced the city to a desert hours before the sun set, after which the Tans, who operated outside every known law and war-convention, roved the dark streets in search of victims or loot. The order of the nights was sleep broken or made shallow by rifle bursts, or by one sudden single shot in the street below which might well be followed by a scream, or by the ominous rumble of a patrolling armoured car or truck with a searchlight sweeping slowly across the faces of the houses, pausing perhaps at one's own particular home or window; and then, it might be an hour later, another crackle of fire followed by the sound of running feet had you sitting up wide-awake, tense, imagining what might be going on, wondering fearfully if Running Feet had got safely away. Holidays were, of course, quite out of the question; indeed, all prolonged respites, and even the smallest of them that one could invent, were likely to be shattered by an explosion of the war of nerves.

One has to work hard to hang on to normal life. I remember the college dances we held in the late afternoons, during those curfew periods, fitting blackout curtains to the tall Tudor windows to create an artificial night. In complete gaiety we would forget everything outside for the first couple of hours. Then the men would begin to look at their watches calculating how long it would take to see the girls home and then get back to their own homes before the lorry loads of military and Tans rolled into the streets to close them down for the rest of the night. I recall one such evening when, having seen my girl to her home, I was hurrying along my already empty quay off Half Moon Street with just five minutes to go. A Lancia truck, wire-netted against bombs, loaded with Tans, drew up behind me; three of them jumped out, revolvers drawn, and grabbed me. Then, while the rest of them leaned over the side of the truck with expectant grins, they searched me and questioned me, told me that all students were fucking Sinn Feiners, laughed at my protests that I was a loyal citizen of the Empire ('Wasn't my own father a Royal Irish Constabulary man?'), threatened to shoot me in the guts, to strip me, to throw me in the river, to kick my balls flat, to throw me into the Lancia as a 'hostage' – a common trick of theirs, meaning that I would be tied with my wrists over my head to the peak of the netting, and that if they were attacked during the night by the IRA I would pay for it – and finally, tiring of their fun, they ordered me to prove my alleged loyalty by singing 'God Save the King'. I thanked my stars for the days when I used to be a good, pro-British little boy, and used to go with my father on Sundays up to the Victoria Barracks to see the church parade, which always ended with the band blaring out the royal anthem. I threw out my chest, in imitation of those days, and sang it for all my lungs were worth:

> Send him victorious,
> Happy and glorious,
> Long to reign over us,
> God save the King.

'Right,' one long black-visaged fellow said. 'Now run, you bastard! You've one minute by my watch to get to that corner.'

Not much assisted by a boot in my behind I ran, remembering how many men had been found with a bullet in the back and announced later to the press as 'shot while attempting to escape.' The truckload cheered and roared with laughter. I reached the corner just as the bullets crashed after me. But they were, after all, humane. They had not meant to shoot to kill. They were just encouraging a little more nerves. It was not even a story worth telling afterwards, except to raise a laugh. The stories that were worth telling produced grim silence or whispered curses: they had blood on them.

The only men to whom the Troubles gave no least respite were our regular fighters or guerrillas, few in number, who carried the full strain of the fight, day in and day out, on their backs, whether in risky ambushes in city streets or in the open countryside. For these men every day was intense, exhausting and relentless: they could never slacken. They had to be few because they had so few arms. One of the most able and active of the guerrilla leaders in West Cork, Tom Barry, records in his published memoirs, *Guerrilla Days in Ireland*, that in his entire brigade area, in that spring of 1920, all he could muster against some three thousand war-hardened British military and police, Auxiliaries and Black and Tans, was thirty-five rifles and twenty revolvers or automatics, with about thirty rounds for each rifle and twenty rounds for each small arm. There never was an Irish Republican Army constantly in the field. The fight was carried through by those tremendously gallant few, darting here and there for an ambush, folding back into their 'normal' lives until they could get another crack at the enemy. They could not, it must always be said, have done anything without the silence, patience, and loyal help of the whole people.

2

Since, then, I did nothing worth recording between 1920 and 1921, when did I ask myself: 'Was that a battle, and if so was it Waterloo?' My 'battle' began after the first stage of the Troubles was over, and we broke into civil war amongst ourselves in bloody disagreement over the conditions of peace accepted at the end of the first stage of the Troubles by the majority. This battle of mine was to oppress me traumatically for many years. It centred and spread out from my growing realisation of our leaders' folly, which reflected the folly of all of us, in having entered the revolutionary fight in the years after 1916 unprepared for its political outcome. But why do I say 'after 1916'? I believe that we do not even yet clearly understand the origins of our struggle, which, one presumes, must have determined its ultimate harvest; and I say this knowing well, and partly because I do know it so well, that nine Irish readers out of ten will at once prove its truth by denying it – by going back, if necessary, to the immorality of the Norman invasion and moving forward in waves of justifiably passionate anger through the Tudors, Cromwell, and the penal laws to the monstrous cruelty of the land laws of the nineteenth century, which resulted in the Great Famines. By 1916, however, all this had become past history. Through one reform after another the British had, under the pressure of Irish agrarian unrest, removed all, or almost all, of the agrarian injustices and disabilities resulting from the original colonisation of Ireland, and the effects still remaining were either so few, or so obviously fated to die away in the course of time, or were even so beneficent – such as the investment of capital – that when we got our autonomy it would have occurred only to our half-dozen crypto-Communists to touch them. Most historical motivations of the 1916 Rising and the armed fight that followed had by that date become purely emotional impulses. As for the other and far more powerful

143

impulses behind our fight – for, since it took place, they must have existed – I confess that I still am unsure about them, since they have not, even to this day, been investigated by any modern-minded historian; that is, by a man concerned only to identify and record the complex of social and economic pressures on the depressed urbanised surplus of the countryside that really decided the beginning of our last fight for freedom, determined its course and foreordained its outcome.

To such matters only one of our leaders, the socialist James Connolly, shot in 1916, paid any real attention. The attitude of the others recalls the wry story of the English journalist who, soon after 1916, plied the general secretary of Sinn Fein, Paudeen O'Keeffe, with so many insistent questions on the lines of 'What are the practical aims of this movement?' and got so many unsatisfactory answers that, in the end, he said in some slight exasperation: 'Mr O'Keeffe, would you at least say what exactly you yourself want?'

At this O'Keeffe, a small, dark, fiercely moustached Celt, banged the desk with his fist and roared: 'Vingeance, bejasus!'

That was about as far ahead as any of us saw the course before us. We took it fence by fence, a rough-riding, indecorous, hell-for-leather point-to-point. Fight first, think afterwards. Get rid of the British, and all the rest would follow naturally.

We began with the noblest dreams of undefined liberty. To recall how noble and how indefinite they were I reread last night *Principles of Freedom*, Terence MacSwiney's essays. They are high-minded essays, their ideals are as pure and generous as the life he gave for them, and nothing that he there said presents a human picture of a demonstrable, different, desirable mode of life in a free Ireland. An early Garibaldian might have written those essays and lived on after 1870 to wonder at the distance between his noble aspirations and the actuality of united Italy. Our leaders after 1916 were not thinkers. They played their revolution by ear. They were almost to a man gallant, idealistic, untutored, inexperienced and unworldly.

It may be asked, in some surprise: 'But surely your leaders had a social or democratic programme for the future Ireland?' I do not know whether to say they had or they had not, because the fact is that they did produce in the underground Sinn Fein 'parliament' or Dail of 21 January 1919, a slight document, in Irish and in English, covering less than five pages of print, called a democratic programme. Since the entire proceedings of this 'parliament' of such elected representatives as were not then in British jails lasted from 3:30 p.m. to 5:20 p.m., and the entire record of everything said and read out during that one hundred and ten minutes occupied some twenty-six pages of print in the published reports thereof, the proposed democratic programme of the Revolution – which was never again reverted to – was listened to and discussed for precisely twenty minutes and fifty seconds, and then buried forever. In any case, its terms were of a purely pious and general nature that committed nobody to anything in particular. The policy of Sinn Fein had always been since its foundation that simple formula: Freedom first; other things after. Not unnaturally what happened after was that when 'freedom', thus undefined, did come a civil war came afterwards. We have not been the only anti-imperialists to make the same mistake. I doubt if any of our successors made it with such a vengeance as we did.

If ever a revolution was run on faith, hope and charity ours was. It was a heartening experience while it lasted. We saw men and women at their best, transformed beyond all mortal frailty. It was a time that made one, afterwards, when the glowing bubble broke, look about one unbelievingly, asking, 'Can these be the same people?' So might a man look at an old love thirty years after it was all over, unable to comprehend her former beauty and power.

The payoff was in proportion on that glorious day when the fighting stopped in the silence of a truce offered by the British and accepted eagerly by our leaders. At that moment we heard a quietly ominous voice in our celestial omnibus say: 'Please fasten your safety belts, we shall be landing in a few minutes.' The first man to alight was Mr De Valera. Behind him, one by one, step by step, we all came slowly down to earth: down, that is, to the cold consideration of what he, after much preliminary sparring in private and public, defined as the problem of 'how the association of Ireland with the community of nations known as the British Empire might be best reconciled with Irish national aspirations.' Then, and only then, did we begin to consider in a pragmatical way how much of whatever it was that we thought we wanted we might reasonably hope to get: a mental and moral adventure which was to prove far more demoralising for all of us than anything that had gone before. Shaw once said to me that Savonarola – whom on the same occasion he rightly called 'a political failure and a fool' – thought that everybody should live forever on top of Mont Blanc because he had found that he could live there for five minutes. In that bitter truce-year of 1921–1922 and more so in the two years of civil war that followed it, my fellow men and myself came down from Mont Vert and revealed ourselves on more temperate altitudes as mortal men. I do not regret the experience – if only because its conflicts gave me something to mull over and write about – but I confess that I have been much more contented since I put things in their place. It took me over thirty years to do it.

The least intelligent IRA man in 1921 I knew that what he ideally wanted in political terms was a free Irish Republic; that is, a completely autonomous, all-Ireland, Republican parliament completely cut off from that source of evil, the British Empire. From the start it became clear that this was out of the question, since, apart from valuable trade connections, which we did not want to lose, neither the British nor our fellow countrymen in the northeast, mainly Protestant and imperial-minded, would tolerate it for other reasons, political, religious and strategic. Mr De Valera frankly admitted as much in his outline draft for 'A Treaty of External Association with the British Common-wealth' which, with the full agreement of his cabinet, he drew up and presented to each of the five envoys plenipotentiary who crossed over to London in October 1921 to negotiate the final settlement with Britain. This draft treaty accepted the principle of 'association', albeit external, with the Commonwealth. He provided, in a later modification, for local autonomy, under an all-Ireland parliament, for the Protestant northeast. Still later, his cabinet agreed that as a symbol of the proposed association the Irish delegates might recognise His Majesty as head of that association. Still later, under the fierce pressure of the nego-tiations, Mr De Valera agreed that he would accept an oath

146

recognising His Majesty as head of the association he proposed. And there trouble at once began.

Somebody has said that we Irish have an Oriental passion for abstract argument, adding that Arabia begins at Dublin. If so, we had our bellyful of it from then on as we began to wonder, to discuss, to argue crossly, and finally to quarrel bitterly over what each of us might mean, and all must agree to mean, by such unfamiliar terms as association, external association, oath of recognition, of acknowledgment, or even of allegiance to a head or to the headship of an association, and so on, blinded and dazzled as we were by our ikons, caught in the labyrinth of our dearest symbols – our Ancient Past, our Broken Chains, our Seven Centuries of Slavery, the Silenced Harp, the Glorious Dead, the tears of Dark Rosaleen, the miseries of the Poor Old Woman, the Sunburst of Freedom that we had always believed would end our Long Night and solve all our problems with the descent of a heavenly-human order which we would immediately recognise as the reality of our never-articulated dreams.

The result was what one might expect. After some three months of negotiations in London, and constant goings and comings between London and Dublin discussing fine constitutional points of honour, the harder-headed men among our envoys plenipotentiary took the bit between their teeth, turned their backs on Mr De Valera's honourable subtleties, broke their agreement to sign nothing until he had agreed to the fine details (he had most unfortunately chosen not to be himself one of the envoys plenipotentiary), and all five of them unanimously signed certain articles of agreement which the British produced as their final offer. The plenipotentiaries frankly signed them under duress after the British Prime Minister, David Lloyd George, entered the council room on the final evening and held up two envelopes, explaining solemnly that one envelope contained his final offer, the other a dispatch which a courier was waiting outside the door to transmit to the British HQ in Dublin ordering 'immediate and terrible war' if the offer was rejected. It was probably a bluff, but it worked.

I hasten, almost with averted eyes, over the rest. When the five envoys returned to Dublin the next day Mr De Valera battled gallantly but in vain to persuade his cabinet to disown them and to reject the articles they had signed on the grounds that they made Ireland an internal unit of the Commonwealth, agreed to an oath of allegiance to His Majesty, and envisaged an Irish Free State which did not explicitly include the northeast. The articles were duly put to the assembled Dail. There an orgy of word-combat between men and women who had once trusted one another like lovers but were now fast turning to mutual hatred and distrust at once began and went on for several weeks. It went on day after day. It was repeated night after night beside every fireside in the country. It was sealed in savage bitterness by the final ratification of the articles by a majority vote.

Perhaps the main reason for Mr De Valera's defeat was that he then was and always remained too abstract a politician for common understanding. Or the popular feeling may have been that he had himself gone so far in subtle compromise that he had reduced everything to sophisms beyond common understanding. His idea of 'external association' with Great Britain certainly puzzled most people. It is said that he was at one stage driven to explain this ingenious casuistry by means of a diagram, like this:

A (B)(C)

Here, A represented the Commonwealth, B represented Ireland residing within it, but in a different self-contained apartment from C, representing Great Britain. As an abstract idea it is quite intelligible. In practice it struck the British as leaving out of account the one small element which they considered essential to all political and many other 'associations' – loyalty to a common interest. They had a point. A priest and his curate could not run a parish on those lines, nor a man and woman succeed in marriage; no confederation of states, or cantons, has ever existed on this basis; and insofar as the British Commonwealth of Nations is approaching or has arrived at this attitude of mutual detachment it is ceasing or has ceased to be a commonwealth. Mr De Valera's Irish opponents were more cynical. They recognised the common interest, but with unstated, private reservations, and treated the hated oath of allegiance to the British Crown, which became the main symbol dividing them from him, as an empty formula implying neither contractual obligations nor loyalty to the Crown. As for our fellow nationalist Catholics in the North – now known as the Six Counties? We sold them down the river. The treaty was not to apply to them.

Civil War now threatened, between the forces of the new government of the Irish Free State and those recalcitrant forces of the IRA who had since the truce occupied public buildings and barracks in Dublin and various parts of the country, claimed the right to represent the symbolical Living Republic first declared during the 1916 Rebellion, and set up as a *de jure* if not *de facto* underground government during the Troubles. I took the Republican side. The only Ireland I knew and loved was the to me romantic Gaelic-speaking West, its hard ancestral memories, its ancient ways, its trackless mountains, small cottages, lonely lakes, ruined hermit chapels, wild rocky seas, and what on earth, I asked myself, had this primordial world to do with oaths of allegiance to rich, exploiting empires? The idea seemed incongruous, shameful, and a base betrayal. If I had been pressed to say for what, humanly speaking, I did stand, I might have held up my ragged gown and said I stood for the historical Underdog – for Wolfe Tone's 'men of no property'. If I were asked what exactly the Republican ideal could do for this old, beloved Ireland, and for these poor, that could not be done under the constitution of the Irish Free State, I would not have quite known how to say it. If some visible, human alternatives had been put imaginatively before us, it might have been different – a choice, say, between slavery, and antislavery as a base for society, like the polarity in Lincoln's day, or between socialism and capitalism, or between privilege and equality, even between clerical domination and secular rule, even between such urgent ideas (had they then been urgent) as freedom of speech and state censorship. . . . No such polarities presented themselves to us in the Ireland of 1921. I had nothing to guide me but those flickering lights before the golden ikons of the past, and a feeling that their natural enemies were all so-called hard-headed men whose ikons are indeed also golden – but not of the value, not all of them put together, of the simplest pieties of the old Ireland

149

for which these same men would once have died rather than by one least compromising word betray it.

But all this is me looking back, an ageing man, 'a paltry thing' as Yeats says, turned to a pillar of salt by bitter memories. All I now know for certain is that all I then had was a feeling for what I considered the side of pride and honour, with a deep suspicion that the men on the other side were letting material things get in the way of principles, or realism smother ideals, and that the upshot of their canny policy of compromise would be to destroy all our symbols. I am not even now sure that I was entirely wrong, or entirely right, for the sad and bewildering irony of this continuing doubt is that it has been both our 'realists' and our 'idealists' who keep it alive by their two different modes of evasion. The subsequent history of Ireland is no great credit to the 'realists', as I shall have occasion to say more fully later. And when I met and worked with a number of our 'idealist' leaders in Dublin, they struck me as being half crazed by the impossible task of holding to their ideals in a pragmatical world.

My final thought now is that as in religion and the arts, so in politics; if men do not balance feelings and intelligence they lose control of both – and worse still, of their object. I fear that in 1922 our realists said goodbye to too many of their feelings. I cannot say that we idealists said goodbye to our sense of realism, because, alas, if we had any worthy of the name I saw but little sign of it in those disheartening days of civil war.

3

Between the July of the truce in 1921 and the outbreak of the Civil War in June 1922 I was in my first job, as travelling salesman for a publishing firm that specialised in school texts: the Educational Company of Ireland. I called that summer of the truce my summer of the spruce. As a salesman I had to abandon my poet's hat and my baggy tweeds. I visited a good tailor, trimmed my hair, and grew a neat moustache to make me look a little older than twenty-one. I bought my first motor-bicycle, a smart little Douglas, the predecessor to a scarlet-red Indian that made a splendid roaring noise and could, if pressed, rise to sixty m.p.h. I came down from my old attic and had my own room, overlooking the School of Art and the square, papered in dark blue with cream woodwork and cream bookshelves. I had my own bankbook, and I know no other possession except a revolver that gives one such an immediate sense of power. Arms became so plentiful that year that even I got a lovely long-nosed Webley with which I found, to my delight, I was a very good shot.

All that year, while the debating and negotiating went on in Dublin and London, I visited and revisited every village and town in the south of Ireland, until there was not a school, convent, monastery, stationery shop, bookstore or country hotel that I did not come to know, with their teachers, lay and clerical, their shopkeepers, waiters, boots and barmaids. I made the acquaintance of their chilly dining rooms, linoleum-lined floors, grim food and damp beds, with a flowered chamber pot under every one of them. I got to know every commercial traveller on the road – and what good company they often were in the bar, or the commercial room at night, or on our long, slow, dismal rail journeys! No modern tourist travelling amongst us in complete comfort can have any idea of how uncomfortable travel in Ireland was in the 1920s. Trains could take hours over the shortest journey and they rarely arrived on time. One often trudged, in every sort of weather, lugging one's bags, from the station to the hotel, unless the town and the hotel were affluent enough to provide a horse-drawn hotel coach, in which I used to feel very grand if alone or with two or three companions, and very uncomfortable if there were more than six. Motorcars were still luxuries; only a very few commercials used them. The food repeated itself, in every sense, from hotel to hotel. I went shivering to bed by candlelight, clutching a brass or aluminium hot-water bottle in the ice-cold bed, washed from a ewer and basin in cold water that was probably the rainwater from a dank butt in the yard, and I shaved with exiguous moieties of hot water in brass jugs brought up by the boots. No town had a café. I cannot recall one with a cinema. There was nothing to do at nights but drink in the bar or play cards in the commercial room.

I enjoyed every day, every night, every minute of this voyage of discovery through my own country, not excluding the awful rail journeys; not even the once notorious, now extinct, West

Clare Railway that went in a slow, grinding, halting half-circle around the wild seacoast of Clare from noon to night, so that after my first experience of it I always carried a candle with me to stick on the window ledge if I wanted to read – no lights in any carriage, and of course no heat. In the winter months the porters lobbed in iron weights as ballast at strategic points along the coastline to keep the train on the rails when the wind was blowing in from the Atlantic. Indeed, at one station, called Quilty, there was an anemometer; when it recorded gale-force winds all traffic was halted there and remained at anchor until the storm abated. The most famous record of this West Clare Railway is Percy French's gay ballad, based on the guard's call to the driver before starting:

> Are ye right there, Michael, are ye right?
> D'ye think we'll get there before the night?

Its other motto is probably apocryphal: 'All third-class passengers get out and push!'

I enjoyed even more the little monorail, called the Artique, or L'Artique, also now extinct, that trundled across the bogs from Listowel in County Kerry to the superb sandy beaches of Ballybunion. This consisted of small carriages, split in two, slung over a single high rail, in which the passengers sat back to back facing outwards. It was the porters' task to balance fat passengers on one side with their equivalent weight of thinner passengers on the other: if there were not enough passengers the porters had to use sacks of sand to supply the equivalent weight. The railway crossings, for cows, were little wooden bridges.

I do not know any better job than that of a commercial traveller to get to know the life-way of a country, the general character of its people and its distinctive personalities through whom one may approach the profoundest problems of the land. I had just previously been reading with delight Gogol's *Dead Souls*; I already began to dream of writing its Irish counterpart; and if I had spent five to ten years as a commercial I might have done so, or tried to do so. But I was still too young, too ikon-minded, and too inexperienced. All that year I crossed the lives of hundreds of men and women who must have talked often about the one subject that was, or should have been, biting into everybody, the shapes of life that would emerge in a free Ireland. If they were talking in this way – but were they? Or were they, too, still caught by the dream? – I did not hear those worried voices of inspectors of schools, teachers, priests, hotel-owners, little shopkeepers, grubby-tailed waiters or the slattern maids who daily dished out the plates of potatoes, cabbage and bacon like a deck of cards around the commercials' table. I was happy, I was not frank-eyed, I was now about to pay for it, dearly.

4

Early one June morning in 1922 the newly-formed legal or Regular Army of the Free State drew its cannon down the empty quays of Dublin opposite the Four Courts occupied by the HQ of the dissident or Irregular IRA and began to bombard them; with, we true-green traditional Republicans savagely said, British-loaned guns; wearing, we snarled, khaki uniforms merely dyed green. I at once offered my sword, that is my long-nosed Webley, at the IRA headquarters in Cork. To my disappointment, instead of packing me off to die for my ancient birthright they enrolled me as a bomb-maker, an essentially inglorious job which girls could have done as well or better. There, all through that warm June and July, with three or four other men, all college men, I sat day after day from nine to five before the benches, among the jars of acid, the heating ovens, the boxes of grey, red and silver powder, making incendiaries out of rolls of cardboard and cotton wool, filling Mills bomb cases, constructing fuses, removing the bullets from .33 cartridges, refilling the charge grain by grain, carefully and tediously, inserting the wads, shellacking the caps, drying them over warmed metal plates – and so on, and so on, while outside in the sun lorries of armed men trundled in and out of the yard to and from the battle-front (between the Official Free State Army and the Irregulars' self-styled Republican Army) a very straggling, loose sparse and much-gapped line, which by then ran diagonally across the south-west of Ireland from the Shannon to the sea at Dungarvan.

In August the Free State Army suddenly landed its troops in

our rear at the town of Passage, just above Cork Harbour, and the bombshop was ordered to remove itself to the hinterland and the hills. We got hold of a truck and drove west, halting first at Macroom Castle, up to a year or so ago an impregnable barracks for Auxiliaries and Black and Tans, there set up our benches and once more and dutifully went to work. Within hours our retreating troops were after us. We could hear them coming all night long, in trucks, private cars, by horse and cart, using anything and everything they could commandeer, and when we rose the next morning we surveyed the image of a rout. Some of these men had been fighting nonstop for a week, and as they had poured into the grounds of the castle they had fallen asleep where they stopped, on the grass, in motor cars, lying under trucks, anyhow and everyhow, a sad litter of exhausted men. The extraordinary sight left us under no illusions as to our 'army's' capacity to form another line of battle. In fact there was nothing left for the majority of them to do but to scatter, go into hiding, slip back at night into the city like winter foxes and lie as low there as a hunted fox can lie in time of animal civil war, which is not at all, since in such times every man's eye is against his brother. All that winter those hunted, beaten, scattered Irregulars, as we all came to be known, were picked up and jailed in their thousands.

That afternoon of the rout we of the bombshop packed our baggage again and drove on deep into the mountains, almost as far as we could go without coming out on the other side, and after us came the few picked men who were to resume the old guerrilla warfare tactics of pre–1921. We set up our little factory in an abandoned cottage a mile or so beyond the village of Ballyvourney, at the start of the wild valley of Coolea, beside the tiny Bardinch River, a few miles east-northeast of that lonely lake of Gougane Barra which had been for so long Eileen's and my best-loved symbol of the Free Country. (The last I had heard of her was that she had been seen working with the women's auxiliary of the IRA, *Cumann na mBan*, passing out cups of tea and sandwiches to the endless files of fighting men retreating from the city, each man taking his ration with an exhausted hand, half asleep, too beaten to utter a word.) In our cottage we laboured over our bombs into the late autumn while the wet clouds lowered on the mountaintops, the rains fell, and the river rose in spate until we could hear the grumbling of its brown waters outside our door above the roar of the spirit lamps, the rattle of our pestles in the mortars, the hiss of the shaken sifters.

Only one incident ever held up our work. One day our captain, Ray Kennedy – he admitted afterwards that he had always warned us against doing such a thing – was experimentally mixing some powders with a spatula on a sheet of brown paper, a notorious conductor, when the mixture suddenly blew up into his face. We feared that he might have been blinded, and for a while there was a danger that his eyelashes would start to grow inwards. He recovered without mishap. The only reason I recall this incident is that I was sitting beside him, paying no attention to what he was doing, and on hearing the big bang I thought, 'The damn fool's been cleaning his revolver and he has shot me.' I felt no fear, just a slight spasm of irritation. He said afterwards that his reaction was, 'It works!'

I can believe that men thrown into action and shot suddenly may feel nothing but annoyance. It is the waiting for action, and the imagination that unmans men. Hemingway makes a similar observation in *The Short Happy Life of Francis Macomber*. An instance of this occurred a year or so later, when I and my friend Sean Hendrick decided to wander around the streets of Cork with a revolver apiece and have a pot at anything that came along. If it had come quickly I know that I would have had a shot at it. After we had wandered around for about an hour, my fore-imaginings so reduced my nerves to shreds that when a truck loaded with Free State soldiers did approach and Sean said 'Well?' I said 'No!' and funked it. They would have shot us to bits, of course, but what the hell had I expected? At first, nothing. Later, too much. No fighter!

During those dark months in Coolea and Ballyvourney I was often reminded of the Great Famine of the 1840s, when, it was said, the browning or blackened stalks of the rotting potatoes sent the smell of death into the air. We could all smell defeat in the air when we heard that the Free State troops were pressing after us mile by mile, establishing outposts stage by stage, until they were as near as Macroom Castle, a bare twelve miles due east of us, and, later, in the village of Inchageelah, nine miles beyond it to our southeast. It could only be, at most, a matter of months before they began to hunt us like wild game through the mountains unless we could hold them to the towns and villages as, formerly, we had held the British. It was unlikely that we could hold them, since during the Troubles the old IRA had been able to do it thanks only to the loyalty of the men, women and children who sheltered and fed them, guarded them day and night and informed them of the slightest British move. Now the people were divided, at best sullen and uncooperative, at worst hard against us. Besides, the fighting urge of the Irregulars was sinking rapidly. These men whom I saw around me were the same sort of men who had faced and beaten the British with an immense dash and courage in such ambushes as Kilmichael and Crossbarry, a hundred odd men against fifteen hundred, fighting sometimes throat to throat in kill-or-be-killed bodily struggles on the open road. They had no such heart for fighting against their former comrades.

I can recall only two attempted or proposed attacks on the Government forces in our area during that autumn and winter. The first was a night assault on the town of Macroom. Now, since towns had never been attacked in the past, this must have been intended as a vigorous thus-far-and-no-farther message to the Free State troops. If so it rebounded on itself, because it was not carried through. So far as we could ascertain afterwards from those who took part in it, all that happened was some distant firing. We of the bombshop had begged to be allowed to take part in this assault but were told, truly enough, that there were plenty of fighting men available and we were a valuable three or four. We were so sulky about it, however, that when a second attack was proposed our captain agreed that we should all take part in it.

It began in this way. Over at Gougane Barra with Erskine Childers, who was then in charge of publicity, was his old friend and relative David Robinson, an ex-British officer who had been in Tanks during the 1914 war, a tall, lean man with an appealing dry sense of humour, a keen zest for adventure, and a glass eye, whom we naturally called Deadeye Dave. Seeing, as was all too plain to be seen, even with his one eye, that we were fast turning into a dispirited rabble for lack of action, he proposed that a bunch of us should now attack and destroy the Inchagee-lah outpost. He took stock of the position simply by walking into the village disguised as a tramp; found that the outpost was a plain two-storey house which could not be approached unobserved because it stood in the middle of a small field; but also found, bordering this blockhouse, the kitchen garden and home of a Republican sympathiser who was willing to hang her linen to dry, on the night before the proposed attack, in such a way that the pendant sheets would form a cover behind which the assault could approach the house without being observed from the front. He also observed that there was only one sentry on the approach road, and he planned to deal with him by approaching him openly in a cart and donkey with two armed men disguised as tinker-women. Having disarmed him, Dave was to strip him, don his green uniform, and then, while his men closed in behind, walk up to the door of the still sleeping blockhouse 'and just blow it in.' He explained this plan in detail to the available men on the spot, fixed the timing carefully, and we all set off across country for billets on the hills north of Inchageelah under strict orders to report for action at six o'clock the next morning. I was in high spirits, facing my first action. I shared a bed and slept soundly with two other men of the bombshop while our captain tried his best to nod asleep sitting on a hard chair. The poor farmer who had taken us into his cabin probably slept on the stone flags of his kitchen.

It was a fine morning, and we four reported to Dave in good time. Below us lay the sleeping village. Dave was already dis-guised as a tinker, and had with him a couple of slightly built youths dressed as women, their guns belted on under coloured shawls. I think a couple of other stragglers turned up about half an hour late. We waited. And we waited. And gradually, and miserably, we understood. By the time the main body turned up, smoke was rising from the blockhouse chimney; its garrison was by now up, and fully on the alert. Under his burnt cork Dave was white with rage. He got up on a rock and addressed his men. He told us that we were not soldiers, and should stop playing at being soldiers. He told us to stop eating the poor people of the countryside out of house and home. He told us finally that it would be far better if the whole damn lot of us went home and did something useful like forking dung or digging potatoes. Then he said, 'Dismiss', and stalked away.

It took me a long time to understand exactly what had happened. Dave has been too ingenious and thoroughly untraditional. In the past all such outposts had been so heavily sandbagged and protected by labyrinths of coiled barbed wire that they could only be attacked late at night when the occupants were asleep. Then one or two daring men would creep on stockinged feet up to the front door, lugging a land mine with a fuse attached, stealthily place it in position, and tamp it if possible with a sack or two of sand. Meanwhile three or four others would as stealthily plant a long ladder against the gable end, climb up to the roof, laden with incendiary and Mills bombs, hauling after them a hosepipe attached below to a petrol pump, and wait for the mine below to go off. When it did go off their comrades would pour a fast and continuous covering fire at the windows of the barracks from positions in the front and rear, while the men on the roof hammered in a few slates, lobbed in the incendiaries and explosives and poured in petrol on the lot. This could go on for as long as four or five hours until the barracks took fire, the garrison would have to retreat from the front windows and the door could be rushed. It could go on that long because for miles around rank-and-filers would have trenched the roads or felled heavy trees across them; also because garrisons elsewhere had learned to be cautious about bringing up reinforcements, fearing to be ambushed on the way.

By comparison with this technique Dave's plan must have struck the experienced fighting men amongst us as completely crazy. A daytime attack? With no supports? They had listened to it sceptically, chewed on it, gone along with him still chewing on it, finally spat it out. They were then too devious or too polite to tell him what they thought, so they simply got up at their ease in the morning, had their breakfast at their ease, and turned up at their ease, too late. I did not feel quite so philosophical about it that morning. As I stood there listening to Dave's tongue-lashing I thought that what he said about playing at soldiers was dead right. After that even the bombshop began to seem pointless. Not that I thought so frankly and explicitly. I doubt if any of us acknowledged the facts. We were like a man in apparently good health and spirits who is doomed in his innards. My memory is now a surgeon performing a cure on myself or an autopsy on my friends. At the time, I went on thinking that I was enjoying my Fabrizian adventure.

Soon after the Inchageelah fiasco Erskine Childers was recalled to Dublin by the underground headquarters of the IRA and Dave went with him. They were captured by Free State forces. Childers was found to be carrying a revolver, and on that excuse he was tried and put before a firing squad by the first government of the country to whose struggle for liberty he had sacrificed his friends and fortune in its most friendless days. He was one of scores of Republicans executed during the Civil War. I do not like to think of those executions. Once, later when I was Acting Director of Publicity in Dublin, I came by an unpleasant photostat concerning them. It was a quartermaster's official issue for a number of bottles of whiskey to be drunk by firing squads. Before? Or after? I was too chickenhearted to publish it: the relatives of those executed men were still alive.

It may be part of my secretly developing trauma that I cannot now recall when, why or where the bombshop ended. On the other hand, it was a characteristic of those days that nobody had any sense of time: the day could have been Monday or Saturday, the date any date, the month any month, even the year any year, for all anybody cared. I think the end of the bombshop must have come shortly after Childers' death, because I was given his post as Director of Publicity for the First Southern Division. It was not as impressive a job as it may sound. He had at least possessed a typewriter, I had only pen and paper; but I had a fine comrade in Bob Langford of Cork City, who could have done the whole job as well and better alone. Bob was a very tall, handsome, aquiline man who had married a beautiful wife, had several children, and owned a sound printing business in Cork; he had sacrificed everything to come out into the mountains with one of his own hand presses to defend the Republic with his rifle or his press, whichever was most needed. We two set up his press in the kitchen of an abandoned, tumbledown farmhouse in a remote and sunless coom called *An Leaca Bán*, or the Grey Cliff, some five miles from Ballingeary village, and there I wrote my pieces and Bob set up the type while the mist dripped through the few leafless trees, or the frost rimed the grubby little windows. We never published more than a thousand copies of a single sheet and it took us a week to do that.

Bob and I got on well except for one small thing. It was typical of the trifles that rile people living on their nerves. Every morning before starting work he used to insist on seeing that day's *Cork Examiner*. Since he and I were supposed to be the fountaining centre of all reliable Republican news, I could never understand why he had the brass to consult what we considered an enemy newspaper, especially since it meant a long trudge every morning out of our dead-end valley down to the village of Ballingeary and back again – the waste of almost half a working day. It is only a small thing, but it makes me squirm at the thought of how arid and unimaginative I was becoming: after all, if I had left a wife and a family in the city, I too would have wanted to know everything I could about what was happening around them.

One morning a courier came to our farmhouse with the report that large numbers of Government troops had steadily begun to move westward out of Macroom shortly after dawn. They were said to be already halfway on the road west. Later, they were said to be moving in a fan sweep across the mountains. They were said to be accompanied by reconnaissance airplanes, and each soldier was reported to be wearing the shiny lid of a biscuit tin on top of his military cap so that the planes would easily recognise their own men. At this point the first ominous blanks began to appear in my memory. Bob and I must have locked the door of the farmhouse, grabbed our rifles and moved back up into the hills. I do not remember how or where we finally separated. All that is left to me after that is a series of disconnected images.

I see myself with about eight other men lining a ditch on a hillside outside the village of Ballymakeera – it was to be the final western village in our area occupied by Government troops – firing downhill at a long straggle of green-uniformed regulars approaching the village. This brief encounter was, so far as I know, the sole resistance offered to Government penetration into our last bit of West Cork. It was also to be my sole experience of warfare, apart from three rounds of forty-five that I was later to fire at a Free State truck in Cork after a long muscular and moral struggle either with my nervous system or the nervous system of a stuck revolver. All I got from either was the knowledge that the whine of bullets over one's head, whether at two hundred yards or twenty, is an unpleasant sound; together with an unbounded hero-worship for those men of the flying columns who faced and routed British forces ten times their number from on occasion as near as five yards, so that they were at times afraid of killing their own men.

After this incident I must have lost touch with my companions scattering back through the dusk into the foothills, because I next see myself, alone under a bright moon, on a blank mountainside. I am beside a tall standing-stone, older than the Bronze Age, lighting matches to try to decipher the ogham inscriptions incised along its sharpest edge.

Some more images return to me. I next find that I have somehow or other joined up with two other hunted men like myself in the low hilly ground to the south of Inchageelah, wandering aimlessly, driven by the winds of rumour, sleeping in barns and outhouses, eating whatever the poorest cottage could give us, usually tea and bread and, if lucky, an egg. It is poor autumn weather, with rain constantly threatening. I remember our coming on a group of men threshing late wheat, anxiously looking up at the flying clouds as they work at top speed, wondering can they get the job done before the rain falls. After that we three are crossing a swollen river on horseback to avoid taking an open road and a naked bridge. We are armed, and we are nervous, and we are only three. If caught while bearing arms we might end up that night against a barracks wall. I plainly see the three of us, later that afternoon, racing across a main road into the furzy field beyond it. Suddenly I hear an army truck coming around a bend of the road, and I fall flat behind bushes and small rocks with my heart pounding. As the noise of the truck becomes louder, and it at last comes into sight, I shoot home my rifle bolt and say to the man lying beside me, 'When are we going to fire?' In a loud, blasphemous whisper he asks me am I mad. At that word whatever little I have left of fighting spirit leaves me like the sneer of a dying balloon. (I later put the events of that day into a story called 'Fugue'.)

When did the odd incident of the parish priest occur? It must have come well after the condemnation of the Republican fight by the Irish Church, which declared that armed resistance to the Government as by law established was immoral, that any man or woman taking part in it was unfit to receive the sacraments, and was, in effect, therefore virtually excommunicated. Having said so, in solemn conclave, most of the bishops rested on their roars, but the then Bishop of Cork, Dr Daniel Cohalan, issued express instructions to his clergy that anyone who admitted that he was a supporter of the Republican Army must be refused the sacraments. This ukase was considered by all Republicans an abuse of clerical power. It was never to be forgotten, or forgiven.

One evening, somewhere in the hills, I am with a young man who is so deeply troubled by some thought or deed of commission or omission that he insists on visiting the local parish priest in his isolated presbytery. As the young man is carrying a rifle and a bandolier, and is patently an Irregular, the old priest at once refers him to his bishop's command and refuses to have anything whatever to do with him. The young man imploringly persists, until in the end the old priest so far relents as to say: 'Well, I cannot give you absolution! But if you go down there to my curate's house – he lives half a mile away, down by the main road – he might be a bit easier on you. He has a brother in the Irregulars.'

My friend at once drives this small advantage home: 'But supposing I run into the Staters on the way? Are you prepared, Father, to take responsibility for my soul if I am shot?'

The old man eyed him for a minute. Then he said: 'I'll go with you as far as my curate's door.'

And did so. I am sure his bishop would, after a brief theological consideration, have grudgingly approved.

I do not know how many more wretched weeks passed before I met with another kindly priest, but I do know it cannot have been long before Christmas. I was by now dirty – I had not had a bath or changed my linen for months – and, like most of us, I was suffering from itch, lice and those disgusting parasites we commonly called crabs. One wet night I took refuge in this priest's house, though why I have no idea: in those days one never questioned any occurrence, one lived like a wandering tramp, gypsy or animal. This curate, whom I had not previously known, fortunately had strong mental reservations about his bishop's theology, because he welcomed me without question, supplied me with a hot bath and a clean shirt, put me to sleep in a comfortable bed, and in the morning his housekeeper fed me a wonderful breakfast of bacon and eggs on a table with a white tablecloth. His reverence silently watched me eat, and then he gently led me to talk about my home, my father and mother, my girl, my years at university, the job I had left.

After a while he said, quietly and kindly: 'You had better go home, Sean. You are not fit for this kind of life. And anyway, there's no more to be done out here. We're whacked.'

'But if I go back to the city I'll be picked up and put in jail!'

'If you stay here they'll pick you up just the same, sooner or later. And if they catch you bearing arms they'll do more than jail you.'

I was only too ready to be persuaded. He gave me a complete change of linen, a clerical suit, a black hat and a black tie, loaned me a bicycle, told me what name to give if I was held up by the Regulars, the name of the seminary in Cork where I was studying, and the name of my uncle whose funeral I had just been attending west of Macroom. Finally, he instructed me in the safest route to follow into the city.

I entered Cork after dark. When I knocked at Number 5 Half Moon Street my mother opened the door, pulled me in at once, and kissed me, and kissed me. Upstairs my father, the old grenadier, the lifelong royal servant of the Empire, who had for the last six years hated all this damned business of the Revolution, held my arms fondly and looked at me without a word of reproach. I remained with them over Christmas, rejoicing in my blue and cream room, my fire, my books, trying to cleanse my mind and body, each of its own parasites, leaving the house only after dark to meet Eileen and get a breath of sanity and fresh air. Then, as gently and uninquiringly as they had received me, my father and mother let me go and I cycled back again to the mountains for fresh orders. My stay there was brief and pointless. I was ordered to return to the city and run publicity from there.

5

My only difficulty in running publicity in Cork was that everything had to be done underground and I knew very few people whom I could trust. I decided to rely entirely on Eileen, who had meanwhile gone back to college to finish her studies, and on two or three of her fellow students. At first she organised a small group of couriers, I wrote my pieces, she and her friends cut the stencils and mimeographed a tiny underground paper in the tower room of the college, and from there the news sheet was taken down to a hired room in the city for distribution. Such was her innocence that she did not find out until afterwards that the house where she had hired a room – it was over a tobacconist's shop in Oliver Plunket Street – was a brothel, known to its clients as the Abode of Love, and that she and her friends were being used as a cover for the nightly comings and goings of its half-dozen whores. When the paper had been wrapped up in bundles it was distributed throughout the south by a girl who openly drove in and out of the city once a week to wherever the divisional headquarters established itself from time to time out west. Later, Bob Langford, who had returned to the city, living there in hiding like myself, daringly proposed to print a weekly paper. We gladly accepted his plucky offer. How he managed it I do not know, for he was a marked man and his printing office was constantly raided.

For the rest of the winter – it was now 1923 – I was immured in my room, visited, briefly, only by Eileen and two other girls with dispatches. Those three guarded my anonymity and my address so carefully that only a very few others knew who the Director of Publicity was, and only those three knew where I lived. The secrecy was necessary. In February, Eileen was arrested and jailed. A month later my second courier, Molly Fitzgerald, was arrested and jailed. My third girl escaped arrest to the end.

What the old grenadier and my mother thought of all these goings-on I never knew and I did not care. By now I was the mad mole who thought he had made Mont Blanc. I was the mouse in the wainscoting of the Vatican who believed that he told the Pope every night what His Holiness must tell the world every morning. I was Ireland, the guardian of her faith, the one solitary man who would keep the Republican symbol alive, keep the last lamp glowing before the last ikon even if everybody else denied or forgot the gospel that had inspired us all from 1916 onwards. I firmly believed in the dogma which had by this time become the last redoubt of the minority's resistance to the majority, that the People have no Right to do Wrong. Like all idealists, I was fast becoming heartless, humourless and pitiless.

I did not miss Eileen in the least. Her replacements carried my dispatches just as well. When she was ultimately released and I met her again, I was shocked to find how deeply she had been affected, not so much by her experiences in jail as by her experience of her father's misery during her imprisonment, wandering day and night under the walls of the female prison, now jammed with women, seeking here and there in the city for somebody with enough influence to get her out of jail, importuning chance acquaintances, total strangers, even old political enemies. In the knowledge of his unhappiness the heart that had become stilled or stifled in me burst alive in her. Walking by my side on that night of our first meeting after her release, along a lonely road high over the city, staring down at the lights far below, she said to me:

'You are all abstract fanatics. You are suffering, if you are suffering, not out of love for your fellow men but out of love for your own ruthless selves.'

It was more or less what Sean O'Casey was to say about all patriotism in his two great plays later on. Staring coldly at the valley's lights, I said that people who thought like that should be shot as traitors.

She said: 'Some morning you will wake up and find yourself standing in the Grand Parade behind a green iron railing holding up the torch of liberty, not a man at all but a statue made of stone or lead.'

After that those two young people walked on in silence beyond the last of the city's road lamps. They walked close together, full of affection, threatened by anger and by hate. I say 'they' because the whole of this thing is no longer with me as a matter of she and me. That 'she' and that 'me' exist now only as figures in a fiction, or a play printed on the sheets of memory, or ghosts that have left indelible imprints on a place they once frequented in passion. I see him and her walking home full of unhappiness at the shattering of their dreams. They went on meeting one another only because their love and loyalty were stronger than Ireland or mankind.

As Easter approached, the first breath of spring flecked the bushes behind the railings of the School of Art below my window with buds of promise. Its soft breath made my cell unbearable, especially with those two unhappy old people, my father and mother, always hovering outside it to advise, comfort or protect me. I stared to take refuge, even for a night or two, in the houses of my acquaintances, even of acquaintances of my acquaintances, even imposing myself on people who I knew were Free Staters by conviction. Not one of them ever refused me hospitality. Then, in late April, an unbearable longing for the earth smells drove me to take refuge in the old, battered country house to which one Republican friend introduced me, high on the hills to the south of the city. In the eighteenth century it would have been a splendid classical residence; it was now a crumbling lodging for the family of a herdsman on the fields about it. By day I saw, away beneath me, the smoky bowl of the city; by night I could see the city's glow on the underbellies of the clouds from the slattern room where I slept between soiled and crumpled sheets. I ate without tasting it whatever the herd's pregnant wife put before me on the kitchen table. The cowfields were becoming lush with tender grass. The ragged lawn was speckled with enamelled yellow celandines; soon the hedgerows would be alight with the may blossom; in the afterlight, when one can barely distinguish man from beast, I could hear invisible cattle breathing and chewing the cud. The twitchy tits darted. A late blackbird sang the night in. The great, slow April clouds dripped lightly on the ash trees' bursting buds. It was a mistake to have gone there. The agonising joy of those few days and nights unmanned me. In my blue and white cell I was somebody; out here I suddenly became nobody. I loathed the idea of returning to my job.

On the morning of the fourth day I was standing in a field

below the house, after a breakfast of peat-brown tea and too fresh baker's bread, looking down gloomily at the bowl of the city's chimney smoke, when one of the small boys of the house brought me out the *Cork Examiner*, saying: 'My mudder says dere's news in it for you.'

I opened it and read a proclamation from Mr De Valera, on behalf of the Republican 'Government', and from Frank Aitken, as Chief of Staff of the Republican 'Army', ordering us all to dump arms and observe a cease-fire. It was a magniloquent message, beginning, 'Soldiers of the Legion of the Rearguard.' I lowered the paper. In the jails and internment camps tens of thousands of men and women were probably at that moment clustering in groups over this bland order telling them to cease fire. In a hundred homes so were the relatives of scores of men who had been executed by the Free State Government. I handed the paper back to the boy. I had brought with me a tin box of watercolours and a sketchblock, and I sat on a fallen stone pillar to paint a twisted, muscular beech as gray as an elephant's leg. The boy watched me.

'You're a clever fellow,' he said. 'That's a good disguise.'

I said nothing.

'So it's all over?' he said.

I looked at him coldly. I said, 'As long as that tree stands the Republic stands.'

'So does my ass,' he said, and walked off to the house, whistling.

Insofar as we were both using metaphors we were both right.

I walked home, an hour later, openly through the streets. I could no longer see much point in concealment, and I doubted if any detective had, in any case, ever heard of me, or ever would hear of me now that it was all over. I found my dispatch girl waiting for me. As usual she turned modestly aside to undo the top buttons of her blouse, drew out the usual small envelope, and handed it to me, warm as usual from its nest. It ordered me to go at once to Dublin, where the Director of Publicity, Robert Brennan, had fallen ill, and to take over there as Acting Director on behalf of the still-asserting Republic. At first I was elated by the challenge, the idea of a change of scene, the chance of being near the centre of things. Then I became so filled with despair that I nearly burst into tears. I knew quite well that all I was fit to direct was the traffic in a one-way street, that by the calendar I was twenty-three, and that in experience I was about twenty. So they were as short of men as this! In the envelope there were also four five-pound notes and a card bearing the address of a house out under the Dublin hills, near Rathfarnham. I let my elation return, packed, and went off by the afternoon train. I stayed first at Rathfarnham with two old ladies who might have been the Misses Markham who gave the Christmas party in Joyce's 'The Dead'; afterwards I stayed in various other suburban and semi-suburban houses, in Ranelagh, Donnybrook, Drumcondra, Bray . . .

I understand that the elliptical three stops, or dots, which I have placed at the conclusion of the last paragraph usually indicate that the writer's thoughts are what might be called trailing off. Mine are, into a darkness dotted with a number of unrelated spots of light. As I now force myself backward over those eight months in Dublin, it is like flying at night from, say, New York to Seattle, peering down and seeing from time to time cobwebs of green, white or yellow light radiating irregularly from a red neon centre, of which the hostess will be able to identify only the very brightest – Cleveland, Chicago, Dubuque. By then we have travelled about a thousand miles, and are mostly half asleep. It we wake up, restlessly, and peer down, we see now only lone and very small stars of life, across Minnesota, South Dakota, Wyoming. Each one of those unidentified clusters of light is a cluster of people, of whom only a handful are awake. Once we are over the Rockies and have only another three hundred or so miles to go we may, if we are on a poor flight, come down at one or two of these small clusters with names like Walla Walla and Yakima, swallow another cup of coffee, light a pipe, see half a dozen people, even talk with one or two. In my memory of those eight months in Dublin, each one of those small spots of light is called the Absurd.

When I began my new job in verbal defence of the Republic I did not even have pen and ink. I had a pencil, some paper and two sheets of carbon. With these, while staying with the old ladies whom I call the Misses Markham, I began to pour passionate cables all over the world protesting against the destruction of the Living Republic by a junta of traitors. I appealed by cable to the President of the United States, to the head of every government in Europe, to the editors of newspapers in all parts of the globe, to the Vatican, to high ecclesiastical personages everywhere. Whether the post office, in Ireland a Government institution, ever sent out these cables I do not know. I drew up messages *To the Irish People* to be printed as display advertisements in any Irish newspaper that would dare print them. I had access to money then, for I recall handling for the first time in my life several big, crinkly hundred-pound notes, and sending various people off, each with one in his fist, to try to place these advertisements with the newspapers. Some of them did appear. I was told afterwards that when Robert Brennan, for whom I was acting as director, read some of my messages to Ireland and to the World in his sickbed he turned to the wall and burst into tears, whether at my incapacity or at the straits to which his department was now reduced I do not know. Yet, as a one-man office I could have done worse, especially since Mr De Valera was now beginning to reorganise the old non-military political party called Sinn Fein and any form of propaganda on its behalf was quite legal. Indeed, at a general election that August of 1923, his revived Sinn Fein party astonished Ireland by winning forty-three seats as against the Government's fifty-three. It was an illustration of Republican tenacity that, even to this day, makes my heart leap. This party he refused to lead into parliament. Nobody, he held, could possibly enter the traitors' Dail which had disowned the allegedly still-living Irish Republic. The Absurd lay in my awareness, now frankly admitted by me in private audiences with myself, that there was not, and never had been, an Irish Republic, living or dead. I continued to write passionately in its defence.

Mr De Valera and his Sinn Fein party held an even more absurd idea. The Dail which since 1921 had represented the Living Republic during the Troubles, but later by a majority ratified the articles of agreement which established the Irish Free State, had been known as the Second Dail. For subtle reasons both now and then beyond human comprehension the Sinn Fein party maintained that the Second Dail had never been really dissolved, that it still was the Government of the Living

Republic, that it was the sole, sovereign parliament or Dail of the country, and that those of their party who had been elected to it were now that only legal Dail for as long as they lived, or until the Living Republic was objectively established. (They refused to pay any attention to the undeniable fact that this 'real' Second Dail had voted by a majority to set up an Irish Free State.) In brief a rump was declaring itself the body of its own parliament. Indeed, during the Civil War, it blandly elected Mr De Valera as President of the ghostly Living Republic and head of its non-functioning Council of State.

During my eight months in Dublin I met several of these men and women of the dream republic. They were by no means stupid people – several of them were able men and proved it later – but I must conclude that at that time either they were temporarily of unsound mind, or I was. The women I met were particularly disturbing – driven by that unfeminine animus which seems always to make the male constituent in women behave like the worse side of the feminine element in men. They were theatrical, self-dramatising, power-hungry, temperamental but with few warm emotions, ruthless, abstract in discussion, and full of a terrifying sentimentality. Yet they sometimes entranced me by their occasional lapses into sound, womanly, commonsense doubts about the practicality of what we were all doing. It was as if a woman don suddenly stopped in the middle of a metaphysical discussion and said, 'I think I'm using a powder a shade too dark, don't you?' or 'That child needs cod-liver oil.' So one of them transfixed the Council of State one afternoon by saying: 'It occurs to me: what would happen supposing all but one of us were to die? Would that last survivor then actually be the Second Dail? Supposing I were the last survivor? Would I then be the sovereign parliament of the Irish Republic? It is a rather disturbing thought, you know!'

We were all idealists, self-crazed by abstractions, lost in the labyrinths of the dreams to which we had retreated from this pragmatical pig of a world. Sometimes, as I dutifully poured out article after article in defence of them and the Living Republic, I used to cackle madly at the role which Dante assigns to all such pure-souled idealists as myself in *The Inferno*. He classifies them as the Opportunists, racing endlessly through the mists of hell after a wavering flag which they can never overtake, led by Pope Celestine the Fifth, who fled alike from his flock and the frets and dangers of his office in order to save his own unhappy soul in pure hermitage. Michael Collins, at the end of that famous word-combat in the actual Second Dail which had ended with a vote for the Irish Free State, had shouted a not dissimilar judgment after Mr De Valera as he proudly led his Republican followers out of the 'traitors' ' chamber: 'Deserters!' Collins had roared. 'Deserters to the Irish nation in her hour of trial.' Generally, however, I took pride in our idealism, and was encouraged by the flattery of the women about me to do so.

The end of all this folly came after my time in Dublin. I recount it briefly, only because it rounds off this narrative of my encounter with the Absurd, although I feel that the subject is more fit for fiction, where the reader will indulgently accept any fable as reality, than for an autobiography, where he may find it difficult to believe that such real things could be true. Mr De Valera, coming slowly to his normally shrewd senses, realised that the only hope for his party was to cut clear of the extremists, get into the Traitors' Dail by some subtle face-saving formula and reform it from within. When he finally announced this intention to *his* Second Dail, it disowned him on the spot, doubtless to his immense relief. Thereupon he at once set up another party grandiosely called Fianna Fail, or Soldiers of Destiny, which has continued to this day as the Purest of the Pure. For a couple of years they and he still stood poised on the brink, and then, in 1927, he persuaded his followers, who needed little persuading, poor men, being by then as desperate for the fruits of office as Tantalus, that the accursed oath of allegiance over which we had all fought a civil war was not an oath at all! And that they could sign the usual formal declaration that they were taking it without a qualm. I refrain from comment, as most Republicans uncomfortably did at the time, apart from wondering why the hell he did not say this long before. From that day to this I have never trusted any politician anywhere.

Within five years his party was in office. They stayed in office for sixteen stolid years, during which they not only stolidly refused to declare Ireland their Republic but, when opposed in arms by the old and young irreconcilables, gave them the same treatment that they had got from the original Irish Free State Government. They imprisoned them, executed them, and let them die on hunger strike.

In all other respects, Mr De Valera did his best to keep to his abstract, legalistic Republican principles: he threw out the hated oath of allegiance – the main effect of which was to let the Republican irreconcilables into the Dail to oppose him and finally overthrow him. He eliminated the office of governor general, the representative of the British monarch, and finally drew up a new constitution which, he held, embodied all the characteristics of a Republican way of life without explicitly asserting that Ireland was, now, a republic. The irreconcilable Republicans, who thought of a republic not as he did in terms of fine forms of words and fine legal distinctions, but in terms of modern social reform and the historical Franco-American spirit of individual independence and total egalitarianism, remained unimpressed and continued to denounce him as, in a new way, a traitor to the old ideals.

In 1948 the inheritors of the original anti-Republican Irish Free State Government party combined astoundingly with those disillusioned, irreconcilable anti-Free State Republicans to put the most eloquent 'Republican' of them all, Mr De Valera, out of office, and it was they who finally and formally declared Ireland a republic. Alas! Gifts too long withheld lose their value. By then the Republican ideal, if it had ever meant anything visible or touchable, any vision of life as men might actually live it or hope to live it, had lost all its content. Every foreign government acknowledged it, the Church blessed it, the people huzzahed for it, and perhaps some dead bones may have stirred to hear the cannons salute the tardy arrival of a stillborn child. It has made no least difference to life in Ireland.

I hung on in Dublin through January of 1924. My only record of my odd adventures during those two years or so after 1922 was a letter from the Acting President of the Living Republic, Mr Patrick Ruttledge – the President, Mr De Valera, was then in jail – thanking me for my services. I tore it into little pieces and let it flutter into the fire. I went home to Cork, and to private life, a more than disillusioned and embittered young man. My job was gone and I had no hope of getting another, since any jobs that were going were now, naturally enough, being earmarked by Free Staters for Free Staters. All I could hope for was a teaching post in some little country town, and that only when the next teaching year began in the following September. I went back to University College, Cork, to work for a master's degree and to lick my wounds. I was twenty-four that February.

11

Barricades

I

I should be extremely proud if I could record that I now sat down to consider calmly what it was that had happened to me since the first day I had entered that college, six years before. It is what Julien Sorel would have done, or rather, it is what Stendhal would have presented his hero as doing in my situation. I note, however, that Stendhal, in considering his own affairs in his diaries and notebooks, blundered around like everybody else, groping slowly through a life-time's conscious, half-conscious and, it is clear, unconscious meanderings towards the conclusions that were finally to be embodied in his idealised mirror-characters Sorel, Mosca, Lucien Leuwen, Henri Brulard and Fabrizio del Dongo. So it was with me. For some thirty years I was to meander around the experiences of my first manhood, recomposing my life in novels and stories wherein I could halt the flowing, flickering river and look at it. I also tried to use what I self-flatteringly called my intelligence by keeping note-books wherein I argued intermittently with myself and the universe.

By the end of the Civil War life had presented itself to me, forever, under the form of a number of ineluctable challenges, or experiences, densely compressed into the one word, Ireland; just as for, say, George Eliot, Arnold Bennett, Somerset Maugham, E. M. Forster, Graham Greene or Kingsley Amis the world condenses itself as England; as for Sherwood Anderson it meant what he saw of it as a youth in Ohio; as for Faulkner it meant the South; and as for every writer it always means the fated field where he is born, unless, alone, he leaves it at an early age forever. Thereafter, in trying to describe our image of life, we may choose other scenes and times – Italy, Africa, Mexico, any outpost of Empire, any passage to India, the Florence of Savonarola or the Rome of Caligula. Our problems will nonetheless always remain the problems of an Englishman, a Frenchman, an American or an Irishman. I might and did look for and find analogies elsewhere, trying to universalise the data I had in my body experienced locally, but the original data remained. We all make only one basic experiment with life. Everything else is tangential to it. I am impaled on one green corner of the universe.

My recent bitter experience, I now realise, had thrown invisible barricades across the main road of my life. Since I did not realise this at the time, I could not know either that for years after I would go on probing for alternative roads towards the full understanding and enjoyment of life. All I consciously did was to shuffle around and around, over and over again, in unabated bewilderment, the pieces of the incomplete jigsaw before me, much as a physician may consider a number of puzzling symptoms in the effort to arrive at a provisional diagnosis of the malady to which they refer.

Some of my interpretations of that time were, I now see, crassly wrong. Here is one such interpretation. It read the data correctly; it drew an untenable conclusion. When I looked around me in and after 1924 gropingly, intermittently, still not at all like the frank-eyed Julien Sorel, far from seeing any evident improvement in the quality of Irish life now that we had swapped British administrators for Irish administrators, I felt a strong smell of moral decay. However vaguely or unclearly, I felt the onset of what I was ultimately to define as a new, native, acquisitive middle class intent only on cashing in on the change of governments. So far I was not astray. The social fact I was then intuiting was to become undeniable and blatant in the 1930s and 1940s. Worse still, this native bourgeois class could not fill the vacuum left by the virtual disappearance of the old Anglo-Irish landed aristocracy and middle classes, the most obvious marks of the best side of whose wealth, taste and traditions are the beauty of central Dublin, many splendid houses throughout the country, such names in art and politics as Burke, Grattan, Lord Edward Fitzgerald, Goldsmith, Sheridan, Parnell, Wilde, Shaw, Moore, Synge, Augusta Gregory, Yeats and Pearse. That vacuum was filled by the Roman Catholic Church, which fortunately for itself – I am thinking of the misfortunes which have deservedly fallen on the Catholic Church elsewhere in Europe – is completely innocent of any aristocratic ancestry, but unfortunately for Ireland is equally innocent of any cultural ancestry. I believed in the years after the Troubles that this combination of an acquisitive and uncultivated middle class and a rigorous and uncultivated Church meant that the fight for a republic as I now understand it – that is, a republic in the shape of France or the United States – had ended in total defeat.

There I was wrong, as any historian of political revolutions could have readily told me, pointing out, with various examples to illustrate his argument, including France in the eighteenth, nineteenth and twentieth centuries, that few social conflicts resolve themselves clearly. They peter out, rather, by becoming subject to new tensions that they themselves create, and thus modified reappear unrecognisably, in the shape of seemingly new conflicts. As I have said he need not have gone farther than life in France or America after their revolutions to make the point clear.

'Your people,' this historian might have said, 'had intimations of a better condition or way of life more suited to the inherited needs and nature of Ireland. Unhappily you lacked an intellectual élite to define them. Under the circumstances all you could do was to push on from one set of circumstances to another, and then stop for a rest. But even to do this much is not to do nothing. Indeed, inside one generation, all most revolutions can hope to do is to move onward from one battleground to another. You, as one participant in the first stage of your revolution – a continuing process which will never stop – considered that the struggle in which you took part ended in total failure. On the contrary it was, within the limits of the circumstances of the time, a successful struggle. If there was any betrayal, my friend, you were one of those who betrayed by failing to carry on.'

176

Very well. Though a rest of two generations after the first *putsch* does seem a bit long?

A modern psychologist could have pointed out to me where I made another misinterpretation. He might say something like this: 'Do you remember the day you have described in your autobiography when you entered your University College for the first time? You first observed some young men and women playing tennis in elegant whites in the lower grounds, and longed to be one of them. Then you observed some leaden labels attached to the shrubs and trees along the avenue, giving their names in Latin. *Quercus pedunculata. Cerasus serrulata.* And so on. You at once longed to be a scientist and to master the study of botany. Then you saw three students in the quadrangle, one wearing a black, tattered gown stained by acid, and you at once wanted to have a tattered gown like his. The triple symbolism is obvious. You chose the tattered gown, and dressed in black poet's hat with baggy Irish tweeds. How disturbing it must have been for your ambitions and success-minded parents, who wished you to rise in the world! (Really? Objectively speaking, what a pain in the neck to them you must have been!) Finally you joined the Irish Volunteers, and went out into the mountains to learn Gaelic among the cottiers of the west. Those gestures put on the one side of the scale wealth, elegance, ambition, worldliness, your parents and the British Empire; on the other side stood the poor and the oppressed, who alone had the secret of the good life, and you. Very democratic. Very satisfactory. Freedom for Ireland, freedom for the oppressed, and freedom for you.

'You overlooked one thing, though. The student in his ragged gown is not a democratic symbol. It is a symbol which contains too many Bohemian implications. And the Bohemian is always a self-concerned rebel of middle-class or bourgeois origin. You must surely have noticed that we rarely find manual labourers wanting to wear black hats and flowing ties or pondering the superior attractions in life in a garret? I agree that aristocrats are also accustomed since birth to wearing the most extraordinary clothes, including red-lined cloaks, ragged coats, tall hats and kilts. You must consider that you may have preferred the ragged gown to the white flannels not through dislike but through poverty? Or even, if I may say so, through envy? Your ragged gown may also have been a form of dandyism in reverse, like the famous *dandyisme* of Baudelaire, also a great rebel but no democrat, if the word democratic carries, or ever carried, for you any suggestion of being a heart-pal of every Tom, Dick and Harry. Wasn't it Baudelaire who said, in his deep hatred of the masses: '*L'artiste ne sort jamais de soi-même*' (The artist never comes out of himself)? Your idea of freedom was primarily one of the mind and the spirit. It is possible that that is what you should have stuck to – like Joyce; fought and lived for that liberty and for no other.'

'I did that for years after 1924 – fighting Irish puritanism and ignorance. Things like the Censorship and the Church. And I paid dearly enough for it.'

'Your type always pays. Your dilemma after your Troubles has long since been identified as the common dilemma of every liberal individualist, especially if he is an artist. When such a man takes part in a popular revolt he is thereafter looked at with considerable suspicion, if not dislike, by the levelled-up-or-down society he has helped to produce. Pasternak?'

If I had asked this unpleasant *Doppelgänger* what, then, I ought to have done in 1924, I have small doubt that he would have replied: 'You could have agreed with yourself that you had done your part, for good or ill, drawn a line, cut your losses, left the future to other men and spent the rest of your life being, happily or unhappily, yourself. To every man his role; to every man his time.'

'Did I not do this by becoming a writer?'

The scoundrel smiles evilly at me. 'May I introduce you to my friend Flaubert. He has been around for some time. Have a word with him.'

I do so, and this is what he said, musing over my early stories:

'Very interesting. They remind me a little of a certain problem I had to deal with in my own work. Some of it is, as you know, very romantic, and some of it is not. I think I did my best work when I was writing unromantically about the damned middle classes, the dull grey level of shabby-genteel bourgeois life. I did it calmly and coldly because I felt that it was essential for me to transcend my anger with that which I described. I did not do quite so well when I romanticised myself away from my anger. It is always a problem. Your early stories romanticised your anger. I observed recently that those Angry Young Men of post-war Britain set out, as it were, to socialise their anger. That is another way towards detachment from anger. No critic has any right to pass judgement on the merits of any writer's technique for surmounting this emotion, but since I do notice that over the years you began to veer towards the technique of humour and detachment, it does occur to me as fair comment that you felt that your first method had its limitations? If detachment and humour come, as I believe they do, with a growing accept-ance of one's human material – which, to be sure, is not the same thing as agreement with what your human material accepts – could it be that you arrived at this detachment and so forth by some gradual process of life-acceptance? I do not know that life-acceptance leads necessarily to a greater realism, but it must always lead us away from romanticism. What do you think?'

So? And, also, so! Meaning that I must agree with my three commentators. What they are saying is that in being privileged to see man at his best I had been given an exceptional vision of the potential wholeness and integrity of human nature in a moment of intense awareness forced on us all, collectively, by a crisis in our country's history; that I had thereby been blinded to the nature of ordinary, average, common life as it is outside such rare hours; and that when the hour passed I felt at first bewildered, then dismayed, and finally filled with a wholly unreasonable anger at my fellow men. If it was as simple as that, why did I take so long to see it? Only those who have not been privileged to see men at their finest, as I did, will have trouble in observing, with pity and continuing love, that while man contains the potential of everything admirable and lovable he rarely achieves it, is for the greater part of his life doomed to live in an obscure *demi-jour* between his long night of apathy and his few, shatteringly few bright hours of grace.

As my anger gradually abated, but with my curiosity still unabated, I was, over the years after 1924, to become fascinated to understand, in sympathy, what flaws in the intricate machin-ery of human nature keep it from fulfilling itself wholly, from achieving complete integrity other than in moments as brief, if one compares them with the whole span of a human life, as a lighthouse blink. I would, then, in my late life-acceptance, embracing as much as I had the courage to embrace of all of life's inherent evil and weakness, try to write, however tangentially, about those moments of awareness when we know three truths at one and the same moment: that life requires of each of us that we should grow up and out whole and entire, that human life of its nature intricately foils exactly this, and that the possibility of wholeness is nevertheless as constant and tempting an ideal as the manifold actuality of frustration, compromise, getting caught in some labyrinth, getting cut short by death.

I do not think that I deceive myself – in such matters one can never be sure – when I speak of my having been filled with an unreasonable anger at my fellow men. I know that when we are angry with others the reason often is that we are transferring to them our unacknowledged anger with ourselves. The psychologist who chided me for mistaking my Bohemianism for a genuine love for the underdog has already made this point cruelly. Another might have made it in another way, impressing on me Jung's well-known distinction between our Persona, a social ideal or outward mask, and our inner Shadow, a natural inner-life instinct, as personal, primitive and primordial as in a child or a savage. He might have stressed that I was – as time would show – a born artist, one of those creatures for whom the Shadow or primordial instincts are the source of all his ideals. Here the great conflict begins.

The artist, certainly if he is a writer of novels or stories, must express his ideals in human images. If men and women seem to betray his expressed ideal, his first instinct is to be filled with anger against them, thereby inviting an equally angry response. If his ideal has been a practicable ideal, then their anger against him is unreasonable. If his ideal has been impracticable, then his anger against them is not only unreasonable, but is, in actuality, the mark of his own unacknowledged anger with himself for being such a fool as to have asked too much of human nature. Jung maintained that this struggle between the Shadow and the Persona involves a moral conflict, and that few of us have the courage or intelligence to resolve it. It is this personal conflict within myself that I have called my psychic barricades or fences.

2

Since for the next fifty years and more my moral war as Jung would have called it turned out to seem not much different, I suppose, to that of most thinking people, namely a nonstop Grand National over various moral hedges and ditches and jumps and fences, a few cleared with skill, most crashed through embarrassingly, and since nobody's fences are quite the same as another's fences, and since the approach of each equestrian therefore must also be a bit different, I feel I owe it to my invisible readers up on the grand stand to give at least one clearcut illustration of the main kind of obstacle that kept me from being at peace with life for as long as I can remember.

The example I choose is not very abstruse – I probably share it with the greater part of mankind. Indeed I have, inevitably, paraded it already when describing the embarrassing discussion I had in my raw student days with an Irish Jesuit (his name unexpectedly flashes on my memory, he was one Fr Aubrey Gwynn) about the unrewarded years of slavery forced on my saintly mother by her devotion to the welfare of her family. That futile discussion had finally culminated, for me, as Dostoievsky's Grand Inquisitor's unappeasable question, *Why should such things be?* I recall that discussion now solely because it recalls another such discussion I had years later with another Catholic theologian, but this time a man of much greater subtlety and sympathy of mind, around Easter in a rectory parlour in the Harlem section of New York City.

This meeting was a result of the merest chance. One week earlier I had been arguing amiably with a group of friends, mostly Catholic, whom I had met at a tea party in Princeton – I was lecturing at the university that spring – about that hoary subject the recurrence of evil as a denial of free will. Catholics, anyway intellectual Catholics, love starting some such argument as this. It is the breath of life to us. After all, theology, as a packed-down kind of philosophy, is one way of describing the nature of life.

181

'Easter is coming,' I said, mockingly. 'We will all celebrate the Resurrection and the Life. Every Christian in the wide world will confess his sins of pride, covetousness, lust, anger, gluttony, envy and sloth. He must know that within a matter of weeks or months he will again be drinking, cheating, idling, raging, envious, fornicating or as full of vainglory as ever before. Surely there can be no meaning to a resolution of the will for anyone – and of whom is this not true? – who over five, ten or even twenty years, if it takes him so long to face the fact, observes this apparently inevitable recurrence?'

Our little group wore out the discussion and we passed on to something else, but one man who, I knew, taught philosophy in New York City pulled me aside and said, passing me a book of paper matches with a name and address written inside the cover: 'You know, Sean, if you didn't start that argument just for the hell of it, I mean if you're really bothered by it, we have some pretty bright philosophers among the clergy in these parts. Try talking to this man. He is well worth a visit.'

For the hell of it? Long before I had gone to University College, Cork, in my teens I had begun to be 'bothered by it' in one form or another. It had started, as I have recorded earlier, when I could not beat the unhappiness of my mother and wondered, like Ivan Karamazov, 'Why must such things be?' In spite of the efforts of years to exorcise them many other things had gone on 'bothering' me ever since; as whom, outside the gastropod molluscs, do they not? Each one of those executions during the Civil War had left a blue bruise on the skin of my heart. There were even occasions when Irishmen were tortured not by Englishmen – this, illogically, one could bear – but by their fellow Irishmen. When Mr De Valera at last entered the parliament of those traitors who had shot those republican comrades of his I was horrified to find him sending some more of those still republican young men to their deaths because *they* were now unlawfully opposing *him*. There had been plenty more 'bothering' things since then – things that had happened under the European dictators, and during the war against them. There were Israel, and India, and Cyprus and Algeria. And there was of course sex. One kept on being 'bothered' and one kept on trying to cope with one's 'botheration'. However, I thought I might as well try this old fence again. On Easter Sunday I found myself sitting in a downtown rectory in New York talking to the man whose name was written inside the cover of the matchbook.

He knew nothing about me and I did not tell him anything about myself. I was to him just one of New York's anonymous millions. Like all such Easter Eve talks ours was at first bitter-sweet, happy-sad. Then it became very serious. As we talked in general terms of good and evil he said, in the run of his thoughts, many things that I found illuminating and interesting; but I had not come for that, so I brought him down to cases and our talk at once became more tensed. As he tried to deal with these cases, and with my 'botheration' about them, he let fall four words at whose touch one of those old barriers or fences of mine revealed itself clearly to me and at the same instant fell as flat as a used-up film set. He was just then talking about the highly complex nature of this created world in which we involuntarily find ourselves from infancy; a world that as I evidently to some degree believed or I would not be there talking to *him*, had originated in a First Cause. (Privately I would have preferred some less explicit words. Creative will? I might even have preferred some purely mythic phrase such as Architect of the Gods.) This First Cause, this Creator, this Will, this Force, this Architect, this Essential Element, call it what I liked, dominated all created life. Nothing that ever happens in this life could, *once it had happened*, be considered contrary to that godly will. Otherwise that will would not be godly at all. In which case what was my Fyodor Dostoievsky belly-aching about? In asking 'Why must evil or cruelty, or any such unjust things be?' Dostoievsky was not thinking about the real world we live in. He was inventing his own Utopia. As things really are, my host went on, we are all involved in everything that happens, involved especially in the old paradox that it had been from the beginning part of the Creator's design to bestow on every human the power to choose, in other words a will that could if it so decided choose quite contrary to the primal plan of God, who nevertheless continues to whisper to us, plead with us, encourage us to go on trying to make those two wills, human and superhuman, coincide. When he said the sentence containing

183

those four wonderful words, 'once it had happened' my hurdle came clearly into focus, my horse rose into the air and my Free Will hurdle became part of my past for ever – I hoped.

What most of all I felt at that moment was the superlative joy of being freed from my own uniqueness. I was suddenly exempt from the awful loneliness of being merely Me, that feeling as abiding as childhood of being as coerced as a mouse mesmerised by the cold eye of God. Oh yes! I had been told countless times that God loves me, that God opens his arms to me as to us all, but always I had felt that I was down here and God was up there inexorably arranging, ordering, judging. Suddenly I was elevated, emancipated, given a vote in the parliament of creation. From this moment onward I knew that Heaven and Earth are one. If God or Fate or Destiny or X, Y and Z wanted things one way and I wanted them another way my vote counted! I would never again feel powerless. But another and far more liberating discovery had been vouchsafed to me – that even if great masses of mankind, even if the whole human race without exception acted against God's will, that universal human revolt, *once it had happened*, left His will intact. At this I rejoiced, as Fyodor Dostoievsky could not rejoice because his image of life could not bear to accept the fact that at every second of time human evil thrives while God, man's image of perfection and of omnipotence, can only sigh, endure, forgive and plead. There is, I saw with relief, no perfection. There has never been a saint who has not been a sinner or a fool. No goodness is free of blemish. As for liberty? Only slaves are free.

When I came out of that rectory that morning into the Easter sunlight I can say with certainty that although I have been on other occasions as gleefully happy I have never been more so. Perhaps what so impressed me about that brilliant man's four enigmatic words was that they vibrated the strings of other not totally disparate truths that over the years had also, though less vividly, left happy marks on my mind, such as Count Mosca's remark to Fabrizio when the youth was complaining about the devious nature of politics: 'But, my dear boy, you do not complain about the devious rules in whist?' Einstein was sure that 'God does not play dice with man.' Whitehead summed up the inconsistencies of this good-bad world, as the missing piece of the jigsaw which when found could make an intelligible picture. That clever Bostonian woman-of-letters Margaret Fuller is reputed to have said, 'I accept the universe', at which Thomas Carlyle is reputed to have said, 'She had better!' adding a sage 'By God!' Why did all those sages say those things? I could only feel that it was through love for the nature of common man and common woman in their ordinary clothes as I stepped into the pure air of Harlem that Easter noon filled with a totally liberating love of guess-whom. I was remembering yet another nudge towards common sense given to me by another philosopher, who happened also to be a priest who had said laughingly, 'If you do not love yourself you can't possibly love anybody else.'

So, there waiting for me in my taxi was an Irish-born driver chewing a five cent cigar and reading the New York *Daily Mirror*? That is what I recorded in my first version of this autobiography – untruthfully because over-discreetly. I had, in full truth, been driven up there by my hostess who lived (when not in her luxurious New Jersey country house) in what used to be called the silk-stocking district of fashionable Manhattan, an attractive, sparkling, life-loving, little woman, looking like a child in a vast, open limousine, happily chatting – as was always her way with everybody and anybody – with three black kids, having I observed, fully completed her regular double-acrostic. Seeing me she said, 'Well? You do look happy! Everything okay?' I thought her, so frank with those black urchins, so competent with her acrostic, so welcoming to me, so very, very attractive at that moment that I said, spontaneously, 'I am so happy I could kiss you!' She raised her eyebrows and smiled a smile as welcoming as a hamburger . . .

But there I must halt and return to where I interrupted the sequence of my life-story way back in 1924.

12

The Full Life

The last time I had seen Eileen before my return to Cork in January of 1924 was in Dublin, when she was returning from Cork after the Christmas holidays to her job as a teacher in Ballinasloe, a country town lobbed from a parachute into that flat, wind-swept and rain-swept land known as East Galway, as often flooded as drained by the River Suck and other lesser tributaries of the Shannon. She had been there since the previous September. In her letters from this Irish middle west she had already evoked the town for me with a brilliant and hideous vividness born of a growing terror that she might never escape from it, or that if she did it would only be to another, identical Ballinasloe. In her talk she now evoked it again, as if warning me of what lay in store for me as a teacher in a similar country town.

Through her eyes I saw the long, wide street, lined by undistinguished houses mostly with shops on the ground floor, climbing the slight ridge that alone seemed to keep the whole place from sinking into the bog to its chimney tops. She described the vast, soggy landscape beyond the top of the town as she had last seen it: an immense mirror mottled and cracked, a gleaming sheet of flood water threaded by long black hedges, with, here and there, a thatched farmhouse huddled under the pale umbrella of one immense cloud reaching from horizon to horizon. No sun; only a diffused pallor, under which nothing ever cast a shadow. From my travelling days I knew this dim occlusion of the west. I knew that it can also be felt as a pensive calm, a perpetual predawn, but I knew, too, that when it persists and persists, for weeks on end, those Irish steppes can reduce a man's soul to fly-size and induce that kind of apathetic torpor described so well by all the nineteenth-century Russians (such as Herzen) that when we first read them we felt they might have been writing about any part of the browning, tattered billiard table of Ireland's central plain.

She lived in a lodging house that catered to the town's bank clerks, a class that at that time was the nadir of depressed gentility. They dined together in a long room 'carpeted' with chilly linoleum, heated by a central stove, and they shared one small fire in one small parlour. She was the only girl in the house and found no interest in any of them, so she had to retreat every evening at seven o'clock to her bedroom after the usual supper of 'tea and something', meaning tea, bread, butter, jam, and an egg or two. When she closed her bedroom door, and thought of the dark, damp land all around her from the Shannon to Galway Bay, and the long, damp, empty street below her window, and the long, empty evening ahead of her, she confessed that she used often to feel within an inch of Ophelian dottiness, sitting there alone, thinking, in fury, of all that was at that moment happening elsewhere in Europe – symphony orchestras tuning up, every man and woman in evening dress, the faint whiff of a cigar in a foyer, red plush seats filling, curtains about to rise on the opera or the play, ballet dancers practising a last preparatory *entrechat* in the wings, cabs driving up to the doors of fine restaurants in Paris or Rome, or London.

Outside, the Irish wind came blowing down the slope of Main Street.

On such nights she sometimes thought, in wonder, of a certain Countess of Clancarty – their vast estate lay to the southwest of Ballinsloe – who had been brought there at the end of the nineteenth century from London, a great stage beauty in her day, known to the public as Bella Bilton, her maiden name or stage name. The legend was that young Clancarty and several other Oxford Corinthians had been madly in love with her, and finally agreed between them to play cards to decide who should first seek her hand. In later years I met a very old man who had been a stable boy in Garbally House, and he described to me how she used to drive a pair of greys with scarlet trappings, herself in a red coat, down through the streets of Ballinasloe, going, he said, he knew not where, and it might be that she herself sometimes did not know either. In Eileen's time the Clancartys had abandoned Garbally House; the house was taken over by religious, stripped and sanctified; such bits of furniture as were left behind auctioned off around the country, and the luscious, erotic frescoes on the ceilings painted over. The theme would have made a perfect chapter for an early novel by George Moore, say *A Drama in Muslin*, which re-creates with such impressive realism the bored, nerve-ridden Chekhovian atmosphere of the Big Houses of nineteenth-century Mayo.

When Eileen and I met in Dublin after that Christmas of 1924, a little incident happened as we parted, she going back to Ballinasloe, I returning to Cork, a defeated and jobless ex-rebel. As a parting gift I bought her a lovely bunch of white chrysanthemums. And right lovely she herself looked when saying a loving goodbye to me across them. Long afterwards she confessed to me that when she got back to her lodgings that wintry night, her landlady stuck the rich flowers into a jam jar in the dining room. They only made her lot seem more drab, dismal and desperate than before. By the following September I also was to be living in a lodging house, a little better but not much better, in the country town of Ennis, in the County Clare, some seventy miles down the reedy Shannon, bedewed by the same rains and blown by the same winds in from the Atlantic coast, teaching in a school run by the Christian Brothers. Soon our letters to one another were like mirror-letters passing up and down the Shannon.

Before I went to teach in County Clare we had one summer, that of 1924, together in Cork City. By then I was penniless. Frank O'Connor, *né* Michael O'Donovan, released from jail before I left Dublin, was back in Cork, and so, also penniless, was my second courier Molly Fitzgerald. Penniless ex-rebels all except Eileen who staked us for teas, cigarettes, an occasional cinema. I borrowed from her heavily. Once, out of the maternal warmth of her heart, she bought Michael a pair of boots. We four often walked and talked as a group, an odd kind of group because Michael and I would walk in front of the girls, absorbed in the poetry or novels we had been reading. He had a magnificent reading voice and a bottomless memory, and he would stalk along reciting Gaelic and English poems of which our audience behind could have caught only the wind of the proud words: Seathrún Ceitinn's *A bhean lán de stuaim (O woman full of wile)*, or Sir Thomas Wyatt's *They flee from me, that sometime did me seek,/With naked foot stalking in my chamber* . . . When we sat together it is likely that we may have talked very little about politics, for what mainly held us four together now was no longer Ireland but the writers, the music, the thought of Europe. We were sense-starved and eye-hungry. The old symbols of the Free Country were fading – which of us would want to go back there? – before the siren whispers of the Full Life.

When that summer ended Eileen went back to the full life of her Main Street and I set off for mine. On our last night together before that parting she said that she was looking forward to Ballinasloe's one picturesque week, when the most unlikely of all things happened to the town – an invasion of buyers from continental Europe for its then famous October horse fair, after which, she sighed, the town would sink back into the silence of its bog grave for the rest of the year.

'You are not cheering me up about Ennis,' I said.

'Ennis,' she said, 'does not have a famous horse fair.'

It proved to be another Rathkeale, except that I did not know anybody in Ennis. There were the same sort of empty roads, with the same wind humming in the telegraph wires, where I might pass, with a nod, the same two or three bank clerks, or another chemist's wife out with her dog and a walking stick, or a slow-pacing priest reading his office, or a cric-crocking country cart. The town had no cinema, no library, no bookshop. For a while I was quite happy. I enjoyed walking the country roads until the fine weather broke in rain and, anyway, I had by then exhausted their slight points of interest – an old castle, a ruined abbey or two, the evocations of Lord Inchiquin's fine house and estate at Dromoland. (It was later taken over by an American as a luxury hotel for tourists.) I enjoyed my solitariness and my independence. I had a salary, a hundred and fifty pounds a year, enough to enable me to pay off my debts and save a little for the summer holidays to come. I tried to keep in touch with the world by taking in the *Times Literary Supplement*, the *Spectator*, the *Irish Statesman* – edited by the poet AE (George W. Russell), a paper of an excellence never before or since equalled in Irish journalism – and the *Labour Monthly*, edited by Rajani Palme Dutt, a brilliant young English rebel, who had been sent down from Oxford in 1917 for socialist antiwar propaganda. I am bound to say that if I had been less solitary-minded, and more enterprising, and had a few more piastres, I might have got much more out of Ennis and County Clare. I could, at least, have interested myself in its prehistoric and Christian antiquities and, as I was to do in later years, have made through that interest a few good friends. My main trouble was lack of cash. Today, being better heeled, and with a few books under my belt, I could lead a reasonably pleasant life in County Clare, with a fast car at my door and Shannon Airport at hand to fly me to any city in Europe whenever I felt in need of contact with the fuller life. Then I was an unknown schoolteacher, so hard up that I could not afford even to buy a push-bicycle. I have no doubt that even then most people lived very happily in County Clare. They belonged – a totally different situation from that of transients like me. So, unenterprisingly, I let the autumn pass and the winter come. I bore up until one lashing night just before Christmas. Then the trap was sprung on me.

That December night I was sitting with my fellow lodger, Paul Moran, also a teacher with the Christian Brothers, much my senior, beside the turf fire in our little sitting room, each of us reading, pen in hand, a pile of children's essays. Growing tired of reading one essay after another on 'The Mineral Resources of Ireland', I laid down my pile of copybooks, lit my pipe, bellowsed the fire to a blaze and looked across at Moran's greying crop.

'You know, Paul,' I said, relishing my pipe, the fire, my lumpy armchair and the Atlantic rain battering the empty street outside, 'these aren't such bad lodgings after all.'

He laid down his pile of essays on 'The Irish Language', took out his pipe and said, sourly: 'I'm glad you like 'em.'

'Paul,' I said expansively, stretching out my legs, 'did you ever think of marrying?'

If I had stuck a lance into his stomach I could not have produced a more violent result. Red rage poured from his mouth, his eyes, his ears, his clenched hands, every hair of his cropped skull.

'Marry? Are you mad? On my salary? With a mother and a sister to support? How the bloody hell do you think I could get married? Do you know anything at all about the facts of life? Next June I'll have been in this job for sixteen bloody years. Since I left college I've . . .'

He poured abuse over me for five nonstop minutes of out-spoken autobiography that filled me with pity for him and terror for myself. He calmed as abruptly as he had begun, lit his pipe and, mentioning a girl whom he had liked but was too poor to marry, said: 'I don't blame her. She saw there was no future in me. She died a year ago. She had four children. I'll have one of them in my class next year.'

He went back to his task and I pretended to return to mine. I was thinking of the long, wet street of Ballinasloe.

Was I trapped? For life?

When Eileen and I met in Cork that Christmas of 1924 we had both made up our minds to resign at the end of the school year. She had already laid out her course: she was spending her last year in Ballinasloe preparing herself for a post in a technical school as an instructor in commerce. (She had taken her college degree in economics.) I decided to save every shilling I could and go back to University College, Cork, for another master's degree which might lead to a better job. The following Easter, of 1925, we met again, in Galway. We had by then both given notice of our intentions to our superiors. We spent the summer in Cork, saving our few pounds.

For all of us it was our year of fate. Molly Fitzgerald, left for her Main Street, where she met and married a senator. Michael O'Donovan was plucked from penury and provincialism by the generous hand of Lennox Robinson and sent off as assistant to the poet Geoffrey Taylor, then in charge of the Carnegie Library in Wicklow town, some thirty miles from Dublin. Through Geoffrey and his wife Norah McGuinness, the painter, he was at once thrown into contact with the literary set in Dublin. Eileen got exactly the sort of post she wanted in a technical school in the pleasant town of Naas, which is only twenty miles from Dublin. I was left alone in Cork, envying the lot of them, feeling sometimes even a little jealous of Michael, who often met Eileen during their visits to Dublin to see plays, or exhibitions of painting, or, on occasion, to attend a symphony concert. That year I was deprived even of the company of Daniel Corkery, who disapproved of my angry criticisms of Republican politics and whose continuing interest in such folly, as I regarded it, struck me as the peak of unrealism. In my solitariness I began to write.

Michael had meantime met AE, talked to him generously and enthusiastically about me, and urged me to send something to the *Statesman*. He was by this time writing excellent poetry and had already appeared there himself, in March 1925, under his pen name Frank O'Connor, which he kept ever after. I did send AE something, and he did publish it, in the *Statesman* of 6 February 1926, beside a translation of a Gaelic poem by O'Connor. It was a short story called *Lilliput*. That day I felt like an explorer who has been pushing on for such a long time, in such bad weather, over such rough country, that he is almost ready to turn back and publicly acknowledge defeat when, suddenly, the fog parts, the clouds rise, and there, far away, very far away, shining clearly in the sun, is his beckoning city.

2

If I know now that I had always been a writer it is not because of my early, boyish efforts (every child wants to write or draw), nor because of my persistence (every writer has met scores of people in their forties and fifties who still 'want to write'). I know it because I have become a writer. Of what quality is another matter, something that not even I know, perhaps I least of all. In these matters there is only one judge who dares not lie, Father Time, and he wobbles a long time before he makes up his mind. Everybody who has lived to be seventy or eighty must know this, having in his span seen too many men and women reach an apparently unassailable peak which they were presently forced to yield, line by line, to their successors and later critics. Few of us can be quite so certain today as we once were about say Galsworthy, Bennett, Gide, Rolland, Gerhart Hauptmann, Somerset Maugham, John Steinbeck. By a coincidence, it has just happened that I have come on two topical reconsiderations of two of those writers. I will quote two sentences from a review by Richard Mayne, in the *New Statesman*, of the paperback reissues of four books by Maugham, including what I still think his best novel *Of Human Bondage*:

> The habit of talking like a Dutch uncle to some imaginary middle-brow reader is crippling for a serious novelist ... The writing is far more uncertain than in most of Mr Maugham's later work – more cliché-ridden, lusher, sometimes sentimental, and occasionally even inarticulate.

In the same paper a long essay on John Galsworthy by V. S. Pritchett opens:

> Galsworthy's imagination was lukewarm: thin, partial, thumbnail sketches of people, poor invention, jogtrot realism, blur when there was a question of feeling, embarrassment or jauntiness when there should be thought.

This about a Nobel Prize-winner, and an OM, who refused a knighthood. Such later reconsiderations of writers whom we once admired are chastening. They warn us that when we attach the word *artist* to any living man or woman our certainty about what we mean is as limited as when we meet a doctor or a priest – we acknowledge a vocation, a title, a claim.

This is all I mean in general by saying that I know now that I had always been a writer. A writer is a personal state of mind endowed with a certain amount of graphic skill, the measuring of which mind and skill rests with the ages chatting over a glass of Olympian nectar an *ingens lustrum* or two after the author has become dust.

But I also mean something specific by the word *writer*. Every writer is a man with one deaf ear and one blind eye, unteachable by anybody except himself; a man who only half hears and half sees the world about him because for half his time he is absorbedly listening at the keyhole to his own Jungian Demon, examining with fascination his primordial Shadow, his female (or male) self that he (or she) adores. From this inner absorption comes the writer's ruthlessness; egoism; readiness to make use of anybody, even of his dearest and nearest, to serve his pen; his insistence on reshaping everything that he thus half sees and half hears in accord with his inner self; and his endless curiosity mingled now with sympathy, now with an almost blind hatred for other writers, who are, meantime, also eavesdropping on their own Demons and Shadows.

I do not, however, believe at all that writers are blind masses of subjectivity. On the contrary I believe that most writers have much more in common with the scientific mind than we realise. Just as every scientist seeks for the inherent order of life in some small corner of nature, surely the artist who wants to understand his whole experience as a man will seek also for an intelligent hypothesis to 'explain' his small corner of human life? Hardy – Dorset, and the President of the Immortals; Jane Austen – Hampshire and Good Intentions; Mauriac – Bordeaux and Greed. Where scientist and artist radically differ is in the nature of their material, not of their pursuits. We can classify crystals. We cannot classify the endless variety of the human psyche. But the pursuit of each seems to me to come from a similar intellectual desire to find order in the seeming chaos of Life.

I have to except, of course, from this intellectual pursuit those writers who are mainly excited by what one may call the Donnybrook Fair side of life – writers who choose disorder as a theme, or the tumult of their own beings, which comes to the same thing. These one might call our Dionysiacs or anarchists. I do not deny their interest. Yet, even including these Dionysiacs, I suggest it is a true image of both scientists and writers to see them all as a scattered procession of explorers, small as ants as compared to the world, each climbing his grassblade to view the universe, uttering triumphant cries, now called a poem, now a scientific fact, one here, one there, until the world we know gets mapped and remapped, over and over, that is to say gets invented again and again in every generation: *made up*, as Isidore Rabi put it much more forcibly that I dare to when he said:

> The universe is not given to us in the form of a map or guide.
> It is made up by human minds and imaginations out of slight
> hints which come from acute observations and the profound
> stratagems of experiments.

Just as the intellectual side of the artist is too often unappreci-
ated by the layman, so is this imaginative side of the scientist.
Every scientist not a hack knows that without imagination he
cannot move an inch when faced by a new problem. When
Newton called space the *sensorium Dei* he was talking poetry;
when he used such words as *force* and *attraction* he was talking
metaphors. I have even heard a scientist say that Newton was
being a mystic when he used those terms, as I have seen it
written by another scientist that Einstein's 'unified field' theory
was a pure act of faith, though no less scientific as an approach
for that. Scientists are always inventing shapes of life, in the
sense that Max Planck invented the life-shape of the quantum
theory by a pure hunch or guess at a time when he had not a
shred of evidence for assuming, that is, imagining-for-the-sake-
of-the-hypothesis, that radiant energy is emitted in particles or
bits, or quanta, and not, as everybody else had thought before
him, in a flowing stream. The scientist who says 'Let's suppose!'
is at that point using the same inspiration as the storyteller
who says 'Let's pretend', and for the same reason – to transform
chaos into meaning.

The image of the artist holding a mirror up to nature leaves
out of account this transformation, by selection and invention,
of the otherwise meaningless jungle of actuality. His good eye,
his good ear, demon-guided, decides fastidiously, intellectually
and imaginatively what, alone among all the eyes and ears of
the world, he shall see and hear in the green wilderness. What
saves him from the banality of seeing and hearing what everybody else has always seen and heard is his God-given infirmities.
They bestow on him his own obstinate vision, which is his Self
in action, making new shapes of life.

3

One revealing experience came my way one morning in the
spring of 1926 when I chanced to halt in the main corridor of

University College, Cork, to glance at the official notices pinned up among the ogham stones and the old stone querns that line the stone-flagged hallway. At that instant my line of fate was crossed by a man named Stephen Harkness, an American who once loaned a poor man named Rockefeller one thousand dollars for some scheme concerning the sale of oil, as a result of which both became in the course of time very rich indeed. In 1926 Stephen's son Edward was also a very rich man, an Ohioan who had been educated at Saint Paul's School in Concord, New Hampshire, and at Yale; was a director of the Southern Pacific and the New York Central railroads; a trustee of the Metropolitan Museum of Art in New York, and of the Presbyterian Hospital; the president of the Commonwealth Fund; and a member of seven New York clubs. He was just twice my age that January morning in 1926 as I read on the notice board that the Commonwealth Fund (later known as the Harkness Fund) was offering valuable travelling fellowships to suitable candidates who wished to do postgraduate work in the United States.

Whether through ignorance or arrogance, or both, I was not much interested in this idea of studying in the United States. At that time very few people were. Nevertheless, on an idle impulse, I went into the president's office for further information, was given an application form and mildlyencouraged to 'have a shot at it.' I filled in the form. I found that I also needed some written recommendations from people who knew me. That Christmas I had been in Dublin, and met AE and Lennox Robinson, so I ventured to ask them if they would be so kind as to sponsor me. They very generously did, and I have no doubt that it was solely thanks to their recommendation that I was asked to come to London for an interview. In due course, I was informed that I had been granted a fellowship valuable enough to permit me to spend two years, studying freely, in any American university which the foundation approved and to travel around the United States, in comfort, for three months.

When Whistler published his *The Gentle Art of Making Enemies* he brightened the margins with little mocking signatures, his famous butterflies. As my narrative gradually progresses from inscience to awareness I have been tempted to drop on my margins from time to time a drawing of a pealing bell, my warning bell. 'Here it comes!' my little bell would say. 'Another of those welling-up moments whose supreme import- ance you failed at the time to recognise, yet years afterwards were to recognise, and change by another speck.' There might well be a whole bombilation of clanging bells in my margin at this point.

Because, when I opened and read the letter informing me that I was now a Commonwealth Fellow I read it between bewilderment and indifference. I was, as journalists say, stun- ned. I told nobody about it for several days. The first person I told was the president's secretary, a young woman whom I very much liked and admired, and her only because I met her by chance in the street and because she asked me eagerly if I had had any news about my application for the fellowship.

'Oh, yes!' I said, with the air of somebody recollecting a matter of small importance. 'I got that thing.'

Delighted at my good fortune, she clapped her hands and cried: 'Isn't that absolutely marvellous? You must be feeling on top of the world!'

When I said that I supposed that it was all right, it was better than nothing anyway, she went pale with fury, turned on her heel, and walked away from me saying over her shoulder: 'You are impossible!'

4

Perversely, Cork became more attractive to me according as the time for my departure from it approached, so that whenever I hear on the wind, nowadays, a church bell in the evening, the fragile memory it evokes, the sense of something lost forever, goes back as swift as lightning to this city of my birth at the point in time when I was, without knowing it, about to leave it forever. We must all in our house have had some third sense not merely of departure but final departure, for my father and mother now, at the last moment, evoked from me an affection that I had not given them since childhood, and on their side poured affection over me lavishly, largely no doubt because, for the first time, they had, or thought they had, reason to feel proud of me. My father kept coming to me every second day with some fresh testimony from somebody he had met to my ability, or my cleverness, hitherto unsuspected but now made apparent in this donation of a valuable fellowship. I was happy that he got so much pleasure out of me in the end who had given him so little in the beginning. My mother took an equal delight in gradually filling my brand-new cabin trunk with my brand-new trousseau, which I had the small wit to make as complicated, that is as interesting, for her as possible.

I had bought a book on etiquette and had discovered, for instance, that the ideal shirt for tennis should be fastened between the legs to keep it from riding up and building out in an ungraceful fashion in the heat of the game. There was also, for some reason now lost to me, a mention of black silk shirts. Her search for these, and her explanations for their urgent necessity in Every Gentleman's Complete Outfit must have spread my fame as an oddball in all the drapers' shops in town. (She did not succeed in buying a black silk shirt.) I sent her off after visiting cards, dress shirts with American-style collars attached, a special and hitherto unheard-of kind of expanding cuff-link, patent-leather pumps, silk under-trunks, riding gloves with cord-woven backs, white woollen socks for squash, Ascot-type cravats for wearing with my dressing gown at breakfast. She was both shocked and enchanted by my needs. I did not dare to ask her to inquire after an opera hat, collapsible. I did ask one hatter, pretended I wanted it for a fancy-dress party. He said, 'I know what you mean, but I don't stock 'em, and if I did dere isn't anyone in dis city would know what dey're for.' Ever since I had read *Raffles* it had been my ambition to have one, and make it go *crac*, and swish it under my black red-lined cloak as I climbed the steps of the Opera in Paris – previous to a night raid on the Banque de France. If it was going to be the Full Life I might as well taste what I could of it. I may add that in due course I did play tennis and squash, learned to ride, rowed sculls on the Charles, and went in tails to the theatre, the symphony and opera, though not, alas, in a tall hat (collapsible), to see – how old it makes me feel! – Ruth St Denis dance (she had 'more charm' but 'poor luck' in Yeats' *His Phoenix*), and Duse act, and hear Chaliapin sing.

I think my father touched the peak of his pride in me the day

I told him, rather sheepishly, that I had been summoned to London, with all the other Fellows, to be presented in Saint James's Palace to His Royal Highness the Prince of Wales, later King Edward VIII, and the Duke of Windsor, at the time the Patron of the Commonwealth Fund. Over and over, on my return, I had to tell him about Saint James's, about the equerries, about HRH. ('The grandson,' he said in sad recall, 'of King Edward VII whose head is on my constabulary medal!') There was only one detail that I suppressed – the dry, this-may-take-you-down-a-peg comment of one of the equerries that just before we scholars arrived the Master Bakers of Nottingham had been presented to HRH, bearing – on their shoulders? – a six-foot-high cake. 'Damn nuisance some of these gifts! The cellars are full of boars' heads, elephant tusks, lions' hides, frightful oil paintings from the four corners of the world, and we have to keep every one of 'em. Never know when the fellow who gave them may turn up again and inquire after his tusk or his hide.' I did retail how cross the Queen Mother was the day she spotted this same young equerry's tennis shoes, freshly pipecleaned, drying on a windowsill of the palace. 'My batman took the blame. Sacked! I got him another job of course. But is she a Tartar!'

My father thoroughly approved of the Tartar.

'Take note of it,' he said. 'If you are ever asked to stay in a rich house never put your boots on the windowsill. That's the spirit that made the Empire!' He looked at me sharply. 'You didn't say anything, I hope?'

It was unkind of me; but we had been over this ground half a dozen times and I was bored with it, so I said: 'Well, he did ask me what I had been doing before I got the fellowship.'

'What did you say?' he asked anxiously.

'I said I had been in the Irish Army.' I waited for him to blench. 'I didn't say which army. And he had no time to ask, because then it was my turn to walk up the twenty-five yards of red carpet to the prince standing at the end of it.'

'You foolish boy!' he moaned. 'You might have lost the fellowship!'

'Why? After all, there is such a thing as the Irish Army.'

'The Irish . . .? Oh, *that*!' – and he walked off in disgust at the idea of a Fellow who had been out with the IRA being presented to the grandson of HM Edward VII.

That day at Saint James's Palace was the first time I mingled with my counterparts, and the last time I met them on their home ground. The experience was both disturbing and exhilarating. Those twenty-odd Fellows, from universities all over Britain – I was the only Irishman – depressed me at first for a reason that I could not have foreseen. Their poise, their polish, their techniques, their name-dropping, their social probes into one another's background, their skill at what might nowadays be called Upmanship, even their real or pretended maturity I could take for granted. We all had read of, met or observed enough British-trained Anglo-Irish to recognise an old and rather boring pattern. What I did find disturbing was their cool way of regarding the fellowship purely as a financial subsidy for continuing their private studies for two years, with, as they considered, the regrettable proviso that these studies must be pursued in America. Their eyes were so firmly fixed on the home groove that to them this two-year trip to the United States was, apart from the financial subsidy, a cul-de-sac. They had no wish to escape; quite the contrary. They did not anticipate any experiences in the USA that they could not overmatch in Britain or the Continent. What troubled me was not that this was part of the effortless superiority of a master race looking down at America: it wasn't – it was the normal attitude of all young Britishers of their class at that date, contentedly aware that there was adequate opportunity for them at home, making straight and hard for their fixed goals.

Listening to them bandying all those names of colleges, tutors, professors, posts in the universities, industry, banking, even the Church, prophesying where Tom would go, or recording where Bill had already got to, their minds moving smoothly over a network of opportunity, I thought back to Ballinasloe, and Ennis, and to my one and only, and extremely doubtful, groove in University College, Cork, and it came as a shock to me that, by comparison, Ireland could offer to men like me at most only an isolated opportunity here, and another there, many miles and many years apart. But after this first painful shock of revelation I began to get an exhilarating feeling, quite effortlessly I may say, and all my own, from the thought that if I was not grooved I was different, I was out on my own, I was challenging life in a way that they had never known and never would know.

One of them probed me delicately about my school. I told him all about my grim-happy Lancasterian National School in Cork, its battered desks, its crowded rooms and malodorous jakes, my barefooted companions, Sloppy Dan with his swinging leather, the glass falling from the clerestory when the ball game was being played in the gravelly yard outside with tightly rolled-up balls of paper. He then probed about my college and I enlarged eloquently on old Professor Stockley – 'The only living professor of English who can write sentences without verbs'; on Feathery Ellen, the professor of education who banned Joyce's *Portrait*; on my professor of Old Irish, a poet and a charming little man, who used to write the Sanskrit roots on the blackboard from cards in his hand because he knew no philology, no Sanskrit, and very little Old Irish. As I talked others gathered around me. Gradually they all fell silent, their mouths as hang-jawed as pelicans. When, finally, I told them I had been with the IRA for several years, they stared at me in at first disbelief, then in confusion, amusement, liking, and at last, I believed, in plain envy. It was as if behind an old school tie and the mild exterior of, at least, another future don, they had suddenly discovered a Brendan Behan or a Jean Genet.

As we rose to leave I said: 'See you fellows in America! If you ever get into trouble there ring me up. I have an uncle who is chief of police in Chicago and a cousin who is the best ward boss in Boston.'

I never did that again. It was too easy and (with all respect and affection for my friends who do it often) too near to the stage Irishman. And funny poses do not cut fine grooves.

In turn, those Fellows aroused envy in me when I found that they had all been travelling in Europe in their summer teens while I had been sitting under dripping hedges in West Cork, talking Irish to old men with mouths full of bad teeth and minds full of primordial memories. One Fellow had been as far as Istanbul; another talked glowingly of Zagreb; another, an architect, had pursued Byzantium from Venice to Thessaly;

while I had not even touched the shores of Europe, and the only foreign language I had ever heard spoken by a native was English. On my return to Cork from London I tried to make up a little travel party. It came down in the end to Eileen, Frank O'Connor and myself, and we did just touch the shores of Europe. We went to Bruges.

We stayed in a little inn called, in Flemish, the Flemish Lion, at Damme, a hamlet about four miles up the canal to the sea. One of the charms of Bruges, as of Ravenna or of Aigues Mortes, is that it has been in the literal sense left behind by the tide – so far that the site of the famous offshore naval Battle of Sluys, where the English beat the French in 1340, is today green grass beside this canal that now joins Bruges to the sea. There for a week we swam as deep as skin divers in our first pool of foreigners, feeling everything, seeing nothing, far too mesmerised by the strangeness of this sensual experience for so cool and clear a sense as sight. O'Connor was not there an hour before he revealed, in his usual spontaneous way, his own secret image of the Full Life. He bought an enormous-brimmed black poet's hat – to my intense envy, because once he had done so I could not do it any more than a lady can buy a frock identical to one she has envied on another. He put it on, sat in an outdoor café, and sank into a blissful coma of narcissism, immobile as a waxwork the livelong day. We saw so little of him in Bruges that I should not be surprised if he spent his entire holiday immobile in that café. It was not such a bad way to spend a holiday. How often in later years have I not spent days and days in Rome or Paris – once I had got the monuments and museums off my conscience – just sitting in a café in a boulevard, or a piazza, or on the Via Veneto, watching the passing crowds, or lying on the brushed and combed sands of the Lido, gazing for hours at the blue of the sea or the sky. Otherwise, we cycled into the adjoining piece of Zeeland formed by the estuary of the Schelde, in order to be at least able to say that we had been in Holland, or out to the long beaches of the popular Belgian resorts around Blankerberghe and Heyst. As dazed as a boy after his first kiss, I brought away from Bruges itself only a few startled visions – the great belfry when the chimes rang out, the silence of the Quai du Rosaire, the tomb of Charles the Bold, a few anonymous Gothic outlines blanched by the early morning or by the late moon.

Eileen and I then counted up our few remaining pounds and shillings and declared that we must go to Paris, even if only for a few days. O'Connor either could not afford it or did not wish to come, so we set off alone, indifferent to such unimportant things as comfort and meals, for our first smell of Paris – as unforgettable as the scent of old cottage roses, verbena after rain or apples in hay – of the Bois at night, the deep Seine, the subways, cheap state-monopoly tobacco, and that happily inimitable smell of French water closets, largely Eau de Javel and garlic, that makes them as indigenous a part of the French tradition as Pascal or Voltaire. We wandered, as happy as only first-run tourists can be, hand in hand around the quays, the island, the old city; saw our first play at the Comédie Française; took our first vast, intoxicated, undifferentiating, overgorged gulp of the seemingly endless Louvre; though for me (who had read every novel I could find about the Revolution) the most impressive building in Paris – and I think it may be this for anybody – was the Conciergerie, in whose cold stones all the coldness of the Terror still lives as if preserved on ice forever. That alone made Paris worth every discomfort.

Social manners have become much more relaxed since those days of the expansive 1920s. I was in my twenty-seventh year, ardent and romantic. Eileen, with her high colouring, brown eyes and black hair, was like a rose with the sultry yet brilliant effect of a dark-red rhododendron. Anybody hearing that such a young man had gone to Paris alone with such a girl would then have raised at least an inquiring eyebrow; today, perhaps, add an indulgent smile. I must admit that if today I had a son or a daughter wandering in Paris in like circumstances my eyebrows might shoot up under my hair at once – until I bethought myself of myself at that time. We were as innocent as the morning star that Lampedusa so exquisitely describes in *Il Gattopardo* as 'hanging like a peeled grape' in the dawn sky over the dews of Sicily. Our days were as candid, in the true and original sense of that gleaming word. It sometimes amuses me now to remember that the Left Bank was then full of Americans in temporary exile whooping it up in ways often far from candid, in any sense of the word; to wonder what on earth they would have thought of us two the night we went to the Grand Guignol. There Eileen became so terrified – how wonderful to be able to be terrified by a make-believe! – that she said, as we trudged home at midnight (no money for taxis, and we would not have wasted a sou on a bus supposing we had known what bus to take): 'I know I won't sleep tonight – will you sleep with me?'; which, we both knew, meant that I might in all candour lie by her to comfort her. When we got back to our obscure hotel we agreed that if she were troubled during the night by red visions of blood, and knives, and old women screaming in madhouses, she would knock at the wall of our adjoining rooms and I would come in to her for a while. If, now, I have any of those momentary doubts about young people going off alone, I have only to remind myself of those blissful, disembodied days spent wandering in wonderment through Paris long after the morning star became the evening star in its pink-dark sky.

5

Such was the youth – turned twenty-six, but still an inexperienced youth – who pushed off one night that September, in the tender chugging out from Cobh to a liner anchored far out in the bay under a full moon. Its long lines of portholes were bright. White specks of seagulls swung over its masts. As we approached it we began to hear the ship's band that had come out on deck to welcome us. Two girls on the tender by me melted into a soft weeping at the tune floating across the still water. It was *Come Back to Erin*. They might never see Ireland again. My own feelings as I heard it gave me a shock. I found that I was hearing it with a savage pleasure at its ineptitude – all my latent disillusion with Ireland, therefore with life in general, welling up in a sudden, bitter satisfaction at yet another instance of human stupidity.

A young friend, who had not shared as deeply as I had in the bright dream or the sad disillusion of the Troubles, had come out on the tender with me. He said: 'I hope, Sean, you won't be too homesick in the States?'

'For Ireland?' I asked bitterly. 'I don't care if I never see the bloody place again.'

He was shocked. 'How can you say such a thing?' he cried. 'Look at how lovely it is, especially now, in this moon. Look at the hills, look at the bay, you'll be dreaming of them, man! You'll be weeping tears of blood to get back to them.'

'Nonsense!' I laughed. 'What is Ireland but a country of grasping peasants? Yeats is right. "Romantic Ireland's dead and gone, 'tis with O'Leary in the grave." And "Paudeen grubbing for his greasy pence." No, son! It's finished for me. Forever!'

I thought of him more than once in the year that followed when I would lie awake at night thinking of that moon-white bay.

I was awakened gently the next morning by a bugler softly playing a few bars of some German hymn. We were on the old North-German-Lloyd *München*, taken from the German after the war but still served almost wholly by Germans. I went on deck. Ireland had drifted away behind us out of sight. I went to the prow and for a long time I stood there, looking ahead. Then I went below for breakfast, took my place at a long table, returning the general good mornings. As I shook out my napkin the woman opposite me, German-looking, blonde, blue-eyed, strongly built, handsome, smiled at me. She was older than I, but not by so many years: perhaps five or six? I smiled back and lowered my eyes. My heart was fluttering a wing that it had not fluttered before. It was a very brilliant wing, clearly marked in the colours of the Stars and Stripes beyond the prow. She was travelling alone. We began to chat. After breakfast we continued to chat, side by side on our deck chairs. I will call her Anna Marie Kauffmann.

Had I then read *Lucky Jim* I might have enjoyed my predicament a little more. If it comes to that, had Lucky Jim read *Lucky Jim* he might have enjoyed his predicament a little more. Mine was not unlike. I have not mentioned that I was accompanied aboard the *München* by, of all people, the registrar of University College, Cork, together with his wife and daughter, on his way to spend a year in, of all places, Harvard. He had already mentioned to me that if I covered myself with distinction in Harvard he just might be able to find a post for me in University College, Cork: meaning none other than the post of professor of English which old W. F. P. Stockley was due to resign in – *figurati!* – five years' time. There was really only one time when I could be safely with Anna Marie – after he retired to his cabin, blessedly early because he had no taste for either bingo, dancing or imbibing German lager at the bar. As a result I had to come clean about all this to Anna Marie, who would not otherwise have understood why I kept on suggesting to her to invade the first-class quarters as being more comfortable, or the steerage as being more matey. My patron was equally puzzled, his favourite remark when we met being to me the most welcome one possible: 'I didn't see you all day.' Fortunately – Or was it unfortunately? I might have been saved, as I would also have missed, a great deal of heartburning if she had straightway covered me with disdain – Anna Marie not only understood the situation at once but enjoyed it to the hilt. She proved to be six years older than I, unhappily married, an Episcopalian – Oh! A first-rate kettle of fish! and I thought her very intelligent, though this may have been only because she had had so much more experience than I. She was sardonic, wistful, eager, pretended to be tough, and was as vulnerable as a girl. Her two interests were modern poetry – from her I first heard of T. S. Eliot – and American politics. She had been born in Switzerland, in the Grisons, and was half Italian; her parents, now dead, had emigrated when she was nine to Boston, where they mixed with the German community; her father had done well enough to put her through Vassar; she had married a German exporter, and had no children. While I was with Anna Marie the *München* went at about a thousand knots. When I was not it chugged as slowly as an old tramp. Whenever I saw her in the year ahead of me she always had the same magically accelerative effect on time.

How did she see me? Not surely as a man of the world! She knew her *métier de femme* too well for that. I did not even know my *métier de clerc*, and as for the world I was not even a tonsured catechumen. It did not, of course, occur to me then, on that crowded, sun-drenched ship, sailing into my future, putting a large sea between it and my youth that she might have liked me most for the very thing I was pretending not to be. Now, if I were writing a story about her, that is how I would picture her: a woman of the world, vulnerable to the world, wounded by the world (as who is not who has tried to tread it down?), drawn to an image of her own ignorant youth. I thought then that I carried it off splendidly. And maybe I did too; not because I actually did, but because she would have wished to hope, and so would have chosen to believe, that I could at least pretend a bit. I love these secret, self-deceiving ambiguities. They are far more honest as well as more tender than the crisp certainties of the world at large, though they can also be far more dangerous as I was duly to find out.

13

Harvard: 1926–1929

———————— ❧ ————————

I

On the liner I had amused myself by composing some doggerel
verses about the traditional Irish climate on the lines of:

> And praise God, too, for summer, with the gutters full of rain,
> When the roses drip down the back of your neck and the trellis
>   falls down again,
> When the turf smoke snakes down the chimney in a beautiful
>   purple vein
> And the uncut lawn is starred at dawn with the fallen lilac's
>   stain . . .

In the heavy heat of Manhattan, how I longed for those soft
silvery Irish mornings! The heat was America's first rap on the
knuckles of my expectations. Others followed. The morning we
docked, on the New Jersey side, facing the splendid architectural
mess of Manhattan gleaming against the rising sun, New York
had looked excitingly beautiful; when I got into the city I was
pained to find so much of it dirty, scruffy, paper-littered, untidy,
and hideously raucous with black-barred overhead railways. It
takes time to realise that while New York can always be an
exciting city it is beautiful to the eye only when one can stand
back from it, as when looking across the Hudson, or the East
River, or from the bay, or when approaching it from the airports,
or from certain vantage points at night such as from 70th Street
and Fifth Avenue looking south and west across an angle of the
Park at its army of illuminated alpine towers. Then it can seem
a city never to be forgotten, one of the most lovely in the world.

But the deeper truth about New York is that its supreme appeal is its mill-race energy, as of an overcrowded smithy where, as Milton said of London, there are 'not more anvils and hammers working ... than there be pens and heads sitting by their studious lamps, musing, searching, revolving new notions and ideas.' In fact, even on my first days, I never felt lonely there except at night, when so much of this energy is switched off – its long avenues, as is true of most American cities, strangely empty, its towers lit only in random dots, its roaring elevated railways giving me eye-level glimpses through domestic windows that made me feel like the eye of a passing wind.

It was quiet Cambridge and Harvard, however, that gave me the sharpest knuckle-rap. On every side, at every moment, good example – or bad, according to your ideas? – I heard the puritan murmur of the eleventh American commandment:

> Then come home,
> Close the door,
> And at your leisure
> Sweat some more,
> And call it pleasure.

In humble recognition thereof I took lodgings at Number 48 Irving Street, a quiet, dusty, undistinguished suburban side street, wholly devoted to students' lodging houses, as was plain to be seen every night by the number of green-shaded reading lamps staining the dusk of every window; every morning by the number of milk bottles deposited with a different jingle on every porch; and every Saturday and Sunday morning by the line of exhausted-looking jalopies waiting along the side-walks.

Two other Commonwealth Fellows joined me at Number 48. One was a lean bouncy Scottish physicist named George Bull, an ex-army man, a born mixer, and a splendid cusser in broad Scots, who always walked as if he were swinging along in a kilt to the nearest pub. Bull liked his beer, so his encounters with Prohibition used up a lot of his cussing-power. He was a keen amateur violinist, so we naturally called him Ole Bull. The other man was Frank Chambers – a handsome, dark, indolent-eyed architect, as big and slow as a black bear, though not quite as formidable: he was a very gentle creature. He later gave up architecture for political history; became Senior Lecturer at the London School of Economics and Political Science; probably best known for his book *This Age of Conflict*, a study of the political and military history of the West from 1914 to the present day. These two were somewhat older than I, both serious-minded students, and although Ole Bull had his occasional outbursts of Celtic revolt, it is honest recording to say that the three of us lived at Number 48 like three monks boarded out from Harvard Abbey. Each had his one room, his narrow bed, his one armchair, his pinewood office desk, his chest of drawers (called 'bureau' in American), and on his bureau – as, I suppose, on every bureau within a square mile of Harvard Yard – his one, unmonkish ikon: his smiling girl waiting for him back at home.

Within days my routine was in accord with my simple lodgings. The first thing I bought was an alarm clock, then a teapot, one cup, saucer, plate, spoon, knife and fork, tea towels and paper napkins from the five-and-ten, to make breakfast and afternoon tea and, if I had no lectures, or if it was snowing badly, a snack lunch. Every morning, including Sundays, my clock buzzed me awake at seven. After breakfast I worked until nine, went to my tiny carrel in Widener Library, or to a lecture, and I was back again in my cage in Widener until dinner time. Each day I squeezed in a fast bout of exercise. I tried rowing on the Charles but found that it took too long. I tried swimming but found that it was not strenuous enough. Anyway – it may be a token of my prudery – I did not like the Harvard convention of swimming naked. In the end I found that I could lose the most sweat in the shortest time on the squash courts. After dinner, mostly in some steamy, noisy, students' cafeteria – we all loathed these places but could not afford better – I either went back once more to Widener or returned home to Number 48, there to add my green lamp to the thousands of other green lamps all about me, many of them burning, like green eyes, into the small hours of the morning.

2

I fell completely in love with this ascetic life. It gave me the feeling that I was sharing in a special and perhaps unique reflection of the New England puritan tradition – high-minded and self-denying, lean-limbed and stout-hearted, privileged yet responsible, hierarchical and leisured, sometimes boringly jaunty, but always chock-full of character, never vulgar, often fastidious, and if Harvard was not exactly a liberal institution (I cannot imagine any university in America being called, like Oxford, the Home of Lost Causes!) it was not bigoted, or mean, or parochial, or shut-minded. I felt I was imbibing the finest wine of old Boston's mandarinism as I had been induced to imagine it by such men as Emerson and Thoreau and William Dean Howells, but especially by those three great Harvardians, Henry Adams, William and Henry James.

This pleasant illusion faded when I discovered that what I was really admiring in Harvard was not Boston but Berlin. I could not have known that all over America, from coast to coast, other students of the humanities were living very similar lives under the same Germanic academic influence; devotedly earnest, pedantically specialised, fanatically rationalist, emotionally arid, fundamentally anti-aesthetic. But I should have seen, and did gradually come to see, that whatever about other places, literature in Harvard at the graduate level chiefly meant philology; as all over America it later meant textual analysis. I know no Harvard professor of the 1920s, except Babbitt, who realised that plays, poetry or novels had ever been written at a higher temperature than an icebox. If I am right in this it is not surprising that the book which then presented the ideal approach to literature was John Livingstone Lowes' *The Road to Xanadu*, an exotic piece of scholarly bravura where every line of *Kubla Khan* is traced to its source, and all the wild wonder of the poem annihilated. ('Our most accomplished sleuth,' Babbitt called Lowes.) Perhaps I came at a bad time; too late for Santayana, Whitey and Foster Damon, too soon for F. O. Matthiessen and Theodore Spencer (both in the graduate school with me in 1926), for Harry Levin, and Archibald MacLeish; and Alfred North Whitehead was not teaching while I was there; too soon, above all, to escape the powerful and, I now feel, baleful influence of that devouring old lion of the humanities in Harvard for some forty years, George Lyman Kittredge.

Like everybody else who sat under him, I never failed to be entranced by Kitty's lucid brain, and depressed to find him invariably remote from his students, to whom he always gave the impression that he regarded everybody under fifty as little better than a schoolboy. I do not doubt that among his colleagues he must often have expanded; I never once saw him do so in class, and as well as attending all his lectures in the Beowulf course – which were of a deadly dullness – I dropped as often as I could into his other classes simply for the joy of seeing that lovely brain and that faultless memory working as smoothly as a precision instrument. A student in his famous English 2 course might, for example, shoot up his hand and say: 'Sir, is there any reason for maintaining a parallel between the story of Hamlet and the story of Orestes?'

Kittredge would instantaneously reply: 'No, sir, for the following six reasons. Number one. We do not know that the mother of Hamlet was privy to the death of Claudius. We do know that the mother of Orestes was privy to the murder of her husband. Number two. The madness of Orestes occurs *after* he has slain his father's murderer, whereas Hamlet . . .'

And so on, unhesitating, clear and orderly no matter what the question. Agreed that he had been doing this sort of thing for forty years!

I only wish I had been in his Beowulf class the day he irritably reproved my friend Moody Prior, later professor of English at Northwestern, for halting his translation with an occasional 'Er . . .' (This was a common practice of Kitty's with all of us: he really was a testy old man!)

'But sir!' Moody had the wit to retort. 'To er is human?'

It would have been something to see Kittredge smile, however feebly.

I have often, since then, heard it proposed that the reason why Kittredge and his colleagues persisted in the grim Ph.D. regime that they imposed on their students – it meant at least two gruelling years of linguistic or philological studies, and one, two, or more years on a thesis of the most pedantically concentrated nature – was not only because they had been trained that way themselves in Berlin, or Munich or Heidelberg, but because they felt that very few, if any, of their students had enough background or brains to be anything but useful language teachers. If there ever was any validity in this idea it could,

212

surely, refer only to the sort of pioneer or backwoods America which they had known in their boyhood. Certainly, by the 1920s, when Kitty's patriarchal beard and leonine mane were white as snow, this argument of despair was fast losing any such validity as it may ever have had. It was nothing but blind militarism to have subjected men like Matthiessen, or Spencer, or Ernest Simmons to this (for them pointless) discipline: men who were cut out to be, and proved themselves to be, perceptive and inspiring literary critics as well as sound scholars. I used to groan whenever I thought of Ernie Simmons toiling over his doctoral thesis on one single folktale at a time when he might have been laying the foundations for his three big books on Tolstoy, Dostoievsky and Chekhov. Instead, in search of variants of that single tale he had to travel all over Europe to satisfy the Kittredgian insistence on absolute completeness of detail irrespective of any other quality whatever. If Ernest Simmons were proposing to be a folklorist, yes. But had Kitty no perception of the young man's real potentialities?

Over the years I have canvassed the opinions of others who knew Kittredge. The general feeling is that his mind was assimilative rather than original: he had, that is, amassed an encyclopedic knowledge of a certain orthodox combination of subjects, and never forgotten one jot of it. All pay tribute to his domineering personality. He built up what Babbitt called the Philological Syndicate in Harvard, which he was also able to control indirectly in other universities throughout the United States. On the verbal precision of his mind everybody is admiringly agreed: as most are about his behaviour as a crotchety martinet in the classroom. No present-day student, one feels, would put up with his petty despotism. His throne did not so much fall as crumble in the late 1930s and 1940s; 'toppled,' says Harry Levin in his monograph on *Irving Babbitt and the Teaching of Literature*, 'by the sheer unbalanced poundage of Germanised scholarship'; or undermined by the gradual shifts of emphasis of younger men like Mattheissen, Spencer and Levin himself, though not without some tough hand-to-hand fighting from the old rearguard. And nobody who has ever taught in any university needs to be told just how tough these gentle recluses can be. Others may consult the reticent novels of Sir Charles Snow, and multiply by ten. A key date for the beginning of the change-over may be the appearance of T. S. Eliot in Harvard as Charles Eliot Norton Professor in 1932–1933.

Is it far-fetched of me to think that, long after Kittredge's era is over, his young-clerks-become-old-presbyters still carried on something of his pedantic tradition under other forms? Such as the lethally mechanical, pedantic and dogmatic application of the so-called New Criticism; i.e., literary 'criticism' by means of microscopic verbal analysis, and the bloodless sport of truffle-hunting under every literary oak tree not now for Sanskrit and Old High German word roots but for symbols and archetypes: like a certain, far from untypical, Ivy League professor of my acquaintance who always explained to his classes on Mark Twain that *Huck Finn* was not about the Mississippi River but about the River of Life, that the fog that descended on the runaways was not a real Mississippi fog but an archetypal soul-fog, that the island was not a real island, that the slave was not a real slave, and so on and on. To all of which, I have no reason to doubt, his young pupils sat enraptured, because it is, alas, true that the one thing all American youngsters love is a rational explanation of the otherwise vague, mysterious and troubling. In justice to Kittredge, this sort of thing would have driven him mad. In full justice to him, it was all inherent in his own refusal to treat the humanities as human. Or is it simply that there is some endemic demon in the academic nature that aches for machine control, even in the arts?

3

This, then, was the reality of the illusion I fell in love with that September of 1926, all unknowing, uncritical, happily deceived. Still, such after all is the way of love, and by the time I saw through my love, undeceived, I had learned at least one thing well worth the experience – the difference between imaginative and unimaginative scholarship.

The nature of the thing-in-itself, as a discipline or as an abstract virtue, apart from all question of its use and abuse, I learned in my first fifteen seconds at Harvard. One single sentence did it, spoken by my adviser in studies, Fred Norris Robinson, whom we all affectionately called either Fritz or Robby, a distinguished Chaucerian with a sound knowledge of early English and Celtic philology. He uttered it after I had outlined to him the project I proposed to work on while at Harvard. This ingenious project was to have been 'The Possible Influence of Old Irish Verse on Anglo-Saxon Metrics,' which was exactly the sort of damn-fool project that young would-be scholars then loved to dream about o' nights – until somebody like Fritz Robinson taught them the elements of commonsense.

Fritz, who over decades of study in medieval history, literature and linguistics had gathered more than a few facts about the places and centuries I proposed to deal with, listened patiently, and I may now well think quizzically, as I eagerly told him all about Iona and Lindisfarne, about the Celtic missionaries who had founded them, and about their possible (I said probable) influence on Northumbrian letters; pointing out to him that Caedmon (whom I regret to say I called 'The Father of English Song') had actually lived and worked in Whitby; which (I explained to Fritz) was a foundation, part hermitage, part monastery, that had grown up in the wake of those Irish missionaries. Having then given Fritz a little lecture on the nature of Irish metrics and of Anglo-Saxon metrics, and declared finally that 'nothing would have been easier' than for the Irish verse mode to have influenced the Anglo-Saxon verse mode, I leaned back and awaited his approval.

For a few moments, Fritz, impassive as a bonze, breathing heavily, pipe-puffing, said nothing. Then, very slowly, in his pleasant double-bass, double-chinned, port-winey voice he uttered *the* sentence. 'Well,' he said, 'it might be worth while. To spend two or three years on it. Just to see. If there is anything in it.'

It is a sentence that every neophyte might well hang over his bed and look at long and ponderingly every time he feels himself about to give birth to a bright idea. I have timed the sentence many times, and if I speak it slowly and breathingly, as Fritz did, it always takes fifteen seconds. Each time it sinks into my bowels like a very, very cold drink. If you care to pour it out rapidly and stir it briskly you will get Instant Harvard; vintage 1926; *very* dry.

I do not pretend that on hearing those twenty-odd words I

was converted instantly to the faith, but I did at once yearn to be a catechumen. If I never did become a member of the community it was because I was no more cut out to be any kind of scholar (whether with or without imagination), either by temperament or by natural endowments, than I had earlier been cut out to be a gunman. I think I might, with training and discipline, have developed at least some of the qualities of mind necessary for scholarship – coolness, detachment, a healthy modesty, a distrust of the flashy, and a terror of all attractive generalisations. Unfortunately I lacked utterly that most elementary scholarly requirement of all – a quick, capacious, accurate and retentive memory, without which no scholar can move an inch. Still, like Saul about to be anointed by the prophet Samuel, I did see the darkness and the light. As from a little hilltop I could at least see henceforth the supreme beauty of accuracy in thought and word, even when actually hearing anything but accuracy balloon out of my mouth, quite effortlessly and indeed quite involuntarily – it is an ethnic gift – like conversations in a strip cartoon.

I became aware that Fritz was still talking in the same leisurely voice, gentle and authoritative, developed, no doubt, over years of dealing with other yearners for the true faith, who (he presumed, possibly quite wrongly) would never rise beyond the degree of married subdeacons with large families in some remote Baptist high school in Mississippi or Alabama. He was saying: 'I think, perhaps, to begin with, you had better join my class in Old Irish. I know you have done some work on this in Cork. It will be no harm to polish it up a bit more. And you might also do some Middle Welsh with me. And I don't see why you should not take Professor Kittredge's course in Beowulf. And it might be no harm to do some Middle English as well. And then,' he concluded pleasantly, 'we will see.'

I had no doubts. Eagerly I set to. Two or three years? Why not four or five? I saw myself going on to Gothic and Old High German with Francis Magoun; to Chaucer under Robby; to Old French under J. D. M. Ford. I thought of my old professor back in Cork, W. F. P. Stockley, who had only a smattering of Old English and Middle English, who never even mentioned O. H. G., who knew no Old Irish or Middle Welsh, whose finest gesture when dealing with Chaucer was to recite the first four lines of the Prologue in a rousing, Harry Lauder-ish version of the Midland-Kent-ish dialect, after which all references to linguistics were firmly dropped. I thought how all this would impress my registrar at UCC. After three years at Harvard, and with its Ph.D. under my belt, I could see myself swishing into the quadrangle of UCC in a low-slung, high-powered car, with a beard just like Stockley's.

I duly attended the classes recommended by Fritz. They were gruelers, especially his own since there were only two students at each, myself and Ernie Simmons. I got an A in my courses. I grew a small beard. I bought a Model T Ford secondhand. And I ultimately got an A.M. in what the authorities called, in kindness, Comparative Philology, which it was not. To achieve even this little I worked as I never worked before or since, and while it lasted I felt as happy and as immortal as a student; for Edward Thomas was right when he said of Oxford that to a student life is forever. My happiness lasted until I found about the middle of my second term that the factual stocks I had accumulated with so much effort during my first term were already evaporating as slowly and surely as whiskey in an uncorked bottle.

It is likely that, just as religious doubts often flower in the mind only after they have begun with a revolt in the body, my doubts about the vocation of scholarship began to proliferate only after I made this discovery of my physical inadequacy for it; though it has to be said, I have already as much as said it, that when I looked at the end results of scholarship among the Melchizedeks about me, their bleakness fed the flames of doubt like dry leaves in autumn. It would be only a matter of time before I would finally decide that while everything good, great and worthwhile that men think, dream and do is based on our knowledge of the world as scientific fact, or is nonsense, so that without even philology a great part of the world of letters would be closed to us, I was not going to add one word to that world of words if I were to devote all my energies under Harvard's antiquarians to the history of words alone.

In my growing discontent, whether it was with Harvard or myself I cannot tell now but I do know that I was suddenly reminded that across the Charles River there is a place called Boston. Coming on a forgotten letter of introduction that I had brought with me from Ireland, addressed to one Albert Kennedy, South End House, Union Park, I mailed it and received by return a warm letter inviting me to visit South End House. I found the place with some difficulty. The 'House' turned out to be a 'Settlement House' (*vide infra et seq.*, as my fellow neophytes at Harvard might say); tall, red brick, sedate, Victorian, one of about thirty others like it. The park was a railed-off, neglected, sub-city square. The surrounding quarter was more than seedy: it was then one of Boston's juiciest Skid Rows, a run-down complex of old-time oblongs, polygons, circles, rhomboids, triangles and elongated ovals crossed or connected by long grimy streets. I found this geometrical paradise for drunks and dope addicts so confusing that even after I had lived there for a year as a Settlement worker (again *v. inf. et seq.*) I was always getting lost even by day, and I can testify that apart from such permanent residents as the Settlement's workers few people knew the way around there after dark except the ancient drink- or dope-filled residents, the overworked priests of the Cathedral of the Holy Cross, the cops, and daring explorers accompanied by talking dogs.

Here Kennedy ran his Settlement House. This he crisply defined on our first meeting as 'an institution designed to fill in the educational gaps of a given geographical area.' It was typical of him to be so practical, and so wrong. I took to him immediately. He was a handsome man with a ready laugh who looked as if he could have been a parson. In fact he could not have been; he might have been; he had actually hoped to be one before he abandoned the seminary for a more humanitarian vocation. I liked his quick mind, his wry humour and the impeccable craftsman's taste with which he had transformed so much of the interior of his ugly old house into a pleasing sequence of livable and even elegant rooms.

His wife, Edith, was disturbingly different. She was a little, greying woman who had obviously once been pretty and vivacious, and gave the immediate impression that she still had far more zest for life than she was able to satisfy. She struck me as being more Beacon Hill than South End, where she was, and I fear felt herself to be, a goldfish in a trout pool; so much so that from our first meeting I was fascinated to know how she ever got there – all the more so because I believed that she spent a certain amount of her time wondering over the same question herself.

I am always attracted by that compulsive quality in men and women that makes them follow a dream. It may be a reticent strength or an eloquent weakness. In either case, it is certain to conceal or reveal a good deal about their inmost natures. When they hang on to the dream to the end, and it becomes a mask that has become a second face, they are by then so much their own imagination of themselves that it is extremely difficult to see the essential private person behind the dream. But if the dream dies in the dreamer you not only sense, even if you only sense the precious problem in the oyster, but you know that at certain emotional tides the crustacean will open to breathe. With Kay – we always knew Albert Kennedy, perhaps symbolically, by the first letter of his name; nobody called him Albert, or Bert or Al – the dream held firm, and very, very few people ever got behind it. If Edith ever had had a like dream of working for, or among, the other half of Boston, it was plain that she had none of it now. She loved nothing better than to make jasmine tea in their agreeable apartment at the top of the house, well insulated from the busy social workers below, and start long probing, wondering, self-revealing, philosophical-analytical talks. She would have made an ideal wife for a publisher or the president of a university. She wrote wry short stories and had already published a few of them in the *Atlantic Monthly*. Was she an American Candida? After all, Kay had very nearly been a parson like Shaw's Morell.

I soon became deeply indebted to these two intelligent and idealistic people not only for their kindness and hospitality, not only because they opened some interesting doors for me in Boston, New York and elsewhere, mainly among people interested in the arts, but because their own talk and their own lives threw so many intimate lights on Boston and America.

Before I met the Kennedys I had not heard of Social Settlements although there is a well-known one in London's East End called Toynbee Hall. After I met them I visited several of these Settlements, and through them, whether in places like downtown New York, South Chicago or the Kentucky mountains, I was to come close up to a feature of American life that was no less vivid, when I thus experienced it directly, for having previously been a common-place in print. I mean the America of the melting pot. When this happened I began to see that Kay had been much too restricted and practical in his ideas about Settlements. After all, Jane Addam's Hull House in Chicago was much more than a house in Halstead Street where a few kind ladies read William Morris to poor immigrants by day and taught them *petit point* by night. (See her *Twenty Years at Hull House*, or her *Democracy* and *Social Ethics*, or her *The Spirit of Youth and the City Streets*.) Hull House taught Chicago, and tried to teach America, what for better or worse Americanism could, should or actually did mean to any Pole, Swede, Irishman, German, Syrian or other immigrant yearning to be part of it. If in the Chicago of the end of the last century, and for a deplorable part of this century, Americanism did not mean much that was agreeable – indeed, very much the opposite – the immigrant had nevertheless to know it, adapt to it and in time learn to improve it or even reform it, as his good friend Miss Addams, and her good friends such as Clarence Darrow and Governor Altgeld, tried to do. Hull House was a lighthouse piercing the fog of America's future, and so was every other Settlement House in America at that time.

5

Now Dear Reader I am about to record my first exploration of those sexual charms that every man has dreamed of since Eve drew Adam's attention to hers by means of a tantalising fig-leaf. I had not given a second thought to Anna Marie since our goodbye in New York in the September of the previous year, and neither had I pursued any of the appealing young women I had observed at those three or four ritual parties given to foreigners by hospitable Bostonians such as, in the case of us Commonwealth Fellows, the anglophile members of the English Speaking Union. I had not even mentioned Anna Marie Kauffmann in my letters to Eileen, assuming that she would be much more interested in Boston's seventeenth- and eighteenth-century relics, in parts so very like Dublin's; its decade of museums, its art galleries, its wide city parks, its weekly Symphony (Koussevitsky conducting at that time) with its ritual (pre-Depression) parade of feminine fashion, low-bosomed, bare-backed, diamonded, pearled, invoking such names as Cartier, Worth, Tiffany, Lalique, Fouquet, all the more impressive when blended in the usual egalitarian American way with students from Mass Tech, Harvard, Radcliffe, Boston University, Wellesley and farther afield. Besides, now that Eileen had happily exchanged Ireland's steppes for Ireland's Moscow, rich with its own theatre, museums, galleries and political gossip, what interest could she have in an unknown Mrs Kauffmann?

I had myself all but forgotten her until there she suddenly was of a fateful March evening in 1927, standing with her husband in the babbling foyer of Symphony Hall dressed in a metallic puritan-grey gown that displayed her splendid, strong, golden shoulders, looking at me between a dozen other shoulders so quizzically yet so coolly that I was unsure whether or not to approach her until her lips seemed to foretell a smile ... And did her right eyelid or did it not flicker? I came forward with a bow, introduced myself as a fellow passenger on the *München* the previous September, since then post-graduate student at Harvard, and was formally introduced by her to her husband, who gave me a sharp look-over. Something about the reserve of all three actions made me instantly feel her fellow-conspirator, however slightly, innocently and involuntarily.

I do not know what I had expected Kauffmann to look like (General von Hindenburg?), but I know he surprised me by being slight, dark, lean and earnest, with a restless, almost embarrassed manner towards his wife, a way of flicking his eyes around all the time as if to see who was listening. At one moment, when she said something which I do not now recall and then did not understand, he nudged her. She was, as always, unconstrained, her spirit flowing in the wind. I found her less demonstrative than on the ship, possibly because I had already become more accustomed to American ways. I cannot say that I was drawn to him and I might not have been redrawn to her at all that night if I had not earlier liked her so much when alone with her on that liner, two overgrown juveniles on holiday, or if the present contrast between these two married people (who possibly had been drawn to one another originally by that attraction of opposites which produces so many marriages and which I now call the completion of complements) did not by their manner that night reveal an undeniable incompatibility.

Just as the intermission ended he was saying that they were going to the shore that week, if the good weather held, to check on the roof of their summer house. She invited me to join them. He rather less warmly added his invitation. That is how I saw for the first time those little woods of the New England shore, alone with her while he fussed with his local contractor. In the late afternoon she drove me still chattering like an eighteen-year-old along the beach to see the first lights of Plymouth across the bay. They moved me deeply, and by her sudden silence I could feel that they also touched her, and for the first time I realised how tense, how hovering, how close the past tense is to us all. In that moment by the monument commemorating Myles Standish – Elizabethan fighter, colonist, Governor – barely aware of the dusking, whispering, dividing Atlantic, I succumbed so far to our fellow-feeling as exiles, to the loneliness of the place, to my first intimate human contact with an antique America, to the feeling of us both being part of all Time that I put my arm around her waist and she hers around mine. I rubbed my cheek to her cheek. She stared at me. Our mouths kissed. She shook me to my marrow by her swift, wild, alert glance around and her warning of 'Not now! Not here!' Trembling at the premise and the promise of that erotic cry I released her.

We returned to the car and to her house in virtual silence. The three of us drove back to Boston, seated in the front of his station wagon (they called them beach wagons then) she between us, her right hand occasionally seeking mine, our shoulders together. I returned to my monk's life to bury myself

222

in the counter-attractions of the paradigms and mutations in Middle Welsh.

6

Weeks passed. One's judgment of people would probably be more accurate if we could feel with them warmly and simultaneously observe them coldly. Between Anna and me this counterpoint of the reason and the imagination never happened even while we still were – or was she ever? – merely playing The Game. Whenever we met for a cosy afternoon tea in Cambridge or Boston, or casually in the Harvard Fogg museum, or in the Isabella Stewart Gardner, or by arrangement one frosty night somewhere on Beacon Hill at some amateur group's gallant struggle with Joyce's *Exiles*, I felt with pleasure, sometimes with delight, her closeness, touch, voice, scent, laughter, her intake of breath if she happened to mention her idealistic youth in Europe or her failed marriage in America. It would only be when we had parted, with a formal handshake if in public, a warm kiss if we were secluded, that I would face such self-questions as what did she imagine was interesting about me or what did I find so attractive about her, and never come to any clear conclusion. Do I hear over my shoulder a one-shot laugh from Dear Reader amused at the hypocrisy of this young man wondering what could possibly be the attractions of a woman when he is apparently on the eve of enjoying her between the sheets? Yeats may answer for me. *We were the last romantics . . . Traditional sanctity and loveliness . . .* And so on.

One precious thing I am sure I got from my experiences as a would-be Irish revolutionary had been the joy of a selfless confederation that transmuted us, elevated us, invaded, wedded us. And I swear that Stendhal's attitude to love had the same source, in his politics – the revolutionary's shattered dream after Waterloo of emancipated Man compensated by his lifelong glorification of Woman. No wonder the author of *L'Amour* and *Le Chartreuse* spent far more years (on the evidence of his own memoirs) idealising women than he spent in the actual enjoyment of them, while at the same time (again his memoirs) finding relief from his lusts in prostitutes at a *louis d'or* a head (or tail) or in (again frankly) those bad habits 'which we all had'.

Like Yeats, like every idealist, he distinguished between the Paphian and the Platonic in sex. I thereby no longer wonder, as I once did, that my infatuation for the splendid shoulders of A. M. K. could feel like a pot simmering, bubbling, seething upwards and that just when it should have boiled over it should collapse as if some celestial hand had suddenly cut off the gas.

It is not that I was too young, virginal, unpractised. After all, Stendhal, who wrote his autobiographical epitaph in the three words *scrisse, visse, amo* (wrote, lived, loved), was forty-nine when fate tore him from his beloved Italy and his adored Méthilde, 'that angelic soul hidden in so lovely a body . . . a woman I adored, who loved me, and who' – the sad words are almost the *leitmotif* of his whole love-life – 'never gave herself to me.' His admirers will remember the continuing sequel to that adoration months later, in Paris. There three of his pals, out of pity for the poor chap's love-lorn depression, plotted a delicious sexy party to comfort him – four girls, as handsome as willing, all warm with hot punch or champagne, in an establishment so elegant that the loveliest girl of the four, by name Alexandrine, black-eyed, shapely, shy ('I never saw anything so pretty') brought her own personal maid with her. When it came to the love-lorn Stendhal's turn to disappear into the next room where Alexandrine awaited his pleasure in the garments of Eve he found her body utterly adorable, but – 'I completely failed her! An utter fiasco!' His pals, furiously informed at once by the insulted Alexandrine that in fact their guest was impotent became so hilarious that one rolled for five minutes in laughter on the carpet and another had to be restored with champagne. The story enchanted their set in Paris for weeks after. I feel that their victim did not lie when he later reported in his reminiscences: 'I was not at all embarrassed. I was merely surprised. I don't know why it happened, but when I entered that bedroom where Alexandrine lay like some charming ornament I suddenly became enveloped by the image of my Méthilde.'

I do not wholly believe him. He was a writer of genius, and writers of genius cannot help but touch up life a little. But I have one very good reason to believe that he just may have told the essential truth. Shortly after Saint Patrick's Day (for the benefit of infidels, March 17) Anna Marie telephoned me one evening to say that her husband was about to leave for New York for five days and that she would be alone. We dined and wined in Boston the next evening; hand-clasping in the taxi we returned to her home; we went upstairs at once to her bedroom and straightway began to don the garments of Eve and Adam. I turned around. I saw my first naked woman. She was smiling expectantly at me. The part of Stendhal's account of his fiasco at this moment which I distrust is 'I was not at all embarrassed', and his assertion that he was 'merely surprised'. I was neither embarrassed nor surprised to find that I was looking at Anna's body without the least interest. But I do believe the reference to his Méthilde because at the same juncture as his I became aware only of my Irish Méthilde's finger tips, slight, tender, and pink. They sufficed. Anna Marie said gently, in tender amusement, 'It is like a boy's'. Then, raising her eyes to my mesmerised stare, it took her less than five seconds of silence to understand fully. She burst into mocking laughter – at me, at herself, at life? – and (it is the only word for her dismissal) threw me out.

It may well occur to some readers that besides my love for Eileen another elemental force may have held me back that night from Anna Marie – the taboo of the remains of my religion. I have pondered on this many times and have finally decided that while no inherited taboo ever dies completely, no matter how often it be submitted to the cold light of reason, and contemptuously rejected by it, it is equally true – and this must be too obvious to need argument – that Sex and Religion may become so subtilised, so intellectualised, so transformed as to become changed from mere negative interdictions into an inspiration that can produce some of the loveliest erotic art and some of the noblest thoughts in the world. Ever since I met and loved Eileen sex, like religion, spelled for us not a coarse prohibition but a sweet promise. Religion had absolutely nothing to say to my fiasco with Anna Marie. As with Stendhal and his black-eyed Alexandrine the only thing 'wrong' about the woman who had stood so invitingly before me was that she was not the right woman.

It was hereabouts that I began to have those dream-experiences that nobody can describe, they are so apparently portentous yet so tenuous that even while they may suggest one shapeless shape of cloud they become other and endlessly other. What could it portend that I was, in one such tormenting visitation, a small boy of the streets of Cork on the quays of the River Lee throwing stones into a rusty old boiler that had lain there on its side, full of holes, of accumulated lumps of ordure, abandoned for years, not recurring to me for years, yet become to me now, in vision, so beautiful, so desirable that my joy at seeing it again woke me? Twice I clearly heard the church-bell of Saint Peter and Paul softly answering another bell coming across the blue, wet roofs and the gently flowing River Dee from Saint Mary's. Another night I woke as if to a bang which, half-awake, I took to be the clear boom of Shandon coming through the dry summer air to my baking hot attic in Number Five Half Moon Street. Leaping from bed to look through the window I saw snowflakes slanting slowly sideways around the halo of a street lamp in Irving Street, Cambridge, Mass. What could a psychiatrist make of these emotional seismorgraphs?

Without further warning I became aware that I had for several half-aware, half-conscious days been working absorbedly on a long story which I later called 'Fugue', based on a couple of weeks I had spent dodging enemy troops during our Civil War in the wild mountain country of West Cork. I called it 'Fugue' because the word originally did mean 'flight' and the music it describes is a contrapuntal, polyphonic repetition of a theme. Of what theme? Danger? Flight? Passion? Death? Salvation? In hours stolen from my continued pretensions to be a scholar the writing of it went on for months. It was ultimately first published in that remarkable Harvard student magazine *The Hound and Horn* – 1927 to 1934. It is still, I find on rereading it, a good story.

A week or two later I got a greeting card from Anna Marie. It was polite-sympathetic-friendly. I could not cope with it. What I replied I do not now remember but I do know that my reply was between the evasive, the portentous and the unskilful because I kept her chilly acknowledgement for years in the usual would-be writer's way of squirrel-storing bits of paper that he has chosen to think may prove to be revealing 'human documents'. Even still I remember one sentence of her dismissive reply: 'What a masochistic race you Irish are, always shaving and whittling bits off of yourselves!' (That sentence made me wonder if she had had some similar trouble with some other Irishman.) She also said something about her never wanting or being able to hurt me even if she wished to. But the one part of her letter that stuck like an arrow between my ribs, and still sticks there, was her quotation from the final quatrain of Shakespeare's 94th sonnet:

> They that have power to hurt and will do none,
> That do not do the things they most do show,
> Who, moving others, are themselves like stone,
> Unmoved, cold and to temptation slow . . .

on down to the terrifying last line of the sonnet: 'Lilies that fester smell far worse than weeds.' Whoever the stinker was to whom that sonnet was originally sent by Shakespeare has my fellow-feeling of sympathy.

7

Easter was coming. Since it was part of the pleasant duty of Commonwealth Fellows to spend some time each year travelling in the United States I called on Albert Kennedy ('Kay') in South End House to ask him where I could most profitably spend Easter. A conventional man might have suggested some touristic place such as say New Orleans. Kay said at once 'Why not go to one of our rural Settlement Houses? What about the Kentucky mountains? Go to Hindman. See the tough roots of modern America.' It turned out to be exactly what I needed: a restful bit of the old, hard, traditional world, very different to the traditional Irish world but just as obstinately stuck in Time. Boston had been chilly that March-April. In Washington the cherry blossoms were in glorious bloom. I paused at elegant Charlottesville for Jefferson's sake, a highlight of bygone Southern elegance; thence to the line that strikes across the Alleghenys, down to some junction point now lost to me where earlier explorers also wanted to press on to some place along a river called The Big Sandy, or somewhere between it and the Kentucky River, and so along the trackless, thickly forested uplands that back on the western side of the Alleghenys. Finally the train gave out at what appeared to be a lumber camp. There, thanks to Kay, I was met by a buggy managed by a capable and pleasing young woman in a split leather skirt who at once proceeded to drive through, that is in, a riverbed deep into the surrounding mountains. There were few roads around there in those pre-Works Progress Administration years.

It was a pleasant, restful and soothing drive. Forests of blue ash, walnut and gum rose tier on tier on every side to the blue sky. Whenever we paused I could just hear the far, faint tinkle of a cowbell. (I still have one of those cowbells, and I need only tinkle it to be whirled back to that moment in that place.) Houses were rare. Cultivation was slight. Looking all about me, I could readily see why Cecil Sharp was once able to collect here ballads and folksongs as old as the seventeenth century: no covered wagon and no covered-wagoners that got this far could have wanted or been able to press farther through so trackless and lofty a labyrinth. When I saw a house and said to my girl-guide (her name was Joan Brandt) 'But there is no glass in those windows!' she laughed and said that there still were houses in the mountains lit by rushlights. 'But,' she added, 'every man has a modern six-shooter.' As we approached the tiny village of Hindman, near the Settlement House where I was to stay, I saw a woman in a field wearing a white coif or bonnet. Joan said: 'She is a virgin.' And the others? 'Always in black.' The she said: 'Some day, roads will get built in here and automobiles will bring in the eighteenth, nineteenth, and twentieth century in one flood.'

I said, 'What do they *do*?'

She said, 'Whittle, and spit and swap Bible quotes – and breed.' Then she said, 'They will be seeing their first cinema tonight – *The Thief of Baghdad* with Douglas Fairbanks. It's a travelling show.'

I said, 'Let's go!'

She shook her head. 'No women! And the machine is old and will probably break down. And they'll shoot the roof off.'

The sun went down early behind the tall hills. Soon they were jet and the cowbells were silent. Fireflies, winking floaters, acknowledged the darkness. That night I slept a deep and dreamless sleep, disturbed lightly, around midnight, by wild revolver-shots down in the valley. The machine *had* broken down.

I spent three blessed weeks in Hindman, idling, taking the sun, exploring the farther valleys, mostly alone, sometimes with Joan as my guide. I rode a sturdy, loping pony, using a long leather and a high-pommelled Western saddle. On those day-long wanderings through hills featureless apart from the woods and the creeks, utterly empty except for an occasional half-lost farm shack, I might have been in the backwoods of South America or Siam. Nothing broke the calm of those blessed days. They were so seemingly empty that I might have become a piece of the perennial sequence of nature itself – that time-filled sequence which is man's prime inspiration for an ever-blossoming otherworld where there shall be no time, no memory, no more events: as when I woke on Easter morning to hear children singing 'The Frog's Courting', a song so old – older than the first Pilgrims – that when I rose to look out at them, a single-file procession lit by the sun that lit the tender spring green of the hillside, down which they wandered and disappeared, I felt that life was here pared to its simplest elements.

On my last night in Hindman a trivial farewell incident underlined the Creationist moral that every Eden has its Eve. I had sometimes varied my guide from Joan Brandt to a hearty, vigorous young woman whose name, even whose features, I have long ago forgotten, but whose bodily appeal I can still vividly realise. As she and I were making our way back that last night from the school in the dusk to the sleeping quarters of the staff up a worn, winding hilly path between darkening pine-woods she directed me, all unsuspecting, off the path some twenty yards into the woods and there suddenly, with a deft wrestler's grapple, she had me on my back on the soft piney earth in no doubt as to what her fiercely groping, tearing hands were after. In a panting silence we fought for my virginity for, it then seemed to me, a long bout until, I, she, we were finally saved by approaching voices from Heaven – which is to say two or three others of the staff gossiping on their tardy way to their night's rest. The whole encounter could, I suppose, have happened just as easily in America's biggest city, but not so nicely placed as in this rural Eden.

8

Back in wicked, slushy Boston I saw the sun melt its candle across the Charles River. The countryside was presently to explode into an instantaneous spring, as it always so dramatically does throughout New England. And I was in everybody's black books. At Harvard I was a backslider; worse, a secret sinner, now merely pretending to follow the Higher Studies. It was only a matter of time before I had to confess to Fritz Robinson that my interest was not in linguistics but in literature and that what I next wanted to do was to study Yeats's philosophy. He was even more sceptical about this project than he had been about my alleged interest in Old Irish and Northumbrian metrics, but he let me have my way.

Within weeks, in fact, I was myself becoming sceptical about my new subject. Yeats had dabbled in all sorts of philosophy from Plato and Plotinus to Nietzsche and Berkeley, but only for whatever inspiration each new encounter gave him to develop another emotional attitude, another state of mind, another momentary inspiration, some new mystical or magical role that excited his imagination as a poet. He had, in practice, only one central faith, simple, clear, forceful and endlessly creative. He believed in the primacy of the imagination. Small wonder that he should to the brink of the grave reject all intellectualism in favour of the purity of the imagination. 'Science,' he declared then, 'is more false than philosophy,' and 'that too is also false.' Small wonder also that so flexuous a hare, throwing up behind him wherever he ran a lovely transcendental dew, should finally turn me into an unslaked, despairing hound.

If, then, Yeats was a philosopher I was patently no scholar. If I was a scholar Yeats was no philosopher. Caught in this critical imbroglio I began to suffer such despair and distrust of all scholarship that I wrote a long letter to Eileen telling her that I wanted to hand in my gun, chuck up everything and return to Ireland, telling her I felt a fraud here, an alien pretending to be one of thousands of keen-minded, keen-eyed young intellectuals, when all I really longed to do was to capture in words certain haunting intuitions commissioned by my imagination. (Just like Old Master Yeats?) The only bearable alternative would be for her to join me say in September in Boston, there taste the lifeway of America for a year and, between us, make up our minds whether to stay here or return to . . . But to what? This I could not, at any rate did not define. To solemnise my reckless proposal of an early union of souls I went that same afternoon into Boston, walked up Beacon Hill to a handicraft shop opposite the New State House, there bought a delicately designed, hand-worked engagement ring in American gold with an amethyst centre flanked by small diamonds, and sent it to her with my letter. It was either Kay Kennedy or his wife, Edith, who suggested this shop as one of the most tasteful in Boston.

Well, I suppose everybody has in the course of his life done something or other that he had later recalled with a specially deep breath of shame, as I do still when I recall that letter to Eileen. I had no right to throw the responsibility for my future on a girl's shoulders. Surely there were other alternatives open to me within Harvard besides philology and a poet's philosophy (real or alloy)? I might excuse myself by arguing that the Harvard of my time was not an aesthetic hive. Even my refined, cultivated, kindly official supervisor, Fred Norris Robinson, was not really interested in literature. If only, I sometimes later thought, I had come later to the liberated Harvard of say Harry Levin, or to the contemporary Princeton of Christian Gauss! Any modern young sceptic will, I know well, laugh at these self-excuses. He will say that my trouble was simply that I was sex-starved.

The full truth is that, while financed generously to as good a university as exists in the world, I was not only throwing my miraculous chances to the sea-gulls but egotistically inviting a lovely, spirited girl, who had worked her way out of the lonely steppes of Ireland, to throw away everything she had so hardily won and join me three-thousand-odd miles away without any prospects whatsoever for herself, solely in order to hold my hand! Eileen's reply was honest, loving and full of guts. She told me in our exchanges of letters that I was crazy to think of giving up my Fellowship; that my future might depend on it; that there was always this half-promise of a teaching-post in University College, Cork; that we both knew how few such openings there are in Ireland; nevertheless if I really and truly was as depressed as my letters sounded, she would join forces with me rather than see me return to penury and loneliness. Meanwhile would I enquire about the chances of her getting a job in Boston? This brought me down to earth or at least within parachuting distance of it, although all I did in a practical way, perhaps all I could do since I knew so few people outside Harvard Yard was to consult Albert Kennedy. He at once made a dual suggestion. When my current term finished at Harvard why continue to reside there? Why not at once come to live in South End House? I could earn my keep there by helping with the immigrants whom the Settlement was trying to serve, and when my fiancée arrived why should she not do the same? It was very gallant of him to have taken the risk, although had we known it the risk was rather greater for Eileen and myself than for South End House. I accepted his offer eagerly.

9

Every artist, I hold, should begin the day with 'Let me dust my mirror,' much as in Roman Catholic devotion there is a process called Examination of Conscience whereby one is expected to recall all one's past sins. Psychologically impossible, of course. I mistrust even more the Examination of the Unconscious, largely because whenever I have gone back in search of some clear memories of the months, not quite a year, that we two migrants spent in South End House I find my mirror mottled by clouded patches of oblivion. Rub these patches as I may I have always hitherto been driven to conclude that my sensibilities as of that time were intermittently either blinded by the joy of reunion with Eileen, or shattered by a frightening sense of my irresponsibility in bringing her all this way to an unknown future, or else that those psychologists are right who insist that our brains deliberately forget anything that our bodies find it uncomfortable to recall.

There are, to be sure, a great many things about our life in South End House that I remember readily and happily, such as Kay's forbearance and efficiency; or the personalities and faces of several of his staff; or the generous hospitality of his wife Edith's drawing-room; but what has come back to me most often is the shock of being transferred from the genteel environment of Harvard Yard to the ghetto life of South Boston, and by extension to the lives of the urban masses of every major city in the USA challenging me close-up with the problems of the Syrians, Latvians, Armenians, Cypriots, Poles and all their latest-come likes who were catered for by South End House. Not that I extrapolated from those isolated variables to any such generalised conclusion as, 'So this is what Kay calls America's underprivileged raw material.' Nor did I think, 'So this is the backside of Beacon Hill, the twentieth-century version of what drove Thoreau to the silent retreat of Emerson's thirteen peaceful acres around Walden Pond.' But I must have unconsciously nourished something like those feelings the day I stopped worrying about Yeats's transcendental philosophy, and began writing about the defeated rebels, embittered misfits and desperate ex-revolutionaries of faraway Ireland.

One circumstance however in that House became for years an almost total blank or fog in my mirror-memory. It was something that Eileen sensed within a week of her arrival there but did not openly discuss with me until we were both in our eighties. That was its factious atmosphere as of some ancient, family feud or feuds such as one scents easily enough in wild highland places, chiefly because there feuds last on for generations. In large cities like Boston or in formal homes anywhere it takes a Henry James or a Jane Austen to smell them out. And yet all that was driving South End was as simple and above board as the Seven Deadly Sins. Kay and Edith were on their polite way to the divorce court.

So whence the feud? If they had been entirely private people and had times been normal their divorce would have been of no concern to anybody except their close friends. This, however, was a time when the United States was on the brink of one of the greatest financial depressions in its history and when Settlement Houses were beginning to feel themselves a part, however modest, of a widespread public network of social relief. In these conditions the divorce was as if some baptist bishop in the old South were found to be leading a double life: sides would be taken, fear felt for the trust, the agreement, the unified effort that creates the *esprit de corps* of every community. Even I ultimately found myself taking sides, partly because everybody else in the house was doing so, but chiefly because much as I admired Kay's taste, readiness and ability to help, my sympathies went to Edith as the weaker of the two. She was no longer young and did not look young. And she was not the one who had initiated the divorce. It was then only natural for me to be touched when she began to confide in me about her girlhood in Boston, her rebellious ideals in her teens, her liberal ambitions as a young woman and her bewilderment when, brought close up to the realities of life, the depressed classes of South Boston became too much for her enthusiasms. It was an easy matter for such a story to fling open the gates of sympathy in any young man who had also nourished his own political dreams and unfulfilled hopes: another failed rebel. Sympathy blended into empathy as I looked at her old photographs of what might then have been thought of as a *petite charmeuse*, and she could even still, in flashes, be attractively vivacious, which made it all the more sad to see her for the most part withdrawn from life, lapsing into sceptical sighs and silences suggestive of the disillusion of a woman who knew that her dancing days were done.

As for her attitude to me? It may, it has since struck me, have mirrored that of Candida in Shaw's play to the young poet, Marchbanks. I am not suggesting for one second that my arrival in South End House disturbed its harmony as the poet did that of Shaw's parsonage – it had been thoroughly disturbed long before my coming – only that Edith may have found in me some such relief from Kay's battles with Boston's immigrants as Candida found in Marchbanks from her husband's battles with London's sinners.

Perhaps I should have been more careful. Or it would have been well if some old hand in the House had given me the tip that once Edith took the measure of Eileen's youthful attractions and of Kay's amiable interest in his latest *protegée* it could only fan a new enmity in the Edith Party of an already sufficiently partisan House. Eileen, as I have said, did feel this unfriendliness but for whatever reason – such as pride, puzzlement, consideration for me? – she did not speak of it at the time. It was one factor that made her first months in America, I now know, a less than entirely happy experience.

One afternoon, many years later when we were in our eighties, having said goodbye to a visitor from Boston whom we had known for a number of years, Eileen and I got to wondering whether people change very much over the course of their lives. I said something like, 'Take Boston itself. I spent three years there. You spent two. I don't believe it had any lasting effect on either of us.' She astonished me by saying that she could not speak for herself but that within a week of her arrival there in 1927 she saw that I had already changed completely since I parted from her in Cork a year before. And she went on unemotionally, disinterestedly, like somebody idly recalling a story of long ago.

'I saw inside a week that I was not the girl you had been expecting. All that time after you had left Ireland you had been living on some ideal image of me that – you suddenly saw – was no longer real!'

The dust on that bit of my mirror-memory did not stir. A trauma of amnesia?

'But,' I protested, 'you did not tell me this at the time. Nor since! You never said one word to me about it!'

She continued still quite dispassionately, quite tranquilly.

'I did tell you. Or have you forgotten the night, about a week after I arrived, when we went to Duxbury to stay with the Kennedys in their seaside home? You drove me down one night to the beach alone in that funny old Model T Ford you had bought for seventy five dollars? It was a mile or so away from their house. A long, lonely spit of beach as I remember it now. Not a soul or a sound. Nothing but the wild sea-grass and the Atlantic. You told me that the night before when the whole house was asleep you had come down there alone and spent the night there crying. You told me why. You said you saw you had made a mistake in asking me to join you in America. That I would never be able to fit in. You begged me wouldn't I please go back home. Of course I said that I could not go back home. I had nothing to go back to. No job. No money. I had not a penny.'

I could not recall it. My only personal memory of that sea-

235

coast evoked one night there with Anna Marie Kauffmann and some pleasant hours spent there with the three Kennedy boys. Since Eileen remembered our confrontation there it must somehow have happened. But why? How could I have felt that she could not 'fit' into Boston at least as well as I did myself? Had that South End House enmity affected me more deeply than I realised? I cursed my age, turned eighty when my wife recalled that scene, and my fading old man's memory. The thing that made her recollection especially impressive was that she was not interested in it. She saw it as something foolish that had happened long ago. So much water under the bridges of our lives.

She went on recalling it.

'Naturally I was upset at the time. But in time I began to understand. I had come to the States as you had done the year before, inexperienced, innocent, knowing nothing about the world. You had been there all that time before me, seeing different types of people, of different races even, meeting many more kinds of people than you or I had met or ever would meet in Ireland, going to all sorts of events, talking, reading, discussing with students from all over America, music, art, politics, drinking in a completely different atmosphere every day, and there is no use in waving your hand now or making little of these experiences. Even if you say you merely looked out at the world through a keyhole the fact is that you *had* looked and I had not. The result was that when you saw me coming off that liner a year later all you saw was a girl like another girl you used to know when you used to live in Ireland.'

I *had* changed. That one year in the States had surreptitiously, for good or ill, or both, done to me what exile is liable to do to everybody. For one thing, and it is no small thing, however dissatisfied one may be with one's native place, with its most exasperating ways, its most boring, narrow-minded, infuriating, nit-picking, provincial, parochial character, sheer familiarity can at least act against all such aggravations like a wasp-killer's protective net. One can walk through the buzzing and the boredom without hearing it. Go into exile and you at once become naked and defenceless against a whole new set of exasperations unless, and this can take years, you adapt, or in other words unless you change. There is, however, one other alternative, which the Irish in the USA have historically taken for all too many generations: you can choose life in a ghetto. And in a way that was what I and every other Commonwealth Fellow did – turning Harvard into a cosy enclave, cushioned by tradition, by cash, by social convention. Thanks to that status and the generous funds of the Commonwealth Fellowship any of us could very easily seem to 'fit into America', to enjoy every aspect of it, to give out the illusion of being quite at home there. Eileen, in her circumstances, could never be anything but an obvious transient. But has any first generation arrival ever seemed anything else?

If, then, an unhappy Edith Kennedy did blow into me a seed of disapproval of my betrothed I can only say that I either did not observe it, or that it is something that my memory has lost. Of one thing only am I certain, which is that her New World's life-experience could be no match for Eileen's native qualities of realism, pride, perceptiveness, warmth, and the patience to wait until the bond that she and I had forged during our idealistic years in Ireland welded itself again as, however slowly or haltingly, it did.

10

Eileen had come off the liner from Cobh, as brown as a berry and looking very much a girl of the 1920s, cloche hat, boyish hairstyle, straight jacket, short skirt.

I had said, 'That hat is like an upside-down saucepan.'

She had looked at my Debussy-Edward VII beard and said, 'That's awful, it makes you look like Landru the multiple murderer.'

After which, I am convinced, she just refused to recognise its existence. (Every woman has an unchangeable image of the man she loves. He may age, grow bald, dye his hair green. She still sees him as she first knew him. Later, when I shaved off my beard she did not observe the fact until I drew her attention to it.) She was delighted when a social worker, female, circled slowly about us and then, with a crooked look at me, asked her if she needed guidance. Having assured the kind lady that I was not a white-slaver, I bundled Eileen into the Model T and drove her off with what dignity was left to me to settle ourselves into our quarters in South End House forthwith – which was a mistake, as I could see by the astonished look on her face as we drove through one seamy street after another. I had, of course, tried in my letters to forewarn her what to expect. All the same it was something of a shock for a girl straight from the green hills of Cork to be lobbed without transition into the heart of Skid Row. If I had had any sense I would have first driven her up to the Hill for lunch at the Bellevue, and then carried the Common and the Public Garden with us down to the grubby South End. However a few days' shopping and leisurely touristic exploration revealed the more elegant side of Boston whose traditional grace had not, even as late as 1927, been as it is now adulterated by overbuilding, highrise monsters, wide motorways and the usual modern curse of noisy traffic. Then we drove down to the sea where the Kennedys had kindly invited us for a week-end. After that we had the old Model T to explore the nearby countryside and so, I can now only presume, gradually dispel the effects of the painful confrontation that I have described in Eileen's words a few pages back, and thus relate things to things, and feeling to feeling in better proportion.

Boston itself did a good deal to hasten this healing process. To live in the middle of a busy city rather than inside an academic stronghold made life feel much less cliquey, conventional, cloistered. One met a greater variety of people, went 'out into the world', got interested in politics, in the problems and preoccupations of a whole country – it was Coolidge's last year as President, the Hoover versus Al Smith contest was just starting. For the first time I felt consciously metropolitan. We were so lucky as to get two half-tickets, that is tickets for alternate weeks, for the symphony; able to go at our ease to concerts of chamber music and to occasional recitals; drop in casually to the galleries of an idle afternoon, or run down to the wharves for a cup of orange pekoe among the smells of gasoline and fish; or, for a special occasion, count up our dollars and dine out. When one is young it takes such a small bonus to brim over into happiness. A skating party on the Charles could do it; a Sunday breakfast party in a friend's apartment after Mass at the cathedral; a few days' skiing with a few of the Fellows in New

Hampshire; a glass of muscatel after the symphony in another friendly house; even one open door at Christmas in Louisburg square, when every railing was white on the windy side and every candlelit window glinted on Aristides' cap of snow. And every day I had Harvard and the Widener Library. I was free of philology and of Yeats's vast ideologies. I was studying German, an essential for a master's degree, I was listening in to Babbitt's antiromanticism, which I always found lively and entertaining, and in retrospect think just a little odd. I found later that he had had T. S. Eliot as a student, but said he considered him 'a poor student', which – if Babbitt meant student as disciple – one might be reasonably certain that Eliot was, even without the tactful wording of his later tribute to his old teacher: 'To have once been a pupil of Babbitt's was to remain always in that position, and to be grateful for (in my case) a very much qualified approval.'

One thing astounds me as I look back at that year of 1927, and the year after it – our utter improvidence. We had decided that Christmas to get married in the June of 1928, when my fellowship was due to run out. I had no prospect of a job, and Eileen had no certainty of one either. (She did, fortunately, the following spring, bespeak a teaching job for 1928–1929 in an interesting progressive school called Shady Hill.) The most I could expect to have in the bank that June was about fifteen hundred dollars, which I was in duty bound, as a Fellow, to spend on travel in the States, and which I fully intended so to spend on a two-month honeymoon.

Our gay lack of prudence aside, the fact is that improvidence was in the air of America during those boom-crazed years before the great crash of 1929 brought an end to the 1920s. Everyone seemed to drink in recklessness. Even the maids in South End House, and the undergraduates at Harvard, were speculating on the stock market, without collateral. Everybody 'never had it so good,' including the gangsters, the bootleggers and the madams, and on every side they showed it splashingly. I do not know what Friday nights at Symphony Hall look like now, but in my memory of those affluent years every woman there had diamonds in her hair, mink or chinchilla in the cloakroom. I do know what Harvard looks like now, and it is very sedate compared with those expansive years, when for every three monks sweating it out on Irving Street for a philological Ph.D. there was at least one rich swell whooping it up in expensive idleness on the Gold Coast. They were at their most enviable on football weekends, when every window of every swank enclave sent out a collective roar of chattering parties and clinking glasses, and every narrow street was a babel of revving-up sports cars filled with pert, fragile, belladonna-eyed boy-girls and precocious youths in ankle-length raccoons – lords of the day, culprits of the morrow.

Since then I have read everything that I have been able to lay hands on about the 1920s in America and Europe, yet one thing about them still puzzles me: that so many people could live extempore at a time when the novels of the period were chock-filled with characters fully aware of the fleeting nature of the good times they so faithfully describe and eviscerate so well. I think at once of the doomed young men of Aldous Huxley's novels or of Hemingway's fine, perhaps finest, novel *The Sun Also Rises*, or Scott Fitzgerald's *The Great Gatsby*, or his *All the Sad Young Men*. Take even one such passage as this one from *The Great Gatsby*:

> Listen, Nick, let me tell you what I said when my daughter was born. It'll show you how I've gotten to feel about things. Well, she was less than an hour old and Tom was God knows where. I woke up out of the ether with an utterly abandoned feeling, and I asked the nurse right away if it was a boy or a girl. She told me it was a girl and so I turned my head away and wept. 'All right,' I said, 'I'm glad it's a girl. And I hope she'll be a fool – that's the best thing a girl can be in this world, a beautiful little fool.' Everybody thinks so – the most advanced people. And *I* know! I've been everywhere and seen everything and done everything. Sophisticated? God, I'm sophisticated!

Surely that is as plain a way of saying *merde* to the public at large as if he had smacked them in the face?

Oh, well! I read *The Great Gatsby* and I did not take its meaning. (Anyway, I was writing stories about my own Twenties.) Any more than I took the meaning of what was happening one June day in 1928 when a broker friend took me into the New York Stock Exchange to see the city's sights. Even before we got into the hall I could hear a rumble like Niagara in spate. When I beheld the floor, all I saw was what New Yorkers might call a hassle around distracted men trying to take selling orders against a ticker that was already two hours behind events. I have since looked up the records to find out what really was happening that day, and I can only conclude that it must have been the backwash of the sudden slump that June on the San Francisco exchange, when in one day the Bank of Italy fell a hundred points and on the New York curb swooped from 200 to 110, followed by this typhoon of selling that for the time being knocked the bull market to smithereens. But how few then saw the all-over picture, or grasped its larger warning, is plain from the fact that within a year the total value of listed shares – with one third more by then on the lists – was to fall by fifty-five billion dollars. Only once – and that was a week before I left America, in June 1929 – did I get a glimpse of what those vast sums (and Fitzgerald's novels) meant in human terms. That was when I dropped in on the old Irish cobbler on Massachusetts Avenue who used to mend my shoes. I made some remark, for the sake of conversation, about the market. He looked at me dully and said: 'I'm not innarested.' Then he added: 'Keep off it, boy. Two months ago I lost fifteen years' savings at that game. Keep off it. Its like hooch or drugs. It gets you, until it kills you. *Keep off it!*'

His eyes were windows into his stomach. I could see a big hole in his stomach, and an ache in it, where they'd cut out all his hope for the future – and most of his interest in the present.

So, perhaps, I was in fact less improvident than most.

II

We got married as secretively as if we were runaway lovers, very early on the morning of 3 June 1928, at the Cathedral of the Holy Cross. It is a big place and it was empty. The young priest was one Father Harry O'Connor. The only witnesses were the chapel woman, Mary Murphy, and the sacristan, Michael Sullivan. The fee was only ten dollars. We drove from the cathedral to Cambridge to a tiny restaurant on Brattle Street, where we sat on a booth with our one close confidant, Ernie

Simmons, who acted like an amused nonagenarian shepherding two teenagers out into the vast, sun-baked continent of life, and of the USA, across the double stream of students coming and going across Harvard Square from nine o'clock and to ten o'clock lectures. We were quite silent until we had left the city behind us, and then, on an impulse, I stopped the car. I looked at my wife, she looked at me, and we both burst out laughing. 'I feel,' each of us said, with one voice, 'so happy!' We sat there for a while, staring first in laughing, then in silent, wonderment at one another under this blossoming tree of happiness that had grown about us as husband and wife. Then, too full of joy to speak, we drove on, south and south, in the sunlight of the gods. Of those eight bemused weeks that followed I remember most vividly our first love-makings, as happy, natural, and simple as the mating of fish, fur or feathers, not that mentally twisted or kinked vulgarity commonly called Sex which is a search for elaborate greedy sensual pleasure, instead of for that simple ecstasy without which 'a prince in prison lies.' Of course there were bright moments meaningless to everybody but us, such as the first night we pitched our tent – we were motor-camping – by a brook on a hillside in Virginia, where Eileen made her first stew, which she thought would take twenty minutes and took three ravenous hours; or the divinely beautiful silence and darkness of a wood in Tennessee when the summer lightning waved mad witches' fingers for hours and hours on every horizon; or the day we came on the greatness of the Mississippi, brown with the mud of a dozen states, sedgy, swirling wrack before it, a vast spread of desert water driving stolidly and ponderously in flood down to the Gulf, one of the greatest sights of America, perhaps in all the world. We had to race it southward for about two hundred and fifty miles below Memphis, where at last we were able to cross it on a cable-straining ferry. I remember vividly the long night we spent under our first mesa, in talk with a little fat priest, sallow, laughing, French-born, who kept reminding me of the good Father Vaillant in Willa Cather's *Death Comes for the Archbishop* as he talked of his vast parish and his horse on which he traversed it, and especially when he talked zestfully and without the least touch of reprobation about wild characters of the Llanos like Billy the Kid, or about Kit

Carson and the old Indian wars. This, I think, was where our journey became most interesting, after we saw that first mesa rising out of the plain, with another ghost or mirage mesa hovering over it in the great heat of aromatic air smelling of sage and juniper, light and heady. The old Model T boiled like a steam engine, so that we had to fill it often from our water bottles as we climbed up the Rio Grande from Albuquerque to Santa Fe. Cave dwellings in remote valleys. Navajo Indians working the symbols of the rain, the thunderclouds and the lightning into their black pottery. Taos, with Mabel Dodge and Tony Luhan in his feathers and his Cadillac, and an odd, delightful character, always dressed in a yachting cap and a blazer, who wrote later for the *New Yorker*, and a number of other lighthearted, oddball people whose identities are now as lost to me as mine is to them. I remember, above all, the apple orchard on a hilltop outside Taos where we camped for two weeks with the Rio Grande at our feet and the Rockies before us in all their ominous splendour that, one evening, did something very strange and final to us both.

We were lying outside our tent, side by side, entirely relaxed and at our ease, gods of all we surveyed, watching the sun set behind the distant mountains. When it had sunk behind them and the light slowly grew cold and dim, we began to talk about a thing we had often discussed during our travellings: could we live in this country always? As we talked I suddenly became aware that, by a trick of the light, a last cut-off peak seemed to stand up quite bare and quite alone across the plateau beneath us. The vast range had otherwise withdrawn itself like mountains in a vision; there was not a soul in sight. The dusk was absolutely silent. We were oppressed by the silence and ceased talking. There wasn't even the least cry of a bird. It was an immeasurable night. And it wasn't in the least bit impressive – because if those mountains had associations we did not know them; if history – that is, if some sort of purposeful life, other than that of missionaries or explorers, ever trod this vastness – it had left no vibrations for either of us.

There in the darkness we made up our minds. We belonged to an old, small, intimate and much-trodden country, where every field, every path, every ruin had its memories, where every last corner had its story. We decided that we could only live in Europe, and in Ireland. The next morning we started on the first leg of the Long Voyage Home.

But to what? I thought a lot that night of what Henry James had said some fifty years before, in the course of his famous lament about the shortcomings of life in Nathaniel Hawthorne's New England, and as I recalled it I wondered about Old Ireland. Here is part of the passage I was remembering that night as I lay in my camp bed:

> The flower of art blooms only where the soil is deep, and it takes a great deal of history to produce a little literature, and it needs a complex social machinery to set a writer in motion . . . If one desires to enter as closely as possible into Hawthorne's situation, one must endeavor to reproduce his circumstances. We are struck with the large number of elements that are absent from them, and the coldness, the thinness, the blankness present themselves so vividly that our foremost feeling is that of compassion for a romancer looking for subjects in such a field. It takes so many things, as Hawthorne must have felt later in life when he made the acquaintance of the denser, richer, warmer European spectacle – it takes such an accumulation of history and custom, such a complexity of manners and types, to form a fund of suggestion for a novelist.

At first thought this may seem quite unapplicable to Ireland. And yet . . .? A complex social machinery? Would I find that in Ireland? If I were Anglo-Irish, like, say, Sheridan, Goldsmith, George Moore, Somerville and Ross, Wilde, or Shaw, and if unlike all these, except Somerville and Ross, I had lived in Ireland, I would certainly have found a complex social life in Ireland of their origin and their day. But since their day a great levelling had begun in Ireland, and I was, though town-born, of the poor peasant stock that was mainly responsible for this modern levelling. All the people I had grown up with were outcroppings of the injured and oppressed who had risen up against England and the Anglo-Irish colonists. Would I find in this new Ireland what James meant by 'a complexity of manners and types'? Or 'an accumulation of history and custom?' In a folk-sense, yes. But in his urbane sense, 'the outlook indeed for an embryonic novelist would not seem to have been cheerful.' I could begin all right. In compiling notes and images for my first novel I had already begun. Perhaps James might have even more pointedly said that it needs a complex social machinery to *keep* a writer in motion . . . But I am incapable now of distinguishing between what I vaguely felt that night above Taos and what I was later to find out when I came to close quarters with my problems as a working writer in my own land. All I know is that when we decided, in that silent dusk of New Mexico, to turn back, first to Cambridge, and thence to Ireland, we knew we were making a grave choice, and I did not make it without grave misgivings.

We were back in Boston just before August ran out and our cash with it. We found a tiny demi-furnished clapboard house, just off Brattle Street, at Number 10A Appian Way, and settled down to domesticity. It had three rooms. It was like an oven in that damp August heat – I used to work in the boiler-basement – and promised to be freezingly cold in the winter. Friends loaned us things to take the bare look off the little place, one bringing us a chair, another a rug, another a bed. We were so poor all that year that we had to limit ourselves to one packet of Luckies per week between us, and to one night at the movies. We never ate out, never drank, and – it was the false economy of greenhorns – lit the furnace only in the afternoon and let it die out during the night, so that we were always awakened early by the cold, hastened to rise and breakfasted in our overcoats. Then, having filled the radiator of the Ford with boiling water, we used to hurry out into the snow and the wind, Eileen to the warmth of her school, I to Widener. Whichever of us was back the sooner would clean, stoke and light the furnace, and by four or five o'clock our houselet would again be as cosy as could be.

It was a good, tough year. I think it was a more than tough routine for Eileen, adapting herself to that unusual type of school, though she insisted that she enjoyed it and never complained. We were able to save enough for our tickets home and the sizable sum of two hundred pounds sterling to boot. I got my A.M. I compiled my first book – very slim, fifty-one pages, a selection of *Lyrics and Satires from Tom Moore* – for the two Yeats sisters who owned the hand-set Cuala Press in Dublin.

(My little book was really a way of finding out once and for all if Tom Moore really was a poet. I decided that he was – for about four or five occasions in his long career as a prolific versifier. He was at his best as a writer of lyrics for a nation's music.) I gave an extension course at Boston College on Anglo-Irish literature. This, too, was a weeding-out process. After I had done it I could have said, coattailingly, yet truly enough, that there was nothing before George Moore in prose, and Yeats in poetry, except minor forerunners, who are now of no interest to anybody but historians. I began to make a collection of translations from Old Irish verse, which was later published under the title of *The Silver Branch*. (Here there were riches in plenty.) But the most fateful thing that happened to me that year was that my story *Fugue* was published in September 1928, in that remarkable Harvardian literary monthly called the *Hound and Horn*.

The *H and H*, popularly known as the *Bugle and Bitch*, had been founded in the autumn of 1927 by Lincoln Kirstein, then an undergraduate student, later the distinguished impresario of the New York City Ballet. With an amazing percipience he chose as editor a frail, Keatsian-looking poet from Maine, Richard Blackmur, whom he found working off Harvard Square in the Dunster Bookshop, owned by Maurice Firuski, a charming Yale man who later had a bookshop in Salisbury, Connecticut. Lincoln and Dick were ably helped by Varian Fry, who, in Dick's words, was 'wonderful at reading proofs.' Another young man, Bernard Bandler, put a lot of money into it in 1929; just in time, I must imagine, because after 1929 few people put 'a lot of money' into anything quite as lasting.

My connection with these and other young men associated with the *H and H* had one delightful effect on me. Listening to them gossiping about their day-by-day lives whenever they came to drink a cup of tea with us in our chicken coop at Number 10A Appian Way; or arguing hotly about literature in the office of the *H and H* in Harvard Square, with its bright red-framed reproductions of cover designs and photographs; or going off with Dick for a coffee or a bootleg beer, I found my image of Harvard changing completely. It was not alone that the eager zest of all these young men counterbalanced the dullness of the

246

Teutons; or that their interests were so wide and contemporaneous; or that, through listening to them, I first really became interested in the modern metaphysicals, in e. e. cummings, Hart Crane, Wallace Stevens, Marianne Moore, the Southern Fugitive group, Ezra Pound and many more who, for various reasons, had hitherto passed over my head. It was that through them I made the elementary but fundamental discovery, so elementary that I do not know why I had not made it long ago, that it is really the undergraduate who makes a university, gives it its lasting character, smell, feel, quality, tradition. You can never know a university, or ever belong to it, by entering it as a graduate student; it may even be that no professor coming to it late from another university will ever know it as well as his new-come sophomores, juniors and seniors. It is these whose presence creates it and whose memories preserve it – its rakes, rapscallions and idlers, its rebels and its aberrants, no less than its scholars, sloggers and bright stars. It is to these that the first toast should be drunk at every university dinner: To every shade who here once was happy, because he was young. I think that it is in recognition of this truth and not from snobbery that your true Harvardian says, with just the faintest emphasis, that he went to Harvard *College*.

I am even more grateful to the *H and H* for another reason. I at once sent off the September issue, containing my story, out of the blue, to Edward Garnett, the most remarkable and influential publisher's reader of his time in England, then working with Jonathan Cape. He wrote back those joyous words that every young writer dreams wildly of hearing some day from some reader of Garnett's calibre: 'You are a writer.' He also asked me to send him everything else I wrote and to call on him if I ever came to London. That letter alone would have made this year a complete success.

It was the happiest of my three years in America; swift as a stream of happiness whose moments I can no longer hold separate from one another. The hard winter died slowly. The spring exploded, the summer leaped on us, and soon Commencement was in the offing. We made our last trip to the shore. We made the last round of our friends to say goodbye; in the street I met my first American beggar; I read in the paper that some big financier had thrown himself off the elevated at Columbus Circle; Widener was packed day and night with students cramming for their examinations; country cottages were waiting for the schools to close and fill them; and all our friends were talking happily of their holiday plans for Europe. We emptied 10A Appian Way, sold the old Model T for twenty-five dollars, packed our worldly goods into four suitcases, and at last walked up the gangway of our liner. It was far from crowded. Because of the calamitous economic Depression more Americans were returning from Europe than going there. We had known total happiness in America, we made many good friends in Boston and Cambridge, but as we stood that evening on the deck and looked out over the empty spaces of the sea, and heard the engines pulsing and the waves swishing, what we mostly felt was the pleasure of knowing that we would soon be seeing old familiar places, back where we belonged.

Seven days later, when the liner dropped anchor in Cobh Harbour, with the same green hills bright across the bay, and the same gulls squawking and wheeling about the masts, and the ship's orchestra playing the same old sentimental tune, we leaned on the gunwale picking out in the bright moonlight the spots we knew along the coast, certain that nothing here would have changed a jot. So far as I knew there was only one change in me. I now knew or thought I knew what I wanted to do with my life. I wanted to write about this sleeping country, those sleeping fields, those sleeping villages spread before my eyes under the summer moon. Whether I did so or not, in any realistic sense of those words, remained to be seen.

Fade in the slow music... *back to Erin, Mavourneen, Mavourneen*... Fade up the music. And as the tender draws slowly away from under the overhanging flank of the ship towards the moon-white shore, fade slowly out.

14

London: 1929–1933

───────── ☙ ─────────

We spent the summer wallowing in Ireland – it was one of those rare, golden Irish summers – until, with a start, it occurred to us that we must have jobs in the autumn. We might have got them in Ireland, but only again in some rain-shotten Ballinasloe or Ennis, teaching in remote secondary schools, and we had had our bellyful of that; besides, my friend the registrar of University College was still encouraging me to keep my eye on the post of professor of English in his college; so, with this will-o'-the-wisp in mind, we postponed Ireland for, as we thought, at most a year, and went to London in search of something better-sounding than an Irish country school.

In those years England was stygian to Ireland. We crossed night-water, often stormy, to get there. On this joyless beach of Acheron – called Holyhead – we were met by cold customs officials; on occasions there were passport checks. Tea in the railways halts was reheated. The train journey to London took long, restless hours through a sleep-drenched land. Over the noise of the train one sensed the silence of the fields. The dawn took a long time to come; its clouds were heavy; the red-brick, half-timbered farmhouses withdrawn behind holland blinds; in the morning dusk the tidy fields, the clipped hedges, the village pubs, the streams, the pollarded elms seemed even more alien. Then the dew was grey on the grass. The cattle rose from their haunches. Euston Station was Erebus. It was a foreign country that finally revealed itself. There was no doubt about this embalmed foreignness of England to Irishmen. Few of us liked it, and none of us loved it. The English had many splendid virtues that we admired, and even envied. They cost too much in terms of the spontaneous and impulsive life-spirit. We damned them with a word. Cold; like Euston in the early morning.

By one of those pure chances that favour the feckless, I at once fell into a most agreeable post in a teachers' training college, not only in the pleasant suburb of Pope's and Walpole's Strawberry Hill but by Horace Walpole's old house on the Thames, teaching English to two classes of young men who were working for the teacher's diploma and to one senior class studying for the extern degree of Bachelor of Arts of London University. I taught on the average ten hours a week, which, once I had organised my lectures, left me plenty of time for writing. Eileen was equally fortunate. She got a part-time post in a big convent school a couple of miles down the river at Isleworth, just across from Kew Observatory and Kew Gardens. We took an apartment in Richmond, midway between both our jobs, on the northern side of Richmond Hill, on Queen's Road.

We could not have been better situated. We had four fine large rooms, one with French windows opening on the garden at the back. We were close to Richmond village, Richmond Park and Richmond Hill, with its fair and famous prospect over the meadows, uplands, woods, and bosky eyots of the winding Thames. I think even Henry James would not have found Richmond wanting. It has always attracted Londoners who love their river. It is rich in historical associations. The park – our park; two and a quarter thousand acres of it at our door – had once been a deer forest, later the favoured pleasure ground of Charles I. Wolsey had lived in Sheen Palace and Elizabeth had died there. Kean had acted in the old theatre on the Green, and is buried in the old churchyard hard by. There are good pubs, restaurants and coffee shops. The river walks are delightful, up to Twickenham, down to Kew. The place has only one drawback: it is not London. It always took us an hour, by bus or underground, to visit friends, theatres, museums, galleries in town. It was what Harvard and Cambridge would have been to Boston if they had been five times farther apart.

This did not trouble us greatly. We were self-contained; I wanted to spend all my spare time writing; and we were, for us, making enough money not only to be able to enjoy accumulating enough household goods and gods to satisfy our needs, if not always our tastes, but to spend the following long vacation partly in Ireland, partly staying with my brother near Dover, and partly on a walking tour in Germany. I must say our domestic needs were modest. I remember my brother being so amused at seeing me carve the dinner joint one night with the breadknife that he made us a present of our first set of carvers; and I recall a very kind neighbour, a Mrs Stenhouse, who lived directly beside Richmond Bridge, forcing herself to suggest, most tactfully, to my wife that if she did not 'care for' rugs and carpets – glancing at our bare painted floors – we could buy attractive woven matting in Heals of Tottenham Court Road. We never did buy a carpet while we lived in Richmond. Until our children came, and created their own demands, we preferred to spend our money on other things – food, wine, books, music, plays and travel.

I know that to many people this may sound a further instance of the improvidence of the artist; but when my values are deplored I always feel that it is my profession that is really being deplored. Even to this day, when I am a successful writer in his sixties, my brother, a most prudent man, sometimes growls unbelievingly: 'You always seem to land on your feet!'

There is in this an echo of the morality of the Utilitarian Society. Artists are not producers. They are mere dealers. They deal in words, the stuff that falls out of everybody's mouths, already ready-made, which they merely shuffle about and polish up, as used-car dealers polish up old cars to resell them. It is in vain that I explain to such friends that I have a small factory, called an Underwood Portable, wherewith I manufacture fine sentences as other men manufacture fine silk, which I sell in the highest market available. It is no use. I am lobbed into the same class as dealers in postage stamps, old masters or real estate; with inventors, actors, ballet dancers, circus performers and con men. I live by my wits. It is a rocky profession. And a very old one?

I at once called on Edward Garnett and he straightway became our best and dearest friend in London. My pet image of him is from a later time when he came to stay with us in Ireland and we drove with him around Connemara. One day we paused at Oliver St John Gogarty's hotel in Renvyle, near which there is a lovely deserted beach with the Atlantic waves always rolling in on its pallid sand. There we bathed, he in his bare pelt. He had always reminded me of 'old Silenus lolling in the sunshine,' large, big of belly, soft of eye, now dreamy, now bellicose, now ironical, now mocking, sunk in an armchair or bowed over a restaurant table, his white locks tousled, his herbal cigarettes dropping ash all over the place. That day he just lay down naked on the sands and luxuriously let the waves roll and rock his big belly and bottom to and fro, a blissful pagan child of the waves and the skies. He was in this sense one of the most romantically tempered men I have ever met; a happy – I stress the word – lover of the body and of nature, in no least way a *malade* of romanticism, quite alien to any of the sick categories of Mario Praz's *The Romantic Agony* except, possibly, if it really be a malady, that of 'La Belle Dame Sans Merci.'

It was as natural therefore for him to wed his romanticism to his paganism, in real life, as it was to demand the closest blend, in fiction, of the ideal and the real; to have an enormous admiration for, say, Conrad, who had been one of his close friends, yet to refuse to include in his admiration that very *femme fatale*-ish novel *The Arrow of Gold*, about which somebody said, and Garnett would have echoed it heartily, that reading it was like 'listening to a performance on the Conrad.' His favourite Conrad novels were those that worked the ideal-real blend – *Lord Jim* (which I loved) and *Nostromo* (to read which, for me, is like trying to swim in the Dead Sea), or even those only novels of Conrad's that are almost wholly realism, *The Secret Agent* and *Under Western Eyes*. These two may reflect his adoration of the Russian realists, so many of whom his wife Constance had already translated. I wonder whether he was not drawn to the new generation of Irish writers because we, too, had been deeply influenced by the Russian novelists and short-story writers.

He lived, when in town, on the edge of Chelsea in Pond Place, a narrow street off the Fulham Road, about three blocks south of South Kensington station, in a tiny maisonette jammed with books, pictures, furniture, signed photographs of such great men of the past as W. H. Hudson, Conrad, Crane, Galsworthy or W. H. Davies; and, of course, with piles of hopeful manuscripts. There he always lolled like a potentate on a chaise longue, giving forth on life, love, literature, and the stupidity of critics. If we were dining we might go out to the Russian restaurant on Harrington Road for whose bortsch he had a particular affection. Otherwise I might join him for lunch in Soho, usually at the Commercio Restaurant. (Italy, where he had been with the Red Cross during the 1914–18 war, was his most admired European country after Russia.) Only once did we go to stay with him in his country cottage near Oxtead.

He always had somebody interesting to meet us at these places, but never a lion, always a cub, somebody young like myself, at the beginning of his career, like H. E. Bates, or Malachi Whitaker, or H. A. Manhood. It would give a completely wrong impression of him if I were to suggest that he introduced me to the London literary set. He had no time for coteries. I do not believe, for example, that he had much contact with the Bloomsburyites, apart from such as were connected with magazines and publishing. He had been born before the age of sets. He admired and loved only the individual writer spinning, like the spider, out of his own guts; such as Doughty, or Yeats, or Conrad, or Davies. He never really warmed to Galsworthy, sensing in him, I think, the cold, English, bourgeois thing, saying of him that he would never be an artist but would always look at life from a club window: in which time has proved him right again. Likewise he had a profound suspicion of all literary success that did not come late, forced on the public by sheer quality.

'The public,' he once snorted to me, 'don't want anything original – they just want to see their own mugs reflected in a familiar mirror.' Adding that I would never succeed – that is, make money. But he was always telling this to young writers. Not that he needed to tell it to me. I was too romantic and arrogant to want that sort of success. This contempt for current public taste was what made him one of the greatest publishers' readers of all time: he smelled the future in his men. He believed in long odds. One day he, unknowingly, illustrated this by saying in his dry, crusty, ironical way of Jonathan Cape's success as a publisher:

'Cape succeeded for various reasons. He started as a book salesman, known to the trade as Herbert J. Cape, Herbert for short, and 'Erb for shorter. When he decided to go into the publishing business he put the J. first and became Jonathan Cape, a fine solid-sounding name – the sort of name that inspires confidence in the English public. His greatest gift was that he knew nothing about books and admitted it. He looked around him for the best reader he could find, chose me, and followed me blind. He had about four hundred pounds in cash. I had always been a great admirer of Doughty. I had made Duckworth publish an abridged *Arabia Deserta*. I said, 'Cape, you must publish this book in full. You will lose money on it, but it will make your name.' He decided to trust my judgement and he did publish it. He spent all his capital on that first book. And it made his name.'

'But,' I asked in mock innocence, 'surely every publisher's main aim is to publish best-sellers?'

'That, my boy,' he growled at me in a proper rage, 'is the quickest possible way for any publisher to lose money! Good writers like good company. They want to be published by publishers who publish other good writers. If Cape hadn't aimed at a good list he would never have attracted the writers who are both good and sellers. If he hadn't earlier had Doughty he wouldn't have got T. E. Lawrence and *The Seven Pillars*, any more than he'd have got Sinclair Lewis or Hemingway or Louis Bromfield or Elizabeth Madox Roberts or Sherwood Anderson! . . . Best-seller publishers! Look at Herbert Jenkins! Who has he?'

'P. G. Wodehouse?' I suggested blandly.

He stared at me through his thick lenses, between disbelief and a sudden suspicion of my worthiness as a disciple. Then he rumbled. He loved teasing, and to be teased.

'Mind you,' he added, 'Cape was shrewd. He was one of the

earliest publishers to go to America in search of books, and he did it off his own bat. From the first American trip he brought home the English rights of three future Nobel Prizewinners, Lewis, Hemingway and Eugene O'Neill, as well as Mencken, Dorothy Canfield, Sherwood Anderson, and others – an astounding haul compared with the meagre results anybody got after him. Before his time the traffic had been all the other way. He did another thing. The get-up of his books was first-class, and something new for the time. All that led authors of repute and staying power to him. Quality, my boy! That's what pays off in publishing.'

Allied to his scorn of the public, of reviewers, and of quick financial success was his enormous love of life. A novel to him was life imaginatively reincarnated. (He could be a near-failure today when the novel is so often about life reduced to abstract atoms and documentary fallout.) He had his preferences, of course, and his limitations. He plumped for spontaneous, passionate, imaginative and unaffected personalities. Within this range or octave of preferences he could equally appreciate D. H. Lawrence and Cunninghame Grahame, who goodness knows had plenty of affectation, though always arising from his zest and romanticism; T. E. Lawrence and W. H. Hudson; or the wildness of Liam O'Flaherty and the infinite delicacy of H. E. Bates. But he had no relish for Joyce, and little for Shaw, or for any intellectuals who spun out of their brains rather than their bellies. ('They'll have one idea today, and they'll be all for another tomorrow.')

H. E. Bates, in his excellent little book *Edward Garnett*, which includes a couple of brilliant pen portraits of an old master dealing with a young writer in the 1920s and 1930s, calls him the last of the great Victorian eccentrics. Signs by, he adored everything in life as in letters, that was off centre, egregious, unconventional or idiosyncratic. As when, one morning in Ireland, he woke early – old men do not sleep well – and went strolling across the grey-green, dewy fields until, to his delight, he saw striding towards him a handsome, dark-haired young woman. 'Like a fairy woman coming to me out of the morning mist!' But he added, with glee, that as she came up to him and talked with him he saw she was nonchalantly swinging a chamber pot. Another day he got in tow with a half-drunken farmer who assured him that there were serpents in his well. E. G. at once went off home with him to see the serpents, standing high up in his salmon-pink creel-cart, by this time a little tight himself. The pair were welcomed somewhat coldly by the boozy farmer's sober wife, and then Edward was led behind the house to look down into the shallow well. He saw no serpents, and said as much.

'Look at 'um domn oor sowl!' raged the boozy farmer. 'My God! Can't you see 'um, man? Dozens of 'um!'

E. G. stooped and peered again. There were no serpents. He said then, satisfied: 'Of course! I see them now.'

As he explained to us, this was just as it should have been. He had been a dull Saxon to have expected to see real serpents. But if these incidents were presented to him in a manuscript, with what savage care he would scan every word and insist that the telling should make him see, smell, taste, feel, and know the life of that woman and that old farmer in all their credible and persuasive realistic detail.

This ultimately was where we fell foul of one another. It seemed to me that anyone who wants realism plus romance wants to have his cake and eat it, and that E. G. was not free of this double-think. I am not going to go into this here. I know that I have used two words which it would take two volumes to define, though I think the reader will be able to form an approximate idea of what I approximately mean. But if I cannot here define those terms, I can illustrate them by saying that if one examines, say, Conrad's *Lord Jim*, one will find no such substantial main characters as we get from realists like Trollope or Balzac. Such realism as Conrad employed is always in his minor characters and in his geography, apart from those two realistic novels that I have already mentioned, *Under Western Eyes* and *The Secret Agent*. If we were to cut the minor characters and the geography out of *Lord Jim* we would be left with one of the squashiest and thinnest heroes in fiction – that is, if we had been hoping for that sort of solid social man, formed by and reacting to his place, time and circumstances, that we get from the real realists. Jim is an imaginative figure out of a legend, illustrating a parable about the nature of bravery and cowardice; and this is precisely how Conrad presents him from start to finish through the memories of those who kept on meeting his fabulous, wandering shade. On these terms *Lord Jim* is a moving, persuasive and conscience-haunting book. As realism it is a fairytale. I am not surprised that W. H. Davies, an earthy man, gave it up in disgust after fifty pages.

I either did not want, or could not hope to achieve, or was temperamentally alien to Trollopian realism. My favourite writers were mainly the authors of the *Lord Jim* kind of novel: Borrow's *Lavengro*, and Theodore Watts-Dunton's *Aylwn* (when I was sixteen), Turgenev's *The Torrents of Spring, The Charterhouse of Parma*, Alain-Fournier's *Le Grand Meaulnes*, all the romantic side of Scott, the bizarre side of Dickens, all Dostoievsky, all Hardy of course, *Dead Souls* and *The Cloak* of course, *Wuthering Heights* of course, any good comic writer, *Don Quixote*, Chekhov, some Peacock, all Waugh. I read the realists for thrills; they were my vitamins; the others were my pleasure, what one might call hovercraft writers, floating just above the ground – indeed *when* and *as* I first read them taking off from it like airplanes. I was therefore all for E. G. in his love of novels dealing with idiosyncratic, bizarre, rebellious and aberrational men and women, transformed, elevated or shattered by their passions and dreams; but I could not agree that the kind of writers I liked depended for their essential appeal on realistic techniques, still less on naturalistic techniques – descriptions of food or furniture, the analysis of incomes, the colour of people's hair, the cut of their clothes, whether they drank Maxwell House coffee or ground their own beans, had or had not been to the London School of Economics or to Vassar, how this character fondled a rep curtain, or that one saw a fly crawling up a windowpane, or put salt in his porridge instead of sugar, and so on – all that, as I called it, 'other stuff'. I wanted to pierce right to the star or moon that gleams deep inside every exterior. I wanted to cut the cackle and come to the essentialist 'osses. I could admire the realistic type of novel with intensity and perhaps with envy, wishing I could do that too. But it *is* another kind of novel – to be judged and enjoyed on other terms. I know only one novelist who has managed to combine both sets of terms, and him I admire this side of idolatry. I mean, of course, Stendhal.

I often brushed with E. G. about this. I could understand his insistence on realism where realism was due. But was it *always* due? For as long as I was writing stories we got along well. The short story is pure essentialism – there is no time or space for more than a minimum of the other stuff: you just use as much of the other stuff as is necessary to create the illusion of actuality, and no more. I did not even clash with E.G. over my first novel, because that was a bulky family chronicle. (It was to be called, in a gesture of adoration towards Turgenev – whose work it no more resembled in treatment than in quality – *A Nest of Simple Folk*.) It was when I wrote my second novel that the fur flew. It lies ahead of my present chronology, in 1936, but this is an appropriate place to speak of it in recalling my more tempestuous relations with E.G.

This second novel, *Bird Alone*, was nothing if not essentialist. Here I wanted to get down to nothing less than sin and salvation in an Irish setting. Now, every reader, except the most disciplined, enjoys in every novel only what he chooses to enjoy or can enjoy according to his nature. Garnett did not give a tuppenny damn about sin and salvation. He hated this side of the novel from the start. He liked his heroic characters too much to have time for this sort of subjectivity. Instead, he went straight for the other stuff, of which I had put in plenty – mainly the social background of the hero as seen through his bizarre family. He tore it to bits in his best fighting-Yorkshire-Irish way, refused to be persuaded by it, told me I was not realistic enough, asked me did I actually know the originals of my hero's father and grandfather, told me that, if so, I was fantasticating my characters, which was true; told me I should see myself as the Balzac of Ireland (no less), and, to shorten many and heated arguments on his side, met obstinately and rather coldly on my side, he demanded that I rewrite the whole story on solid Balzacian lines or scrap it entirely. I refused to alter a line; he washed his hands of me; and we were both wrong.

He was dead right about the social background. It was Quilpish stuff written by a non-Quilpian. It would have taken a Dickens to make some of those people credible in the wild, romantic way I overpainted them. If I had to take that part at all I should have approached it far more humbly, built it up slowly, steadily, calmly, even coldly. But I was in a state of heat over my essential theme, which simply could not be done in the way E.G. recommended, and in which he was not interested anyway – a young man's and a young woman's passion in a community as merciless and alien to passion as Hawthorne's Salem. I *knew* that this part of my novel was good. I have just reread it, without complicity, as if it had been written by somebody else, as, in fact, by this time – thirty years after – it effectively was; and I am still in no doubt about the quality of this part of the novel. The total destruction of those two young people is as true, honest and inevitable as the destruction of Hester Prynne and Arthur Dimmesdale in *The Scarlet Letter*.

Alas! I did not have Hawthorne's inspired wisdom. Henry James might, quite rightly as for himself, lament the uncomplexities and simplicities of Hawthorne's community, seeing there no material suitable for a social realist. But Hawthorne never wanted to write that way. In *The Scarlet Letter* he cut down, virtually cut out, all that 'other stuff', and wrote a short, black, oppressive, poetic, symbolist Gothic novel concentrating wholly on his subjective theme. What I should have done, what E.G. should have advised me to do, was likewise to cut down, or cut out, the 'other stuff' for which I had no real taste or talent. Instead of working up to my theme from a semirealistic basis, I should have begun with the theme, harried it, complicated it, been inventive about it, developed it and finally blown it up like a balloon, as Hawthorne did with his theme, which he then sent sailing off into the night-skies of his magnificently morbid imagination. I occasionally wonder what E.G. would have said to Hawthorne's manuscript! Or to Alain-Fournier's?

It all goes to show that not even the finest critic – and in his age there was no finer critic of the novel than Garnett – can help a writer unless he can get into his skin the way a psychiatrist does with a patient. No writer, he least of all, can himself get into his own skin. If he were to try he would merely confuse himself utterly, and so destroy himself. Yeats gave me the only sound general advice I ever got from anybody about writing. I was saying to him that I was sick of the usual (that is, current) techniques of novel-writing: the dog that barks in the distance, the train whose chug somebody hears at night, the graphic details of dress, tics, food, furniture, all the usual paraphernalia of naturalism. 'I want,' I said, incoherently, 'to be able to do something different, with pins stuck on human maps, or with birdmen flying around on leashes.'

He intoned, or moaned, in his vatic voice, his delicate right hand slightly raised as if to give the papal *urbi et orbi* blessing: 'You must write yourself into yourself. There is no other way.'

It is why the early death of a promising writer is always so sad. Writing is a long, long lifetime's study.

Bird Alone was published as written. It got an honourable reception. It was banned in Ireland as indecent – and subsequently, when out of print, unbanned. Gogarty, of all people, recommended the Irish Academy of Letters to give it a prize. It still circulates. So it must have some merits. Of all its critics only Cecil Day Lewis said something helpful: he observed pungently that in places the style peeled off like wallpaper. I took that to heart. Perhaps it is only writers who can really help other writers. They see one's work with the eyes of fellow workers.

After that I had little contact with E.G.; anyway, I had by then left London; though I doubt if we would have met very often even if I had stayed on – he tired of his ducklings as soon as he had launched them. And to my next book of stories after that I find I have appended a dedication to him, in Avalon. It ends, sadly, with the words: 'Alas, that we can no longer contradict one another.'

I will always revere him for his boundless generosity of mind and his gallant independence of the world. His son David, in his autobiography *The Golden Echo*, truly describes him and his wife Constance as puritans and rebels. It was a puritanism shot through with the lofty epicurean belief that all true pleasure is pure, lasting and imperishable. He was a poor man all his life. I remember, once, saying something to the effect that I found it heartening that his great work for English letters was so widely appreciated. He growled back at me:

'Yes? And I suppose that's why Cape wanted to cut my salary only last week? Some stuff and nonsense about times being bad.

I roared at him: "Do you want to reduce me to the level of a packer?" He said, "Let it go, let it go, it was just a passing idea." '

And for the twentieth time he warned me that there was no living to be had from letters, and told me again how Conrad had said furiously to him, 'I can't live all my life in a garret!', had begged for assurance that he really could make a living from writing, and was told ruthlessly, 'No! There is no living to be had from letters unless you become a hack. Or are one of few lucky ones.' In which, as in (almost) everything else, he was right.

3

Only one thing disturbed our peace of mind in Richmond. I kept thinking of that chair of English in University College, Cork, mainly because it seemed to be my only chance of living in Ireland in anything like a decent way, but also because I was confident I could do good work there, and I felt a great pity for the youngsters passing out of that place with minds as disorganised as mine had been, and to some degree always would be because of it. I fear my handling of the problems surrounding this chair of English will show how untrained and how inexperienced I still was.

My main and lasting difficulty was that I could not find out whether anybody at all wanted me there. My friend the registrar seemed to consider me a serious candidate for the post, but although he was always most amiable, and kept on encouraging me to apply for the post, I could never get him to the point of saying what the odds were on my getting it, not to speak of saying whether he wanted me or not. Looking through some old letter files, I come on a letter from him, evidently an answer to a letter from me trying to find out. It goes:

Dear Sean,
  I am replying promptly – if I defer I may never answer! The Governing Body is considering the English Chair on 21st March. That will be the first bit of news. They may decide to advertise it or they may postpone it. I will let you know immediately. Mrs O. is still in bed, not a bit better. No servant for the past few days – her father died. Kids have measles. I

need make no comment. Prof. from St. Louis stayed with me two days recently to discuss matters. I may go out temporarily next year – permanently if I get salary and security. Any man under 35 ought to leave this country. No influence, no peace, no elbow-room. Kindest regards to Mrs O'F. Let my promptness excuse my brevity. Consider yourself very lucky. Best wishes.

A.

It was a very friendly letter and I was glad to get it, but I do remember reading the sentences about leaving the country many times over. Was this a broad hint to stay away? And yet, if he knew that I did not stand any chance of being elected, it would have been so simple to have said so? Perhaps, I thought, he is just in a melancholy mood because of the illness of his wife and children, and having no servant, and that Prof from St Louis staying with him? On the other hand, I had been rather disturbed by a rumour from Cork that my former friend Daniel Corkery was also in the running for the chair, though I found this hard to credit, since Dan had never been to any university and had no degree whatever. I was much more disturbed to hear that UCC had bestowed an honorary degree on him. If it had been a D.Litt. for his work as a writer I would not have been puzzled. But it was only an honorary B.A., which one would have expected any writer to reject with scorn. My doubts greatly increased when Dan wrote a book on *Synge and Anglo-Irish Literature* – not, to put it mildly, a very good book – and was given the degree of M.A. on the head of it. This ought to have been enough for me if I still did not find it easy to believe that even UCC could appoint to a chair of English a man whose only previous teaching experience had been with small boys in a primary school. It would have been different if UCC had been a big university with a number of English professors, associate professors, assistant professors, tutors, graduate teachers, and visiting professors, where any man such as Daniel Corkery would have been a valuable supplement to the purely academic staff. But where the entire English faculty consisted of one unassisted professor? When UCC remedied Dan's lack of experience in university teaching by inviting him to deliver a series of lectures there, it became clear even to me, living at a distance in London, that Dan had some strong supporters on the spot, that I did not know who they were, that I did not know if I had any, and that it was high time I found out. I crossed over to Ireland to ask my friend the registrar whether I should or should not apply for the chair. He received me amiably, gave me tea, chatted, was most friendly, urged me warmly to apply, to canvass for my election, and let the best man win. I took his advice, and went into the bull ring like a lamb. In the months following I had one of those experiences, like being shipwrecked or falling through the ice, about which one says grimly: 'We'll all be laughing over this in five years' time.'

There were, I found, three stages to the election of a professor in colleges of the National University of Ireland. The Governing Body votes; then the Academic Council votes; then the matter finally goes to the Senate of the National University, of which each college is a constituent, for confirmation or rejection. I found, further, that every candidate for a professorship is expected, though not obliged, to introduce himself, by means of a printed brochure, to each and every member of these bodies, and if he so wishes to present himself in the flesh for inspection by each and every one of them; which is a polite way of saying that he may discreetly plead with each electing member for his vote or, in short, canvass them. When I procured the lists of members I was appalled. It was democracy gone dotty. The Governing Body alone numbered thirty men and women, of whom all too many could be expected to know nothing at first hand about academic matters. They included country shopkeepers, tavern owners, members of county councils, members of the Cork Corporation, farmers, three mayors, two bishops and four men elected by graduates past and present. The Academic Council numbered about fifty, of whom perhaps half-a-dozen knew something about the teaching of English. The Senate numbered thirty-four or thirty-five. I saw that to reach, from London, all these ladies and gentlemen was going to be a bit of a task, but I decided to do my best. So, on various occasions, I set off, by boat, by train, by bus, by car, by bicycle, on foot, over hedges and ditches, up avenues and cart tracks, into various remote parts of the not-minute Province of Munster.

My adventures would have enchanted Gogol. I remember

interviewing, or being interviewed by, one stout farmer who was so hard at work saving his crop of hay on a day of high wind that to talk to him at all I had to walk along beside him shouting into the wind while he vigorously plied his hay fork. When I explained what I wanted of him he shouted: 'A professor of English? Can you talk Irish?'

When I shouted that I could and started to talk in Irish to him he declared that that was 'something', but added sadly that he did not himself, God help him, know 'the Irish'. I mentioned, in a series of discreet, peripatetic roars, an article that I had just written for the organ of the Folklore Society, a proposed (and insupportable) emendation in the text of Beowulf that I had communicated to the *Times Literary Supplement*, and my little book on Thomas Moore. At this name he faced me.

'Him?' he cried. 'Yerrah, sure, Tommy Moore wasn't Irish at all! That English toady?'

I ventured to shout into his left ear as he gazed about the sky, wondering if the weather was going to hold, that Moore had at least claimed to be a poet, and that such claims needed, at the very least, to be examined. My stout farmer paused at this, told me he was very fond of poetry himself and always read the poetry at the back of *Old Moore's Almanac* . . .

I preferred the gloomy attitude of a county councillor whom I interviewed over the long mahogany counter of his musty pub, drinking more whiskey than was good for me while he wandered sadly to and from me to attend to other customers. This melancholy man gave me his considered opinion that anybody could teach English, and that it was only a deplorable waste of money to be paying professors for bloody nonsense like that . . .

I presented myself dutifully to the Lord Bishop of Cork, who, a few years before, had virtually excommunicated all Irish Republicans like Dan Corkery and myself. I found him courteous and uncommunicative. 'Ye are both very good men for the post,' he kept assuring me benignly, evasively and unhopefully. Only one man of all those I talked to refused point-blank to vote for me; and that was when he discovered that I had taken 'the wrong side' in the Civil War. His frankness made me feel that I was wasting my time talking of my degrees and my sponsors. One letter from a bishop or a politician, five lines from a former commandant of the IRA, would have been worth more to me than all that stuff. Only one man promised me his vote, not because of my merits but because of my mother, who hailed from the same part of the country as himself. He laid down one condition, that I pay for the car to drive him to and from the election. So it went, on and off, for months, during which I alternated between bitter amusement and bouts of rage at the folly of all concerned, not excluding my own as it gradually became apparent to me that I was an innocent abroad in my own land.

In the event I got two votes and Dan Corkery got all the rest. The man who voted for me told me that the second vote came from the registrar. I find this very hard to believe. Some thirty years after, when he had been president of that college, and retired, and I had become a well-known writer, we met by chance in an airplane, and he said, out of the blue, 'I made a mistake over Corkery.' If this meant, as it seemed to mean, that he had preferred Corkery to me, which he was, of course, fully entitled to do, why on earth should he have given me his vote? Out of pity? I would hate to think so. But I have never understood any part of the whole foolish affair, in which from start to finish I played such a foolish part myself. Not that I have, or ever had, the least reason to feel aggrieved at the result of the election. The foolishness of the thing was that neither Corkery nor I should ever have wanted to be elected; and I least of all, who had my life before me. If I had, by some mischance, been elected I can only believe that I would have been out of the place within three years, or else stayed on and gone to seed. Kingsley Amis's hero Lucky Jim was lucky to have been rejected from his job. I was lucky to have been rejected for mine. It is a novel that I often reread with all the bitter pleasure of dismayed self-recognition.

4

How devotedly and happily – faithless lover – I now toiled, back in London, at that handful of stories which I had begun while at Harvard, in the spring of 1927, and was not to complete until the winter of 1932. I used to rewrite every sentence a dozen times over, reading aloud to my wife any sentences that gave me particular pleasure, showing each completed story to Garnett for his criticism or approval. I was learning my trade in the only way any writer can learn his trade, by practice, by experiment and hard work. I count this the happiest time of my life, married blissfully, full of hope, self-belief, ambition, free of that stupid academic will-o'-the-wisp in Cork, self-reliant, very occasionally enjoying, or being distracted by the lights and delights of London, for we were now living farther up the Thames, near Teddington Lock. Our first child, Anna Julia, called Julie for short, was born on 6 June 1932. We were then completing our third year in London, and were in no hurry to return to Ireland, the latest plan now being to publish my first book of stories; if it had a *succès d'estime* to ask Jonathan Cape for a subsidy to enable me to start a novel; and if he granted it to drop teaching, go back to Ireland and devote myself wholly to writing. As may be guessed, this plan came from Garnett, who had already done the same thing with Liam O'Flaherty, to whom, as to me, he pointed out that for every writer, as for every horse-breeder, the sensible place to live is near his stable. Liam had amply proved the truth of this by producing in London, as his first efforts in fiction, some pieces of such embarrassing badness about the amours of London society women that Garnett roared at him that he had no business writing about things beyond his knowledge and experience and ordered him to go home and write about the sort of things he really did know.

'But,' Liam had said, miserably, 'all I know about is things like cows and seagulls!'

'Then write about your cows and seagulls!' E.G. had said, and packed him off to Ireland, where, to Edward's delight, he began to write those lovely, delicate stories about birds and beasts which are to be found in his volume *Spring Sowing* –'The Cow's Death', 'The Black Mare', 'The Rockfish', 'The Blackbird'. In Ireland Liam further fulfilled E.G.'s ideal pattern by running away with the handsome wife of a professor in Trinity College and living with her and their child in a deep glen called Glencree, in County Wicklow, in a small whitewashed thatched cottage, where his main recreations, as duly appeared in *Who's Who*, were 'breeding goats and playing the melodeon'. I am afraid I did not do so well when my turn came: my recreations in *Who's Who* were duly to appear as 'daydreaming', which is God's truth, and my devil's vice, and could not have given E.G. half as much pleasure as Liam's bearded goats and wheezy squeezebox.

My book of stories, called, after its first story, *Midsummer Night Madness*, appeared late in 1932, with a preface by E.G. To my delight, and his, its literary success was all that any young man could desire for his first book. I do not know how many copies it sold – they cannot have been very many or I would have remembered – but, in the technical jargon of the time, it broke through. It did not, in any big sense, make my name, but from that day on every editor in London at least knew about me. I remember my wife saying to Edward, as one enthusiastic review followed another: 'But you have always said about the critics that they don't know a good book when they see it!'

He growled: 'It was too damn good – even for *them*.'

Looking back, I feel the critics were more generous about me than he was about them. I remember the mingled satisfaction, irony and scepticism of his voice the morning he said to me: 'The great J. B. Priestley is handing you the bays in the *Evening Standard* tonight.'

I felt grateful to J.B., and, I think, so did E.G.: the puritan in him just did not want me to feel involved in all that sort of public thing.

In the middle of my satisfaction I read that *Midsummer Night Madness* had been banned by the Irish Censorship Board as obscene. Outwardly I laughed at the news. In my heart I felt infuriated and humiliated. Above all I felt frightened at the thought that I was soon to return to live with these stupid, boorish, dispirited people who publicly disowned and insulted me. Was Henry James right after all when he said that the flower of art blooms only where the soil is deep? That 'the coldness, the thinness, the blankness' in the life surrounding a writer can only evoke compassion for his lot? Was I mad to propose to spend the rest of my life rooted in this sour and shallow soil?

Today nobody in Ireland is greatly troubled by, or much interested in, the activities of the Irish Censorship Board. It is almost a law of nature that censorship will always sooner or later make a fool of itself by its own excessive zeal, and as an example of this law of self-stultification the Irish board now takes a high place in the long history of the follies of unenlightened licensed proscription. Over the years there can scarcely be a good writer in the world some work of whose it did not list as obscene – practically all Irish writers since 1930; Tolstoy, Shaw, Dreiser, Balzac, Proust, Malraux, Romain Rolland, Colette, Graham Greene, Sinclair Lewis, Montherlant, Marcel Aymé, Saroyan, Gide, Giono, Moravia, H. E. Bates, Ignazio Silone, Thomas Mann, William Faulkner, Robert Penn Warren (*All the King's Men*), Hemingway (*Across the River and Into the Trees*), Steinbeck, Apuleius, Boccacio, Plato – I could go on, the names coming to me at random, for pages and pages. Not even the most thick-skinned government could face the mockery such folly invited the world over. From this comes a secondary reason why the censorship now only rarely riles us. Thanks to the persistent fight put up against it by Irish writers, from Yeats on, and by liberal-minded public groups like the Irish Civil Liberties Association, the censorship has within recent years so far reformed itself that it now confines itself mainly to the exclusion of American paperback pornography, and does not often make such stupid blunders as its banning of, say, Danilo Dolci's casebooks on the social miseries of Sicily, or Frank O'Connor's fine translations from the Irish, *Lords and Commons*, or Muriel Spark's profound and witty novel *The Bachelors*. Also, there is now, as there was not in 1932, an appeal board. It has to be said, unfortunately, and to our shame, that the long lists of books banned during the board's fanatical period – thousands and thousands of them – still stand as the official demonstration of Ireland's contempt for literature.

But the board was only getting into its stride when I was banned in 1932. Censorship was then a novelty and front-page news; so that I felt very much like a man suddenly plucked from the privacy of his study and shoved naked into the pillory to be pelted by his fellow citizens with rotten vegetables. Some of the missiles were pretty smelly. I am thinking of the anonymous letters I, my wife and my mother now began to get, on the lines of, to mention one typical effusion: 'No detractor of Ireland's fair name must whine because we Irish want to clean our house after dirty little dogs like you have dropped your filth on our clean carpet, as a pup is whipped so shall you be.'

Only one letter, not anonymous, amused me: it was from some chap in Cork I had never heard of ordering me to appear forthwith before a court-martial by the Irish Republican Army. It must also be remembered that I had now been living for almost seven years out of Ireland and had lost touch with the feeling of the country as a whole. It was not until I went back to live there and began to meet old friends and make new friends that I realised that all this unpleasant stuff emanated from a fanatical minority maggot-bred by the decay of national morale during the years following the Civil War, a time when the Catholic Church was felt, feared and courted on all sides as the dominant power. As soon as this became evident to me my heart rose. I even felt happy. It was as when a fog lifts suddenly from a battlefield and one can with clear eyes deploy for the fight. Besides, I was by then already deep in my first novel.

Cape duly agreed to pay me a three-year subsidy of two hundred pounds a year as an advance against future royalties. In return I contracted to offer him whatever other books I should write. By June of 1933 we had managed to save a couple of hundred more pounds, and with Edward's warmest blessings, and direst forebodings, we set off for Ireland and the Life of a Man of Letters.

15

Home

I

That July, Edward visited us to see how we were faring, looked about him at my menage, threw up his hands and cried: 'You are lost!'

His reasons for this dismal prophecy were threefold.

'You are living,' he growled, 'like a lord! You have a car! Your wife has a French maid! And you are living in a mansion! You will either never write a line, or you will become a hack!'

It is true that we had had to have some domestic help in Teddington in the year after our first child was born, and it had happened that a young Frenchwoman, who wished to learn English, had proffered her services in return for her keep and a small fee. She had come with us to Ireland for a short visit. It had also happened that somebody told us that if we purchased a motor car in England and transported it to Ireland we would – owing to the operation of something called the McKenna duties – make a profit on the resale. It had also happened that we had earnestly, but in vain, searched all over County Wicklow for a whitewashed cottage like Liam O'Flaherty's and, for want of better, and seeing our money being wasted on hotels, had had to settle into a modest house, about two miles from Liam's Glencree, called Killough House, at the foot of the Wicklow Mountains, about fifteen miles from Dublin. It had a neglected orchard, a crumbling glasshouse with vines, therefore a vinery, and a lawn with a swing. Edward glared about him, took it all in, and disapproved. I knew him too well by this time to take umbrage at his attack. I was, in fact, writing many 'lines' in his exacting sense of that word. I was finishing my novel, *A Nest of Simple Folk*, and feeling well pleased with it. Life was good. If he had complaints, I had none.

As for my becoming a hack, it was true that I was now living by my pen. I was doing what every successful writer I have ever known or know about did, at some time or other, to some degree or other, from Yeats, Joyce, Wells, Greene, or Katherine Anne Porter back to Chekhov, Dickens, Scott, Thackeray, Balzac, George Eliot, Dr Johnson, Steele and Addison. I was doing what Renoir did when he painted designs on commercial dinner plates or murals on the walls of cheap cafés, which their idiot owners duly painted out in favour of something newer and brighter. I was working for what I call the Small Cheque, in memory of the day Graham Greene asked me 'Are you writing?' and I, as if I were a cloud that is asked 'Are you raining?', said 'I have to!'; at which he sighed, being then infinitely more successful than I: 'Ah! those mornings when I used to hurry down to the letterbox hoping it would contain even a Small Cheque!' Though, in real truth, what I was working for was Time – to write what I most wanted to write.

When young would-be writers now approach me and ask me 'Can I earn a living as a writer?' I show them the tattered blue notebook, marked on the cover *Presentation Brothers College*, in which for years I was to enter my earnings in Time. It is ruled in seven columns, filled in like this:

No.	Title	Nature	Editor	Payment	Words	Date
1	Boccaccio	Review	*Spectator*	£5.5.0	750	A.4th
2	First Love	Story	*Mercury*	£15.0.0	2000	A.10th
3	The Irish Road	Talk	B.B.C.	£20.0.0	1750	A.12th

And so on. At the end of each month the first thing I used to do was to add up the number of words I had written to assure myself that I had written an average of at least five hundred words a day during that month. Then I added up the Small Cheques. If both totals were satisfactory I had earned two, three or more weeks of Time during which I was at liberty to write what I most wanted to write. I followed this simple and infal-

lible system for many years. I abandoned it only when my fees
rose high enough to make the Small Cheque entries unnecessary. I did not, of course, sell all those words; and when I say
five hundred words a day I mean five hundred that stood after
many rewritings; and we lived modestly; and if fees were lower
then, so was the cost of living. It was a good life and there were
many compensations. I could idle on a sunny day and work on
a wet day. Many a fine morning we were on the eighteen-hole
links of Kilcroney, all by ourselves, until lunchtime, and I would
do my five hundred words in the afternoon or at night. Had I
lived in London I might have had to write fifteen hundred or
two thousand words a day, and even at that, many of London's
compensations – theatres, fine restaurants, elegant entertaining
– would have been beyond my means. In Ireland Time is for
next to nothing. It is a good country for a writer – provided he
is willing to live in solitude and can create his own inner heat.

If a writer does not care for this way of life he must have the
foresight to be born of rich parents from whom he will inherit
unearned Time, or work at some other job which will earn
Time, or marry a rich wife. There are no other alternatives.

I have to say that my system – and every freelance has, I
presume, some such system – depends for its success on four
qualities in the practitioner. He must be fluent, versatile, self-
disciplined, and a writer. The need for fluency is obvious. The
self-discipline will show itself in his promptness; for every
editor cleaves to the contributor on whom he knows he can
rely, and at once blackballs the contributor, however brilliant,
whose manuscript is not in his hands when the printer asks for
it. I can best illustrate the quality I call versatility by the first
entry in my Time Book (not Cash Book): a review of a biography
of Boccaccio.

I remember this item well because it taught me so much so
quickly in my very early days when I was making the rounds
of the London periodicals in search of reviewing. One day,
shortly after the publication of my first book, I called on one of
the most brilliant literary editors of that time, Derek Verschoyle
of the *Spectator*. He received me most kindly, and congratulated
me on my stories, while admitting that he had not yet had time

to read them all. This surprised me so much that I mentioned it to Garnett, who laughed and said:

'He will read them all. He probably has read them all by now. But anyway, he is a very good literary editor and knows all about you without reading you, even without reading the reviews. He is on the grapevine. He is part of the grapevine. That's the way all solid reputations are really made.'

He was right, as usual, as I have long since found out by experience. If we want to find out what writer in, say, England, France or Italy is well considered we must go to the grapevine and ignore the reviews. These are always liable to one form or other of ambiguity, equivocation, and even adulteration, through kindness, or the topical appeal of a book, or the reviewer's natural anxiety to excite or to amuse his readers. We must, that is, drop in to some pub or café, in London, Paris or Milan and ask its literary habitués, 'Who is the latest star?' or 'Is A.B. really as good as the reviewers are saying?' One half-hour in, say, El Vino in London is, in this way, worth columns of reviews. But I learned the really important thing from Derek when he ran his hand along the shelves full of recent publications, picked out as if at random this new biography of Boccaccio and said: 'Try your hand on this.'

When I said that I did not know very much about Boccaccio he gave me this sound advice:

'I could get a dozen scholars at the drop of a hat to review that book for me. They would be learned and dull. That is not what I and your readers want. You have written stories. Boccaccio has written stories. Write as one writer on another. What any man needs to be a good reviewer is to be versatile, responsible and have a graphic pen. Reviewing can only be, at best, an approach to criticism. For close criticism the public should, but won't, go to the monthlies, quarterlies and learned journals.'

I took the book and I wrote what must have been a good review because for years after I did regular reviewing for the *Spectator*. Nevertheless, to show that I did not learn my lesson fully, I may here add another piece of advice I got from Edward Garnett's son David, when he was on the *New Statesman and Nation*. He tested me for three weeks as a reviewer of novels. They were, as the majority of topical novels are, poor stuff, so much pap for the lending libraries, and I said as much. After the three weeks were up David dropped me. I asked him why. He said, honestly and bluntly, as his father would have done: 'All you say about these novels is that they are poor stuff. That is not interesting for readers.'

'But,' I said, 'if a book is not interesting what else can I do?'

He said, dryly: '*You* can be interesting.'

He was right. There is nothing on earth that is not interesting if one has curiosity and wit enough.

2

Before I returned to Ireland in 1933, literary Dublin had meant little to me other than a night or two in Yeats's living room, a couple of clubs, such as the Arts Club and the PEN Club, a couple of journalists' pubs, and gossip galore. When I now set out to explore it as a permanent base, I found that 'literary Dublin' meant the half-dozen Irish writers who lived there, and the occasional good play at the Abbey Theatre and the Gate Theatre. For the rest I could hear Mentor Garnett saying it:

'Literature isn't produced by Dublin, London, Paris or anywhere else. It's produced by a few men sitting alone in their rooms before the blank page. You will find a few, and damn few, doing that in Dublin: a few more writing about literature; and a lot of fellows talking about those few. Stick to your desk, my boy!'

All the same, Dublin, like every other city, has its atmosphere, and groups that can, if they are sophisticated, intelligent, informed and keen enough, work on it like a hotbed, forcing it, as a gardener would say, by a constant fermentation of criticism and discussion, not only about the arts but about everything else surrounding the artist in his studio or his study. I would not go so far as to say that literary Dublin in the 1930s deserved all those four adjectives, but for about five years or so I thought it a lively and stimulating place, and I was well pleased to be part of it.

Those of us who belonged to the Irish Academy of Letters were privileged. It had been founded the year before by Yeats and Shaw, when I had been elected a founder-member on the strength of the promise of my one book of stories. Its membership list would have been a remarkable roll of honour for any country much larger than Ireland, though I have to admit that it lost much of its first impressiveness for me as soon as I realised that half our members lived in England and elsewhere.* As long as Yeats was with us his Academy – it really was *his* Academy; Shaw merely lending his name – had an interesting life. There were lectures in the Abbey Theatre, dinners or, as we sometimes called them, banquets, prize-givings and council meetings, with their inevitable small conspiracies and their lively, and as is also inevitable in Ireland, occasionally bitter controversies. I want to try to recall, quickly, three of those dinners, which, spread as they are over five years, may re-evoke the sense that I gradually got of a receding tide.

The first dinner, because of Yeats's health, gave me a slight forecast of what the Academy would be without him. This dinner, at the Dolphin, was stage-managed by Gogarty with Yeats at the head of the table. A number of ladies were present at this dinner, which was given in honour of the Harmsworth family, who had recently bestowed some very welcome prize money on the Academy. That night, whether it was the presence of ladies that restrained us or not, Gogarty thought we were all being much too dignified and sedate. He kept puckishly trying to put some ginger into the event, hopping about from one part of the table to another, inciting us to start an argument, to show

* The membership of the Irish Academy of Letters in 1932 was: Austin Clarke, Padraic Colum, St John Ervine, Oliver Gogarty, Frederick Robert Higgins, Brinsley MacNamara, George Moore, T. C. Murray, Frank O'Connor, Peadar O'Donnell, Sean O'Faolain, Liam O'Flaherty, Seumas O'Sullivan, Forest Reid, Lennox Robinson, George W. Russell (AE), G. B. Shaw, Miss E. (E. Somerville, James Stephens, Francis Stuart, W. B. Yeats.
Those were the full members. For some reason there were also, at first, associate members, a distinction later abandoned. These included Ernest Boyd, Lord Dunsany, John Eglinton, Stephen Gwynn, J. M. Hone, Sir Shane Leslie, Walter Starkie, L. A. G. Strong, Helen Waddell, Eugene O'Neill and Aircraftsman T. E. Shaw. (It was drawing a rather long bow to claim these two as Irish; but they did agree to join the Academy.) We were later joined by Elizabeth Bowen, Shan Bullock, Alice Milligan, Rutherford Mayne, Desmond McCarthy, Robert Lynd, Lord Longford and others. As the original members died, others, such as Enid Starkie, Kate O'Brien, Mary Lavin and Denis Johnston, came later still. Sean O'Casey refused (violently) to join. Joyce also refused. Corkery and Douglas Hyde declared that an Irish Academy should be confined to writers in Gaelic.

the English visitors our paces; proclaiming, with a splendid gesture towards the head of the table, 'We have seen Shelley plain!'; or, whenever Yeats – who was silent for most of the evening, and had recently had the Voronoff treatment – was obliged to retire now and again, muttering such Buck Mulligan-ish remarks to the ladies as 'Read his latest?' and after reciting a few bits, 'Pure prostatic verse, my dears!'

We were also in the Dolphin for the next dinner. That night I found myself at the head of the table, feeling far too much like a nervous hostess to pay much attention to anybody but the guest on my left, who was Lord Dunsany, and the guest on my right, Francis MacManus, on whom the Academy had just bestowed the Harmsworth Award for his historical novel *Travelling Men*. Dunsany was in one of his most difficult moods. He first rejected the salt because it poured. ('Takes ten years of your life, that stuff! Full of chemicals!') Instead he produced from his waistcoat pocket an envelope of his own home-ground rock salt. ('If your butler,' he warned me, 'is too lazy to grind your salt for you he's a washout. Get rid of him at once.') He then rejected the ashtray because it bore an advertisement for somebody's ale. 'Am I,' he demanded hotly of the head waiter, 'to be made the butt of free advertising? You can hardly be married now-adays without some oaf trying to introduce a bit of cheap adver-tising. Bring me an ashtray with daisies painted on it!' He next rejected the cream, smelling it, lifting his glasses to peer into it. ('Full of chemicals. Look at the top of it. Borax! If your dairymaid,' he warned Frank MacManus across me, 'is too lazy to bring you fresh cream every night for your dinner, don't hesitate. Get rid of her at once!'). I liked Dunsany, who was odd, original, honest, hospitable and sensitive, but that night I was afraid *he* was going to make the scene when he asked me as the coffee was about to come: 'Do we not toast His Majesty?' I said, 'There is only one toast – to the Nation.' Hastily I gave the toast and said, 'You may smoke, now, gentlemen.' As everybody broke into chatter he rose quietly, unnoticed, unobtrusively lifted his brandy glass and whispered softly to himself, 'God bless him!' It was done very tenderly. I recall the whole night a little sadly. It was pleasant, and dignified, but there was no

Yeats to give it glamour, no Gogarty to give it sparkle. The best days were going, if not gone.

Here I would like to pay tribute to Oliver Gogarty. Joyce did him an immense and cruel injustice in *Ulysses* by presenting him to posterity as something approaching the nature of an insensitive lout whose only function in life was to offset and emphasise the exquisite sensitivity and delicacy of Stephen Daedalus. Gogarty was a kind and generous man, full of verve and zest, as well as being, especially in later life, a curiously lonely man. When he retired to New York, where I met him three or four times, he was a pathetically lonely man. His essential nature, which nobody could ever possibly gather from *Ulysses*, was his nature as a poet – he was a genuine poet – and it must have hurt him deeply that from the time *Ulysses* appeared everybody knew him as the original of Malachi Mulligan and only a very few as a poet. He had his insensitive areas. (So had Joyce – large areas. So, no doubt, have we all.) He could be cruel, above all if he could be cruel wittily; he would, as we say, have sacrificed his grandmother for a joke; and in Ireland, where the bitter joke is treasured, this could do for others exactly what Joyce did for him. I will not say that he was a gentleman, not because he was not but because it is a period word, and his period was the eighteenth century, when he might have been called a Corinthian, or as Joyce accurately dubbed him, a buck.

The next dinner, or banquet, was held one August night in 1937. Yeats made a short speech which was later printed (seventy copies, dated December 1937: *A Speech and Two Poems* by W. B. Yeats), and it is worth giving in full if only to recall the dignity and imagination with which he could invest every public occasion. It reads:

Guests and Fellow Academicians,

    Mainly through the help of Dr MacCartan I was able to collect in America money enough to pay for the beautiful Gregory medal, the principal award of the Academy, and for certain working expenses. Dr MacCartan has himself paid for the O'Growney award, and I think we owe to his influence with his friend, that generous Irishman, the Marquis MacDonald, the Casement award. These are the reasons why we entertain him at a banquet – but for him this Academy would not exist.

I have a reason for gratitude of which you know nothing. A year ago Dr Gogarty told me that Dr MacCartan and certain wealthy Irish-Americans wished to show their appreciation of what I had done or tried to do; they knew, he said, that my wife and I had sufficient for our necessities, sufficient to educate our children and to place them in life, but they wished, he said, that I should have that something more which is precious to an old man. I said that I accepted, with gratitude, but that the gift must not be secret. I must be permitted to tell my friends and associates. You are those friends and associates, and I tell you that I shall be given for the next few years enough money for dignity and ease. Standing amongst you, I thank Dr MacCartan, but I do not yet thank those others. I have not yet got all their names, and, when I have, I may still have to wait a little time. I think though I cannot yet be sure, that a good poem is forming in my head – a poem that I can send them. A poem about the Ireland that we have all served, and the movement of which I have been a part.

For a long time I had not visited the Municipal Gallery. I went there a week ago and was restored to many friends. I sat down, after a few minutes, overwhelmed with emotion. There were pictures painted by men, now dead, who were once my intimate friends. There were the portraits of my fellow workers; there was that portrait of Lady Gregory, by Mancini, which John Synge thought the greatest portrait since Rembrandt; there was John Synge himself; there, too, were portraits of our Statesmen; the events of the last thirty years in fine pictures: a peasant ambush, the trial of Roger Casement, a pilgrimage to Lough Derg, event after event: Ireland not as she is displayed in guidebook or history, but Ireland seen because of the magnificent vitality of her painters, in the glory of her passions.

For the moment I could think of nothing but that Ireland: that great pictured song. The next time I go, I shall stand once more in veneration before the work of the great Frenchmen. It is said that an Indian ascetic, when he has taken a certain initiation on a mountain in Tibet, is visited by all the gods. In those rooms of the Municipal Gallery I saw Ireland in spiritual freedom, and the Corots, the Rodins, the Rousseaus were the visiting gods.

With this speech is printed a dedication in verse to MacCartan and the well-known poem 'The Municipal Gallery Revisited'.

Yeats died two years later and proved to be, in every regard, irreplaceable. He had been our inspiration and our justification in the sense that all the rest of us younger men and women could not, between the lot of us, represent literature with anything like his achievement and authority in the eyes of the public. When he retired to Menton to die, and most of his generation had passed away or gone into exile one by one – George Moore, Russell, Forrest Reid, Robert Lynd, Gwynn, Gogarty, Shaw, Desmond McCarthy, Hone, Seumas O'Sullivan – the vitality of the academy oozed away and, as Lennox Robinson used to say – he was one of the longest-lived of that remarkable generation – there was nothing to do but wait until Time, if it ever did, created new reputations of equal authority.

It was not a matter alone of literary achievement. Had, for example, Joyce returned to live in Dublin his presence would have made no difference. For the source of Yeats's authority, like the source of his poetry, was the extraordinary union in his nature of a powerful imagination, the will to enforce it, and a persistent self-image of himself as seer and leader. It was his plasma, nobody else's. It was the blend that at once bestowed greatness on him and condemned him to loneliness. At this point I have arrested my pen as it was about to write that few knew him as a man; it is more likely that nobody did; indeed, it is unlikely that there was, in the common implication of the word, a man to know. His intimates may have known him as a poet, or a colleague in the theatre, or in the Senate, but it can only have been very much as they might have known a prime minister or a cardinal who, to use a crude phrase, never came off it, never unbuttoned. As there are priests who move, who live within the aura of *l'esprit ecclésiastique*, Yeats moved and lived within *l'esprit poétique*. He had created a mask and become it, in his every nerve and artery, thought and mood. He was writing an autobiographical testimony, not merely making a poetic flourish, when in 'The Tower', in 1926, he made that part-Hegelian, part-Platonic, part-Kantian declaration that *Death and life were not/Till man made up the whole,/Made lock, stock and barrel/Out of his bitter soul* . . . and so on.

This is not solipsism, though it is extravagantly near it. He did truly believe that man can not only make 'a super-human, mirror-resembling dream' but can make it come to pass as reality, if he has the accompanying will. He imagined a theatre, and it grew, not quite his dream yet one that without his dream would not have come to pass at all, and that now, when there is nobody like him to keep on imagining it into life, has virtually passed out. He imagined his Academy, and it became a kind of fact for a brief while. The strange thing is that he never seemed to realise that his mirror and his dream were indivisible, so that when he was about to leave the fray he could say to Frank O'Connor, 'You will save the Abbey Theatre, and O'Faolain will save the Academy,' as if we could dream his dreams as passionately as he did. We might dream some other dreams but not his. Does this make him a bad builder? I think it makes him a bad parent. He left no Peter and Paul behind him. He prepared no disciples. He was too busy, and rightly so, making himself.

Most of Dublin's many stories about him, and it does not matter whether they are apocryphal or not, rose about his aloofness. Here is Mrs Padraic Colum telling us with asperity how she, just back from the United States, meets him unexpectedly in Nassau Street and says with delight, 'Why, good morning, Mr Yeats!' – only to hear him intone:

'I hear a voice. It comes from beyond the seas. I know it not.'

I can enjoy the impishness of that, for, as Molly Colum remarked, 'He knew damned well who I was!' But it is aloof. Here is his small daughter Anne walking or playing near his gate in Rathfarnham. She sees papa approach, pause, look slowly at her and murmur: 'And what is *your* name?' In another man that could be pose or puckishness, not in him. It may well have been sheer absentmindness. Here he is introducing Daniel Binchy, one of the finest Celtic scholars in the world, to his wife: 'This is Michael Tierney, the finest classical scholar in all Ireland.' Wrong man, wrong subject, and even Tierney, later president of University College, Dublin, would not have made such a claim.

Yeats loved Ireland, and in a sense knew Ireland better than most people, but I do not believe he knew the people of Ireland. MacCartan once said an odd but true thing: 'Yeats is much more of a nationalist than Gogarty, but Gogarty is much more Irish.'

Meaning that Yeats had Ireland in his soul, but that Gogarty had it in his bones. Here is the great Yeats, during the riots over Sean O'Casey's play, coming to the footlights and declaring to the audience with all the magnificence of poet to peasant: 'You have disgraced yourselves again! You have rocked the cradle of a new genius.' But how else could he rule them, how else preserve his soul in their 'rude, unmannerly town', except by refusing to know them other than in his imagination of them? As in his passionate poem 'Easter 1916', where he recalls how he used to meet some of those sixteen executed rebels in the streets before the Rising, and pass on with a nod of the head, or 'polite meaningless words', or think of them as a mocking story to be told at the club:

> Being certain that they and I
> But lived where motley is worn:
> All changed, changed utterly,
> A terrible beauty is born.

I have said poet to peasant, reverting to an odd phrase in his 1937 speech describing an IRA ambush as 'a peasant ambush'. It is an old-fashioned word, and the wrong word – there are no peasants in Ireland, there are small tenant farmers – and it is a revealing anachronism. I, as I have recounted, once took part, in the hills, in something remotely like an ambush. Many of my friends really took part in serious ambushes. Ministers of state, friends of MacCartan, had taken part in ambushes. All peasants? It was not, of course, that Yeats looked down on peasants, of whom, as a boy, he had known many, and had been inspired by many, as a poet. It was his way, his poet's way, wise for him, necessary for him, of being deliberately undated, of holding every common fact at a slight distance. It has been observed by critics that he would even, for this, deliberately make some slight, seeming mistake of nomenclature when writing about Irish things, which other readers have too readily ascribed to ignorance; as when his Hag of Beare – in Gaelic, as he must have known well, *An Cailleach Beire* – is called *Clooth-na-Bare*, because he preferred the sound of it that way, or the Fianna, or even the Fenians, are called Finians, or the placename

Doona is altered to suit his ear in 'The Fiddler of Dooney'. It is interesting to go from that poem which accompanied his last speech, 'The Municipal Gallery Revisited', to the actual pictures he saw and slightly reconstituted. That peasant ambush is not an ambush at all; it is a studio painting of three west-of-Irelanders provided with rifles. Casement is not, in the painting referred to in his poem, half hidden by the bars. He speaks of 'an Abbot or Archbishop with upraised hand blessing the Tricolor.' Why an Abbot? I am not carping about a fine, warm, passionate poem. All I am saying is that this way of moving all things a little out of focus into a slight distance was part of his art of living as well as of writing. It was his need of his nature, as poet and man, to live a foot off the ground, a foot or two, or more, away from common life, more or less, I have to say it, in the English nineteenth-century romantic tradition of Shelley, Blake, Byron, Swinburne, Dowson.*

> Dear fellow artist, why so free
> With every sort of company,
> With every Jack and Jill?
> Choose your companions from the best;
> Who draws a bucket with the rest
> Soon topples down the hill . . .

But we had marched with Sheila and Sean, taken refuge with them, gone to jail with them, been poor with them, bitter with them, fought with them, toppled with them at times very far down the hill. We had know nobody else but them. We could not walk away from them in his aerial footsteps. We must, at times, have bristled at this withdrawal of his. In those days, heaven help us, we thought of ourselves as the new realists, which we certainly were not in comparison with any other writer in the world, apart from him. We had to deal with much more intractable material than he. His fiddler of Dooney was, for us, at every street corner, in every shop, every office, not at all larger than life, just irreducibly life-size. We knew too damned much about the Jacks and Jills of Ireland.

* But selectively: see his *Oxford Book of Modern Verse*. Hopkins is in, but not Morris; and not a line by Browning. Too realist, too sociable, too gregarious?

I would like to have known him, but for the few times we met and worked together in his Academy I never did know him. I suppose his oldest friend was George Russell (AE). I knew Russell in the common, intimate, unbuttoned sense in which men know men, and it was apparent that even Russell never knew him in that way. One of his latest close companions in Dublin was F. R. Higgins, a good poet and one-time manager of the Abbey Theatre. Fred, a fat, amiable, nerve-ridden, devious, earthy man, and a genuine poet, had many puckish stories about their encounters; but they were all those little sidelights with which the favoured companion of a great man tries, without much success, to suggest humanity behind greatness. As when he recalled how, while he, Yeats and a third man were discussing some problem, perhaps of the theatre, or of poetry, two Persian cats kept frolicking in heat with one another in a corner of the room, quite unobserved, it seemed, by Yeats, but much to the amusement of earthy Fred; yet when the deep discussion ended and Yeats and he were in the taxi driving away, Yeats murmured as if to himself: 'Yes, Higgins! Cats *are* very interesting creatures,' and resumed the discussion where it had left off. For that matter, I feel sure that Yeats also knew Higgins only in his imagination of him, as when he once said of Fred's frequent visits to his home, 'He comes to me here sweating from his whore!' – a fantasy-image that gave much amusement to the good and most uxorious Higgins when it was repeated back to him; as every such remark made in Dublin is always repeated back to its victim.

He lived on a peak: but there was no pose about him, although he did sometimes act his play and the Dublin gossips always said he was a poseur. Garnett, who met him often in his young London days, was quite certain that he was just a natural dreamer. 'No pose at all!' he once said to me. 'The first time he came to stay with us at the Cearne he had no luggage whatever. I asked him about it. He put his hand absently into his pocket and produced and gazed at a toothbrush. He had no sense of place or time. I have walked from my place in London to his late at night; he returned with me; I saw him home again; he returned again, talking, talking, completely lost.'

Other poets descend from their peaks to common earth; he

never. Even as a critic he was best when to the point, the word, the line, the phrase, the image. Other poets can be men of the reason and the intelligence; he never, except when he unwillingly had to for the purposes of the theatre or to make some philosophical statement, pronouncement or hazard pertinent to the course of his thinking as a poet. Apart from that he loathed Reason, that generalising, abstracting power that takes from the object its intimate particularity by relegating it to its dull social purpose and category; as was plain also to men like T. E. Hulme, Flint, Bergson, Ezra Pound and all the imagist poets who must have influenced him, also, in the early 1900s; and is something every artist recognises instinctively: not to see a 'priest' or a 'soldier' or a 'dustman', but to see the faces of Thomas, Richard and Henry; to concentrate on the particular until it becomes almost hallucinatory, to avoid at all costs the purely rational, which turns the hallucination into an essay. (As I, writing like this – inescapably in this kind of book – know that it would be much more interesting to try to describe the peculiar, slanting shape of his eyes, or the long droop of his fingers so well observed by O'Sullivan in the portrait that used to hang in the foyer of the Abbey Theatre.) Yeats, protecting his hallucinations, would never wish, or be able, to communicate with intellectual, organising men whose role and habit is to turn everything into a generalisation, into the sort of blueprint picture of life that, of its nature, obliterates that most interesting part of experience, the particular and the exceptional. He was a poet, for poets, about poetry, a Blakeian creation of his own imagination. I think he probably communicated best with his own like, poets and contemplatives. And yet he might, I have often thought, he just might be a good man to live with marooned on a desert island. Or would I prefer old dirty Jack or sweaty Jill?

3

La cera di costoro e chi la duce non sta d'un modo . . . The wax and the seal that marks it are made of different materials, and all too soon, and too easily, his mark on the Academy became illegible, except for one word which I lived to deplore. I mean his *haughty*, unbending attitude to the Censorship. We inherited this attitude and it was to have a profound effect on my life, for years to come. It involved bitterness and anger.

His attitude to it was exactly the same as his attitude twenty years before in his poem 'To a Wealthy Man Who Promised a Second Subscription to the Dublin Municipal Gallery If It Were Proved the People Wanted Pictures'. This poem, translated into non-Yeatsian language, angrily asked this man: 'Who the hell are the people that we should bother about them?' He invoked Duke Ercole, Guidobaldo and Cosimo de Medici, who, before they sent the mummers to the marketplace of Ferrara, or set up a school of courtesies on 'Urbino's windy hill', or plotted the library of San Marco with Michelozzo, did not inquire what the onion-sellers thought or on what side the *popolazzo* stood. (Yeats was no democrat!) In his wake we asked the same angry question, with the result that it took us twenty years of battle to persuade the politicians to set up an appeal board and replace the fanatics, who were making Ireland a mockery, by a half-dozen sensible men and women. We could have achieved it far earlier if we – or if he, which of his nature he could not – had, of our right as partakers in and inheritors of the Revolution, gone before the people and the Government immediately the idea was mooted and said: 'Either ask the police to administer this thing, or ask us.'

In the first solution, the censorship would then be open to the rule of law in the courts, and every man could plead his rights in public, as happens in England, France, America and other democratic countries. The only difficulty in this solution would be that, since no books worth counting were published within Ireland, the English publishers and printers would have taken no part in such trials, and the Irish booksellers and writers would have had to bear the whole brunt. Whatever about the writers (and many of them were living out of Ireland), this the booksellers were not prepared to do; and, in view of the vast numbers of books the fanatics then wanted banned, I find it hard to blame them – they would have been in court every day of the week. Accordingly, the Government decided to operate a censorship by ukase, administered by an autonomous board responsible only to a minister, which meant that the writers were left to bear the whole brunt, had no appeal to the courts

– unless they cared or could afford to impeach a minister, who was covered by his own law – were therefore publicly insulted, without appeal to the courts, deprived of their Irish market, cut off from communication with their own people and virtually outlawed. It followed that if there were to be any kind of sense or justice in a censorship so operated it could only be operated cautiously by wise and prudent men. With Yeats and the Academy talking like Duke Ercole, Guidobaldo and Cosimo de Medici to our lay zealots, to our puritanical priests and our inexperienced politicians, some of us refusing to as much as recognise that any censorship has any right to exist anywhere, the game fell like rotten fruit into the hands of the zealots, and stayed there until the thing became a public scandal. At that point a few of us, detaching ourselves from the two extremes, were able to approach the more intelligent and cultivated men among the politicians, who took the first steps toward reform. It is worthwhile recording that there were two other much more potent reasons for the reform of the Censorship. One can be nutshelled in the appeal an Irish ambassador to the USA made to me in the 1940s: that while I might reasonably say anything I wished in derision of the Censorship while I was at home, in deriding it publicly throughout the United States I was damaging my country's reputation abroad. The other and perhaps most potent enemy of our Censorship was the arrival of television. Since no government can censor the air it is pointless for it to attempt to censor print.

All this is now with the years, and I have long since lost interest in the Censorship, believing that with the passage of more years it will, as elsewhere, become a purely sanitary operation, and, as such, ultimately, as elsewhere, be handed over to the courts where it belongs. All of it that now interests me is its heritage of anger, and the division it created between the artist and his people. These were two grave challenges with which we artists all had to cope since anger in an artist is of itself at best a barren emotion and at worst a blinding one.

This I had realised very early on. In a 'Letter from Ireland', sent to the *Hound and Horn* soon after I left America in 1929, I quoted Stendhal on Anger from his *Promenades dans Rome*. For several years I carried the quotation in my pocketbook, and used occasionally to take it out and read it. Freely translated, it says:

> For all our anger the Government will be much the same in twenty years as it is today. Since by then the world will be almost finished for many of us, it isn't very intelligent to postpone until such time as the perfect Government will have been established the joys of nature and the delights of art. There will always be something to drive us mad in politics, and one of the saddest ways to spend one's life, I feel, is in a state of impotent rage.

It is true that an artist can canalise his anger, but if once he begins to do this it will by then cease to be more than the trigger that sets him to work, and he will once again be subject to the cold controls of his craft and the warm feelings that belong to his creative nature. No man can paint, or write, or do anything fruitful in a state of rage. If, however, the anger of an artist is directed against and held against the very protoplasm of his art, his own people, he is in a terrible danger of quarrelling with the very paint on his brush, the plaster in his hand, the words on his tongue, his model on the dais, his own vision of life, his whole being both as man and artist, and there is really little left to him — unless he is an enormous genius, and slightly mad at that, like Swift — but to become a psychopath, or fall silent, or become an agitator or a prosecutable pamphleteer.

There were times, during those years, when I used often to think of Henry James on Hawthorne, and say to myself: 'He didn't know the half of it!' For here I was, not well settled back into Ireland, torn already (and once more) between love for it and hate of it, and a longing to get out of it, and a cold, bitter feeling that I was not going to be driven out of it. I was looking a few nights ago at an old notebook of those years which formed the basis of my second novel, *Bird Alone* (1936), odd thoughts, wonderings, and problems of the soul, and I am not surprised that they all look slightly daft to me now. This novel was the one Garnett did not like, saying it was not real enough. He did not know the half of it, either!

'You see, Edward,' I should have said to him, 'it's not a question of whether the stuff is real. The question is: Am I sweet?'

287

'Sweet?' he would have growled.

'Yes, Edward. That's the real problem of every Irish writer, to keep sweet about his material, not to go sour on it.'

'Give Ireland hell!' he would have roared.

'But, Edward,' I would have had to say, 'I don't want to do that. In my divided heart I love my people.'

Somewhere Scott Fitzgerald describes a fellow as laughing mockingly with a hang-jawed, half-moon mouth. Imagine you see me making a half-moon mouth, saying to Edward:

'Aw! Edward! It's not the conflicts I mind, they are good for a man, so long as he can face – no, not them, they are easy! – *himself*, without evasion. The conflicts are all right, they are useful, they are part of living, so long as you can use them, for as long as you can keep your sense of humour, keep your distance, your focus, keep sweet. Look at Henry James. A few more conflicts wouldn't have done him any harm. They might even have made him as a good a writer as Nathaniel Hawthorne, who faced so many problems – and kept sweet.'

Yeats knew it all, had said it many times in many ways, thinking of how often the angers of Ireland had threatened or broken his dearest friends.

> Out of Ireland have we come.
> Great hatred, little room,
> Maimed us at the start . . .

Or when, after quarrelling with some once beautiful woman whom 'this blind bitter town' had reduced to angry rage, he cried, 'Where had her sweetness gone?' and answered where:

> Somewhere behind the curtain
> Of distorting days
> Lives that lonely thing
> That shone before those eyes
> Targeted, trod like Spring.

Old master! Be with us always in this blind bitter town, seeking, longing for, remembering that lost spring.

Thinking of Yeats, and the Academy, and our angers, I have been led ahead of myself, and in a sense I have also been led out of my Self by those public things happening in Dublin. Certainly, most of my life during those years was domestic, rural, private and subjective; which is to say that I lived in my house and garden in County Wicklow, and that I lived for the greater part inwardly. When I came out of my cave or wilderness of self it was not always to engage in public controversy; it was to collect fallen apples, or to see why there was no water in the taps, or to rake the gravel, or to play golf, or to dig the garden, or go for a drive with my wife and child, or collect a friend from Dublin coming for supper and a long talk over the turf fire: Fred Higgins, the poet, or Sean O'Sullivan, the painter, or most often, for he was my closest friend in those years, Frank O'Connor.

I do not know what I would have done for intimate companionship in those years without Michael, as I called Frank O'Connor, having grown up with him in Cork when he was Michael O'Donovan. I used often to say that he was the only man in Dublin with whom I could talk about the things that really interested me; that is, any sort of prose fiction, its craft, its aims, its living sources, possibilities and limitations. We were complementary in many ways; his imagination was a ball of fire, mine was less combustible but steadier; his memory was infallible, his interests more confined; his brain was first-class but completely untrained, and discipline was a word he had never heard; his intuitive processes were something to marvel at, to distrust and, if one was wise, to respect profoundly, because if you were patient enough to discard the old boots and bits of seaweed that he would bring up from his deep diving he was certain, sooner or later, to surface with a piece of pure gold. I do not think he ever reasoned out anything. He was like a man who takes a machine gun to a shooting gallery. Everybody falls flat on his face, the proprietor at once takes to the hills, and when it is all over, and you cautiously peep up, you find that he was wrecked the place but got three perfect bull's-eyes. I remember one time when I was proposing to write a biography of Daniel O'Connell, the Liberator, the man who, at the head

of what one could only call an Irish rabble, won political emancipation for all the Catholics of the British Isles. We talked of
it, and talked of it, and the machine gun rattled, and the walls
of my living room became riddled with bits of the eighteenth
century, and the nineteenth century, and bits of Dan O'Connell
were shattered all over the floor and the ceiling until, exhausted,
and utterly bewildered, but wildly stimulated, I drove Michael,
as usual, down out of the hills for his last bus at Bray. When I
came home the fire was gray ashes, the shooting gallery was
wrecked, but there in the room I found exactly what I needed
to give shape to my book. It was the echo of Michael's superb
voice reciting his fine translation of the Irish poem 'Farewell,
Patrick Sarsfield' – written in praise of Lord Lucan, when with
the rest of the Irish aristocracy, known as the Wild Geese, he
had to fly to the Continent at the end of the Williamite wars,
leaving the common folk behind to endure for centuries the
dire effects of that defeat. Dan O'Connell was the first *popular*
leader of those helots; a hundred years later. I had the title and
theme of my book – *King of the Beggars: A Study of the Rise
of Modern Irish Democracy*. I rightly dedicated the book to
Frank O'Connor. On the other hand, after I had spent some
three or four years over a biography of the great Earl of Tyrone,
he insisted that I had made a mistake in not handling Tyrone,
one of the ablest diplomats and generals of the sixteenth
century, as a comic figure. Michael's great gift for simplification
had its corresponding weakness in oversimplification, as my
preference for winding myself into a subject with a blend of
thought and sensibility has its weakness in overcomplication.
For years we stimulated one another. If he did a good story I
wanted to do a better; if I did one I am sure he felt the same
healthy spirit of emulation. Our quarrels were the quarrels of
colleagues; our arguments were the arguments of friends; we
supported one another in our public controversies; we chose to
imagine that the responsibility for the future of Irish literature
was on our two backs. Unfortunately, as we grow older we
become indifferent, call it tolerance, and get more intolerant
than before. Over the years Michael and I grew weary of one
another's ways and more attached each to his own way. Ultimately the friendship died, to our mutual loss.

In such ways – walks, talks, friendships, days on the beach in summer, gardening, paintings and mendings, all the usual dear simple domestic things – the Life of the Man of Letters revealed itself as being very much the same as any other life except in one vital respect. I was often struck, as so many artists have been, by the immense difference between these simple things, which are so large a part of everybody's life, and Art, which leaves so many of them out. This sense of the disproportion between art and life which then first started to grow in me has bothered me all my life, and I see no answer to it except to regard all life as a blend of many arts, of which what we call Art is only one art among those many; and one to be considered less than any of them – such as cooking, or joinery, or plumbing, or fencing, or chess, or politics – if it is of less human import and interest than they.

This is why my first novel, *A Nest of Simple Folk* (1934), which was not really a very good novel, gave me much satisfaction while I was writing it but less after it was done. It was a historical novel, or family chronicle, based on everything I had known, or directly observed in the countryside, of my mother's people, and the city life of my mother and father away back, some twenty years ago, in Cork City. So that, in this book I am now writing, that novel, *A Nest of Simple Folk*, links these pages with my earliest pages describing my childhood. It was, or was intended to be a child's view of the world brought into relation to a grown man's view of the world. The grown man was, in his cave of Self, explaining to the child he once had been what it really was that he thought he saw as a child. It was a relating of aspirations nourished in innocence to the world allegedly experienced in knowledge. While I was working at it a friend might have asked me, 'What are you writing about?', and I might, for short, have said, 'About Limerick and Cork between 1840 and 1916.' But it would not have been true. Just as a critic reading the novel might have said, 'He here describes life in Ireland over three generations,' and it would not have been true. I was writing about my own youthful dreams; and whenever I went upstairs to my study in Killough House, and looked out over the soft roll of drums of the Wicklow hills, I was hearing every time – no matter what I was writing about

– the drums of those boyhood dreams. Because of this I felt less disjunction between myself at my table and the countryman passing along the road outside, or the girl in the kitchen humming over her work, or the old tramp we called Forty Coats pausing at the gate to talk to my small daughter Julie playing inside it on the lawn. I felt very close to the old Irish poet of the eight or ninth century, who wrote of his cat:

> Pangur Bawn and I,
> are each at his own trade;
> he intent on mice,
> I on my wordy craft . . .

because I felt no disjunction of time, or place, or purpose between him long dead and me at my table.

Yes, that prentice novel made me feel less separated from life than some other far better things I have written. Whenever I left it I felt a jolt not greater than the opening and the closing of a door, as when I would leave my table to see why there was no water in the taps – it was always happening to us: one of the unjoys of country life! – or why the snow was leaking through the valley of the roof, or to burn leaves, or do any small domestic chore. But, of course, there *was* that jolt. It would be delightful if all our lives were an absolute unity, like a crystal ball, a man's work and his child, his book and his wife, his business and his friends, his private Cave and his open Fireside. Certainly for an artist such a crystal unity cannot exist. No artist dares wish it to exist. Constant flickers of detachment from his subject are essential to keep on reminding him of whatever it was in its internal shape that made him think he felt some special significance there in the first place. For it is always Shape that speaks most clearly in a life or in a work of art.

Across the hedge of my orchard, dividing me from his orchard, there lived a man who became a close friend of mine for many years. It was only after a couple of years that I discovered that he also was secretly writing a novel. When he showed me what he had so far written it was already of immense length. It was all about his childhood and boyhood dreams. After we parted company he still went on writing it until it must – I will not say 'in the end', because there was no end to it – have reached a quarter of a million words. He was Michael Farrell. His immense novel, very expertly cut to a reasonable size by his friend and mine, Monk Gibbon, appeared in 1963, after his death, as *Thy Tears Might Cease*. It had a great success, which, I have to say, it only partly deserved, because it has no form, no shape. Over and over I used to say to Michael: 'But the shape, Michael? You are not giving it any shape! Where are you leading us?' I ceased to say this to him when it gradually became apparent to me that within himself his private life had taken no shape, and that this was his deepest personal torment. When his novel appeared I seized it with excitement hoping that, before he died, he had at last given form to his chaos. Alas! For as long as he was dealing with his past, with his childhood dreams and boyhood innocence he wrote like an angel; once the crude chaos of his adult world entered in he began to fantasise, to romanticise, to sentimentalise, that is, to invent fake forms, that is to say forms that do not eloquently reflect his own life-shape – if he had, in actual fact, any life-shape to reflect, which I finally began to doubt. And if any reader of these pages asks me for examples of *eloquent* form I answer, 'Very easy! Think of the forms of Mozart's Violin Concerto Number Five in A. Or think of the *eloquent* form of any famous ballet when well performed. And if my reader still protests that words are expected to be more explicit than music or than the dance I first repeat that the essence of a poem is not what it says but how it says it, and as for the novel I suggest Conrad's *Lord Jim*, or Stendhal's *Charterhouse*, or *Daniel Deronda* as plain, straightforward, implicit, formal demonstrations of each of those writers' personal *manière de voir la vie*. If my friend across my orchard's hedge had developed his personal way of 'taking' life he did not display it. He had courage however. He knew his failing. He could not overcome it. He refused to publish while he lived. Ironically his novel was widely acclaimed, and translated into half-a-dozen languages after his death.

I sympathise deeply with him. The reader who will have had the patience to follow me thus far must have rightly decided that I also lingered an unduly long time between a groping boyhood and a shaped manhood. It is something that Ireland has had a way of doing to its children. Or is it only Ireland and not also her unmanning conquest by the empire at her doors? Yet, other countries have had a like retarding effect, chiefly old countries but also parts of modern countries which the mainstream of European civilisation might seem to have only lightly touched if not actually bypassed – isolated parts of southern Italy, or Turkey, of those areas once called the Balkans, those wastes of Australia that fascinated Patrick White, large chunks of the Middle West and the deep South of the United States. Accordingly I have so far in this book done little more than record a semi-isolated youth's efforts to amass some basic information about this globe, these genes, this body, this place that destiny wished on him. From this on I must come to some conclusion about it, which is what I dare to call my tardy coming of age.

16

Turgenev and Eliza

I have in my time written too much. So have some of the most distinguished writers – Balzac, Goethe, Joyce, D. H. Lawrence, Hugo, Tennyson, Dostoievsky, Proust, Scott, Wordsworth, Browning. But it is eminently true of those who instead of living the exclusive life of the devoted artist have lived the versatile life of the Man of Letters.

After our return to Ireland in 1933, to live in that rustic ramshackle retreat grandiloquently called Killough House, Kilmacanoguc, I produced nine books in six years almost without taking breath. In 1934, a quite unnecessary biography of Countess Constance Markievicz, that lovely revolver-fondling gazelle of Yeats's *The light of evening, Lissadell,/ Great windows open to the south,/ Two girls in silk kimonos, both/ Beautiful, one a gazelle*; and also my first novel (that Markievicz job had kept us alive while I was writing it) *A Nest of Simple Folk*. In 1936, I wrote a second novel, *Bird Alone*, banned at once by the Irish Government as 'obscene and indecent' presumably because the heroine had a baby out of wedlock; in 1937, a second volume of short stories, *A Purse of Coppers*, and a potboiling abridged edition of the autobiography of that gay and gallant United Irishman, died 1798, Theobald Wolfe Tone. 1938 saw my Abbey Theatre comedy *She Had to Do Something*; *The Silver Branch*, a collection of The Best Old Irish Lyrics Variously Translated; and a quite admirable biography, considering that I had no scholarly knowledge of its subject, Daniel O'Connell, the Irish Liberator, entitled *King of the Beggars*. In 1940 I produced a third novel, *Come Back to Erin* to which I shall have to return later since, in time, it revealed a turning point in my life. I note that in addition to these writings Professor Maurice Harmon records in his scholarly *Introduction* to my output up to the 1960s some 220 items that he benevolently calls 'Minor Works' and 61 portentous manifestos written between October 1940 and April 1946 as editor of the monthly magazine *The Bell*. He lists after 1939 thirteen more books, including two more biographies, two travel books on Italy, two books of literary criticism, seven volumes of short stories and the first incomplete edition of this autobiography. Dr Harmon does not, I am relieved to note, list scores of controversial letters dispatched to the press, or talks given through the radio or from platforms all over the United States and elsewhere from Switzerland to Sicily, not to speak of various unclassifiable trivia that I would be more than happy to forget.

The main interest I now have in this reckless abundance is that it impresses on me yet once again that the personal (i.e. biographical) interest of any artist's work can vary in inverse ratio to its merits. It is as if the spectacle or the reading or the listening to any master-work drives all thought of its creator out of one's mind, whereas some piece of defective art invites one to think about the personal circumstances responsible for its imperfection. Recall James Joyce's *Exiles*, a failure as a play but a clear-as-daylight mirror of his passionate nature, his satanic pride, and some contrary complex that may have been born of a conflict between his pride and his sexual masochism, about which he is so explicit in his private letters to his wife. It is one of the great reliefs of his (justly) acclaimed masterpiece that the private author stops pitying himself after the opening chapters of *Ulysses*, leaving the reader happily immersed in the public cartoon.

To descend from these Icarian heights to my own modest *Come Back to Erin*, I only realised some ten years ago, on rereading it for the first time since it had been published in 1940, how clearly this botched novel presaged my ultimate development; for although I found it impressively real in parts, and quite shrewdly observed, I did botch it by giving the general subject such a 'realistic' melodramatic treatment as to reduce the whole thing to fustian. Nevertheless the connection between this fustian and my development after 1940 is almost too neat, as neat as the title of the novel with its obviously satirical implication that its theme is exile of mind as well as body, loneliness of soul, isolation of the will. I had been unconsciously wondering about exile for years. After all, my seven years in the USA and in London had been a form of spiritual as well as bodily uprooting. The mere title of my second novel, *Bird Alone*, had already stressed this theme of personal isolation from one's social origins. And even while I was conceiving *Come Back to Erin* I was writing a longish story called *A Born Genius* motivated by the same obsession. It was about the son of a man who had fled from Ireland (symbol?) abandoning his wife and children (symbol?) including this gifted son (symbol?) who ultimately visits him in New York only to find that his father has there become a bigamist (symbol?) with an Italian-born wife, i.e. another exile and a new family. The gifted son returns home in despair and disgust to spend his talents making a boat (symbol?) in which to sail *inside* (symbol?) the enclosed expanse of Cork Harbour whence years ago his father had sailed to freedom across the Atlantic. This story was published as a slim book by Schumann of Detroit, who subsequently asked me to sell him one of my manuscripts. When he asked me to put a price on the manuscript I said airily, 'Oh, give me a complete set of Turgenev.' (Meaning Heinemann's Library Edition of 1920 in fifteen volumes, translated by Constance Garnett.) Now I had, of course, dipped into Turgenev in my student days in Cork but only as everybody does who is at all interested in literature at that age when we rage and ravage, blindly and hungrily, to devour all art and life in one indiscriminate meal. As I now slowly savoured my fifteen yellow-backed Turgenevs I found myself simultaneously engulfed in the delicately exquisite *The Torrents of Spring* of Volume Eleven, while being irretrievably committed to my own ongoing melodramatic treatment of his favourite themes of love, loyalty, betrayal, moral damnation and the shadows of impending loneliness falling across the bright dreams of youth. Later when I reread my sad *Come Back* and remembered that supreme Russian story I realised that I should have sat at the feet of Ivan Sergeyvich Turgenev for ten years before even thinking of writing a novel about such clashing differentials in Irish life as nationalism and self-interest, loyalty to the hearth and the lure of liberty abroad, the snobbery of the cautious middle classes and the conviviality of the garrulous pubs, and above all, the conflict that absorbed countless young Irish people during the 1930s, struggling, despite their inherited peasant puritanism, to celebrate in total joy love's elemental passion (else a great prince in prison lies) namely that ideal love which more subtly than any other European writer Turgenev explored so frankly, so delicately, so tenderly, with such intense compassion and spontaneous emotion and yet almost always with an astounding reserve and a calm, cool, undeceived eye.

As I pushed aside that unworthy-of-me third novel it was not that I wanted henceforth to write novels like Turgenev. I knew I could not, possessing neither his great talents as a novelist nor enjoying his fortunate circumstances, though I still felt that I could (and later did) write as good and sometimes better short stories than he; just as Joyce must have seen that he could never write plays as ably as his admired Ibsen – he courageously used the word 'a fiasco' for *Exiles* his solitary dramatic effort – but that he could write infinitely more exciting prose. What made me embrace Turgenev was not his art but his artlessness – though to recall how embarrassingly artless he could sometimes be try again *his* fiasco *On the Eve*, or the melodrama of his *An Unhappy Girl*. What drew me to a stunned admiration of the man's work was not his devotion to any ideas of a social or political nature – he was no Dostoievsky, no Gogol, no Gorki, no Bakunin – but his modest acceptance of his own given nature. I was especially impressed, as so many others have been before and after me, by the patent honesty of his portraits of his feminine characters, but what affected me even more was the unpretentious honesty of his casual self-portraits, his looks into his own mirror – see page after page of *A Sportsman's Sketches*. He is so unaffected, trustworthy, guileless, modest, spontaneous that at its best his work seems to be a product not of art but of nature. He becomes then one of those rare hybrids from whom one wants nothing more than the self-revealing sensations that rise like vernal exhalations from his pages.

Why precisely, to speak like a footrule critic, is this so? Because, in the one word that was to make him my exemplar for life, he knew his *range*. He accepted his limits and thereby triumphed over them. And, again to speak by the card, how and where did he learn what his range was? He tells us himself, or rather he lets it slip out in that prolix story *First Love* when he says that Meidanov, the writer in that story, was 'a man of rather cold temperament *like almost all writers ...*' He learned his range from himself. All passion curbed, a horse reigned well back, is Turgenev's hallmark.

But to return to my *Come Back to Erin*, no longer wondering, as I did when I finally read it as a printed book, why I had had no Irish Turgenev to waft a cooling breath over its lurid style. I should never have wondered. A couple of years earlier had I not written my study of Daniel O'Connell which I had called *King of the Beggars?* And what else was I but one of that beggared host of the tail-ends of an ancient people, the most ancient between the Himalayas and the Atlantic, so insulated for centuries from the rest of Europe that during the Dark Ages this island had been able to preserve cultural traditions engulfed elsewhere by the invasions of Asiatic hordes. Alas! – it is the central tragedy of the Irish – this same isolation barred them from subsequent European developments. Caught in the web of prehistoric custom and outmoded tradition, they proved to be no match in war or diplomacy for the ultra-modern Tudors. Generation after generation, acre after acre, we were conquered and colonised so thoroughly as to be all but obliterated as a separate race. Shakespeare and Spenser, who lived for a time in Ireland, might have heard Ireland's first death rattle. A century later Swift's image for us was a chained lion with his teeth drawn and claws cut. In the following century, O'Connell's century, famines and emigration reduced the population of the island from some eight million souls to around four. By the coming-of-age of Queen Victoria nothing but sheer racial pertinacity, equalled in Europe only by the Slavs and Jews, kept the Irish serf proudly aware, however dimly, however uncritically, of his island as the only living memorial to what the historian Arnold

Toynbee felt nevertheless obliged to call an *aborted* Celtic civilisation. Under these chaotic conditions it was unlikely that any traditional Irish art could continue to subsist let alone develop and flourish. Nor did it, barring a few Last Minstrel lays from homeless poets, a handful of doomed harpers, an anthology of popular fireside songs at times of a startling beauty, the gay music of part-time fiddlers, and a goodly harvest of rebelly political verse that on occasion flowered into real poetry. But as for an Irish Novel? If we are using the word generically – the French Novel, the Russian Novel, the English Novel – it was inconceivable in a population cloven in two as irreconcilably as the white landowners and black slaves of the American south before 1865. Even today – I am writing these pages in 1984 – there is no such genre as the Irish Novel.

The governing factor in all this is – to take France as an example – that the traditional novel, say between Rabelais and Proust, always depended for its subjects and distinguishing characteristics on the society in which the novelists found themselves; which society they always accepted as sufficiently coherent, complex and complete for their purposes. It is not irrelevant that this social nexus was sometimes not at all to their liking. Quite the contrary. Conflict, bewilderment, efforts to escape, imagined alternatives, can be inspiring. Nonetheless the relationship of human beings as a community is always there – to be felt under the surface of every European novel composed between the mid-sixteenth century and the first quarter of the twentieth after which our society began to fall to bits as a system like a tumbled jigsaw puzzle.

At no period in the lifetime of the traditional novel has the social consensus had a more dominant influence on techniques and attitudes than in Czarist Russia, where the social infrastructure of the traditional novel was clear, tight and literally inevitable. To describe this social infrastructure one need only recall the status of any of the best-known Russian novelists before the Revolution. Count Tolstoy. Doctor Chekhov. Goncharov, one of a family of well-to-do merchants. Lermontov, raised in total comfort. Gogol, descended from modest landowning noblemen. Turgenev's father a cavalry officer. His mother a wealthy landowner. Dostoievsky, son of a surgeon of lesser noble rank.

Maxim Gorki stands out as an untypical vagabond. In short the czarist Novel was written by an élite, about an élite, for an élite. Naturally its interests, its themes, its back-reference, its whole mental attitude to life tended to be, certainly could afford to be, singular, personal, intimate, idiosyncratic, detached, rarefacted, refined, exalted, subjective so long as its authors operated within the limits of ruthless imperial tyranny.

To sum up: I saw that the basic elements of my situation as a budding Irish writer were three, although it took me several years of self-doubt and torment to identify them as clearly as I now can. One: like every artist I needed a dozen illustrious predecessors to point out to me my way home. Two: they did not exist: the Irish life-way before my time had been far too elementary to feed a Novel; one might as well hope to grow a whole garden in a flower pot. Three: I was, thanks to that elementary Irish life-way, inexperienced in the worldly sense of that word to a degree that Turgenev could never have been. How, for example, did he who as a man was so dominated by his mother and by Pauline Viardot ever come as a writer to understand women as intimately and penetratingly as he obviously did? The answer can only be that the Russian life-way under the czars, however unsatisfactory it may have been for the serfs and the liberal upper classes was, from the novelist's point of view, as complicated as French society had for so long previously been for generations of French writers.

This course of thought I do not here propose to follow farther than to record its climax. As I set off once again from Kilmacanogue, County Wicklow, for London (where life, i.e. society, *is* complicated) I found myself reading a novel that seemed to me at the time to solve all my problems by demonstrating that one actually could be a Turgenev when writing in holy, simple pietistic, peasant, bogtrotting, jansenistic, lower lower middle-class agricultural Ireland. This novel had been published eight years before I had heard of it. It was sited in a remote corner of . . . Where? Not the Balkans, nor in Moscow, or the Dordogne, nor the Ukraine, nor the Yorkshire moors. It was exotically placed in my own County Cork and it was a beautifully written work of romantic genius composed realistically. How had she achieved this miracle? For it was a woman who wrote it – name of Bowen. It was, like my own first stories, about the Irish Troubles, but as experienced largely, but not wholly, by the élite in their final autumn of power, which gave the novel its title – *The Last September*. Before my train drew into Euston Station the next morning I was bleary-eyed from reading, but I was excitedly wide awake to the realisation that I had fallen utterly in love with this author who had Turgenev's triple trick of presenting reality to me as close-up as if it were a ball balanced on her five finger tips; transubstantiating this globe of fact into its artistic essence; remaining both compassionate and ruthless about all those people in whom she presumably found, as every artist does, her subjective mirror. My mind was in a state of turmoil. Come Back to Erin? Every artist both inspired and limited by his social conventions? The artist as an élitist snob? Illustrious predecessors? Could E.B. be one such for me? Every artist has his own given range, his own accepted self, a Turgenevian altimeter. The novel or the story? Cold hand, warm heart? Writing had hitherto seemed such a simple, spontaneous thing, like living. As I stepped down to the platform at Euston, mingling with the stream of other sleepy travellers I could not have foreseen that I was not so much ending a familiar journey as beginning a new, troubling and bizarre one.

2

The first person in London to whom I had the chance to unburthen myself about the skill, plus sensibility, plus humanity of *The Last September* was Derek Verschoyle of the *Spectator*. To my great delight he at once agreed that Elizabeth Bowen's novels were, at their best, yes say *September* or *The Death of the Heart*, fully equal to Turgenev's *Fathers and Children*, *Virgin Soil*, or, yes indeed, especially my favourite *The Torrents of Spring*. (It was only later that I was assured by his colleague Goronwy Rees that he had never read any of them. But then Goronwy Rees, I found, was not himself all that reliable.) Derek also agreed with me about *A House of Gentlefolk*, and some of his short pieces like *The Two Friends*, or *The Brigadier* or *Punin and Babarin*. And this was true, he judicially agreed, even after allowing that today's' tempo – what between air-travel, radio, the telegraph, telephones, the cinema, fast cars and so forth –

does tend to give his nostalgic style the beat of a slow march in the wake of lost happiness. As for E. Bowen he was so amused by my confession that I was already half in love with an unseen authoress that he promised to arrange a meeting at once and inside forty-eight hours he did fix a *partie carrée* at his club. The second woman was his own strikingly beautiful wife who, however, proved to be more outstanding for her beauty than her brains. In fact while we awaited Elizabeth's arrival, she provoked me by her repeated tiny warnings that I must not expect a woman who was lovely as well as clever. The most incongruous of her warnings about our awaited guest's looks was embedded in the adjective 'horsey', which made me at once anticipate something between a muscular scout mistress and an Irish Diana, 'lover of the woods and wild chase over the mountains?' I was accordingly disappointed presently to gather from Miss Bowen that she had never been on a horse in her life, had no interest whatever in any sport and, to my deep regret, did not swim either at dawn or midnight or starlight in the river near her Irish country house, Bowen's Court.

Actually, when my Turgenevian examplar did finally arrive at my table, that day in the Savage Club, what I saw at first was a tall, sturdy, bejewelled, fashionably dressed, just perhaps a bit over-dressed, capable-looking woman smiling at me in an amiable if collected way, her fair hair parted centrally, gracefully waved, her hands rather mannish, her eyes unusually small, peering at the three of us like the helmsman of a yacht in a crowded harbour. I saw, all in all, a figure of worldly self-possession. My second or rather my overlapping impression was very different. It was of a personality rather than of a person, a dramatic character, strayed from perhaps *The Last September*, one of its young Irish girls become fifteen years or so older, married – Derek had introduced her as Mrs Alan Cameron – more aware, though not yet, and perhaps never to be quite worldly-wise. This impression of an unknown past, this present waiting, asking even, almost begging to be defined, this possible future must not suggest that I am trying to disguise history as clever insight or foreknowledge. She had herself already revealed her essential character away back in 1929 in the Proustian epigraph to her best novel. '*Ils ont les chagrins qu'ont les vierges*

303

et les paresseux.' It would be the elegy of all her virgins, all her romantic dreamers, all her idle heroines whom, however sympathetically, however tenderly she so often doomed to disaster, intimating thereby that those dreams which alone make life worth living can prove to be illusions that cost life itself.

I never did disengage those two Elizabeths, the romantic woman who so warmly celebrated young love and her realistic double who step by step, hint after hint, simultaneously ordained and finally engineered love's inevitable dissolution. It says a lot for her attractions as a woman and a writer, both of whom I found irresistible, that it took me a score of affectionate encounters to decide that her strength and her weaknesses were at least in part born of a division in her personality; for that, I would ultimately decide, was what she was, a dreamer and a sceptic, a romantic and a realist, sometimes a yearner but as often a toughie. Some duality is certainly evident in the contrast between her inexperienced young dreamers and their grown up counterparts. Recall those two threnodies on youthful love, *The Death of the Heart* and *The Last September*, books as persuasive, as appealing, as sympathetic and above all as lucid as anything of their kind in fiction; and compare them with, say, *The House in Paris* and *The Heat of the Day* where adult love has eaten the apple not of knowledge but of bewilderment and confusion, sailed into frightening fogs and unstable winds, has to cope with misleading forecasts, unreliable compasses, deceptive maps and all with small hope of ultimate salvation.

Not that those words 'frightening, confused, misleading, bewilderment, deceptive' reflected the slightest counter-shadow of indecision or timidity in Elizabeth's public character after she had led her imagination's Pegasus back to its stable. As woman and wife she accepted and coped with every challenge. To give one simple example of her determination as a social person it was characteristic of her to insist on living in central London beside her husband during the whole of 1939–1945 war rather than retire to the security of her ancestral home in County Cork, even after a ritual midnight blitz bombing drove them both out of their elegant London house on Clarence Terrace. I have occasionally thought that her character was if anything too strong, deliberate and stubborn to the point of weakness. I once inadvertently came on her (this was before the war) working at her desk in Bowen's Court. I have never seen anybody so engrossed, so concentrated. Sweat beaded her forehead. But which was driving her? Her imagination or her will? Of her book on Rome she said that the only way to see that city is on foot, hour after hour, until one has to lean against the nearest wall in exhaustion. Her husband Alan so admired her powers of endurance that he, to her amused delight, described her as 'an animal'. Long after the war our ways crossed a couple of times in the USA when, like so many other writers, we were on some parallel lecturing circuit: on one such evening she joined Oliver St John Gogarty, myself, Lord Dunsany and Denis Johnston, five of us on the same platform at the University of Virginia in Charlottesville. She told me she had arrived that morning at 2 a.m., had by then already spoken at two other colleges during the day, and would have to take off early the next morning for a luncheon *conversazione* somewhere else in the deeps of Virginia. Would many other writers have had the energy to undertake this strenuous type of circuit? I met her later on in Pennsylvania while she was conducting some course in the English Literature Department at the Bryn Mawr College for Women: when I congratulated her on having a restful residential post this time ('And you can write when you are not teaching') she snorted comically. 'Those children suck you dry! All I'm fit for after a couple of encounters with them is to sneak off to my room, put my feet up on a chair and relax over a glass of sherry and a detective story.' Admittedly those were among the toughest years of her life, after Alan had retired on pension from his job with the BBC in 1952 and it had become plain that his pension and her literary earnings could no longer support both the elegance of Clarence Terrace and the dignity of a country house as big as Bowen's Court, built to house a score of occupants between family and servants. (Her father had been one of nine children. An earlier ancestor had twelve children. She was barren.) Forced to economise they abandoned London and moved to Bowen's Court. Within months Alan was dead. At this the realistic side of any other Elizabeth might well have advised her to throw in her hand. Not she! What I call her romantic side prevailed. For seven years after 1952 she kept

Bowen's Court alive on her literary earnings, and on these alone. Then, being just short of sixty, she had to sell. Bowen's Court has since been levelled to the grass.

This melancholy image of another Cherry Orchard halts me. I return to the happier memory of my first sight of her in Derek Verschoyle's club, feeling a trifle awed at first in the presence of Ireland's only equivalent to the masterpieces of Russian fiction. However I discovered, or invented, a different role for her before the lunch was over. Why might I not learn as much from her about Woman as I had already learned from Turgenev about Writing? This extravagantly romantic idea was flashed to me twice over that lunch table if only for a mini-second each time by the merest upward flicker of her eyebrows at some passing word. It intimated a far younger creature, girl rather than woman, vulnerable, more sensitive, private, percipient, at all events a quite different person to the citizen of Vanity Fair who had so graciously accepted my introduction. The flash had been of the briefest. Had I seen it at all? I was seated to her left, the flicker had crossed my right eye as lightly as a pendulum. The same woman? Another woman? Invisible? Mirrored? The closing and opening of a shutter between illusion and reality? Something simultaneously accepted and denied? All I knew, or guessed, or intuited was what I would now call a wavering in her when seeing a thing outside herself and when seeing the same thing within.

It was not until many months later, when our intimacy became as complete as, in our circumstances, it could ever be, that I dared to ask her a question whose answer might turn a key and provide the reason for this division in her being, this illusion-reality oscillation, this split personality that I continued to intuit in an otherwise clear-cut mind. I finally dared to ask my key question one warm September afternoon about a year after our first encounter, both of us lying on a sloping, grassy bank outside Bowen's Court. I asked her why on earth had she, with so impressive an Irish home as this, chosen to establish a second home in London? Of her long reply my memory has speared only two sentences, each of which flummoxed me to the total exclusion of its context. The first reply was the proud and vehement declaration:

'I wanted to be as good as the best of them!'

The other came as forcefully and struck me as being even more astonishing and revealing:

'I see no reason why any writer should not be a man of the world as well as an artist!'

Even to this day I can only make sense of that 'as good as the best of them' bit by treating it as a Cork joke at the expense of some absurdly pretentious Londoner. For was she not as E. Bowen of Bowen's Court, Ireland already as good as or better than 'the best of them'? Would it have mattered if she had never owned Bowen's Court, if she were James Joyce (bum and bankrupt), or Sean O'Casey (a labourer), or Dylan Thomas, or D. H. Lawrence? As for the ambition to be a man-of-the-world it had not been difficult for George Sand, Jane Austen, Colette, Shaw, Shakespeare, Thackeray, Thomas Hardy (father a stonemason). But again one could go on. Why had she fussed about it? For a moment I wondered was she pleading with provincial me to become 'a man of the world'? Or could she be voicing a painful personal lack in herself? Or boasting a proud possession? Or anything, rather than see her revealed as a mere split personality? Again and again I thought, 'Why had she fussed about it?'

What a fool I was! A split personality. I now know it as an essential possession for all poets, politicians, philosophers, theologians, actors, authors, in short for everyone who is not a monomaniac. We may control but we cannot cast off our natures any more than we can get rid of our bodies. She must have known that she had not been born a shattering beauty, a ballet-dancer, a film star, an orator – not with that stutter passed on to her, as she records, by her father's mental breakdown – but she must also have felt that she did have a vivid imagination, a strong will, pride, eloquence, ambition, enormous energy and conviviality; and was she to waste these gifts as the childless chatelaine of a disproportionate mansion in the extremities of County Cork, with an income so small as to have evoked from a less sensitive, a less arrogant woman a daily laugh at her bad luck in inheriting such an anachronism and her folly in feeling obliged, purely through pietas, to preserve it? For whom? Instead, she wisely divided her loyalties. England was blessedly near. Constant oscillation became part of her life-pattern. If the prime Geomorphist had only planted her island two hundred miles further west! Things being as they are her London had been established long before her time, its countless paths beaten all over these islands, especially deeply once the compound of a common language became as universal in these western isles of Europe as it now is in the United States. The effects of geology, geography and history on this girl's life were that a crossing to or from London soon came to mean little more than a broken night's sleep. No hiatus. No breach. No bump on arrival at either side; yawn for England, smile for Ireland's green fields, one just changed gear.

A possible alternative would have been to have swopped Bowen's Court for Dublin. They had kept house there for seven years at one stage of her father's legal career – she was born in Dublin at 15 Herbert Place, on the Grand Canal. She wrote a charming little book about it called *Seven Winters*. It is pleasant to conjecture how she might have developed if they had ultimately stayed on in Dublin. She would as likely as not have gone to Alexandra College, Prod.; from that on to Dublin University, so much more pluralist then than now; imbibed something of Dublin's mid-Yeatsian, early-Joycean atmosphere, lived where the sun rises twenty-four minutes later and where Queen Victoria was still alive in 1916. But whom might she have married? This last thought stunned me some thirty years after those seven Dublin years when I brought her one afternoon to tea at the Yeats's, he then being around seventy. She made such a hit with him that George, his wife, kept imploring me in whispers every time I rose to go not to take her away. 'He likes her! He likes her!' George was mother and wife to him, and more, almost his procuress; she was understanding about what she sympathetically called his 'girls': as when for example she once advised him when they were discussing the logistics of one of his romantic excursions not to ignore his mistress on the railway platform and occupy a distant carriage until the train moved out, as he was proposing to do, but rather to go forward to her and greet her joyfully before the world. And what other wife would have had the wit on their own honeymoon to 'distract her preoccupied husband' (Richard Ellmann's words) 'by faking automatic writing': a game she then had to keep up for several years, and long after his search for more cosmological insights had become as wearisome for her as a vision of the ultimate result of their strange collaboration is likely to prove for most of its readers to-day. He may however have warmed to my Eliza that afternoon for other reasons. He liked the landed gentry – it was part of his proud feudal snobbery. ('My father served their fathers before Christ was crucified!') If Eliza had her own touch of snobbery it was purely social. ('I wanted to be as good as the best of them.') Ambition? Dreams? Realism? My thoughts keep repeating themselves. Only realist-romantics like Liz and Turgenev can dream so passionately, marry so sagely, observe so sympathetically, sum up so logically and pass final judgement without a tear.

All this is, of course, the thought of an old man, all passion spent. W. B. would never have suited her nor she him. She had too much of an astringent sense of humour. She was more than amply romantic but the black cap was always near. Was she ever whole-heartedly in love with me? Or I with her even when I called her Liz? Good reader! I hear an intake of breath and its sighing expulsion. Yours or mine? I admit it, in schoolboy language, I had a crush on Eliza. She attracted me as keenly as I attracted her. But if any man can fully recall the blinding, enchanting emotions of his first fine careless rapture he will know that even when my feelings for Eliza were at their warmest they could never come near to recapturing the joy-ache that had overwhelmed me in my teens at the mere thought of those brown eyes, that midnight head, that tiny mole on the right side of a mesmerising smile, the tips of the delicate pink fingers of my first girl. No man's or woman's boyish or girlish experience of love can ever be repeated, copied, described, painted. Only music might partially evoke it. It is, yet once again, the Turgenevian assertion of the crystalline power of ideal love to make life worth living – his master theme. Eliza's tremulous-to-terrible theme is that although love is, indeed, the one experience worthy to be crowned, its mask carries death between its lips. When I was eighteen I never asked any question about my loving. I did not know I was in love. I did not need or want to know any more about us two than any young man or girl in

rosy health wants to know about health. To ask myself prob-
ingly now whether I was or was not in love with Eliza is therefore
in itself its own answer. I came by chance a few days ago on a
perfect wording of this unquestioning nature of love in *The
Life and Opinions of Tristram Shandy, Gentleman*, where that
nominal hero speaks of his 'dear, dear Jenny'. 'Nor is there,' he
declares, 'anything unnatural or extravagant in the supposition
that my dear, dear Jenny may be my friend. – Friend! My *friend*?
Surely, Madam, a friendship between the two sexes may subsist
and be supported without – Fy! Mr *Shandy*! Without *anything*,
Madam, but that tender and delicious sentiment which ever
mixes in friendship where there is a difference of sex . . .'

That tender and delicious sentiment. Oho? Yes, Mr Shandy.
Yes! But then comes what? Why then comes the pure, clean,
clear cry of animal passion – pure because as we know animals
do not sin, feel no guilt, utter only the cry of triumph of another
prince released from prison. Was there ever as neat an image of
duality as that final call of love to love to die that it may live
the more.

With the outbreak of the 1939–1945 war Elizabeth virtually
disappeared from my life. During those six years I saw her only
once. That was in Dublin when I took her to lunch at Jammet's
restaurant in either 1941 or 1942. It was not a happy lunch. She
did not say why she was revisiting our well-fed and neutral
Dublin from her bombed and spartan London, and I did not ask
lest I should touch the nerve of some private crisis at Bowen's
Court, and a lunch is a lunch even if between foiled lovers. As
it was I blundered almost with my first words, saying with a
gush of a false gaiety as I shook out my table-napkin, 'Well,
Elizabeth? So it is taking a world war to divorce us?' As I uttered
these insensitive words I remembered that I had tried to make
the same joke during a final visit to her in London on the thirty-
first of August, 1939. That day, as we lay-abed, passion-sated,
Alan had rung from his office to tell her that the British fleet
had been ordered to mobilise, 'Which means war.' She had
thanked him unemotionally. I had jested, and she had replied
dryly, 'It *is* the sort of thing that war 'does to people', isn't it?'
She gave me exactly the same answer at our Jammet's lunch.
Presently we outdid one another in fatuity. For some, or for no

reason that I can now remember, I said floridly, 'I am afraid, Elizabeth, that I am content too often to let life ride me down. Whereas I always imagine you riding down life astride a power-ful, prancing dapple horse.' Her reply to this idiocy was com-placent. 'I have never before felt so completely a leader!' Some weeks later I gathered that Dublin gossip was insisting that she had revisited Ireland not for any domestic reason but solely at the suggestion of the British Ministry of Information, conveyed to her by the Honourable Harold Nicolson, to help them in the compilation of a dossier about the unwillingness of the Irish Government to grant the British Army, Navy and Air Force free access, presumably fully equipped, to our neutral ports.

All this is now over forty years ago but I can still wince a little at us all – at Elizabeth, at myself, at some patriotic woman who wrote to the press about visiting spies disguised as harm-less visitors, at Harold Nicolson, at the British Ministry of Infor-mation; or else I see the whole trivial incident as a tiny symbol of the sort of thing that war does to people. It puts an end to that civilised balance of values that normally encourages us to see everybody's dilemma from other angles besides our own. The extreme contrary symbol is, I suppose, an actual battlefield with, say, a Wellington and a Napoleon on horseback at the edges of their last encounter, their eyes focused on distant dust (cavalry), puffs of smoke (artillery), masses slowly moving toward masses, horsemen, belching cannons as each leader calmly moves his human chesspieces. If the British had found it necessary to seize our harbours and pour in men, guns and planes they could have done it, and would have had to do it if the Germans had forestalled them. The very thought of Ireland at war would have torn Elizabeth's heart apart.

After the war I met her only once, apart from those chance encounters in the United States. Once was on my invitation to dinner in my daughter's London house, with a couple of other writers of our maturing generation, of whom I recall now only that kindly man Johnny Betjeman with whom I had become friendly during the war when he was at the British Embassy in Dublin. Elizabeth scornfully, and I think unnecessarily, dis-missed him the next day as that 'silly ass Betjeman' when I took her to lunch at the Café Royal for old time's sake. That lunch was a pleasant reunion. We each enjoyed the other's chat, but our sense of intimacy was quite gone. Bowen's Court was by now sold, Clarence Terrace bombed, and in her person there was an absence of that sense of almost masculine vigour that had once appealed to me so much. She still seemed to feel to some degree Irish but she was no longer a Londoner. She had resided for a while in Oxford; she was now on the south coast, off the social map or on the rim of it. Our lunch over, I taxied her to Charing Cross where, gracious as always, she shook hands warmly, thanked me for the lunch and said, 'I did enjoy it! But, then, the company was so good!' For a moment I wished we were both in our warm thirties again.

It was our last meeting. She died (it so happens on my birthday) on 22 February 1973.

I did not go to County Cork for the funeral. That night I took down her novel *The Last September* but I could not bear to reread it. It is her loveliest novel, written when Ireland was still, in some sort, her home.

17

War and No Peace

This chapter should both negate and confirm everything that has gone before. It should be filled with toil, tears, blood and sweat (the famous phrase that Winston Churchill swiped from Byron who possibly swiped it from John Donne) embodying that appeal to male masochism which has motorised every blood-stained adventure that man has ever invented to his gory glory. It could also be a boring chapter, but so can most martial chapters, and the final preparations for all wars, by which I mean that it will probably manage to tell only a little of the truth.

Because of our Irish neutrality my keenest memories of those six years of war have one merit, far from being martial they are thoughtful. They circle about an abstract problem which was to engage me for the rest of my life. You are not expected to take it seriously, but I do want you to visualise me as taking it as grimly seriously as some half-looney Thurber-ish character chasing his problem around and around himself like a kitten chasing its own tail. I am referring to my problem of the just relation between any modern John Citizen and that impersonal solemnity we call the State.

My first conscious and physical acquaintance with the Problem of citizen v state, the part v the whole, *alpha* (me) v *omega* (them) dates from a breakfast table scene in our home in or around late 1940 or early 1941 when in my normally cheerful domestic way I asked my beloved Eileen crossly why couldn't I have a banana with my cereal.

This little breakfast scene occurred inside the walls of a brand-new house which we had decided, just before the war, to build for our quiet, calm, cosy, peaceful, philosophical old age on an acre of virgin grass, as green as ourselves, but many centuries older, which Eileen was to transform into a most pleasant garden in the quiet, i.e. undeveloped, i.e. unspoiled suburb of Killiney, whose lower slopes my Blue Guide of 1932 describes as 'justly favoured as a residence by the more prosperous citizens of Dublin.' This word 'prosperous' reminds me that James Joyce told my wife, when she piously visited him in Paris, that he remembered – as if he would ever forget *anything* – how as a child riding a tricycle he had careered wildly downhill through the public park whose gates directly faced the six-foot wall around the site of our future prosperous residence, raced out of control at 60 m.p.h. across the public road and bashed his head against 'our' wall. This bash may well be embedded in one of his rare Full-Stops in *Finnegans Wake*.

We had made our move to this suburban site, so much closer to Dublin than our first house in Country Wicklow, for the sake of our two children's, Julia's and Stephen's, education. (Stephen was born in 1938.) It may convey some idea of the inequalities of those pre-war times that, poor though we were, we were able to do it because the Irish building business was then in its babyhood; that is to say, a new house even allowing for inflation then cost very little. Ours was a two-storey house of four bedrooms, one large living room, a modest study, bathroom and kitchen, all fully wired. Later on an enterprising young carpenter built me a private wooden study at the bottom of the garden, sacred from all interruptions, overlooking many acres of green fields, and, away down at sea level, some seven or eight miles away below me as the crow flies, the tiny roofs, spires and domes of Dublin. If my presence were *urgently* wanted in the house somebody up there would clank a cowbell that I had brought with me from my sojourn in the Kentucky mountains. (I had refused to have a telephone extension.) My retreat contained one table, one chair, one sofa, one shelf of reference books, one scythe, two garden spades, one shears, one typewriter, one box of paper and a rug under my feet. I christened the house *Knockaderry* (meaning in Gaelic 'The Hill of the Oakwood') in memory of the nearest hamlet to my mother's impoverished birthplace.

It was in this house, then, that I petulantly asked my wife at breakfast, 'why can't I have a sliced banana with my cereal?'

She replied dryly, 'Because there is a war on.'

My mind leaped at once to that cluster of insignificant insects called wartime rations.

Every day for about ten years – rationing was not finally abolished in Great Britain until 1960 – they kept crawling over one's subconscious. They did not sting. They merely annoyed a little. They left no outward mark, but they did gradually begin to have for me a haunting symbolical force. Today, forty years after, I see those privations as trivial. Twenty cigarettes each week, one ounce of tea each week, one quarter-pound of butter, tiny moities of sugar, soap, spirits ... All clothing was controlled by coupons. Imagine a pretty (or other) woman surveying her last laddered stockings or her torn panties. Imagine a housewife short of fuel adverting to those novel professions of Glimmermen and Glimmergirls, officials entitled to pounce into her home, hand outstretched to feel the tell-tale warmth of cooker, range or oven, so as to determine whether she had been using as much as a glimmer of cooking-gas outside the hours permitted by law. We had, agreed, sufficient to eat. But no frills. (My son, born just before the war, was seven before he saw a live orange.) One could call it the simple life or, if petulant, the boring life. On a different level I recall the hoarse groans of a neighbouring violinist echoing his long outworn G string. And I recall the kindness of a friend at the British Embassy who smuggled in some kind of brush that a portrait painter of my acquaintance needed acutely for his profession. When I began to edit our monthly periodical *The Bell* some Dublin wag said truly that it was a most distinguished production if for no reason than that it was the only magazine in the world printed on lavatory paper with ink made of soot. It *was* bum paper. We were lucky to get any from a Britain so hardpressed that its own publications soon dwindled every year in number, size and quality.

Other people around me, I now suspect, felt the same discomfort showing it from time to time by their defensive reactions, ranging from the cynical, 'Well we are not being bombed anyway!' to the judicial, 'We simply have no option but to keep

315

out of Europe. We are a nation in its infancy. We are like the United States when their first President, George Washington, declared for neutrality in order to preserve the new-born state.' In *The Bell* I never dared to argue either for or against Neutrality – I was not permitted to by the Government's official Censorship whose operations added their own anaesthesia to the demoralising atmosphere in which by then any thoughtful citizen might well have begun to look questioningly at his State from under lowered eyelids and his State look at him, meaning – each to t'other – 'What *are* your values?'

I had, up until then, I realised, loved not a real Ireland but an idealised Ireland. I do not regret it. Enthusiasm is the prerogative of youth. But I had come, with the years, the long, fumbling years, simultaneously both to love and hate my dream-love when, in the Civil War and after I experienced the (to put it mildly) deviousness of her offspring. Once a slave always a slave? Could it be true of my once gallant countrymen? Joyce's libellous cartoon-figure Malachi Mulligan put it more savagely: 'Their backs are still aching for the lash.' I had seen my trust silently edged aside by my quondam heroes, such as our leader De Valera, two-faced about that Civil War, gutless either to disown it or to back it.

The descent was painful for myself and my fellow countrymen when we finally came down from Mount Sinai carrying two battered tablets of stone. The first line on *my* new tablets as a disillusioned nationalist said: 'Join mankind!' But how? By – common sense replied – constantly exchanging, even blending cultures from all over mankind's world.

Your obsessed nationalist is not eager to ponder on the interdependence of cultures. The idea is reductive. It makes one's beloved country look like a mere piece of history's jigsaw. My own record as a nationalist illustrates. Previous to the Irish Rebellion of 1916 I had been a contented citizen of Britain, one of the largest empires in history. Suddenly stirred, as I have already recorded, by the blood-spattered flag of the Irish Rising I felt as if generations of my impoverished ancestors had begun to murmur appeals to me from their graves. In that instant I became a perfect subject for conversion to the dogma of the old faith of *Sinn Fein*, (founded in 1905), *Ourselves Alone*, meaning that only in national separateness is there complete freedom to live, to love, to create. For over a quarter of a century I clung furthermore to the implicit, idiotic *Sinn Fein* doctrine that there can be such a thing as a complete indigenous unblended culture. World history kept nudging me in vain to observe that all the greatest cultures known to man have been the creation not of separate racial units but of blended hordes of peoples of various ethnic origin, as in such countries, empires or kingdoms as Greece, Egypt, Rome, Britain, the Ottoman empire, or, most precocious of all, that cosmopolitan empire of Babylon which was flourishing five thousand years before that great new prophet Jesus Christ was a baby fated to found a world-wide polymorphous, polyglot, polyandrous culture in his name.

Not that size or numbers alone can establish and sustain a true life-way or culture. Some vast expanses of the globe such as Greenland or Siberia, or the beautiful North Western Territories of Canada, may be considered, in cultural terms, wasteland, compared with one lively crowded microscopic islet in the Mediterranean. My own thought is that the essential ingredient of a living culture is undisturbed Time. How wise of the Roman segment of Christianity, the Vatican, to have as one of its mottoes, *Qui pensiamo a secoli*: 'Here we think in terms of centuries.'

Empires are not born: they grow. Nations are conceived, achieve youth's promise, tend to turn inwards, content with the habits they have formed, and in due course are then culturally intimidated by their more developed neighbours, or simply absorbed. No Celt needs to think twice, be he Irish, Scot, Welsh, or Breton to answer the question: 'Have your people retained their virginity?'

All empires are polygamists. One has only to listen to their languages. Of them all the late British Empire must have been the largest verbal rapist in history. Off hand there are a dozen English (?) words that twirl the globe faster than Ariel: *Cashmere, bungalow, shampoo, huzzar, calico, diaper, tulip, gum, hammock, elixir, avatar, skunk, whiskey* and I may as well add that stout Saxon word *banana* which, pages ago, started me off on all this guff about cultures allegedly exclusive, indigenous, dissociated, autochthonous, national, fully developed without any external help or outside pressure at all. It would seem safe to deny their existence. Even if one thinks of those dots of islets scattered far apart in the Western Pacific, so tiny as to be illegible on any map smaller than a football field. Surely these must have shared the same – not always admirable – cultural whetstones?

There is no such thing as an independent nation. It took a war to teach me that obvious fact.

An unrealized chapter? Sadly, yes.

It should have dealt with the years (1940–1946) when, from his garden 'hut' – now equipped with a telephone –, Sean edited a monthly magazine. He called it *The Bell* in homage to Herzen, the 19th-century Russian exile whose *Kolokol* (bell) aimed to keep Russian revolutionary thought alive. Sean, in internal exile in war-sealed Ireland, hoped to rouse *his* post-revolutionary readers to think again. To do this, he wrote polemical editorials and published work by people as well known as Elizabeth Bowen, Cecil Day-Lewis, Flann O'Brien and Patrick Kavanagh and as unknown – at the time – as Brendan Behan and the ex-convict who signed his account of prison life with our telephone number. Alas, when Sean, in his eighties, came to write about it all, the memory no longer roused him. The public man had gone private and readers eager to know more about those years must turn to old issues of *The Bell*.

(Note by Julia O'Faolain)

18

Avocations

September 1945. War over. Ceasefire, but *still* no bananas, still no lots of things, even ten years later. In the following April I was glad to hand back my baton as editor of Ireland's only polemical monthly and retire to the somewhat less controversial solitudes of Irish literature. I was then just past those middle forties which the experienced man will recall as the end of his first youth and the beginning of his second. That second youth, between say forty-five and sixty-five or even seventy-five must count, if it counts for anything, as the real harvest-time of life – commanding, considering, concluding, and with any luck triumphantly mature. After that? An evergrowing blissful irresponsibility. The smell of the delta. Ship your oars mates. Lie back. Leave it to the river to wind you safe to sea. No more worry. Violence and fate apart you won't die. You will just crumble quietly, like an old house or an old tree or a long memory.

I never kept a daily diary, merely vest-pocket booklets for *Don't Forgets*, but I feel certain that if at this moment I had four score diaries of any kind scattered over my desk nothing in them could help me in the writing of this autobiography. For example, how could I have transferred to a mere diary the sweetness, the beauty, the force, the calm, the courage of the farewell smile of trust I got a few days ago in a Dublin hospital from a departing fellow-traveller of my own generation? (Nov 9th. Gerry died yesterday.) A diary merely records, an autobiography interprets, although either can involuntarily deceive: the first squeamish about one's future, the other fishy about one's past. Indeed, I perceive that since I approached this chapter I have been shilly-shallying about something crucial that happened to me in 1945 as that second World War ended. This was an involvement with two very incongruous people: one a smart businessman, the second a charmingly unbeautiful fatal woman.

The three of them floated like ghosts across the cinema-screen of my memory a page ago, all the more unexpectedly and challengingly because at the period I am now describing, the time of our first encounters, I had not the smallest premonition that they were to influence my life. But I halt. Had I in fact no premonition of this? No inarticulate wish? No desires born of that growing dissatisfaction with Ireland that I have been intimating in the last chapter? Should I call a plague once again on that deceptive slut Mistress Memory whom I have surprised so often in the arms of Master Desire? All I have learned after many times betraying the truth is that the only way to protect myself from a self-indulgent memory is to write fiction at the top of my form – and I stress those last six words. It is so with all the arts. The memory of every artist is incorrupt-ible only when it is steeled against subconscious wishes in the furnace of his imagination going at full blast ... At which point my pen has again stopped dead. *Question*: How do I know this? *Answer*: By trial, by success or failure.

I have spent the last few hours turning the pages of my three volumes of Collected Stories in search of self-evident illus-trations, and I have come on several stories in which outer appearance and inner essence are persuasively contrasted for this express purpose of getting behind extrinsic memories to intrinsic essences. This I have done not by describing character but by imagining situations that reveal it. If any reader cares to test this I suggest that he read either my story *An Inside-Out-side Complex* or *Dividends*, both of which happen to be moti-vated by an actual businessman like the first of the two, known to all his many, his great many Dublin acquaintances as 'J. J.', his initials, whereby he insisted on being addressed by everyone, sometimes with an embarrassingly genial back-slapping gust of laughter.

As to J. J.'s career before I met him nobody was clear about it. His past was wrapped in Irish tact. Had he married? If so what happened to the marriage? Certainly nobody ever mentioned children. After I met him I visited his house several times but there was no sign of a wife, although it appeared to be a roomy, well-kept, comfortable, established home; nor did I see a house-keeper, although I do seem to recall either hearing him once mention a sister, or informally mention her when introducing me to her as 'The Sister'. That was one evening when he and I supped there together with his brother Willie. Incidentally that 'supped' rather than 'dined' placed him socially. The rash-ers-and-eggs-and-tea implied that his main meal every day would have been a businessman's restaurant lunch, and that his evening meals were often as meagre as they were solitary.

One reason for this could have been that he was not a born Dubliner; like so many other city men in every country he had come to the capital from an unpromising hinterland, in his case his native County Wexford. I gathered that the first fish this Dick Whittington had succeeded in landing in Dublin had been a minor clerkship in one of the Departments of our infant Civil Service. He did also let drop one day that he had been an ama-teur actor with Barry Fitzgerald who later became an outstand-ing Abbey Theatre and Hollywood comic. Either ambition or penury must have driven J. J. from the Civil Service into busi-ness. Precisely why or how it should have been the printing business he never divulged, but by the time we met he either had the luck or, as I suspect, had the wits, drive, guts and ingenuity to have made himself the owner or manager (I never discovered which) of a quite efficient – no, a highly efficient Dublin printing works which turned out our magazine *The Bell*, in between lots of profitable and complex jobs of a very different and more difficult nature, ranging from the printing of Bibles for Africa – I was told that he had achieved a monopoly of the market for Bibles in every African language – to the printing of bus timetables, the breakneck late-night printing of each day's Dail debates for early morning distribution, the printing of con-fidential end-of-term scholastic examination papers, of each month's the *English Digest*, which he imitated with his own the *Irish Digest*, the ruthless abridgment of famous novels in paperback, ranging from *Robinson Crusoe* to *The Last of the*

Mohicans to cheer up Britishers starved of fiction during the war. And so on. If this random list of a few of J. J.'s activities suggests a versatile character (I do not say a versatile mind) it points also both to his flair for spotting the urgency of a public need and his salesman's skill in simultaneously promoting himself as the best man to fulfil it.

Was he always as alert? The most likely guess I heard was that he began his career when young enough to undercut older established firms at the price of being ready to wait for his hard-earned rewards until he was middle-aged and established. He had one other priceless gift – he did not mind being smiled at by everybody. If there had been an Irish caricaturist to exploit him, a Cruikshank, a Dickens, a Gogol, a Forain, a Toulouse Lautrec, or a Phiz he would have greeted their teasings with grateful laughter. Anything to be known! Anything to be remembered! His other prescriptions for success were as revealing. The first was that real profit comes not from a finished job but from the idea behind it. Henry Ford did not get rich by selling cars: anybody could have done that. He became a millionaire by selling *cheap* cars at the rate, after 1920, of a million tin-lizzies a year.

'Think!' He said in awe to me on one otherwise boring evening, 'Think of the fellow who first invented the wheel! If that fellow could only have patented the idea he could have conquered the world! That's why one of Ford's closest pals was Thomas Edison – the man who perfected the idea of the printed telegraph, the phonograph, the wire in that electric bulb over your head. They say he had fifteen hundred inventions to his name before he died!' Here J. J. groaned. 'But he knew nothing about selling his ideas! He couldn't sell ice cream in hell!'

As to where J. J. got his own ideas the answer is that he borrowed them. I recall being driven home in his own tin-lizzy one evening, down Dawson Street, past the Mansion House which he noticed was advertising some exhibition of commercial goods. He stopped the car, turned to his brother Willie in the rear of the car, issued the order, 'Go in there, Willie, and feck a few ideas. You can come home by bus,' and drove on, telling me with such a blend of self-satisfaction and solemnity what his own recipe for success had been that I wondered for a moment if he was training me to become another of his idea-feckers.

J. J. did have one failing, a tiny if revealing one: he was given to sudden microscopic lapses into parsimony. These rare fits I could not understand until a wealthy neighbour of mine in Killiney who, unlike J. J., and unlike so many modern Irish businessmen – as distinct from pedigreed Anglo-Irishmen – had *inherited* both his wealth and his business, revealed the simple key to J. J.'s lifeway when he suggested that 'our friend' had probably been originally floated or assisted into commerce by some astute bank-manager with an eye for a customer worth backing.

'Have you,' my wealthy neighbour asked with an inverted smile, 'noticed the very modest sort of car our friend drives? His banker would approve. No bank likes to see its loan-money being splashed about on luxury living. J. J. is shrewd. He is a realist. He keeps his head down. Occasionally a bit too far down.'

If I had not chanced to make the acquaintance of J. J. and his print-works, if he had never seen the *Literary Digest* nor invented the *Irish Digest*, nor been inspired with the idea of publishing a *Digeste Français*, to be followed by a Spanish *Digest*, and possibly a German, an Italian, even an African or an Arabian *Digest*, if he had not offered me the job of General Literary Editor at L1000 per year which, impoverished as I was by the recent World War, I gladly accepted, if he had not therefore ordered me to find for him an accomplished linguist to start translating for his first foreign *Digest*, which I did with the help of the British Embassy in Dublin and the Ministry of Information in London, and if all these chances had not coincided smoothly I would never have met Miss Honor Tracy – in which event the rest of my story might be very different. So much, by the way, for freewill!

After this preamble I trust that no romantic reader has been tempted to anticipate the entry into my life of a beautiful *femme fatale*. 'Beautiful' is the last term most people would apply to the thirty-five-ish or so English woman whom I duly met off the Holyhead-Dunlaoire mail-boat one fine morning in 1946 and guided frugally on a slower double-decker bus into

323

Dublin to the introduced to her new employer. Miss Tracy was plain of feature, buxom, which word can imply radiant as well as plump, eyes small but very bright, voice delightful, hair red or reddish, expression most pleasant when she was not feeling bored or grim, her laughter a cheerful blend of mockery and satire, scorn and admiration, all adding up to a watch-your-step mixture of the courage of a Stoic and the equanimity of an Epicurean. So then? Unbeautiful? Tough? No illusions? Excellent company on her own terms? These were my impressions of Miss Honor Tracy by the time I showed her into J. J.'s office; and they could well have been anybody's lasting impressions of her but for two other qualifying elements in her nature. If anyone summed her up as an amazon she would have hooted with laughter at the idea unless it implied an amazon who would have enjoyed relaxing on a sofa while being coaxingly fed with chocolates, delicate food and vintage wine. Absolutely impregnable then? Only some other woman – it was to take me a long while to realise it – might have divined that deep within her she was as vulnerable as a girl of fifteen.

J. J. had already expanded his premises, to match his new role as an international publisher, by renting and furnishing two rooms in a sunless side-street in one of the older parts of Dublin behind the Bank of Ireland. There his *Digest* staff of four or five young men occupied one large room to the rear while I and Miss Tracy, or plain 'Tracy' as she soon became popularly known to Dublin's inquisitive and gossipy journalists, were installed in the outer office – she for the usual office hours, I only for the afternoons since I was still in the process of parting company with *The Bell* preparatory to devoting myself once more wholly to literature. That trope about Honor's being better known to other pressmen as 'Tracy' without the Miss reminds me of the fact that Joyce's Dublin had long since expanded from the 310,000 inhabitants of his day, thereby possessing an ample sufficiency both of purely social saloons in its local peripheries or boroughs and of professional pubs to cater at its centre for every profession. Honor being a chummy creature soon became a familiar presence in such journalists' drinking holes as The Palace Bar, or The Scotch House, Davy Byrne's, or The Pearl. Otherwise she had only one other entry into Dublin's restricted social life. She was British, and had come to us straight from the Ministry of Information where she had been secretary to that distinguished sinologist Arthur Waley. It also helped that she had been recommended to all who deserved the honour by John Betjeman and Reggie Ross Williamson of Dublin's British Embassy. Nevertheless throughout her first year she had many lonely hours and empty nights; for while its days can be a delightfully sociable experience for foreign visitors Dublin can also be, outside its pubs, and especially at night, a desolate town. I am here reminded of one of our *Digest* staff, a youth, really no more than a boy, just arrived in the city from some remote country town whom Honor, deducing his lonesome nights from her own, twice invited to be her guest at one of the town's four theatres. On her third invitation he baulked.

'Oh?' she asked. 'The play no good?'

'I suppose,' he confessed, ''tis how you have nobody else to ask?'

One could compose an ironical little tale called *Lonely Hearts* about those two transplants, one from a small Irish village, the other from a vast capital, not forgetting the countless lovers whom Hot Pants Tracy (so our highly-imaginative pub-gossips said) had sifted through her chubby fingers all over Britain, and this loyal youngster's one-and-only love weeping for him among the buttercups of County Limerick.

But such incidents were to come to an end and indeed finally abort the *French Digest*. One morning – some versions said at one o'clock a.m., some at one-thirty a.m., some at three a.m. – the telephone woke the sports writer, an expectant father, again various versions, 'screaming, trembling, fearful, hopeful', not to the happy news about his wife and their baby but to the stern voice of our generalissimo J. J. shouting, 'What is this monstrosity you have just fathered? Do you realise that this is the most miserable caricature of the *Irish Digest* that has ever appeared?' The report was that the father of the as yet unborn child fainted with relief. I, when informed of the generalissimo's behaviour, took umbrage. I sent a protest by hand to him that afternoon to the effect that any criticism of anything done by anybody on the staff of my department should be made to me or through me *and me alone*. Otherwise my staff could have no respect for me. Furthermore the manner and the hour of the complaint was intolerable. It therefore was necessary for me to let it be known to all concerned that I was asking for a guarantee that this manner of going over my head would not occur again. J. J. promptly refused by letter despatched to me by hand. (It was only long afterwards that I understood his disability; being in effect a one-man firm he had never learned how to delegate responsibility – he had to have his finger in every pie, a born meddler.) I repeated my terms. He repeated his. Our letters passed to and fro between my Killiney home and his in Salthill, borne by my daughter, whom he always left standing on his doorstep while he wrote his despatches. After several such communications I sent him my resignation. Meanwhile the journalists' pubs were agog over the whole thing, The Palace Bar, The Scotch House, The Pearl, MacDaid's, Scruffy Murf's, Dwyer's, The Bailey ... It was the sort of back-stage story beloved of all such institutions, the reason we all look at *Private Eye, Le Canard Enchaîné*, the *Village Voice*.

The day I sent my dramatic resignation to J. J. was a neat blend of Chance and Fate. Honor did not come back from her lunch until 4 p.m. instead of 2 p.m. She was accompanied by Reggie Ross-Williamson as her apologetic alibi. Both were blindo. I made nothing, of course, of their joviality although I knew that tomorrow every embassy that might be mildly interested in one another's, let alone in Ireland's plot to invade European journalism, would be smiling at J. J.'s Matty O'Hara. All I said to her was, 'Ah! Courvoisier? Or is it Hennessy? He took you to Jammet's I divine.'

'Nashur'ly,' she confessed in a charmingly boozy-woozy voice, while I remembered that the last time I had lunched there had been with Elizabeth Bowen in the role of another Dublin Matty O'Hara carrying in one large hand an Irish tricolour and in the other a Union Jack? I also noted that Honor was offering me an apple, doubtless from Jammet's table, and that she was saying politely, 'Is it permissible for me to ask you what you are proposing to do about the rather prolonged difference that has been rumbling through these offices for the last ten days?' I calmly took a bite out of her apple, savoured its excellent flavour and replied that I had, much to my relief, sent my final resignation to J. J. while she was boozing with the British foe. 'In fact,' I added, moved by a number of emotions, 'I can't tell you how relieved I am. I am profoundly happy that the whole stupid thing is over. I feel so happy that at this moment I could even kiss *you*!'

She said in her tiny baby-voice, unsmiling, unmoving, leaning on my desk for support, 'Why don't you?'

We were now two feet apart. 'I might if I weren't afraid that in your present condition you would give me a crack in the jaw.'

She challenged me ever so sweetly.

'Why don't you try?'

I did. To my astonishment her eyes filled with tears and she blushed like a sunset. For the first time I saw how handsome she could be when moved, and what a splendid figure she had. She then sat to my desk. To *my* desk! She drew out a sheet of paper, wrote a single sentence to her employer resigning her post at once. I was so overcome by her loyalty that I kissed her cheek again. Afterwards I was informed that when J. J.'s personal secretary opened this letter she exclaimed aloud for the whole office to hear, 'Jasus! Miss Tracy has resigned now!', and that J. J. was furious with her for, as he put it, not keeping her bloody gob shut which meant, I took it, that he might otherwise, at any cost, have persuaded Tracy to keep his great money-making scheme going while the going was still good. As things now stood every pub in Dublin, every printer in Ireland, that had been even half aware of our plans, our ambitions, our struggle for power would know by five o'clock – every journalist's gossip hour – that this was The End. Within a week J. J. surrendered, closed the office and abandoned his great dream of cornering the entire Digest market of Europe.

We parted amicably. And why not? He had not sinned mortally; he had, as one pub-critic said, merely been too small for his boots; another pub-critic talked of Greek *hubris*; another wag said that to be ambitious in Ireland is like planting an oak in an eggcup; another said we Irish are all born exiles, like Swift who stayed to curse or Joyce who left to bloom; although I thought the best remark I heard about him was also the kindest! 'The truth is there's a touch of the artist about old J. J. It's something every good businessman has to have. But only a touch, mind you! Only a touch! More than a touch and . . .' As he solemnly turned down his thumb I suddenly remembered J. J.'s younger days when he used to act with Barry Fitzgerald in amateur dramatics.

1946. A question presents itself. When did I first suspect and finally accept that some special events made the later 1940s the turning point in the establishment of my personality? Imagine, good browsing yawning reader of these pages whoever and wherever you may be, that you have for the last few moments been observing that when I take up my pen I lay it down again unused; or that as many times in as many days I write a score of words then crumple them up and discard them again. The fact is that I have been slowly surrendering, finally, to the humiliating truth that it is not until this year, this month, this moment of 1985, now an old codger on the brink of taking flight into nothingness, that I realise the truth for the first time that my tardy emancipation as a clear-eyed adult might be traced back to some forty years ago and to a savoury apple and one forward kiss. As for the ups and downs that have followed, and the whys and hows of them, and their thrusts and parrys, doubts, certainties, self-deceptions and self-acceptances, each and all of those entanglements of the mind that mankind endures, mine over those last fourscore years and their decoding have been . . . Well, my good fellow-liar, *mon semblable, mon frère*, wipe the mirror, read on.

Certainly, Honor had, quite unconsciously I think, a lot to say to my self-recognition. What most attracted me to her was, I do believe, her self-honesty – she had been perfectly christened – plus her sardonic sense of humour. As to what made her that way nobody on earth but the gods in heaven can know this, although I may have got a stout hint of one element that structured her from her cradle onward; namely her mother's remark, consoling, slight, casual yet never forgotten. 'But you have a very nice expression.' She knew she was no beauty; she compensated for it more than beautifully: whence the courage, the honesty, the sense of humour, the sheer force of her personality, so arresting once you took its measure that I never paid any heed to her appearance; a fact which reveals a blend in the raw material of my given nature that I have taken some fifty years to identify.

Honor remains in my memory's storehouse neither a beautiful object nor, in the American sense of the word, a homely one but in Yeats's happy words for that goddess of his youth and abiding illusion of his middle-age, Maud Gonne, 'a phoenix in my youth and an engine of delight.' I may first have achieved this transcendant way of ideating all actuality in the womb, or, in the cradle, or at the very latest in my impressionable boyhood when I thought I was beholding real life upglowing like sunrise from behind the rising footlit curtains of the Cork Opera House. The idealising ceremonies of the Church may at times have rivalled the theatre. Illumination may have come in my eighteens when I fell in love with the aura that surrounded like a halo the personality embodied in the loveliness of the girl called Eileen who was later to become my revolutionary comrade and later and for ever and ever since my wife.

I had at first sight formed my idea of Honor as a strong-minded, realistic, sardonic woman of affairs. The moment she blushed at my gamesome kiss I not merely transformed her, I transmuted her. My idea of her acted on me like an illuminated stage-curtain that rose on a shining, warmhearted, responsive girl who to my astonishmcnt fclt warmly about *me*! In my elation at this transformation-scene I swept half the photographs of J.J. off the mantelpiece to the tiled hearth. There we both laughingly slammed our heels though face and glass.

I found that Honor lodged in a tiny roof-top flat, a single room about twelve feet by twelve, in Nassau Street. Its kitchen-plus-bathroom consisted of one electric ring and a black-based bath, never once repainted, or so I guessed, since it was installed there in the reign of George V. Her solitary room contained one bed and one chair. Her window offered a fine view northward over the grounds of Trinity College and the valley of the Liffey beyond. I was still admiring the view when I heard her say impatiently, 'Well? Are you going to make love to me?' I said to the landscape, 'Yes.' She said, in some bewilderment, 'Then what are we wasting our time for?' Her bared figure would have delighted a Rubens, a Breughel, a muscular Maillol, a fat-loving Titian ... Two minutes later she was sighing, or one might say purring in frank delight. She murmured, 'If I had known you were as good as this I would have had the trousers off you long ago.' I was shocked at this coarse flattery. Dammit, I had been brought up on Keats and Yeats and Arnold and Tennyson. I told her that I *could* not know whether I was what she so vulgarly called 'good', to which she replied that it was enough for me to know that she thought so, because 'I know! And believe me *I KNOW*!' Later encounters substantiated her claims to erotic expertise. They also replaced my prissy word 'coarse' by the more appropriate word 'frank'. After all coarseness is a state of mind. True, it can also be of the body. A highly-skilled surgeon could be coarse in the bedroom, but the same man's delicacy in the operating theatre . . . But, no! The right word for her was *frank*; or clear; or disabused; or realistic, even though she could also talk and think nonsense as eloquently as I or anybody else – but when she had a truth to tell she told it as clearly as a full moon in May.

This total frankness, this uninhibited clarity, this purity of thought was precious to me still struggling to free myself from the cobwebs of my inherited pietism, puritanism and patriotism, my youthful idealism, my dated romanticism, my later platonism and Berkeleyism and, of course always, those faint, far-off but unquenchable bagpipes everlastingly sobbing of Ireland's tortured gore and lore.

'How nice!' Honor laughed at me one afternoon as I propounded some such profundities to her in her super-elegant, lovely, adorably simple flat. 'Life as a sandwich between Heaven and Hell? And, come to think of it, Purgatory is not such a bad invention either? Total Purification after a few thousand years of fiery discomfort? Really, what masochistic swine all you pietistic Irish are!' And as if on the spur of the thought she announced that she was going to Japan to report back on the success of post-war America's noble ambition to bring civilisation to the Far East. She must have been able through her connections at the Ministry of Information, especially through Arthur Waley, to persuade a good English publisher to finance her, for go she did, and in due course duly produced a highly entertaining report called *Kakemono*, published by Methuen. (The title word is Japanese for a long, narrow wall-picture on silk, hanging between two rollers.) A single paragraph from her first page, sited on the steamer sailing out of civilised and pious San Francisco for the pagan, benighted East, may suggest her quietly lethal style. She is speaking of American missionaries mainly from the super-civilised Middle West of America:

> These missionaries were most interesting people. With no knowledge of any language, any thought, any country but their own, with no preparation indeed of any kind, they were going to spill out over China and Japan, bringing to those ancient and complex civilisations the simple interpretation placed upon Holy Writ by their own communities or sects. Their confidence was sublime and disheartening. They held meetings all the time and all over the ship, uttering their prayers and exhortations in a low murmur, out of consideration for others. Once only was I able to catch a few words. 'Let us pray now for Johnny, the Chinese boy we saved yesterday afternoon,' they were chorusing: but alas! The next morning came news that Johnny had leaped overboard in the night. The incident made a deep impression on me, and I was to think of it often during the months to come . . .

19

Honor

I cannot now exactly remember – there was so much to-ing and fro-ing on everbody's part during those early post-war years – by how many moons my escape from Ireland preceded or succeeded Honor's plan for a book on post-war Japan. My escape was quite unplanned. All I can remember about its origin is that while I was in London trying to get the hang of the new British post-war editorial network I found a message waiting for me in my hotel from a publishing firm called Eyre and Spottiswoode telling me that their Mr Graham Greene had heard that I was in London and that he would like me to lunch with him some day. I had met Graham only once before, in Dublin, accompanied by a very beautiful young woman, very volatile, very vivacious, among a bevy of his, and I have no doubt also *her* admirers. I had been taken by his relaxed, boyish, devil-may-care style, surprisingly different to his grim novels, films and plays. I rang him at once at Eyre and Spotiswoode, had a few social words with him and said I would be delighted to meet him the following day in his office at one o'clock.

He was not there when I called. There was nobody in the place except the girl at the switchboard who directed me to his empty room. Presently the same beautiful woman whom I had met with him in Dublin appeared, obviously accoutred for a relaxed lunch – that is to say no business-woman, somebody who might have been created by an Evelyn Waugh, or a Virginia Woolf, or even a benevolent P. G. Wodehouse. She did not mention her name, which I had forgotten, nor ask mine. She just appropriated his chair behind his desk and began the sort of chat that women who are aware of their attractions pour out like champagne after the cork has hit the ceiling, a gift I envy but cannot emulate being the reserved sort of chap who can only froth after his third Martini; or a half Veuve Cliquot might do. Within minutes the lovely creature had my measure. She whirled her chair at right angles to me, stretched out from behind the desk her crossed legs (absolute Greek perfection), glanced at my still orientally impassive eyes, snorted, 'I don't believe you are interested in girls at all' and in silence started to read Graham's correspondence. He duly arrived, introduced us, and led us to a nearby French restaurant where, warmed presently by a Martini and the wine we all three got on much better, especially so when he abruptly made me a most exciting proposal.

'Sean, why don't you write a book for us in Eyre and Spottiswoode?'

'A book? The last thing I would have associated with a publisher! What kind of a book?'

'Say a travel book?'

'The last travel book I wrote was about Ireland and it got me into no end of trouble with an Irish bishop! A crude creature, but powerful.'

'Well this time write about some place where bishops however crude are not powerful. Say Italy?'

'I have never been to Italy!'

'Then go there.'

'I have no money.'

'I will give you £500 in advance of future royalties in exchange for a travel book on Italy.'

At which words – £500 at that time would be £5000 today – I looked with mild surmise into my wineglass from a peak in Darien.

Things fell into place beautifully. Eileen and I had for some time been hoping that Julia, our first-born, could spend a while in France to improve her convent-school French, so we were delighted when her French teacher told us that she had been asked by the widowed father of a family of girls living near Chambéry (Savoie) to recommend to him a pupil, aged fifteen or so, who might like to stay with him as his guest for a couple of months to improve his daughters' convent-school English. Eileen and I were simultaneously eager for a reviving draught of Europe after all those disappointing years in this alien Ireland that we had never known in our romantic youth – now gone puritanical, priest-ridden, bigoted, isolationist, nationalistic, mentally starved by Church and Censorship, in short (as I so often said to myself and to others) set 'free' too late to save it. And, lo! Here I was suddenly invited by Graham Greene to share in and to describe the life-ways and the traditions of one of the most civilised countries in history. We did not hesitate to grasp the life-rope. We left our small son Stephen to stay with neighbours, left Julia with the family of the Morandys, a lively bunch of young girls living a few miles west of the town of Chambéry, and pushed on to Geneva for our first post-war holiday. Eileen then returned to Dublin and I faced south Italy.

To this day the two legible results of my first adult exploration of Europe, the twin volumes *A Summer in Italy* and *An Autumn in Italy* (entitled in Britain *South to Sicily*) are, of everything I have published, the books I most cherish – not because of their literary merits, if any, but because in them for the first time I could be spontaneous and unrestrained about every element, attractive and unattractive in the life-way I was describing. In them I felt emancipated as man and as artist to a degree I had never experienced in Ireland where ancient loyalties and a constant awareness of the sensibilities of one's fellow country-men keep us all from being completely objective about our homeland. Besides nobody anywhere can take the full measure of his own country until he has experienced life in another at close quarters.

From those two books I offer just one striking example of this. We Irish think that we have an agonising ethnic problem in Northern Ireland, due to prolonged and ruthless colonisation. Well, so we have! But so have other countries. Once we leave the tourist track with what intensity one can feel it in Italy! Any Italian will agree that there are two Italys, the north and the deep south. But I have heard nationalistic Sardinians insisting that there are three Italys. And some hold that there are furthermore two Sardinias within Sardinia itself – those patriots so isolationist that they want to revive the old native language of the island, Sard, as against those islanders who follow the policy of Cavour who discouraged Sard in the interest of the primary importance of creating one single United Italy.

Sicilians encourage this concept of four if not five Italys in so far as they have already won their own measure of political autonomy. In Palermo, the bastion of an international Mafia, ask any Palermitano how many Italys he knows and he may well produce without a smile his pocket calculator. As for the *far ouest* of Calabria (see the last grim sixty pages of my *An Autumn in Italy*) it is still the same tangled region that it inextricably has been over the last fifteen hundred years because so many Byzantines came there from Byzantium, and Muslims from Arabia, and Normans from the north, and the Barbarossan pirates sowed it, and the Fredericians had their bites at it, as had the Angevins, and Aragonese from Spain, and Spanish Bourbons, and even the Austrians came there. One recalls also that Napoleon sent Murat from France, and there were the Bourbons, and was it not Sophocles who enthused over the whole territory of the Ionian coast whither, long before it was deforested, ships from Athens and Carthage came for the finest timber for their fleets? And so the peoples come, on and on, even after Garibaldi landed in Sicily and tramped north to hand the whole splendid ethnic mess to the royal and ruthless house of Savoy, meaning by this time for the peasantry a half-bald wilderness to sweat in to this day – those unrecorded generations whom Euripides described as the sole preservers of every nation.

Our Irish ethnic problem scarcely compares. But I pull myself to a halt. Have I not earlier been arguing the need for ethnic blends in the making of a society? Can Italy offer no example of such a successful process? Yes. One. Inside greater Italy, a no less nationalist dictator than Mussolini established in the centre of his country, in its very capital, the totally independent temporal power of the free State of the Vatican City whose religion, although founded by a Jew and staffed by men and women of every race under the sun is nevertheless blandly considered and called Roman by all concerned, even Americans. What a pity that Belfast was not made from its earliest age the ruling capital of all Ireland! Or is it still too late?

Small wonder that those two amateur travel books of mine

plus my later Italian wanderings, year after year, opened my mind to the successful complexity of a culture so different to my Ireland – stranded on the rim of the Atlantic, virtually isolated, ultimately conquered by the British and simultaneously colonised to the point of declining into the sad if lovely tomb of what Arnold Toynbee legitimately called the 'aborted' Celtic civilisation. All of which is merely another way of saying that my wanderings taught me that every real traveller travels out of his mind; as I take it every armchair traveller also does provided that he is sure that what he is reading is substantially true. For I do not insist that it be wholly true! As Pilate said, 'What *is* the truth?' And mark that he was not jesting; that word was added to *John* 17:38 by Lord Bacon in his essay 'Of Truth'. Truth is as volatile as a scent, or the weather, or this rolling globe; always there, always accommodating itself to time and the times, as many-faced as birth, love, marriage, age, death.

I think affectionately of an American priest-friend who as soon as he found himself again on holiday in Rome donned the traditional long cassock and the flat, broad-brimmed, black hat that Roman priests of the time had worn. Alas, *tempora mutantur* . . . In my boyhood I was not surprised that priests wore silk tall-hats. I have lived to see them all now wearing caps! Even the stern Roman collar has disappeared. I wanted suddenly to possess or be possessed by something more than my American priest's Roman hat. Mesmerised by Italy I suddenly felt that I must return to the warm bosom of this Church that some twenty years earlier I had spat out of my mouth for spitting me out of her mouth, that is to say for formally excommunicating me and thousands of Irish men and women like me because we refused rebelliously, often under arms, to accept a treaty of peace with England that we considered shamefully dishonourable.

If only I had waited another year or two! I would have known better by then both about papal Rome and about its Italians. I would have realised that most Italians regard the Church of Rome much as they regard some splendid Italian monument, as a celebratory presence – and not much more. They marry inside the Church, proudly baptise their children in church, make much there of their children's Confirmation, are buried from it and may there be prayed for once a year; but that is the whole routine, or in slang English that is 'it'.

But the Vatican is, nonetheless, composed of human beings and I got a tiny object-lesson to this effect a few years ago when I was scripting a television programme about the Vatican city state and proposed to demonstrate, among other mildly interesting human items, that its Swiss Guards may marry and have children, that it has a little prison, and a bank, and a post office, and its own railway station, and shop. Two priests fine-combed my script. They barred the shop. 'Why on earth?' I asked. A smile. A shrug. A gracefully wagging finger.

'It might give the wrong impression.'

They did not explain in detail but their meaning was plain. We might give the impression that priests and bishops, even His Holiness the Pope, occasionally blow their noses, go so far as to scratch a knee, or even hiccup, are in short human, by showing pictures of socks for sale, or cigars, or soaps, or hair-oil. We might even show a picture of a bottle of Irish whiskey! In a word we might convey the impression that priests, bishops and popes are wholly human. I felt very sarcastic about these censors until a young Irish priest who was stationed in Rome at the time disabused me by being even more scornful and cross than I was but for a different reason – to wit, that if it were not for the Vatican shop, where goods are duty-free, poorly paid priests like himself would be hard-pressed to live in Rome at all. At this a great light exploded within me. I realised that those two censorious priests were right and that he and I were wrong. Celibate priests are *not* human. Their profession makes them more than so many merely human shepherds. They are devoted to, are sacrificed to mysteries more than human. So many mortal truths are written in cipher that we need these black-coated, or brown-frocked, or white-robed interpreters to break the codes, or else all the religions of the world from pole to pole are . . .

That decade 1946 or so to 1956 or so was, I now feel certain, the crucial turning point of my life. During those years my road of fate was finally being mapped out for me. I still would have to turn maps into facts, lay down my road and tread it, experience it bodily day by day, go beyond it to meet with, blend with, become an ultimate self-contained *moi* and, this above all, consciously do what I am trying to do even at this moment as I write on these blank white pages – define in images, or perhaps more modestly say *illustrate*, or even be content to suggest the essence of this homogeneous personality that I call *moi*. Essences challenge definition in words. Ultimately my essence had better be searched for in images within those few of my successful stories that when I read them now give me the satisfactory feeling that I am conversing with an unself-conscious double, a captured mirror, an otherwise elusive, secretive me. Every good portrait is primarily a portrait of the artist. Every essay in criticism of merit is as much a judgement on the critic as it is a judgement by the critic. Examples? Much of Ruskin. What a wonderful blend of depth and prejudice. Or start a discussion some day in Florence of the comparative merits of Donatello's charming *David* in the Bargello and any of Michelangelo's powerful public brawny *Davids*. What interesting depths and shallows one uncovers in each beholder! It is the same in literature. I find James Joyce's *Portrait of the Artist* unforgettable. His vast cartoon *Ulysses* is more memorable. (Alas!) The spirit of the artist pervades the first: the self-conscious skill of the craftsman dominates the second. Whom do I condemn or approve by saying so? Myself?

I return to my crucial decade. I have mentioned its earliest outward signs – those two Italian travel books. They had a secondary effect on my career as a writer. There flourished at that time an admirable American periodical called *Holiday*. Its title defines its appeal. After the claustrophobia of the war there was a widespread longing to travel in peace again. Until one could afford it *Holiday* travelled for us by proxy, and in style – employing the best travel-writers, the best photographers, designers, and general staff. It was an elegant magazine, sophisticated and reasonably well informed. Its commercial weakness was that it had standards – and was ultimately killed by them. It was unable to stoop to the level of invention now known as the Package Tour which has destroyed everything that had once made one reasonably dream of what we used to call 'Abroad'. Take the very simplest of those dreams: that empty, unspoiled, sunbathed, silent beach on which your father and mother once rediscovered Eden. Today that beach is as crowded and noisy as a wasps' nest. The moral? If the masses want anything they will get it, mass-produced and, in every sense of the word, proportionately cheap. And this is not an anti-Marxist growl. Champagne for everybody is not feasible.

The editors of *Holiday* spotted my travel-books and were sufficiently impressed to invite me to write an intimate close-up of the hill-towns of northern Italy. They liked what I wrote well enough to commission me to write similar close-ups of any other regions of Italy that appealed to me, or challenged me, until, over several years, I had explored the peninsula criss-cross, up-down, from the northern Lakes east to Trieste, south to Sardinia, to the 'toe of the heel' of the mainland, to around and within Sicily. Eileen generally came with me but not always – it was concentrated work and when off the tourist-track in the south, far from comfortable. I have just looked, in Dr Maurice Harmon's book about me, at the bibliography of *all* the material I wrote during those ten years and am shaken by the variety of his list. In addition to my work for *Holiday* I published a studiously researched biography of Cardinal John Henry Newman called *Newman's Way*; a volume of short stories called *Teresa* (in Great Britain, in America *The Man Who Invented Sin*); a character study called *The Irish* which is still available in paperback; a variety of such semi-literary work as a study entitled *The Short Story*, still available in paperback; topical reviews and articles galore; and there had been further abortive efforts at a novel. Thus in a *Year by Year* notebook, full of a hotch-potch of memorabilia I find an entry that says '1945, Saturday June 28. The weight has lifted...' (This refers to my release from *The Bell*)... 'I got down today to my novel.' I had been tinkering with that novel all through the war. There are many later references to it which ceased only when I took a bundle of manuscripts down to the end of our garden and burned it.

From that day on I seem to have clarified my ego. I knew what I could and could not do: write good stories, deliver honourable public lectures – these began in the spring of 1954 at Princeton University as part of the Christian Gauss Seminars in Criticism published under the title *The Vanishing Hero*;

occasional serious reviews out of my deeper self. Everything else came from my surface self.

A proof that this is a fair judgement is what happened when *Holiday* ultimately closed shop and its Editorial Director, Harry Sions, offered all my travel essays to my Boston publisher as material for an interesting book on Italy. My literary agent in New York agreed that one 'could' (his word) make a book out of them. But he added politely that they would not advance my reputation. I agreed: they had not come out of my essential self. Harry Sions accepted the judgement of that word 'could' and to my relief killed the proposal. From that time on I knew my destined road. Whenever I stepped aside from it to cook up a picnic lunch, i.e. to keep the domestic pot boiling. I knew that I was boiling well, but that the real chef was not in charge.

It was years before I saw Graham Greene again. J. J. had long since played his minor part. Honor had left Dublin for London, but she had not left my memory, although to this day, to this moment so near the end of my life I cannot find the words to suggest, let alone to define the qualities in her that for several years within that fateful decade made me long for her company and her person. Oh! I know very well – we all do, always what produces our bewildered cries, 'What on earth does she see in *him*? He see in *her*?' We know well also that answer which is no answer: 'She must have something he lacks; he must have something she wants.' So. Every lack loves another lack? And they will separate with sighs of, 'She changed! He is not the man he was!' A lass and alack! But what was it in Honor that I at least imagined I enjoyed to the last drop of her glass? This I *can* answer. It was her warm-hearted sense of the sardonic element in life – that is to say in people, or as she would have said in *peepoo* – that could make her mockery of it, her Beethoven-browed seriousness, merge with her love of laughter.

How deeply I envied that blend! How badly I needed it! I too could love people and places. I too could caricature them. *But to love them and scorn them in one breath?* This I could not. It takes a special kind, a special breadth of genius to do it. James Joyce, for one example, was unarguably a man of genius but there is in his entire opus only a flicker or two of that pity, that warm human love, that forgiveness that makes for the greatness

340

of such satirists as Sterne, Twain, Gogol, Rabelais, Swift, Dickens. Honor's mockery was never cruel. Indeed it was almost a mark of the gratitude she felt she owed to her victims, the vessel of her maternal pity for them, that when it savagely, however briefly, turned to anger it was not in the end anger with some *person* so much as with the nature of *life* itself. The great worth of such satirical laughter is that it is the midwife of Reason, mankind's shield against blind rage, the saving glass that drugs or drowns despair for at least a little while. My reader may well wonder whether two such different people as she and I, the realist and the romantic, must not often have quarrelled with one another. We did inevitably – I the subjective idealist, she the objective realist – but never for long since it was her favourite relaxation to revel with other *peepoos'* dotty dreams and crazy fancies and I had just enough commonsense cowering behind my overt idealism to sustain for us both a tolerable relationship with tedious convention. So, whenever yet another tiny storm had passed over us we would find ourselves embracing again in some high, dim canvas-green corner of the circus-tent of common existence, content once again now that the lions, clowns, acrobats, sad monkeys, smug parents and hideous children had gone back to the vulgarity of the real world outside. Oddly enough, sardonically enough, what pried us apart in the end was not her rebellious realism but her vulnerable imagination; not my idealism but my submissive respect for plain consistency of behaviour – a boring, uncolourful, quality (if it really is a quality) that I have not the least doubt I inherited from my association as a child with the British Empire through my policeman father's admiration for Law and Order.

Two illustrations of this swing-swong will suffice. The first occurred somewhere on the coast of Sicily; it could be Agrigento where there are Greek remains beside the vast African Sea, winter storms that block the railroads, floods, downpours of autumnal rain, ruined temples, three or four with such names as the Temple of Hercules, or of Concordia, or of Juno, or of Zeus. That of Agrigento is said to be one of the largest Greek temples left by antiquity. At this period of her career Honor was writing for the *Sunday Times* of London from various corners of Europe. I was delivering a brief round of lectures for the British

Council between Torino, Genoa, Rome, Palermo and Catania. She promised to intercept me somewhere early along that line, found to my disappointment she could not and *lo!* (Gadzooks! '*sdeath*! *O gemini*! *Who would have thought it*?) we find ourselves together at last totally cut off by sudden storms from the world, at least as far as trains were concerned, by floods of non-stop downpouring rain, thunder and lightening in this farthest south Sicilian port, redolent of ancient crime and time-battered beauty, in an old, candle-lit and perforce cold-water hotel from which we are informed (incorrectly – to our ultimate relief) no train or car can possibly release us sooner than a week.

But who cares about such things when young and hot-blooded? In the bar we celebrate with hot reviving drinks. In the large, dim dining-room, candle-lit, we perceive the only other guests – two young men. We eat well. We keep touching hands. We join the two young men for coffee. One was a man who at the outbreak of war had been captured by the Japanese together with his beautiful young bride, imprisoned and separated. When he heard that like other female prisoners she was being slowly starved to death he chopped off his fourth or little finger, and sent it to the Japanese commandant of the prison with the request that he should have it boiled and given to his beloved to eat. The commandant had been so impressed that from that day on she was well fed.

Minutes after we had left them for our room, sharing one candle, Honor, already bare as a very large baby, realised with a shriek that the bath-water into which she sat was storm cold. 'But the gods will provide!' she cried joyously and flung open the French window on the balcony. She stepped out there, a red-haired pagan goddess upstretching her breasts to the black downpour, the rolls of thunder, the flashes which intermittently evoked and extinguished our Greek temple's come-go-light-go as the rain steadily fell on us both without stop. That night there were no swing-swongs of roles between us: the storm, the place, pagan myths that with every flash of lightning evoked and suspended time, made us harmoniously one.

I once, during my Honor period, wrote a little five-page story called 'Passion'. It was inspired by her. It is about an old man who grew lilies in his tiny garden, his one unappeasable passion.

One wild night a storm wrecked them. I wrote it as a comedy. It was the only way to be bitter enough about his comic tragedy. It is a charming scrap. It is really all about the terrible folly of love, and the price that love exacts. It also amuses me because to give the lilies their erotic significance I set the little sketch into the frame of a love-letter by means of a couple of opening and closing despairing lines. It begins *Dearest Love, When will we meet again*? And these are the last lines.: – *The moon is going down. The lights of Dublin are still bright. The shadows are long and pale. You are asleep with your dear red hair spread on your pillow . . . Dear Love, when will we meet again! Let it be soon, Dear Love, let it be soon.* Honor was enchanted by it for two reasons. She knew all about the lilies of love and the moons over Dublin. But when the story first appeared it was not red hair that spread on that pillow. It was Eileen's black hair. It was only when Honor and I parted that I could safely tell the truth and make that hair go red again.

After our happy, harmonising storm, it was many months before we met again, this time also beside another Italian temple – the church of Saint Mark in Venice. This time we were not a unity of being. I do not recall the actual date: it must have been either late July or August because the sad thing that happened to us happened in connection with the Roman Catholic Feast of Portiuncula, which during my childhood in Ireland always occurred during August. Here, in the Piazza San Marco, where we paused, glad of the shade, glad of the open space of the piazza, I suddenly uttered a happy laugh, pointing to a large printed poster beside the entrance-door of the church announcing the Feast of Portiuncula. I explained to Honor that my very pious mother had had a special regard for this festival because of the vast number of indulgences she could earn by repeated visits to our local church of Saints Peter and Paul in Cork.

I had laughed, not in mockery but partly from pity and partly from despair, as I went on to explain to Honor how my mother, and all such simple souls like her find consolation and happiness by innocently translating or, rather, being taught to translate what was originally a technical term in Roman law for secular amnesty (*indulgentia*) into a clerically invented system of post mortem book-keeping. My mother did this by accepting the notion that one could amass a vast number of amnesties or indulgences, to be noted by God's celestial bank in her favour – one hundred or a thousand days' remission of purgatorial pain, or ten thousand weeks, or twenty years. Unscrupulous clerical characters of the past have been recorded as selling for cash hundreds of thousands of years of such indulgences. My mother would accordingly 'visit' her church as frequently as possible; say therein one Pater Noster and three Ave Marias; quickly leave the church by the epistle door; toddle into the church by the gospel door, quickly mutter another four prayers; again make a quick exit, a quick re-entrance, pray quickly again . . . and so *da capo*, piling up credits or scratching out debits from heaven's ledger until she was exhausted. This whole procedure was, I remembered as a coda, popularly called *The Ins and Outs*.

To my total astonishment Honor was so enraptured by my revelations that she burst into joyous laughter.

'Let's do it, Nicky!' she cried, clapping her paws like a child. 'What fun! The Ins and Outs! We *must* do it!'

(She used to call me Nicky, short for Nicholas, after Dostoievsky's Nikolai Stavrogin who committed suicide at the end of *The Possessed* by hanging. Honor was quite certain, or so she averred, that I would certainly end my life by my own hand – God alone knows why she entertained this fancy!)

In vain I protested that this whole business of indulgences was a patent swindle. It was an embarrassment to every sane member of her church. Even the Council of Trent had dealt with it laying down, particularly, that indulgences should never be sold for cash. To turn her off at once I pointed to the bottom lines of the poster, saying coldly: 'In any case, dear child, you have failed to read the small print.' She read it. It said that the faithful could share in the fruits of the Feast only on condition that they first formally confessed their sins in the sacrament of Confession, solemnly promised never to repeat them, and partook of Holy Communion. Honor read this coda and at once tushed it over every lagoon in Italy.

'Ho! Just the sort of nonsense those black beetles of priests love to invent to show their power. You must, you must, you must if you love me . . . But I have always suspected that you don't really!'

I pointed out that I had already made and broken my peace with Rome largely because of her, and was I now to make another treaty for her sake and break it again tonight? Tears budding slowly raised my flag of surrender just as slowly. We entered the cathedral, found the usual list of confessors. *Italiano. Français. Tedesco. Inglese . . .* I pressed the latter, correct button. We knelt into the tripartite confessional, I in the farther compartment weaponless, she in the nearer compartment, fully armed for battle. The English priest came from the presbytery, lean, tall, white-haired, robed in the black and white of the Dominican order of Spain, sat in judgement in the central compartment, swished its curtain closed, and drew open the grilled slide for me. I saw only his ear and a dim profile. A child again, I confessed, recanted, forepromised, expressed contrition, lied, was forgiven, emerged doubly apostate into the church and out to the heat of the piazza, vacant but for its pigeons and a few sweaty tourists. Presently she, tardily, *most* tardily – what on earth could be delaying her? – emerged. She was radiant. I seized her treacherous wrist and challenged her. I felt, I knew that she had betrayed me.

'You promised?' I challenged.

'Not I! He said I must. I said I could not give up my loved one. He insisted. He would not absolve me if I did not. He argued. I burst into tears. I begged. I implored. He argued more. I wept more. In the end he said the best he could do for me would be to give me a Conditional Absolution. So I won! Now, Nicky! I won! Let's go across to that café and have a whiskey. I am worn out!'

Honor was so happy that afternoon in Venice that if the fall of Rome happened beside her left ear she would not have heard it – she was so gleeful at her triumph over this Venitian Rome that she would not have known what I meant if I had said 'You have betrayed all three of us. You are behaving like a policeman's daughter. You have made me behave like a bobby's son. Sweet God! Shall I never, never, never be free of the Irish womb?' We went to Mass and received Communion the following morning. She was as happy as a child. I was in despair. The morning after – my task in Venice uncompleted – I took a train or, rather, I *fled* by train to Paris.

There I had a few hours to spend before taking off for Dublin. I found myself by pure chance near the church of the Madeleine. I thought to myself, 'This church probably attracts the most *mondaine* congregation in Paris. Idly I went in. My eye caught a light in a confessional, and a large, fat priest seated in it reading a book – which might be his breviary, or might be a detective story. I passed on. I paused. I returned. I entered his confessional. I said to the grille which he slid open: – 'Mon Père, 'suis pas Français mais je crois que vous pourriez me comprendre assez bien?' To my horror he replied in the purest American: 'If you wanna say it in French that's okay. If you wanna say it in English that will also be alright.' I said that I did not want to make a confession. I was in a fix and I would be grateful for a bit of advice. It is probable that he guessed my dilemma before I had described it in four or five sentences because he summed up *very* flatly:-

'Are you proposing to divorce or otherwise get rid of your present wife?'

'Certainly not! I am devoted to her. I love her. We have known one another for forty years. Eileen is the only woman I have ever truly loved.'

'Well? There it is! You don't want to leave your wife. You can't make this other woman happy. So what is the point of it? You just gotta make your choice.'

I thanked him sincerely. I stepped out from his confessional exhaling deep breaths of relief. He had humanised the mystical. Love has nothing whatever to do with religion, nor religion with love. Puritanical Dante had no right to lob poor tormented Paolo and Francesca into the murk of hell with vulgar sluts like Cleopatra. Love loves. Lust lies. Love lasts. Lust dies. I had to make my choice. I have never ceased to cherish Honor in my heart. She wanted more. I have long ceased to love Eileen with my body – an old man of eighty-six! We are both content, knowing well that whichever of us dies first the other will dearly love the lost one until the dark falls on the end of our dual story. That's life. And if by some accident she discovers any of all this – I have arranged that none of it be published during her lifetime – it will be a duty of my daughter Julia to

346

make it clear that she had always been my one true beloved. Which also is life!

20

An American Lady

I

I am now suffering a few moments of discomfort thanks to an uneasy backward glance at my last chapter. Have I done it again? More bloody Irish eloquence? Worse still, more of the Irish gift of the gab? What would have satisfied me? A cool clarity.

But has any Irish writer achieved clarity otherwise than by going into exile at an early age? Shaw was a prime example. Joyce made such a god of words that he came out at the other side of clarity with *Finnegans Wake*. Yeats in his last bout of self-chosen exile (nobody will know how many years of time he spent outside his beloved Ireland until all his letters are published) admonished his juniors to learn the cold discipline of brick-laying. 'Scorn the sort now growing up. All out of shape from toe to top.' He should know! He had in his time often enough been vague enough as well as eloquent enough to satisfy anybody reared in the wildly oratorical Irish mode.

But come! Am I sure that I know what I mean by 'a cool clarity?' I am. I mean thought that replaces the superficial by the fundamental. Few of us achieve so much compression. Only that one Irish writer did it (from time to time) in my lifetime and he did it only on the usual terms that we thereafter called Joyceian – that is by sacrificing, apart from two or three early short stories, all such vague, therefore to him suspect emotions as pity, tenderness, warmth, compassion. Sam Beckett, lesser Joyce, followed suit. We may, and in admiration should, go back to martyred Joyce again and again but we know well that, for better or worse, his ruthless concept of clarity is not within normal human power. It is certainly not within mine and this is not said in modesty; it comes from my final awareness that every one of us should be advised to know well *and soon* – as Joyce did – the gods' price for being whatever one was born to be, and to pay up before it is torn out of us as a dripping red lump. America, as I presently hope to show, thus returns to centre-stage in my story as a renewed challenge to me to admit and define and accept my own *donnée*, my ordained *moi*.

My return there in 1953 was not exclusively a matter of chance. There do, I protest, exist from birth some small grains of sand known as the will, neither wholly free nor completely a slave. My fateful return to America links with those chequered and strenuous years in Ireland before and during the war insofar as by my fifties I had achieved by my own efforts a modest reputation as a versatile man of letters. The autonomy that I had won by 1956, was largely my own hard-won autonomy even if there were, agreed, some small interwoven elements of chance; such as that when I had been a student at Harvard some thirty years previously I had made the acquaintance of one Dick Blackmuir, then working in a bookshop in Cambridge (Mass.), later chosen with great perspicuity by Lincoln Kirstein as editor of *The Hound and Horn*. Dick, having as gradually as myself built up a reputation – his as a poet and critic – was now Director of the Christian Gauss Seminars in Criticism at Princeton University. He had apparently followed my career with something like fraternal interest and accordingly invited me to deliver at Princeton a series of Gauss Lectures in the spring of 1956. These were later published under the title of *The Vanishing Hero*. It was only after I had subsequently prepared these Gauss talks for publication, enlarging, reconsidering, modifying, emphasising, that I discovered that in them I had, quite involuntarily, touched a personal nerve of supreme importance to me. Even today I am not sure that I can convey the how and the why of this vital discovery but I know it centres on the essential unifying thesis of those lectures.

This thesis was and is that the literary character once known and universally accepted as the Hero of a novel has gradually lost caste; inevitably so insofar as the old-time fictional Hero never had been anything more than an artificial convention representing a *socially approved* norm, just as his opposite convention the Villain had represented a socially disapproved abnorm. These elementary images of 'heroism' and 'villainy' had, I suggested, bit by bit lost all credibility because of a gradual relaxation in European moral values and a greater egalitarian sense of social realities – a double process one of whose results has been that those two stereotypes, the Hero and the Villain are now to be found only in such unsophisticated quarters as cowboy films and whodunits.

One might think off-hand that this has made life rather difficult for writers accustomed to make their stories pivot around at least one morally noble 'heroic' character. Not at all! The novelist has simply retained the invaluable axis of a central hero by dropping his or her morality while retaining his or her nobility. That this double-think process had quietly begun quite a long while ago is evident from such amoral tales as *Manon Lescaut*, or *Le Rouge et Le Noir*, or *Anna Karenina* or almost anything by Balzac, especially so when one observes how deftly your amoral author could keep on and on chewing the pseudo-nobility of his pseudo-heroes or pseudo-heroines before sticking them under his desk-top like bits of chewing-gum to be used again in his next volume.

But to return to 'chance'. I do not remember when I first began to get the uncomfortable feeling that my own liberty was governed by a series of chances – or bulk these chances together and call them Fate, or Destiny, or the Wheel of Fortune, or the Fall of the Dice, or Environment, on the *Zeitgeist*, however the fancy takes you – rather than by my own free will. But I do recall vividly and happily not only the year, the month, the day and the hour but the very second when I at last realised with joy that what is most often called Destiny has its own limitation, that Destiny is itself destined, makes and obeys its own warnings to itself of 'Thus far and no farther', respects its own signs of 'Keep off the grass'. In short, Destiny, sometimes called the Will of God, or of the Gods, acknowledges laws for itself as well as for mankind.

Some humans have dared to defy, condemn or scorn the whole idea of destiny – among modern writers rebels such as Dostoievsky or Joyce, Faulkner or Hemingway – the first was driven to speak out by his horror at the tyranny inherent in the mere shape of life itself; the second by his Miltonic scorn of man as heaven's slave; the third by his terror and horror of the Furies raging through his Mississippi woods; the last by what the hero at the end of *Farewell to Arms* calls, at the climax of his amorous adventure, when his beloved dies of a miscarriage: '*Another of their dirty tricks!*' One may admire the skill, the courage and the plausibility of select swathes of all four of them and in that sense enjoy such, and yet be far from wishing to have been a Joycean or Dostoievskian hero. (Joyce's 'heroines' do not arise. He had none.) Far better one may wish to have been Jane Austen's Emma or Mr Knightley rather than any of those futile rebels against the despotism of fact. But has one the choice? Had Molly Bloom any more than Emma? Which of us is free of our natal destiny?

I first recorded my own solution in Chapter Eleven where I described a confession to an unknown priest, in a downtown church in New York City. I was, however, not being wholly truthful. Far from being unknown, he was recognised internationally as a distinguished philosopher; and we met uptown in Harlem in the rectory of the Church of the Incarnation on 175th Street.

There I discovered that Man, meaning of course all mankind including me, really is free to his last breath. (I hope that Saint Augustine really did say to God, 'Make me chaste – but not yet!') I felt so happy about predestination and free-will that I wanted to share my freedom universally. I felt so much in love with life, myself, the day, the Easter light, all Harlem, all Manhattan, this whole wide world (I am quoting my own not absolutely complete account of that moment from the first 1965 edition of this book) 'that had there been waiting for me outside by the sidewalk not a taxi-driver chewing a five-cent cigar and reading the New York *Daily Mirror* but an attractive woman I doubt if I could answer for the consequences.'

Alas, or Huzzah, depending on your mood and convictions – that last sentence is not completely history. I was in no position when I wrote it away back in the 1960s to tell the truth about the long-distance effects of that fateful morning. There was no taxi-driver, as I revealed here in Chapter Eleven, what *was* waiting for me was a shining, black Cadillac. Admiring it were three small black boys, and engaging them in conversation was my hostess, an attractive smallish woman who, had she stood up, would have been no more than the tallest of them. When my shadow fell across the four of them she looked up at me, smiled her wide, wide smile and said in astonishment, as if I were a complete stranger, 'You look absolutely radiant! I see that all went well. Sit in and tell me all about yourself.' She imperiously patted the seat beside her. I sat in and she drove off at speed southward to the for-some-reason beflagged geometry of crowded, worldly, rumbling, busy Manhattan for, I insisted, a celebratory champagne.

Eileen and I had earlier been introduced to Mrs Alene Erlanger years before, in Dublin, by Lennox Robinson, then manager of the Abbey Theatre, in his charmingly sited home on the fringe of Killiney Bay, one of the more picturesque bays south of Dublin city, on the rocky shore that commands a long wide seaview of the high hills of County Wicklow. She was accompanied either by a sister or a cousin. She was, as later we always found her, vivacious, open-eyed, friendly and welcoming beyond our experience then and, we were to find, even beyond that of the most expansive, open and unreserved of the large variety of Americans either of us was later to meet when residents in or as visitors to the United States after that first encounter. Here I return, not for the last time I fear, to the obsession I have been gassing about for pages back – Freedom, Fate, Fortune, the Dice, Chance, Destiny as against the Creative Will planning consciously in total liberty. Had Lennon Robinson not chanced to invite us to 'help him out', as he phrased it, with those two 'odd' – his provincial word – American visitors, a vital part of my mature development would either have been postponed indefinitely, perhaps have never occurred, or been . . .

But how can an old man even begin to imagine alternative might-have-beens with a mind and body that has long since had its hour? All I can now do is to appreciate my good fortune, give thanks to the Great Dice Thrower and to myself for ultimately following this vivacious lady's kind invitation to knock at her door in New York whenever I visited her beloved city while I was in the United States, as at that time I soon expected to be. I had duly done so, but I did so as a visiting Irish student, unable to take the measure of a married woman probably ten years my senior in years and twenty in experience. She was most kind to this (I acknowledge the evidence of old photographs) handsome if dopeish Irish youth. She took me, with her chaperoning mother, that first night to *The Pirates of Penzance*, and when I left her she most eagerly begged me to visit her again during any later visits I made to town from rural Boston.

Once or twice in my far later years as an established writer I have been tempted to expand on that situation, as a Maupassant might have done, but a moment's thought has always shrugged it aside as banal. It would have been even more banal to have tried to dramatise our second meeting when aged fifty-three. Not even Chekov could have extracted a sigh from that. Perhaps a Daudet might have managed a perfumed breath; a Turgenev winced; Flaubert shrugged. The fact (I found out many months after) as usual stranger than any smoothly amorous fiction was that by 1953 she had no least recollection of me. Nevertheless we did meet then, because one bored afternoon in Princeton I came on her name and telephone number in my address book, with some difficulty remembered her, rang her in her home in New York City and she, through sheer American hospitality warmly invited me to afternoon tea that day at 117 East 64th Street. People of wealth – somebody assured me that her address alone, upper Park Avenue, stank of money – do tend to assume that nobody worth knowing has anything to do that cannot be postponed or forgotten; least of all anything to do more pressing than to sip a cup of tea with them at a moment's notice. She went far to demonstrate it by ringing her manicurist – a female doctor at 'Charles of the Ritz' – and some dim relation – to meet me. I am not given to arrogance, certainly not to rudeness, but I could not help showing a more keen interest in her library than in her guests. Her collection covered an entire wall and included among other remarkable treasures a full first-edition set of Jane Austen. This and other rarities spurred me to plumb her interest in the contents as well as in the value of her collection. She was name, scene and character perfect. I was in time to discover that her memory was phenomenal; and not only visually but aurally. Mention any opera to her and she would burst into song; sometimes to the embarrassment of her grown family, none of whom possessed an atom of her vitality. Nor did it need to be some specially melodious operetta: she would as happily sing you a swathe from Verdi's *Falstaff* until halted once more by her family, or anything you cared to mention out of Wagner's *Ring*, the whole of which she several times assured me she used to be taken to hear in Bayreuth every year by her mother between the ages of twelve and sixteen. Once, the sixteen became fifteen. That was when she regretted not having gone to Radcliffe for her A.M. after graduating at sixteen. (Or was it for her doctorate?) But, such was her fate, or her good luck, to have married in her early teens to her dear, dear, loving husband. In fact, I never did discover her true age, or whether she ever had been to college or to Bayreuth. I confess to wondering occasionally whether all this about Wagner and Jane Austen and college might not have been a series of inventions to counteract her husband Micky's modest history – third generation of a family of poor Jews from Eastern Europe who made good by very hard work.

I will have done an injustice to a life-loving, warm and generous woman if anything I have said about her in her mid-fifties should have given the impression of a featherhead devoted solely to the art of killing time gracefully. I admit that my first impression of her was of that order, but the more I saw of her the more clearly did I realise that behind her felicitous exterior there sighed some keen unfulfilled desire. This sounds sentimental. Poor little rich girl! Sad little brave girl! What was it that finally impressed me so favourably about her? It was that extraordinary sense of complicity that flashed between us on my exit from the Church of the Incarnation when she looked up at me beside her car. She had cried out in astonishment, 'Why, you look absolutely radiant! I see that all went well.' Then, throwing open her door she patted the seat beside her and cried, 'Tell me everything about yourself.' One single word in that excited rush of words revealed her heart to me. No! One half-word did it. Not even that! The inaudible, faintest stress on the first syllable of the one word 'yourself' did it, became to my suddenly hypersensitive ear a comrade's plea. I told her everything as we drove out of Harlem, passed through the Park, on down into the super-crowded lunchtime Fifth Avenue. I unrolled before her all I now knew about my former sense of slavery and my newfound independence. Just as I came to the end of it there occurred a tiny incident that in part reconfirmed, in part challenged my dénouement. We were halted in our race, as were batallions of other automobiles right, left, and away behind us by a traffic cop's uplifted hand hurrying a mob of pedestrians to cross the Avenue. I was astonished to see Kick exchange a handwave and a laugh with one man hurrying across the street. Those two laughs transformed the Avenue into a cosy village street as that empty street in Harlem had for a second opened the gates of eternity for both of us. The cop waved a casual hand. The traffic shot forward *en masse*. For a moment she was as silent as a seed. Then she said, 'You were saying?'

'I had finished. All it boils down to is that I was asking that priest why I, you, he, every living thing can't be just himself lone, uninterfered with by some forces with all sorts of fancy names from the Fates to the Gods. But I suddenly feel that I asked him the wrong question. I should simply have asked him are we free or are we not free? Or is there any such thing as complete personal liberty in this world that he says God made?'

She was slowing down to turn into a side-street away from the madding crowd. She jerked a thumb back to them. 'All free?' She laughed. 'You anarchist.'

'Nonsense! I simply want to owe nothing to anyone. Isn't that fair? Where are you driving us to?'

'For a bottle of champagne in Mickey's club. Don't blench, he will pay for it.'

2

I suppose it is obvious that one can never get to know any strange country merely by mooching around in it: one has to select a spot, dig in there, plant a couple of friendships and cultivate them at one's ease. Two friends are enough; a bit of loneliness is excellent for intimacy; and one does well not to stay too long anywhere – at most a year. First impressions are vital. Whenever I was commissioned by *Holiday* to write another of my travelogues about some place in America I found Kick an invaluable help because while she never had since childhood stayed for long periods in any one place except New York, and her own bit of New Jersey, she had travelled around the United States widely and often, was an infinitely sociable creature, had made friends wherever she went, and was filled with human curiosity; her endemic passion for horses, dogs and birds had become living passports through a widespread number of boundaries, social, racial, political, geographical. But her most appealing virtue of all as a guide was her apparently inborn humanist faith in the oneness, or call it the homogeneity of America as just a place, one place.

I told her one day in dismay that my Philadelphian editor had invited me to write 'a lively, informal but also informative impressionistic synthesis' of the city of Chicago in some two-thousand words. As I told her this I slapped my palm around my brow to signify my despair at the contrast between so few words, plus my own vast ignorance of this third largest city in America, the seventh largest city in the world, housing some nine million humans situated six hundred miles (by air) from the cultural capital of its country; and confessed to her that I had been within this forest only three times as a passerby, and for a few brief weekend visits when lecturing for some six weeks up the line in North Western University. She looked at me in surprise and said, 'But they talk the same language as you do! All you have to do is to talk to them. It's not a foreign city.' I stared at her in equal surprise and said – 'Talk to eight million people?' She simply said scornfully, 'Of course you must select.' If I really wanted to become socio-political about Chicago's vast population of Blacks she suggested I could locate them quite easily, through the local equivalent of Boston's slummy South End House (from which Eileen and I had married one June morning a quarter of a century before); and of course she had horse-dog-and-bird contacts galore; whereat I humbly observed that I had indeed seen birds flying over the foreshore of Lake Michigan, which she identified, breed by breed; and, I forget for what reason, she had an open entree to the whole French community.

In the end, I suggested that we might enjoy a few days together trying with our swords to prise open the mental oyster of this capital city of the Middle West. She came. We wrote my piece. My editor seemed delighted with it.

It was during that mutual Chicago exploration that I first began to wonder in earnest what was the accurate word to define the spontaneity of my cicerone. It proved for a long while to be a fruitless search in so far as nothing can exist unarguably without knowledge of its antecedent cause, or causes, which I would never in her complex case be likely to unravel. And yet there was no denying that this inborn spontaneity of hers was the first thing that impressed everybody who met her – her gusto, her instantaneous response to every challenge, pleasant, or otherwise. More important and specific was the central character of that response – spirited, forcible, what I have more than once heard described as 'gutsy' which is simply another slang synonym for dash, or go, or spunk, or grit. Not that she ever looked or acted gutsily. Quite the opposite – certainly, if one met her strolling slowly down her bit of upper Park Avenue or on the equivalent stretch of Lexington Avenue near her home; perfectly accoutred, pausing, as any villager might pause in a rural Main Street at some favourite small shop (she would say 'store'), as often to chat as to purchase, unless she might be in 'her' village *Irish Bookshop* or 'her' wine merchant's, or 'her' music store. She would be carrying gloves, but never wearing them; expensively dressed, or so I would guess; selectively spartan about jewellery; and she always wore the identical same type of shoe, specially designed for her countless years ago – or so she alleged; but she was rather given to concocting those pretty fantasies – their heels slashed diagonally in rose-red and April blue. (Could these have been her racing colours?) With her not ungraceful gait, her toes swaying out a little right and left, and her constant smile, she looked like a pint-size Queen of Manhattan or a very self-possessed czarina.

There was however one Thing that could suddenly transform this air of calm and smiling self-possession into a storm of nerves. This one Thing was what the family amusedly called Nothing – meaning boredom. One magical word, however, could just as quickly demolish this mood – to wit the word 'Let's' if applied to anything novel, such as a new film, or a new play,

357

especially if it were recommended by the *New York Times* which she read every morning in bed over her breakfast tray after fastidiously donning white cotton gloves to protect her fingers from printer's ink. A new restaurant could revive her curiosity, a new book, a new scent, even old things that had become novelties to New York by becoming rare, ranging from some special exhibition of old paintings to the arrival of a travelling rodeo in Madison Square Gardens. She would eagerly seize on a visitor's most casual reference to something not part of the amenities of his own home town. 'No aquarium? Now we have a very pleasant one in Coney Island. Let's go!' I once said – this was pre-Chicago – that baseball is not an European game, and unwisely added that she was probably not a baseball expert. She laughed at me.

'I know *all* about baseball! Every New Yorker does. No baseball fields in New York? There are probably twenty! Let's see what the Yankees are up to. Yes! Goody! Let's run up there this very day.'

And when we got there she did seem informed about the art of baseball. But, I have wondered since, suppose there actually were no aquarium in her beloved city? Or that NYC contained no baseball field? She would have invented them, being as fertile a Let's Pretend woman as a Let's Go woman. Is this a polite way of saying that she could tell fibs? Towards the end of our story, when we had become as close as crossed fingers and I was afraid that I would never see her (alive) again I told her, to amuse her, that she was a terrible liar. She agreed calmly but said, 'I only tell you these fibs, dear Sean, to amuse you.'

How stupid of me not to have guessed long ago that her world was a vast vinery on Prospero's island, a place of witches, Calibans, Ariels, Mirandas. I should have intuited this whenever her personal maid showed me into her library and, before my name was announced, there was this small lady in a big chair before a vast desk, bent over her leather-bound *Appointments* book or her warning *Don't Forget* book, specs on nose, concentrating on her daily battle against empty daylit hours, or in the creation of afternoons warmed by chosen allies always happy to 'drop into Number 117' for a chat or/and a drink, or to join a couple of dozen other music lovers listening to an after-dinner piano recital (I recall vividly one given by Yehudi Menuhin's sister, and the passionate cons and pros after she had left); or listening to a recently-formed trio whom she had discovered and helped to sponsor. They were ultimately to play over her ashes – one of her last requests – that happy-pensive *andante cantabile* that she had so loved, from Mozart's *Fourth Concerto in D*. After that first year in Princeton with Eileen and during the following years that I spent lecturing alone around the US to earn a living – that is to earn enough time to write the stories I constantly wanted to write – few years passed that I did not, however briefly, descend en route a dozen times on Prospero's island – so that our rude joke became not when next I would be in America but in Amerikick, still searching like a passionate Proust for the elusive heart of this elusive lady.

For a while I consulted the secret crystal called time which, taken crudely, meant that I became madly curious to establish her age as a key to her charm. Was she still see-sawing between two roles, the débutante dreaming of power, or the mature woman aware that she had achieved it? One day while I idly fiddled with her handbag as we chatted I discovered the folly of my question even with the answer in my hand. I opened the bag in an idle way while we chattered on and on. When her passport peeped out at me, like Eve's apple, I fingered it and opened it, not as a spy, merely responding to that weary old Balzac-Zola syndrome that impels all realistic writers of fiction to stand in awe of facts rather than rely on their imaginations, to stress the human document, visual testimony, literal proof. My eye fell on the date of her birth. It revealed that she was sixty-two, a vast age to me at that time. I pointed to it with a gleeful laugh. At last I had come on one snatch of actuality in an elusively complex work of female art. She glanced at it unperturbed, shrugged away this piece of stupid American officialdom with, 'I could easily have had it corrected', and went on with her happy chatter. I said to her, 'As if I cared!' – which was, I realised, exasperatingly true.

Her charm remained indefinable, immune to almanacs, chronometry, the rise and setting of the sun. This was put to me as a common feminine technique by a seemingly elderly lady whose own technique was revealed to me by Kick as that of deliberately dressing much older than she was, thereby inducing newcomers to say, 'She is *much* younger than she looks!' Kick once most wickedly alleged that her friend dyed her hair white. My beloved daughter Julia, when still an author in the making, young, beautiful, clever, inquisitive, finally put the delicate question of Kick's actual age to this lady one summer evening as they both sat sipping aperitifs on the terrace of the Albergo Villa San Michele, looking down over distant Florence of so many lying, lecherous, long-lasting Dantesque loves. The elderly (seeming) dame yielded Kick's secret to Julia most diplomatically.

'Alene Erlanger? How old? Take your choice my child. Thirty? Forty? Fifty? Sixty? Eighty? Ninety-nine? The fact is she does not herself know her own age. She sold her soul to the devil years ago. How long ago? She has long since chosen to forget how long ago.'

When Julia smilingly retailed this secret to me I thought 'How beautiful!' *If only I could unweave the web of days that wove your fate, Faustine*! Dear Kick! Let's foil your satanic master. Grow young along with me, the best is yet to be. But only on one condition – that we both also accept that 'despotism of fact' which Matthew Arnold said the Irish have always refused to notice, namely that it is a basic fact that nothing, simply nothing lasts. Arnold said it of himself in that superb poem 'Dover Beach' – one of the greatest love-poems in all English literature. So did that wise old lady when talking to my Julia on the terrace of the Villa San Michele, pensively turning her invisible little hour-glass as she gazed unseeing over the valley of the Arno. She had laid her finger on Kick's one fatal misjudgement – that of putting all her bets on *Bird of Time*, failing to note that her tipster Omar Khayyam had added the warning that time flies. Here today, gone tomorrow. 'The bird is on the wing.' How true! Nothing lasts. Except memory and dreams. Sophocles heard those ebbing tides long ago on the Aegean. 'My love let us be true to one another . . .' So this was her Achilles heel? She, a realist *au fond*, loved to play with the illusion which Arnold rejected?

It became plain to me only when I noticed her apparently irresistible liking for the Irish even while, as a realist, she must have seen right through us to our bare back bones. Two examples will suffice. The first was her indulgence towards that talented, prolific, inflammably emotional child of nature, Liam O'Flaherty, to whom she gave the hospitality of her home for so prolonged a season as to have raised a few suspicious eyebrows. He was strikingly handsome when young, splendidly made, born and reared on the wild, remote, rocky, and at that time still primitive Aran Islands. His mind see-sawed between the obtuseness of an inexperienced child and the inflammable susceptibility of a genius. I once dared to tease Kick about old-time gossip as to the scandalous nature of her experience with this blend of angel and bore. She rose from her chair, went to her bureau in the next room and presently produced an old letter from him to her. I recall only one sentence of it – the final line – 'My one regret is that I did not make you my mistress.' Years later their paths recrossed. They were both flying from London to Dublin. She became aware suddenly of the head and profile of a passenger on the seat behind her leaning forward to her ear. It was Liam whispering: 'It's not Kick? You can't surely be Kick? I wish there was room in your row for me to come and sit beside you! Do you think that if I gave the girl beside you a pound note she would exchange places with me?' And possibly Kick was half-amused, half-pleased in a vestigially girlish way when, as he walked beside her from the plane to the customs hall he said to her, 'You still have lovely legs, Kick.' She smiled at that word 'still' and remarked to him that he was a very handsome fellow when they first met.

My second recollection of her Irish contacts is Ria Mooney. One could not but be puzzled by her friendship with this well-known Irish actress of Sean O'Casey's heyday, later the chief producer at the Abbey Theatre. Several times Kick invited Ria to stay in the Erlanger's rural estate in New Jersey when the Abbey went dark during the summer; paying Ria's travel-fare by the route that Ria preferred, by steamer, first-class, slowly and restfully between Southampton and New York. This friendship I found bizarre only in so far as Ria, though wholly pleasant to chat with or to dine with in company, had no informed interests beyond the Irish Theatre, and was as virginally innocent of the world as a cloistered nun. I still chuckle at her chance encounter one morning, on Dublin's elegant Stephen's Green, with Brendan Behan. He was then the town's most Bohemian toughie, jail-bird (for wholly patriotic reasons), play-boy and occasionally brilliant author. Ria greeted him most amiably with a 'Good morning, Brendan, and where are we off to this lovely spring morning?' His equally cordial passing reply was, 'Ah! I'm just going down to the Flagellation Club for an hour or two.' Ten minutes later Ria, still wide-eyed, was asking her assembled actors, 'What and where is the Dublin Flagel-lation Club?' I can only conclude that Kick simply had, among other qualities, a vulnerable heart as well as a cool brain, as well as often being more bored than Eve down there on that New Jersey farm where she and her husband were legally obliged for tax purposes to spend a specified number of summer months with no other more congenial company than cows, racehorses, and those damn chirruping birds in her aviary gathered from all over the world. I could add other Irish links, ranging between one Ita O'Leary, a girl in exile from Cork, one of New York's million typists, a jolly, talkative girl; her Dublin Bloodstock Agents; a successful jockey turned trainer in County Kildare; an Irish diplomat who became chairman of the League of Nations; a Dublin picture-dealer from whom she bought her first Jack B. Yeats . . .

Oh, well! All now part of my long ago. O'Flaherty long gone. Ria preceded him. Ita, the typist girl, went back to Ireland and now lies there for ever. The hands of the clock move invisibly for us all. You, dear Kick, so life-loving, gallant, fighting, whether as a tough realist or a passionate romantic, are trans-formed into a breath of air, as invisible and as immortal as the breath of the billions of the entire world's dead, merged now into the immeasurable void above us. I surrender. I fear I have failed in the essential thing: to do justice to your most outstand-ing characteristic – your persistent fight for your independence, its emblem that invisible little dagger in your garter ready for anybody who might however faintly dare to challenge your liberty, even though its most dangerous enemy of all was yourself insisting arrogantly on your divine right as the Empress Kick to reign over all of us below your throne.

Even I once felt her steel on what proved to be our last

intimate meeting in New York. Within an hour or so we must for many months to come put the Atlantic between us, I leaving by taxi for the airport, thence by plane home to Ireland, she by taxi home to Sixty-fourth Street. As I hastily packed I had to pass behind her where she knelt groping for a stocking and I could not resist giving her a hearty smack on her bottom. She whirled to her feet at once and her two little fists went bang-bang into my face. We grappled furiously on the carpet for perhaps ten seconds. I let her go and quietly said, 'Go on! Hit me again!' She replied in a voice of disgust, 'Don't be so submiss-ive!'After that not another word was spoken by either of us until our bags were packed. I had checked us both out, and had called two taxis. Then on the sidewalk, she confessed and explained. It was all because of her size. She had been fated to feel handicapped. I said I understood. She said she knew I would. We drove apart, I hearing and seeing nothing of the bustling roar of the city and certain only that her dagger-thrust would leave its mark for ever. Most oddly it reminded me of Honor's insistence on going to Confession in the Basilica of Saint Mark's in Venice.

During that prolonged aerial journey towards an Irish sunrise contracted by the unfelt turning of the globe, a strange thing happened to me that I was not to understand until several months later. I then clearly realised that when the brain is asleep its dreaming ghostly dogs still may dance, growl and jerk. Dreaming is like hearing a dog far-away in the woods barking for what reason the dreamer may never recognise, or will at best identify only months or years later. I was more fortunate insofar as although my recognitions took a long time to pass through partial revelations, whimperings, guessings and mis-leading inspirations, they did, almost as soon as I sat into that Irish plane, at least begin to approach the status of a thought, encouraged by noticing that the man beside me, obviously a practiced traveller, had immediately pulled a periodical out of his briefcase, whisked its pages expertly until he came to its crossword and begun to cope intensely therewith. This did not, as you might possibly imagine, remind me of 'her' weakness for crosswords; still less remind me of the forenoon outside that church in Harlem when I emerged all aglow with the theological revelation that had been granted to me within it, to find that my 'she' had laid aside her crossword to chat with the three little black boys who had halted on the kerb in admiration of her Cadillac. On my plane I was too numb for such memories. It was not until a hostess gave us permission to unfasten our seatbelts and another had offered us drinks that on hearing my neighbour gently utter a 'Damn' I glanced again sidewards at him, and at his crossword puzzle, and heard him murmur *one word* that started me out on a long subconscious trek that was to end months later as a rational thought. Not that I was searching for meanings to his crossword – or not consciously so. It was not even part of what was presumably a sentence. All I heard the man say was 'Conjoint in nine letters starting with an S.' He spoke in tones of frustration. With these words in my ears I nodded into sleep until I became aware of lights, a hostess gently shaking me, and saw morning light outside. I heard a reference to Shannon, and then there was queuing for the lavatory, and suddenly quite close to us rising green fields, and Shannon's airport. I was in Dublin airport, ultimately with Eileen and the beauty of her welcoming smile that in all our seventy years together never fails to bewitch me.

Now, I am too old and practised a writer not to know that the greatest obstacle every artist has to cope with – and this applies to every type of artist – is the scepticism of his audience. Here I am my own sole audience, trying to remember accurately and understand not what happened but why and in what form it happened, and if my reader is incredulous I am indifferent to his or her response to the following pages which carry my private story forward to a new year and ultimately to my life's crucial conclusion. One morning, then, when I was back into the normal routine of my Dublin life, domestic, social, public, professional, I pulled down a volume of my encyclopedia to check some purely literary detail about Symbolism. All I now remember of that article is that it reminded me that a symbol is an outer sign of some inner quality; as when a lion symbolises strength; or in Christian churches a wafer made of flour and water can symbolise God; or some Christian churches such as the Roman insist that the wafer can be transformed into God. Be this, I thought, as it may I was about to close my encyclo-

364

pedia, having established whatever secular detail I had been pursuing, when my eye caught the neighbouring heading, SYM-BIOSIS.

I paused. I frowned. I felt alerted. I suddenly recalled my neighbour on that plane from Kennedy, years and years back, muttering crossly, '*Conjoint* in nine letters starting with an S?' There certainly are nine letters in SYMBIOSIS which, my fat volume informed me, is a process in biology that excited me as much as if I were the look-out man on Columbus' *Santa Maria* screaming 'Land Ho!' at his first sight of a new world. What I had read was that two different species of organism may conjoin, living each for its own good on some desirable quality in the other, as when some wild grass rich in carbon but short in nitrogen may link with some other grass lacking in carbon but having nitrogen to spare. Those symbionts or conjoiners live happily ever after, each as unaware of the necessary other as a newborn infant is of the source of the sweet life it sucks – until, of course, some quietly grazing cow chews up both the carbon and the nitrogen, and until again the butcher's boy duly drives the cow to the slaughter yard at the rear of the butcher's shop, and we partake of the cow and the grass and the wind in the willows and the clouds overhead, until in due time we in our turn fall before wind, weather, age, and time into somebody's very occasional memory.

I found my own memory thinking at once of Venice, and the Basilica di San Marco facing its vast piazza, and Honor clapping her absurdly small fat hands in joy at my memory of my poor mother in Cork during the Feast of Portiuncula trotting in and out of her basilica to pile up enough Ave Marias to shorten her centuries in the fires of Purgatory after she – surely sinless? – died and was judged. She had had a hard life. Honor, for all her bravery and gaiety I felt, had not symbiotically conjoined with some other wind-torn plant, but she should have. We all need additions. I had wronged Honor. She *needed* the Virgin. She had needed more than that squalid alien room under the tiles in Dublin, living alone. She would have been happy as that carpenter's wife in that obscure village in Israel. Being a mere human she needed the fullest possible extension of herself. In Venice she had admitted the need and filled it. Have I not myself needed that extension whenever I have as artist looked into my white mirror searching again and again in vain for my deepest self. We are all of us looking always not for some actual ship's compass but for something more than actual, call it an utter friendship, or call it a weather vane responding to every least breath of air, a lodestar, a lighthouse that will securely guide us after no matter how prolonged our voyage to the destiny marked for each one of us while still in the womb. It is the oldest story in the world since Adam sat alone in Eden wondering and waiting for 'her'.

At which I bethought me, as at the click of a finger, of the day I tried to pass on to Kick my theory that Heaven's desire is that every human creature should in his and in her lone heart be free, which had brought from her as she drove on down through crowded Fifth Avenue that flick of her little finger at the madding crowd. All of those free? Any one of them free? I closed my encyclopedia on Symbolism and Symbiosis. If Eve had been born before Adam she would have been just as eager for company as he was. A strange but powerful foundation for all religions? Loneliness.

That winter, approaching Christmas, as I was walking down Grafton Street I paused outside Dublin's most famous antiques shop, saw an unusually long rosary hanging in a corner of the window, the beads coral, on a fine gold chain; seven groups of nine Ave beads, separated by the usual larger beads or the Pater Nosters, thereby adding up to sixty-three *Aves* or *Hail Marys*. It was a rather lovely rosary but what interested me was the sixty-three indicating that this was a rare rosary, an Irish one, of the type known as a Saint Bridget rosary, that saint having lived for sixty-three years. I bought it and sent it to Kick. She, I later established, began again to go to mass on Sundays alone until she was ambushed by the usual fell disease.

She lived with her cancer to the last round, governed the sale of her home at 117 East 64th, coped with her complex last will and testament, directed the scattering of her library, the dismissing of her servants, ordered the details of her body's gradual reductions to dust and its requiescat. She then lay waiting in the wide, large, lofty suite of a fashionable hotel looking out over the Hudson River – it was already almost a national monument. I heard somebody, perhaps a taxi-driver, say that Jack Kennedy had stayed there, and the Pope, and fabulous wantons like Marilyn Monroe. Her waiting there at the gate of night was prolonged and painful. Even so she would preside over little friendly lunches from her bed. Gutsy to the end.

Driven at last to the defeat of asking her physician, 'How long more?' she presumably divided his 'Two weeks?' by two and requested a Catholic priest. That way her Basilica di San Marco, her Portiuncula, her symbiosis. I have learned only one clear lesson from her life: Saint Matthew's advice to take no more thought for tomorrow than those lilies of the field that briefly outshine Solomon in all his glory. It was her motto. *Carpe Diem*. Now that I am become eighty-seven years old it is time I dusted my wings. The stars, visible and invisible, need, will always need, have always needed a little polishing. I must remember the password. Symbiotic.

Index

Flynn, Christy 99, 122
Foch, Marshal Ferdinand 99, 100
Folklore Society 264
Ford, Henry 322
Ford, J.D.M. 216
Forster, E.M. 9, 54, 174
Forster, Morgan 113
Forty Coats (tramp) 291–2
France, Anatole 9
Free State Army 153–4, 155, 156, 159, 161
French, Percy 152
Fry, Varian 246
Fugue (O'Faolain) 162, 226, 246
Fuller, Margaret 185

Gaelic League 131
Galsworthy, John 193, 253
Galway 191
Gamble, Danny 24
Garbally House 188
Garnett, Constance 252, 260, 297
Garnett, David 260, 273–4
Garnett, Edward 247, 252–61, 266, 267, 269–71, 273, 274, 283, 287–8
Gate Theatre, Dublin 274
Gattopardo, Il (Lampedusa) 203
Gauss, Christian 231
Gentle Art of Making Enemies, The (Whistler) 196
Gibbon, Monk 292
Gide, André 193
Gilbert, W.S. 9
Gissing, George 9, 54
Gogarty, Oliver St John 252, 260, 275–8, 280, 305
Gogol, Nikolai Vasilievich 152, 263, 300, 341
Golden Echo, The (Garnett) 260
Golden Treasury of Lyrical Poetry (Palgrave) 125
Goldsmith, Oliver 9, 176, 244
Goncharov, Ivan Alexandrovich 300
Gonne, Maud 133
Gorki, Maxim 301
Gougane Barra, West Cork x, 112, 154, 156
Gould, Jo (father-in-law) 115–20, 126
Gould, Pierce 119
Grahame, Cunningham 9, 255
Grand Meaulnes, Le (Fournier) 257
Grattan, Henry 176
Great Famines 87, 143, 155
Great Gatsby, The (Fitzgerald) 240

Great Lafayette, The 8
Great War 52, 65, 66, 67, 101, 136
Greene, Graham 174, 271, 332, 333, 334, 340
Gregory, Augusta 176
Guerrilla Days in Ireland (Barry) 142
Gwynn, Fr Aubrey 181
Gwynn, Stephen 125, 278

Hardy, Thomas 9, 129, 194, 257, 307
Harkness, Edward 196
Harkness, Stephen 195–6
Harmon, Professor Maurice 296, 339
Harmsworth family 275
Hartigen (trainer) 32
Harvard University 128–9, 209–17, 230, 231, 237, 239, 349
    S gains fellowship 26, 196, 197
Hauptmann, Gerhart 193
Hawthorne, Nathaniel 129, 244, 259, 287, 288
Heat of the Day, The (Bowen) 304
Hedderman, Constable 29–30
Helen, Bob 115, 116
Hemingway, Ernest 155, 240, 254, 255, 351
Hendrick, Sean 155
Henty, George Alfred 25, 28, 52, 84, 88, 101
Herzen, Alexander 187
Hidden Ireland, The (O'Connor) 133
Higgins, F.R. 283, 289
Hindman 227–9
His Majesty's Commissioners of Education 38, 46, 96
His Phoenix (Yeats) 198
Hogan, Gus 32
Hogan, John 12–13
Holiday (periodical) 338–40, 356
Hone (writer) 278
Hoover, Herbert Clark 238
Hopkins, Gerard Manley 275n
Hough, Jer (cousin) 63
Hough, John (cousin) 63
Hough, John (uncle) 62, 86, 103, 104
Hough, Maggie (aunt) 62
Hound and Horn, The (Harvard student magazine) 226, 246, 247, 286, 349
House of Gentlefolk, A (Turgenev) 302
House in Paris, The (Bowen) 304
Howells, William Dean 211
Huckleberry Finn (Twain) 214
Hudson, W.H. 253, 255

371

Hulme, T.E. 284
Huxley, Aldous 240

Ibsen, Henrik 9, 129, 298
Idea of a University, The (Newman)
    125
Inchageelah 108, 109, 155–6, 157,
    159
Inchiquin, Lord 189
Inferno, The (Dante) 170–71
Informer, The (O'Flaherty) 140
Inside-Outside Complex, An
    (O'Faolain) 320
IRA 100, 134–7, 139, 141, 142, 149,
    153–73, 199, 269
Irish,
    S learns 102–3, 104–6, 110, 111,
    177
Irish Academy of Letters 260,
    274–80, 284, 286, 288
Irish Censorship Board 83, 267, 268
Irish Civil Liberties Association 268
Irish Digest, The 321–5
Irish Free State 149, 169, 170, 171
Irish Party 118
Irish Republic, declaration of 172
Irish Republican Brotherhood 133
Irish Rising (1916) 46, 101–2, 110,
    143, 280, 316
Irish Statesman 190
Irish, The (O'Faolain) 339
Irish Volunteers 100, 101, 135, 177
*Irving Babbitt and the Teaching of
    Literature* (Levin) 213
Italy 334–9

'J.J.' 320–29
James, Henry 19, 211, 233, 244–5,
    250, 259, 267, 287, 288
James, William 211
Jane Eyre (Bronte) 39
Jenkins, Herbert 254
Johnson, Samuel 96
Johnston, Denis 305
Josephus, Brother 40, 41
Journey of the Magi (Eliot) 18
Joyce, James viii, xv, 91, 92, 114,
    125–6, 129, 132, 133, 137, 168,
    201, 223, 255, 276, 277, 279, 296,
    298, 307, 314, 316, 324, 327,
    338, 340–41, 348–9, 351
Jung, Carl Gustav 180, 181
Juvenal, Decimus Junius Juvenalis
    95, 96

Kaakemono (Tracy) 330–31
'Kauffmann, Anna Marie' 205–7,
    220–27, 235
'Kauffmann' (husband of 'Anna
    Marie') 221–2
Kean, Edmund 250
Keating, Ned 49
Keats, John 330
Kennedy, Albert ('Kay') 218–20, 227,
    228, 231–5, 238
Kennedy, Edith 218–20, 231–5, 237,
    238
Kennedy, Ray 135, 155
Kerstein, Lincoln 246, 349
Killiney, Dublin 314, 323, 326
Killough House, Kilmacanogue 270,
    291, 295
*King of the Beggars: A Study of the
    rise of Modern Irish Democracy*
    (O'Faolain) 290, 295–6, 299
Kingsley, Charles 40
Kittredge, George Lyman 211–14,
    216
Knockaderry 62, 63, 78, 314

Labour Monthly 190
Lamb, Charles 20
Lampedusa, Giuseppe di 203
Lancasterian National School 36–47,
    90, 201
Langford, Bob 159–60, 164
Larkin, Philip vii
Last September, The (Bowen) xii,
    302, 303, 304, 312
Lauro (Julia O'Faolain's husband) xvi
Lavengro (Borrow) 257
Lawrence, D.H. 255, 307
Lawrence, T.E. 107, 254
Legree, Simon 8
Lermontov, Mikhail Yurevich 300
Levin, Harry 211, 213, 231
Lewis, Cecil Day 260
Lewis, Sinclair 254, 255
*Life and Opinions of Tristram
    Shandy, Gentleman, The*
    (Sterne) 310
Lilliput (O'Faolain) 192
Limerick 59
Literary Digest, The 323
Little Women (Alcott) 54
Livy 95
Lloyd George, David 147
Lombardi (statue-maker) 17
Longfellow, Henry Wadsworth 20
Lord Jim (Conrad) 252, 256–7, 293